E-Z MICROCOMPUTER HANDBOOK FOR ELEMENTARY AND MIDDLE SCHOOL TEACHERS

50 Programs in BASIC for Math, Science, Reading, and Language Arts

for Apple II+, IIe, and IIc and TRS-80™ Models III and IV

Margaret B. Hackworth, M.Ed.
Sonia Forseth Helton, Ph.D.
Gloria A. Kuchinskas, Ed.D.
David F. Vera, M.Ed.

Prentice-Hall, Inc.
Englewood Cliffs, New Jersey

Prentice-Hall International, Inc., *London*
Prentice-Hall of Australia Pty. Ltd., *Sydney*
Prentice-Hall Canada Inc., *Toronto*
Prentice-Hall of India Private Ltd., *New Delhi*
Prentice-Hall of Japan, Inc., *Tokyo*
Prentice-Hall of Southeast Asia Pte. Ltd., *Singapore*
Whitehall Books Ltd., Wellington, *New Zealand*
Editora Prentice-Hall do Brasil Ltda., *Rio de Janeiro*
Prentice-Hall Hispanoamericana, S.A., *Mexico*

©1986 *by*

PRENTICE-HALL, INC.
Englewood Cliffs, N.J.

ProDOS is a trademark of Apple Computer Inc.
Apple is a registered trademark of Apple Computer Co., Inc., and is
    not affiliated with Prentice-Hall, Inc.
TRS-80 is a trademark of Radio Shack, A Division of Tandy
    Corporation, and is not affiliated with Prentice-Hall, Inc.

Library of Congress Cataloging-in-Publication Data

E-Z microcomputer handbook for elementary and middle
    school teachers.
    On t.p. the registered trademark symbol "TM" is
superscript following "TRS-80" in the title.
    Bibliography: p.
    Includes index.
    1. Education, Elementary—Curricula—Computer
programs—Handbooks, manuals, etc. 2. Middle schools—
Curricula—Computer programs—Handbooks, manuals, etc.
I. Hackworth, Margaret B.
LB1028.68.E15   1986   372.13'9445   86-8168

ISBN 0-13-298415-6

Printed in the United States of America

ABOUT THE AUTHORS

Margaret B. Hackworth, M.Ed., has more than twenty years' experience as a mathematics teacher, compensatory mathematics specialist, and computer education supervisor. She has been trained in three programming languages (FORTRAN, COBOL, and BASIC), has received funding for numerous grant proposals in mathematics and computer education, has written several articles for the journal of the Florida Council of Teachers of Mathematics, and is an author for the University of Chicago School Mathematics Project.

Sonia Forseth Helton, Ph.D., is professor of Childhood Education at the University of South Florida in St. Petersburg, teaching methods courses in computer literacy and mathematics. In addition to writing articles for many professional journals in elementary mathematics and language arts, Dr. Helton is the coauthor of units in the MINNEMAST project (University of Minnesota, 1964-1970) and the author of *Creative Math/Art Activities for the Primary Grades* (Prentice-Hall, 1984).

Gloria A. Kuchinskas, Ed.D., is an educational consultant and writer in reading, language arts, and microcomputer education. She is the author of *Micros in Your School* (Learning Publications, 1984) and the software programs, *Learning Through the Fourth Dimension* (Barnell-Loft, Ltd., 1983), *High Frequency Conceptual Vocabulary* (Florida Department of Education, 1984) and *The Semantic Mapper* (Teacher Support Software, 1985). She works extensively with school systems in Florida and nationwide and has been a frequent contributor to professional journals.

David F. Vera, M.Ed., is a computer programmer and head of the mathematics department at Northeast High School in St. Petersburg, Florida. Trained in the use of assembler language and the computer languages FORTRAN, BASIC, and Pascal, Mr. Vera has had several of his programs published nationally and has been involved with both personal and freelance programming.

ABOUT THIS RESOURCE

The *E-Z Microcomputer Handbook* is written for the teacher of grades 1-8 who has access to an Apple II+, Apple IIe, Apple IIc, TRS-80™ Model III or Model IV microcomputer, and who has had little or no computer experience. The simple instructions in this book will help you in operating and programming the computer by actually entering ready-made mathematics, science, reading, and language arts programs into the computer for immediate use in the classroom.

Each activity provides you with the following information:

- Suggested file name
- Suggested grade levels
- Description of the program
- Explanation of data lines
- How to change the data (optional)
- The actual program

A special feature of this book is the "Skills Index of Programs" on pages 275-276. This index provides you with a complete listing of the microcomputer programs according to skill, program number, program name, and grade levels.

The Handbook uses the self-instructional, learning-by-doing method as you enter the programs for classroom use. By following these step-by-step instructions, you will also be learning simple programming techniques. This hands-on approach enables you to operate your microcomputer, to design simple programs of your own, and to enhance the programs given in the book.

Keep in mind that the *E-Z Microcomputer Handbook* does not present a complete course in BASIC computer language or in how to solve specific programming problems. It does, however, help you become familiar with operating the computer and beginning programming in the most practical way. These two elements are essential for communicating with and using the microcomputer as an instructional aid in your classroom.

WE'RE OFF AND RUNNING!

Margaret B. Hackworth
Sonia Forseth Helton
Gloria A. Kuchinskas
David F. Vera

ACKNOWLEDGMENTS

The authors wish to thank Nancy Buckles and Mary Ann Harrell for typing the manuscript, and Cheryl Vera for proofreading it.

A very special thank-you to Kevin M. Kay of Shorecrest Preparatory School, John L. Buckles of Meadowlawn Middle School, and Tammy Buckles of George M. Lynch Elementary School in St. Petersburg, Florida, for field testing the programs. We also want to express our appreciation to the many students and teachers at the University of South Florida, St. Petersburg Campus, and in the Pinellas County Schools for their helpful field testing of the text.

In addition, a special thank-you to Robert Godown, Boca Ciega High School graduate, for his insightful comments, and to Wayne Helton for his assistance.

HOW TO USE THIS BOOK

If you have an Apple II+, Apple IIe, or Apple IIc, read "Section One: Learning to Operate and Program Your Apple" (Chapters 1-4). If you have a TRS-80™ Model III or Model IV, read "Section Two: Learning to Operate and Program Your TRS-80™" (Chapters 5-8).

You will need the following materials as you work with this book:

- a microcomputer (Apple II+, Apple IIe, Apple IIc, TRS-80™ Model III or Model IV)

- two blank disks (also called diskettes)

- the System Master diskette or the Pro DOS™ User's Disk (©Apple Computer, Inc., 1983), whichever comes with your Apple II+, Apple IIe, or Apple IIc computer

- the TRSDOS disk that comes with your TRS-80™ Model III computer

- a Model III TRSDOS Disk Operating System and Basic Interpreter for your TRS-80™ Model IV computer. This disk (catalog no. 26-0312) is available from Radio Shack. It will permit you to operate the Model IV in Model III mode with a screen display of 64 characters in width and 16 lines from top to bottom. The programs in this book for the TRS-80™ are written to work on a 64 × 16 display. The Model IV TRSDOS disk will produce an 80 × 24 display. REMEMBER: You must use a Model III TRSDOS in order for your TRS-80™ computer to run these programs properly.

STEPS TO FOLLOW FOR OPERATING AND PROGRAMMING A MICROCOMPUTER

1. Begin by reading the first chapter in either Section One or Section Two that teaches you how to operate your particular microcomputer. Apple users should begin with Chapter 1; TRS-80™ users, Chapter 5. You will learn how to operate the keyboard and to initialize a disk for storing programs.

2. Read either Chapter 2 or 6, "Beginning Programming," for your particular microcomputer. You will be introduced to elementary statements and commands in BASIC.

3. Begin with the first program in either Reading and Language Arts or

Mathematics and Science for your particular microcomputer. Apple users should proceed to Chapters 3 and 4; TRS-80™ users, Chapters 7 and 8.

4. Enter the program by typing it *exactly*, line by line, as shown in this book.

5. Read the accompanying explanations regarding the logic and reasoning behind the program structure.

6. After the program is *completely* and *exactly* entered into the computer, try it out by typing RUN.

7. Play around with the program. Explore possibilities of what can be done. Change it by adding new data or by altering existing data if this option is offered.

8. If the program is the way you want it, save it on a disk.

9. Give the program to your students to run. Specific copying and saving instructions are provided in Chapter 2 for Apple users; in Chapter 6 for TRS-80™ users.

10. Review the "Skills Index of Programs" to select other programs to store on your disk.

CONTENTS

ABOUT THIS RESOURCE... iv

HOW TO USE THIS BOOK.. vi

SECTION ONE: **LEARNING TO OPERATE AND PROGRAM YOUR APPLE**..... 1

Chapter 1: **How to Operate an Apple II+, Apple IIe, or Apple IIc**......................... 2

   DOS 3.3 System Master Instructions for the Apple II+, Apple IIe, or Apple IIc ● 13
   ProDOS™ User's Disk Instructions for Apple IIe and Apple IIc ● 19

Chapter 2: **Learning to Program and to Copy Programs for Classroom Use on Your Apple** .. 26

   Beginning Programming ● 26
   Instructional Steps for Copying Programs ● 37
   Helpful Hints ● 39

Chapter 3: **25 Programs for Reading and Language Arts on the Apple**.................... 43

   1. Flash Cards for Sight Words ● 44
   2. Alphabetizing ● 47
   3. Writing a Story ● 49
   4. Synonyms ● 50
   5. Using Context Clues ● 52
   6. Alphabetical Order ● 54
   7. Pronouns ● 56
   8. Guessing Letters ● 58
   9. Matching the Characters ● 59
   10. Suffixes ● 60
   11. Practicing Faster Reading ● 61
   12. Spelling and Typing ● 63
   13. Plurals ● 66
   14. Signal Words ● 67
   15. Visual Memory ● 69
   16. Multiple Meanings ● 71
   17. Antonyms ● 73
   18. Contractions ● 75
   19. Making Comparisons ● 77
   20. Analogies ● 79
   21. Showing Possession ● 81
   22. Playing Concentration ● 83
   23. Writing Poems ● 85
   24. Verb Tenses ● 87
   25. Sentence Transformation ● 89

Contents ix

Chapter 4: 25 Programs for Mathematics and Science on the Apple **91**

    1. Guess the Mystery Number ● 92
    2. Some—More or Less ● 94
    3. Greater Than–Less Than Symbols ● 95
    4. More Than–Fewer Than ● 96
    5. Choose the Largest Number ● 98
    6. Understanding Multiplication (Rows and Columns) ● 99
    7. Understanding Division ● 101
    8. Fun with Decimals ● 103
    9. Perimeter and Area of Rectangles ● 105
   10. Computer Rounding Aid ● 106
   11. The LCM Challenge ● 108
   12. Basic Number Facts ● 110
   13. Reducing Fractions ● 112
   14. Addition of Integers ● 114
   15. Subtraction of Integers ● 116
   16. Multiplication of Integers ● 117
   17. Division of Integers ● 118
   18. The Concept of Percent ● 119
   19. Computer Challenge ● 122
   20. Reading a Scale ● 124
   21. Feet Per Second and Miles Per Hour ● 126
   22. Abbreviations for Elements ● 128
   23. Solving Proportions ● 131
   24. Estimating Measurements ● 133
   25. Twenty Science Questions ● 135

SECTION TWO: LEARNING TO OPERATE AND PROGRAM YOUR TRS-80™ ... 141

Chapter 5: How to Operate a TRS-80™ Model III and Model IV **142**

    Initializing a Disk ● 149

Chapter 6: Learning to Program and to Copy Programs for Classroom Use on Your TRS-80™ **155**

    Beginning Programming ● 155
    Instructional Steps for Copying Programs ● 166
    Helpful Hints ● 167

Chapter 7: 25 Programs for Reading and Language Arts on the TRS-80™ **171**

    1. Flash Cards for Sight Words ● 173
    2. Alphabetizing ● 175
    3. Writing a Story ● 177
    4. Parts of Speech ● 179
    5. Synonyms ● 181
    6. Using Context Clues ● 183
    7. Making Sentences ● 184
    8. Pronouns ● 187
    9. Compound Words ● 188
   10. Guessing Letters ● 190

11. Suffixes ● 191
12. Practicing Faster Reading ● 194
13. Plurals ● 196
14. Signal Words ● 198
15. Visual Memory ● 200
16. Multiple Meanings ● 202
17. Sentence Combining ● 203
18. Antonyms ● 206
19. Sequence ● 208
20. Contractions ● 210
21. Showing Possession ● 212
22. Playing Concentration ● 214
23. Making Comparisons ● 216
24. Writing Poems ● 219
25. Verb Tenses ● 221

Chapter 8: 25 Programs for Mathematics and Science on the TRS-80™ **225**

1. Guess the Mystery Number ● 227
2. Some—More or Less ● 228
3. Greater Than–Less Than Symbols ● 229
4. More Than–Fewer Than ● 230
5. Choose the Largest Number ● 232
6. Understanding Multiplication (Rows and Columns) ● 233
7. Understanding Division ● 234
8. Fun with Decimals ● 236
9. Perimeter and Area of Rectangles ● 237
10. Computer Rounding Aid ● 239
11. The LCM Challenge ● 240
12. Basic Number Facts ● 242
13. Reducing Fractions ● 244
14. Addition of Integers ● 245
15. Subtraction of Integers ● 247
16. Multiplication of Integers ● 248
17. Division of Integers ● 249
18. The Concept of Percent ● 250
19. Computer Challenge ● 253
20. Reading a Scale ● 255
21. Feet Per Second and Miles Per Hour ● 256
22. Abbreviations for Elements ● 258
23. Solving Proportions ● 261
24. Estimating Measurements ● 263
25. Twenty Science Questions ● 266

APPENDIX **271**

Apple II+ and Apple IIe Video Display Worksheet ● 272
TRS-80™ Model III and Model IV Video Display Worksheet ● 273

BIBLIOGRAPHY **274**

SKILLS OF INDEX OF PROGRAMS **275**

INDEX **277**

section **ONE**

LEARNING TO OPERATE
AND PROGRAM
YOUR APPLE

chapter 1

HOW TO OPERATE AN APPLE II +, APPLE IIe, OR APPLE IIc

OPERATING THE KEYBOARD

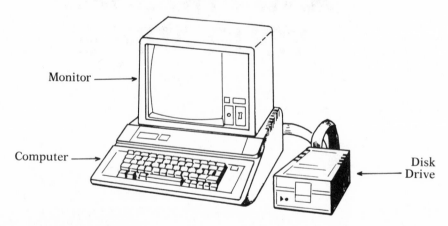

Monitor

Computer

Disk
Drive

STEP 1: THE EQUIPMENT

Examine your equipment. The illustration above shows the microcomputer. The microcomputer has three main parts. The first and most important part is the *central processing unit* (CPU). It is the piece that does all the work. The CPU is hidden from view within the case of the machine. It is made up of chips and circuitry. The CPU is accessed by typing on the keyboard.

The computer is attached to a *monitor* or a TV set. The monitor or the TV set is the piece that shows all the work. Some monitors are in color; some have only one color such as green or amber. The monitor may be attached to the computer, or it may be an independent piece of hardware attached to the computer with a cable.

2

The third piece of equipment, the little rectangular box usually attached to the right or the left of the computer, is called a *disk drive*. The disk drive is the piece that reads, writes, and saves all the work on a diskette. Some computers are equipped with two disk drives and some with one disk drive. The Apple IIc has the disk drive built into the system. It is the slot on the right side of the machine.

The disk drive is the piece of hardware into which the diskette or "floppy" is inserted. The diskette looks like a little square flat plastic record. It is inserted into the disk drive so that the information the user is placing into the computer's memory can be recorded and saved.

The CPU, the monitor, and the disk drive are all called the *hardware* of the system.

If you must fool around inside your computer, *make sure your computer is unplugged!* Never reconfigure your equipment when your computer is plugged in and/or on.

The information on the diskette, this book, and any paper on which you scribble ideas while learning to use the computer are called the *software* of the system.

STEP 2: TURNING THE COMPUTER ON

Turn the monitor switch on. A red light will appear over the switch.

Next, turn the Apple on. The switch is on the back side of the machine next to the power cord on the left side of the computer. Push up to turn it on. The power light on the keyboard will illuminate.

When the switches are turned on, "APPLE II" will appear on the screen.

You may hear a whirring sound in the disk drive, and the red IN USE light will be on.

Hold down the <**CONTROL**> key while pressing the <**RESET**> button on the upper right corner. (If you have an Apple IIc, the <**RESET**> button is on the upper left corner above the keyboard.) In the lower left corner of the screen you should see a "]" with a small blinking square. The "]" is called a *prompt*. The small blinking square is called a *cursor.*

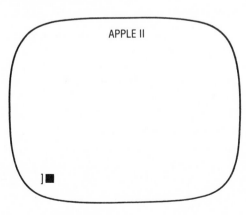

By this time the whirring sound in the disk drive should stop, and a cursor should be on the screen.

Check the red light on the disk drive. Do not begin STEP 3 until the little red light on the drive is off. If you still hear a continuing whirring sound and the red light is on, hold the <**CONTROL**> key down while pressing the <**RESET**> button. If things still do not appear to be right, turn the machine off and wait fifteen seconds; then turn it on again. Repeat <**CONTROL**> <**RESET**>.

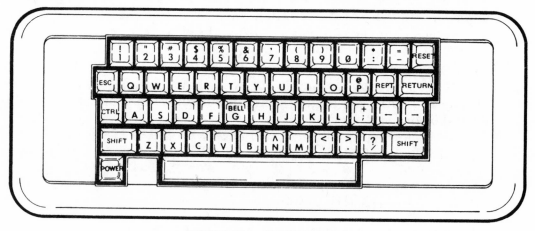

APPLE II+ KEYBOARD[1]

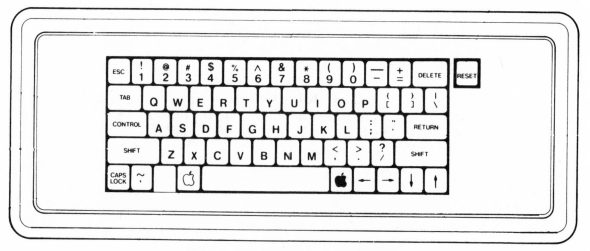

APPLE IIE AND IIC KEYBOARD[2]

---

[1] Raskin, J. and Richardson, C. *The Apple Tutorial*, Apple Computer, Inc., Cupertino, California, 1981, p. 7.

[2] Owners Manual, Apple IIe. Apple Computer, Inc., Cupertino, California, 1983, p. 33.

STEP 3: LEARNING THE KEYBOARD

Study the keyboard for the computer you are using. One difference between the Apple II+ and Apple IIe and IIc keyboards is that the II+ is a standard *teletype* keyboard, and the IIe and IIc are standard *typewriter* keyboards. Both are used in the same way. Notice that the <**RESET**> button is on the upper left of the Apple IIc whereas it is on the right of the keyboard on the Apple IIe. Another difference is that each has special keys unique to the machine, such as arrow keys and keys marked with the Apple logo. The first thing you notice is that there are no lower case letters on the keyboards. The <**SHIFT**> key is used in the same way as it is used on a typewriter. Press it down to type a character that is shown on the top of the key. Keep it in an up position for the main character shown on the key.

If you are learning on an Apple IIe and IIc, press the <**CAPS LOCK**> key down. That is all you need to do to communicate with the machine.

Now, type a few letters. Type your name. Don't worry about the spacing or lines. Just keep typing. *Do not push the* <**RETURN**> *key until you are instructed to do so.*

STEP 4: THE CURSOR

Now, you have something on the screen—your name. You are probably looking at it and wondering what to do next. You should also see the cursor blinking at the end of what you typed. That cursor tells you where you are on the screen. It is a location indicator.

STEP 5: SPECIAL KEYS

The letters M and G are exceptions when you press the <**SHIFT**> key with them. *Apple II+ user:* Press the <**SHIFT**> key and M. You will see a right bracket appear on the screen. *Apple IIe or IIc user:* Find the special key with the] on it, and press it.

Press the <**SHIFT**> key and G. A "G" will appear on the screen. Find the <**CONTROL**> or <**CTRL**> button. This is a special button. When you press it nothing happens on the screen. When you press it with another key and hold it down, it gives that key more operating options.

Hold down <**CONTROL**> and press G. You will hear a "beep." Try it again until you are tired of hearing it.

STEP 6: REPEATING A CHARACTER

Find the <**REPT**> button on the Apple II+. This is the repeat button. It makes the key character repeat on the screen. To use it, press any key; then hold the <**REPT**> button down.

Apple II+ user: Press B and hold <**REPT**> button down.

Apple IIe or IIc user: Holding any character key down for a period of time will cause it to repeat.

STEP 7: DIFFERENCES BETWEEN O AND 0; 1 AND L

Press the L key. An upper case "L" appears. It cannot be used as the number 1. The number 1 is the first key in the set of numeral keys at the top of the keyboard. The same is true of 0. An upper case O cannot be used for zero. Press both keys to study the difference in characters. Press 0 and press O. Remember that the alphabetic symbols on the keyboard are different from the numerical symbols in the top row of the keyboard. You cannot interchange them just because they might look the same.

STEP 8: SCREEN WRAPAROUND

Type the following on the screen and *do not* press <**RETURN**>.

Type: Your name followed by your address, and then "The quick brown fox jumped over the lazy dog" and "4 + 6 +10"

Notice that as you came to the end of a line the computer went automatically to a second line below. This is called *screen wraparound*. Perhaps your screen looks peculiar. That is okay. If you have familiarized yourself with the keyboard, GOTO STEP 9. If you still want to try out every key, do so.

STEP 9: CLEARING THE SCREEN

Look for the <**ESC**> key. <**ESC**> means Escape.

Apple II + user: To clear the screen: Press <**ESC**>: then <**SHIFT**> and press P to get the "@" symbol. Again, press the <**ESC**> key and hold it down while you type the "@" by pressing the <**SHIFT**> key and the P key. The screen should clear.

Apple IIe or IIc user: To clear the screen: Press <**ESC**>: then <**SHIFT**> and press 2 to get the "@" symbol. Again, press the <**ESC**> key and hold it down while you type the "@" by pressing the <**SHIFT**> key and the 2 key. Remember that you will need to press and hold down the three keys in the order shown to clear the screen.

Apple II +: Clearing the screen: Press <**ESC**> <**SHIFT**> and ⧅

Apple IIe or IIc: Clearing the screen: Press <**ESC**> <**SHIFT**> and ⧅

STEP 10: CORRECTING ERRORS

Look for the ← and → keys. These keys move the cursor to the left and to the right.

Type your name and misspell it.

Backspace the cursor by pressing the <←> key to the first wrong character. Type in the correct character over the wrong character. Find the <→> key and press it to move the cursor to the end of your name.

The Apple IIe and IIc have <↑> and <↓> arrow keys. Try them and see what they can do.

Type a few words and misspell them. Correct them using the left-arrow key and the right-arrow key until you are familiar with how they work.

STEP 11: SYNTAX ERROR

At this point you should be familiar with the keyboard. You can begin to learn how to get the computer to print on the screen for you. Clear the screen. Press <**ESC**> <**SHIFT**> @. Now press <**RETURN**> and you will see:

? SYNTAX ERROR

This is a message to you that the computer had a bunch of meaningless characters in its memory and did not know what to do. In other words, it did not understand the message you were sending to it. You and the computer were not communicating.

Clear the screen before going on to STEP 12. Press <**ESC**> <**SHIFT**> @.

STEP 12: TALKING WITH THE COMPUTER

The word PRINT is called a statement. It is an instruction to the computer. Type in the statement below exactly as shown:

PRINT "THIS IS FUN!"

Note that " " are used around the message you want printed. This is very important.

Now, press the <**RETURN**> key. The computer will print:

THIS IS FUN!

Remember: At the end of every statement or command (commands are terms you will learn later), press the <**RETURN**> key.

From this point on, no mention of pressing the <**RETURN**> key after every statement or command will be made. The <**RETURN**> key always tells the computer when you have completed the instruction, which will be either a statement or a command.

PRINT was the statement. "THIS IS FUN!" was the message. Pressing <**RETURN**> told the computer that that was the end of the statement.

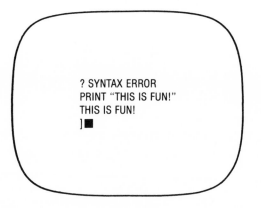

```
? SYNTAX ERROR
PRINT "THIS IS FUN!"
THIS IS FUN!
]■
```

STEP 13: PRACTICING PRINT STATEMENTS

Try typing in more PRINT statements. Remember to use your quotation marks at the beginning and end of what you want printed.

Type: PRINT "your name, address, city, state, and ZIP."
Press: <**RETURN**>.

```
PRINT "MARY ANN HARRELL,
ST. PETERSBURG, FLA. 33701"
MARY ANN HARRELL, ST.
PETERSBURG, FLA. 33701
]■
```

Before beginning STEP 14, try another way to clear the screen. The command HOME will also clear the screen. Be sure the cursor is flush left before you try this command. Press <**RETURN**> to place the cursor in the left margin.

Type: HOME and press <**RETURN**>.

HOME is a system command that you will be using often when you copy programs. You now know two ways to clear the screen.

There are differences between BASIC Statements and System Commands. *BASIC statements* are special words that provide the instructions to the computer in a program. *System commands* are special words that tell the computer to process the set of instructions given in the program. For example: PRINT is a statement in BASIC, whereas in this context HOME is a system command. HOME may also be used in a program and, in that context, HOME is used as a BASIC statement.

STEP 14: IF YOU MAKE AN ERROR USING THE PRINT STATEMENT

If you misspelled PRINT, you will get an error message. Try:

PRNIT "I LOVE YOU."

You receive:

? SYNTAX ERROR

You need to correct PRNIT to read PRINT. Now try:

PRINT   I LOVE YOU."

READ CAREFULLY!

Notice a quotation mark (") is missing in front of the I. A zero (0) will appear on the screen. This means you forgot the first or both quotes around the message. Check your Apple owner's manual for the meaning of error messages.

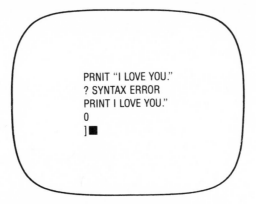

```
PRNIT "I LOVE YOU."
? SYNTAX ERROR
PRINT I LOVE YOU."
0
]■
```

STEP 15: PRACTICING CORRECTING ERRORS

An error in a program is called a *bug*. Use your ← key to correct your errors. Before you press <**RETURN**>, you can use this key to correct any error. Try it.

PRINT "I LOBE YOU."

Correct this before you press <**RETURN**>.

A BUG! A BUG!

Try some other PRINT statements with errors in them, such as:

PRNIT "HELLO, I AM HAPPY."
PRINT "THISIS A BUG"
PRINT "THIS IS A BUG TOO

STEP 16: THE PROGRAM LINE

You are now ready to understand the meaning of the term "line" in computer lingo. A line on a computer is different from a line on a typewritten page. On a computer, the line begins when you start typing at the PROMPT signal "]" and ends when you press <**RETURN**>. A computer line can hold up to 240 characters, about 6 typewritten lines on the screen. You will be able to use the PRINT statement to tell the computer to exhibit any message you wish. If you type 240 characters in one line, the computer will begin to beep. Find a paragraph in a book. Type the statement PRINT, a quotation mark ("), copy the paragraph from the book, and close with a quotation mark (") if you can. See what happens? When you type 240 characters, the computer will beep. The computer will not remember any letters after the beep even though they are on the screen.

STEP 17: NUMBERS

Tell the computer to:

PRINT 43297 <**RETURN**>

Notice that you did not use the quotation marks. The computer will print numbers without quotation marks.

STEP 18: THE APPLE CALCULATOR

The computer can be used as a simple calculator. The basic operation symbols are:

addition: +
subtraction: −
multiplication: * (asterisk)
division: /

Study these. Try the statements below. Don't forget to press <**RETURN**>.

PRINT 3 + 4
PRINT 16 − 10
PRINT 439 * 48
PRINT 45 / 6
PRINT 972 / 4 + 18 − 306 * 31

A "∧" can be used to multiply a number by itself any given number of times.

PRINT 2 * 2 * 2 * 2 * 2 * 2 * 2

can be written:

PRINT 2∧7   (∧ is <**SHIFT**> N or <**SHIFT**> 6)

Now try:

    PRINT " 8 + 9 "
    PRINT 8 + 9

Notice the difference between the two.

STEP 19: PRACTICE SUMMARY OF KEY FUNCTIONS

Practice this summary of Key Functions before you go to STEP 20:

1. Turn on the computer. Press <**CONTROL**> <**RESET**>.
2. Type <**CONTROL**> G.
3. Type capital O and a zero, capital L and the number one.
4. Type your name, address, and a short message.
5. To clear the screen: press <**ESC**> <**SHIFT**> @.
6. Type a PRINT statement.
7. Type a PRINT statement with an error in it.
8. Use HOME to clear the screen.
9. Correct an error by using your ← and → keys.
10. Type some PRINT statements using numbers.
11. Remember to press <**RETURN**> after every statement.

Having fun? If you feel secure with operating the keyboard, you are ready for bigger and better microcomputer experiences. This was your introduction to the keyboard. The next section, beginning with STEP 20, will teach you about diskettes and how to initialize a disk so that you can save the programs you will copy from this book.

Turn off your machine.

INITIALIZING A DISK

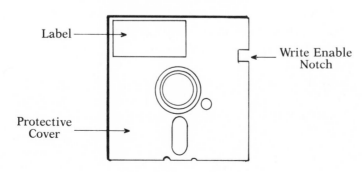

Label

Write Enable Notch

Protective Cover

STEP 20: LEARNING ABOUT DISKETTES

Inside the square cover is a thin, floppy circular disk, about the size of a 45-rpm record, on which information is stored by a magnetizing process. A diskette is reliable and should last for years. However, it is also vulnerable and subject to damage. These rules should be followed in the care of your diskettes:

1. Never write on the diskette with a ball point pen or pencil. Doing this may make an indentation on the diskette that will prevent it from running. A disk problem in computer lingo is sometimes referred to as a *glitch*. If you must write on your disk, use a felt tip pen. It is much safer to write on a label and then affix the label to the diskette.

2. Keep diskettes away from magnets and magnetic fields such as the screen on your monitor or a TV set.

3. Do not bend the diskette. Any creases in the diskette will prevent it from running.

4. Keep fingers off the shiny part of the diskette, which is not under protective cover.

5. Protect the diskette from extreme heat or cold.

6. Protect the diskette from dust by keeping it in its jacket when it is not being used.

7. Never insert or remove a diskette when the red disk drive light is on.

You need to purchase two blank diskettes in order to proceed efficiently with this chapter. Blank 5 1/4-inch single-sided double density diskettes cost less than $4.00 each from any computer store. Once in a while you will run across a faulty diskette. Your computer will not write on it, and you will get a message on the screen. Take the faulty diskette back to the dealer and exchange it for a good one.

A manual and a diskette were delivered to you along with your computer. You need to find this diskette. It is called the "SYSTEM MASTER" or the "ProDOS™ USER'S" Disk. There are two kinds of diskettes provided for an Apple microcomputer. One is called a DOS 3.3 SYSTEM MASTER which is used with an Apple II+ or IIe microcomputer. The other is called ProDOS™ USER'S DISK which is used with the Apple IIe or IIc microcomputer. Look at the disk that came with your microcomputer and see which system was enclosed. If your disk is named DOS 3.3 SYSTEM MASTER or SYSTEM MASTER, continue with STEPS 21 through 30. STEPS 21a through 27a are for ProDOS™ users. If your disk is named ProDOS™ USER'S DISK, turn to page 19 and follow the steps indicated as STEPS 21a through 27a.

DOS 3.3 SYSTEM MASTER INSTRUCTIONS FOR THE APPLE II+ OR APPLE IIe

STEP 21: BOOTING THE DOS 3.3 SYSTEM MASTER

The procedure described in this step is called *booting* the diskette.

1. Turn the computer on.
2. Press <**RESET**> or <**CONTROL**> <**RESET**> to turn the disk drive off. The red light will go out, and the whirring sound will stop.
3. Open the disk drive door and, holding the diskette so that your thumb is over the label, gently slide the SYSTEM MASTER diskette into drive 1 horizontally, label up and oval slot to the back of the drive.
4. Close the door.
5. *Apple II+ user:* Type PR#6 (# is SHIFT 3) and press <**RETURN**>.

   Apple IIe user: Press <**CONTROL**> <**OPEN APPLE**> <**RESET**>.

The red light will come on, the drive will whir, and, in a few seconds you will see a message on the screen. If you have trouble or the procedure hasn't worked, take the disk out, press <**RESET**> or <**CONTROL**> <**RESET**> and begin again.

The message you see on the screen should be:

APPLE II+   **APPLE IIe**

```
DOS VERSION 3.3          08/25/80
APPLE II+ OR ROM CARD    SYSTEM MASTER
```

```
DOS VERSION 3.3 SYSTEM MASTER
JANUARY 1, 1983
COPYRIGHT APPLE COMPUTER, INC, 1980, 1983
```

©Apple Computer, Inc., 1980

STEP 22: THE CATALOG OF PROGRAMS

In order to see what programs are on your SYSTEM MASTER, type: CATALOG and press <**RETURN**>.

Almost immediately you will see a list (catalog) of names of programs. On an Apple II+, it is a partial list. Press any key to see the rest of the list. On an Apple IIe, the list is complete.

For now, the programs you will run are the ones with an "A" in front. To learn about the programs preceded by a "B" or an "I," consult your owner's manual.

STEP 23: USING THE RUN COMMAND

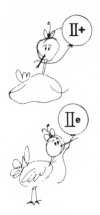

Try one of the programs on the SYSTEM MASTER. Ignore the letters and numbers preceding the program.

Type: RUN (followed by the program name).

For example:

Apple II+ user: Type: RUN COLOR DEMOSOFT and press <**RETURN**>.

The red light and whirring sound indicate that the computer is reading the program, COLOR DEMOSOFT, into its memory.

Apple IIe user: If you have an Apple IIe, you received two diskettes. The second one is called "SAMPLE PROGRAMS." Take out the SYSTEM MASTER disk and insert the SAMPLE PROGRAMS diskette.

Type: RUN COLOR TEST and press<**RETURN**>.

COLOR TEST on the Apple IIe and COLOR DEMOSOFT on the Apple II+ are the same program.

Follow the instructions on the screen. Watch what happens. If you have a color monitor or a color TV set, the kaleidoscope pattern is particularly fascinating.

When you are finished exploring this program, press any key to return to the program menu. On an Apple II+, to exit the program, press <**RESET**> or <**CONTROL**> <**RESET**>. On an Apple IIe, press menu option #5 to exit.

Now type: CATALOG and press <**RETURN**> to see the catalog. RUN other programs on the diskette that have an "A" in front of them.

STEP 24: MAKING A BACKUP COPY OF YOUR SYSTEM MASTER

You should make a backup copy of your SYSTEM MASTER. You need a blank diskette as well as your original SYSTEM MASTER. The SYSTEM MASTER will be the "original" diskette. The blank diskette will be the "duplicate" diskette.

If you have two disk drives, the SYSTEM MASTER should be in drive 1 and the blank diskette in drive 2. If you have one disk drive, the SYSTEM MASTER should be in drive 1. With one disk drive, you will have to switch diskettes several times while the copy is being made. However, all the directions you need will be given on the screen as you run the program that instructs you in making a copy.

COPYA (©Apple Computer, Inc.) is the program that lets you copy diskettes if you are not prevented from doing so by a password protection. Be sure the SYSTEM MASTER is in the disk drive.

Type: RUN COPYA and press <**RETURN**>.

Now give the information requested on the screen. Note that the terms "slot" and "drive" are different. Original and duplicate slots are both 6. With two drives, the original drive is 1 and the duplicate drive is 2. With one drive, the original and duplicate drives are both 1. (If your interface card is not in slot 6, you will receive an error message, "SLOT VACATED." Check with your dealer or some knowledgeable person about which slot the interface card is placed in your computer or try typing PR#2. Your interface card may be in slot 2.

For two drives, the information to the computer is

```
ORIGINAL SLOT:  6
         DRIVE:  1
     DUPLICATE:  6
         DRIVE:  2
```

For one drive, the information to the computer is

```
ORIGINAL SLOT:  6
         DRIVE:  1
DUPLICATE SLOT:  6
         DRIVE:  1
```

Press <**RETURN**> to begin the copying process. You will want to refer to the Apple manuals for more information on making backup copies of diskettes.

STEP 25: LABELING YOUR COPY OF THE SYSTEM MASTER

Put your original SYSTEM MASTER away in a safe place and save it to make another copy should you need one. Write "SYSTEM MASTER" on a gummed label. *Do not write on the diskette.* Affix the label to your new copy. You will use your new SYSTEM MASTER in the next step. If you have two drives, put your new SYSTEM MASTER in drive 1.

STEP 26: PREPARING A DISK TO SAVE PROGRAMS

You will follow the procedure in this step and in STEP 27 only when you prepare a diskette on which to store the programs that you type into the computer.

Begin by putting your new SYSTEM MASTER (the one you made) into the disk drive (drive 1), if it is not already there.

Type: CATALOG and press <**RETURN**>.

The first program on the list is a curious one called HELLO. Run the HELLO program.

Type: RUN HELLO and press <**RETURN**>.

You will see the same message on the screen that appeared when STEP 21 was executed. This message is the output of the HELLO program. It greets you when you boot up your diskette.

The HELLO program is used to identify the diskette and initialize it. The initializing process puts the Disk Operating System (DOS) on the diskette and lays down tracks similar to the grooves on a phonograph record except that the tracks are applied magnetically and can't be seen.

A blank disk must be initialized before your programs can be stored on it.

STEP 27: INITIALIZING A DISK SO PROGRAMS CAN BE SAVED

(Please read STEP 27 completely before attempting anything on the computer.)

A blank diskette is initialized by using any simple computer program which is followed by the command, INIT HELLO. Insert a blank disk into an available drive. Use the program below.

```
10 PRINT "Type your name between quotes"
20 PRINT "Type the correct date between quotes"
30 END
```

If you have an Apple IIe, make sure the <**CAPS LOCK**> key is down. To begin this new program, type: NEW and press <**RETURN**>. Line numbers shown must be included when lines are typed. Put your name between the quotes in line 10 and the correct date between the quotes in line 20. Remember to press <**RETURN**> at the end of each line.

When you have typed each line of this program, including the line numbers, type INIT HELLO and press <**RETURN**>.

When <**RETURN**> is pressed after INIT HELLO, the red light will come on and the disk drive will whir. The initialization process takes a while, so don't be alarmed when the drive seems to whir on and on. It will stop eventually and, when it does, your diskette will be ready to use with this book.

When the initializing process is complete, boot your diskette.

Apple II + user: Type PR#6 and press <**RETURN**>.

Apple IIe user: Hold down <**CONTROL**> <**OPEN APPLE**> <**RESET**>.

Your name and today's date should appear.

Type: CATALOG and press <**RETURN**>.

HELLO should be the first program in your catalog.

Refer to the Apple manual for more information on initializing blank diskettes.

STEP 28: PRACTICING SAVING AND RETRIEVING PROGRAMS

In this step you will write a short practice program to learn how to save and retrieve your programs. Your initialized diskette should be in the disk drive. If you have two drives, then it should be in drive 1.

Boot it up . . .

Apple II + user: Type PR#6 and press <**RETURN**>.

Apple IIe user: Press <**CONTROL**> <**OPEN APPLE**> <**RESET**>.

This enters the disk operating system into the computer's memory so that you can store programs on the diskette.

Now . . .

Type: NEW and press <**RETURN**>.

This command will clear the memory to receive a new program. Continue by typing the following lines. Notice that each line is numbered so that the computer will execute the lines in the sequence determined by the order of the numbers.

```
10 HOME          (HOME clears the screen)
20 PRINT "HELLO";  (The ; makes HELLO repeat
                    horizontally.)
30 GOTO 20
```

Now you need to RUN the program.

Type: RUN and press <**RETURN**>.

The program will continue to run until you stop it.

Press: <**RESET**> or <**CONTROL**> <**RESET**>.

This will break into the program and stop it.

To save the program on your diskette, you must give it a name. For example, name it EXAMPLE.

Type: SAVE EXAMPLE and press <**RETURN**>.

The red light and the whirring sound mean that the program is being written on your diskette. When this process ends and you see a blinking cursor on the screen, list the catalog.

Type: CATALOG and press <**RETURN**>.

EXAMPLE should appear right below HELLO.

STEP 29: LOADING PROGRAMS INTO THE COMPUTER'S MEMORY

Type: LOAD EXAMPLE and press <**RETURN**>.

This command will *transfer* the program, EXAMPLE, into the memory of the computer.

When the cursor appears, type: RUN.

You can see that your program is back in the memory of the computer.

Stop the program from running. Remember how?

To stop the program: Press <**RESET**> or <**CONTROL**> <**RESET**>.

Then type: LIST and press <**RETURN**>.

Did you get a listing of the program? You should see what you typed in STEP 28.

One more exercise. Type line 25 like this:

    25 PRINT "(your first name)"

Press: <**RETURN**>.

Then type: RUN

What do you see?

Is the computer saying HELLO to you on the screen?

Stop the program from running and list it. Remember how? You should see line 25 between lines 20 and 30.

STEP 30: DELETING A PROGRAM FROM A DISKETTE

EXAMPLE is probably not a program you want to save for posterity. To erase it from your diskette,

Type: DELETE EXAMPLE and press <**RETURN**>.

After the disk drive stops, list the catalog.

Type: CATALOG and press <**RETURN**>.

EXAMPLE should be gone from the menu.

SUMMARY OF STEPS 20 THROUGH 30
YOUR DOS 3.3 SYSTEM MASTER*

A. Booting (STEP 21)

B. How to list a CATALOG (STEP 22)

C. How to run a program (STEP 23)

D. Using COPYA to make a backup of a diskette (STEP 24)

E. How to label your new diskette (STEP 25)

F. Using INIT HELLO to initialize a blank diskette (STEP 26)

G. Giving your program a name (STEP 27)

H. How to save, load, and list your program (STEPS 28 and 29)

I. How to delete a program (STEP 30)

---

*© Apple Computer, Inc.

GOTO Chapter 2 to learn some elementary statements in BASIC. After completing Chapter 2, you will be ready to copy the programs in Chapter 3 (Reading/Language Arts) and Chapter 4 (Mathematics/Science).

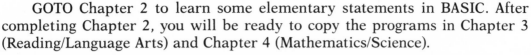

ProDOS™ USER'S DISK INSTRUCTIONS FOR APPLE IIe AND APPLE IIc*

STEP 21a: ABOUT YOUR ProDOS™ USER'S DISK

The ProDOS™ User's Disk uses a set of programs to help you manage the information on your disks. It is a very simple disk and easy to use, but you should read your Apple II *ProDOS™ User's Manual* carefully along with this book.

The ProDOS™ User Disk is designed to manage information in a hierarchical manner. A *volume* is another name for a disk. It contains a collection of files.

A *file* is a collection of information stored on a disk.

A *pathname* is a path the computer takes to find a file. It always begins with the name of the volume and ends with the name of the file.

After completing STEPS 22a to 25a, read Chapters 3 and 5 in your owner's manual to help you better understand how to add and delete files to and from your volume.

STEP 22a: BOOTING YOUR ProDOS™ USER'S DISK

The procedure described in this step is called *booting* the diskette.

1. Turn the computer on.
2. Press <**RESET**> or <**CONTROL RESET**> to turn the disk drive off. The red light will go out, and the whirring sound will stop.
3. Open the disk drive door and, holding the diskette so that your thumb is over the label, gently slide the ProDOS™ User's Disk into the drive horizontally, label up and oval slot to the back of the drive.
4. Close the door.
5. Press <**CONTROL**> <**OPEN APPLE**> <**RESET**> or type PR#6 and press <**RETURN**>.

The red light will come on, the drive will whir, and, in a few seconds, you

---

*©Apple Computer, Inc., 1983

will see a message on the screen. If you have trouble or the procedure hasn't worked, take the disk out, press <**RESET**> or <**CONTROL**> <**RESET**> and begin again.

The message you see on the screen should be:

```
+---------------------------------------------------------+
|  _____       |
|                                                         |
|               ProDOS™ USER'S DISK                       |
|           COPYRIGHT APPLE COMPUTER, INC. 1983           |
|  _____       |
|                                                         |
|                                                         |
|  YOUR OPTIONS ARE:                                      |
|      ? TUTOR: PRODOS EXPLANATION                        |
|      F — PRODOS FILER (UTILITIES)                       |
|      C — DOS  —  PRODOS CONVERSION                      |
|      S — DISPLAY SLOT ASSIGNMENTS                       |
|      T — DISPLAY/SET TIME                               |
|      B APPLESOFT BASIC                                  |
|  PLEASE SELECT ONE OF THE ABOVE   — — —                |
|                                                         |
+---------------------------------------------------------+
```

Read the information on the screen.

Press ? and read the TUTOR: ProDOS EXPLANATION.

After you have read this section, press <**ESC**>.

You will see the original menu on the screen. Let it sit on the screen for now and read STEP 23a before continuing.

STEP 23a: MAKING A COPY OF YOUR ProDOS™ USER'S DISK

You should make a backup copy of your User's Disk. You will need a blank diskette as well as your original ProDOS™ User's Disk. The ProDOS™ User's Disk will be the "original" diskette. The blank diskette will be the "duplicate" diskette.

If you have two disk drives, the ProDOS™ User's Disk should be in drive 1 and the blank diskette in drive 2. If you have one disk drive, the ProDOS™ User's Disk should be in drive 1. With one disk drive, you will have to switch diskettes several times while a copy is being made. However, all the directions you need will be given on the screen as you run the program that instructs you to make a copy.

1. Press F for ProDOS™ FILER (UTILITIES) MENU from MAIN MENU.

2. Press V for VOLUME COMMANDS from FILER MENU.

3. Press C for COPY A VOLUME from VOLUME COMMANDS MENU. You will see:

```
                      ┌─────────────────────────┐
                      │      COPY A VOLUME      │
   —COPY—             └─────────────────────────┘
           The Volume IN SLOT:  (6)
                        DRIVE:
           To Volume in SLOT:
                        DRIVE:
           NEW VOLUME NAME:
   —PRESS <RET> TO ACCEPT: <ESC> TO EXIT—
```

©Apple Computer, Inc., 1983

4. Type the slot number of the source volume or accept the default number by pressing <**RETURN**>.

5. Type the source drive number or accept the default by pressing <**RETURN**>.

   SLOT 6

   DRIVE 1

READ CAREFULLY!

6. Type the slot number of destination volume or accept the default by pressing <**RETURN**>.

7. Type the destination drive number or accept the default and press <**RETURN**>.

   FOR TWO DISK DRIVES   FOR ONE DISK DRIVE

   SLOT 6   SLOT 6
   DRIVE 2   DRIVE 1

You will see the message:

   INSERT DISKS AND PRESS <RET>.

DO THIS NOW!

8. If you have one disk drive, put your source disk (User's Disk) in your drive and be ready to do quite a bit of disk inserting and taking out. Messages will appear on the bottom of the screen telling you when to insert the source volume (disk) and when to insert the destination volume (disk).

9. Press <**RETURN**>. It will be blinking. (If you are copying other disks using this step procedure, type the name you want to give the destination volume [disk]. Type right over the default. Your new volume or disk name must begin with a letter and can be no longer than 15 characters made up of letters, numbers, or periods. Press <**RETURN**> when you are finished.)

Press <**RETURN**> and follow the instructions displayed at the bottom of the screen.

10. You now will hear and see FORMATTING, READING, WRITING as the disk is copied.

Follow the insert—extract directions if you are using one disk drive to copy. Remember that this procedure will require several exchanges. Keep on exchanging until you receive a copy complete message.

When the FORMATTING, READING, WRITING is completed you will receive the message:

COPY COMPLETE

11. Press<**ESC**>to return to the Volumes Command Menu.
12. Press<**ESC**>again to return to the Filer Menu.
13. Press Menu option Q to quit ProDOS™ User's Disk.
14. Press <**RETURN**> to go to Main ProDOS™ Menu.
15. Press B to go to Applesoft BASIC.

This long sequence of pressing buttons and selecting options was required to get you to Applesoft BASIC from the copy routine. It is *not* required every time you want to create programs or get to Applesoft BASIC.

STEP 24a: PREPARING A DISK TO SAVE PROGRAMS: FORMATTING A DISK

When you buy a blank diskette, it is not formatted or initialized. Formatting is also call initializing. *Formatting* a disk means preparing the disk to store information on it. All disks must be formatted before you can store information on them. The formatting procedure places tracks on this disk and divides the tracks into sectors. The tracks on the disk are magnetic tracks in the form of concentric circles. There are 35 tracks on each disk. The tracks are then divided into sectors. There are 16 sectors to a track.

Please try to remember that if you want to store information on a disk, it must be formatted before anything can be saved on the disk.

1. Press F on your main menu. A Filer Menu will now appear on the screen. Remember that volume is the other name for disk.
2. Press V for Volume Commands from the Filer Menu.
3. Press F to Format a Volume from the Volume Commands Menu. You will see:

```
┌─────────────────────────────────────────────────────────┐
│                  ┌──────────────────────┐                │
│                  │   FORMAT A VOLUME    │                │
│                  └──────────────────────┘                │
│                                                          │
│  —FORMAT—                                                │
│            The Volume in slot:  (6)                      │
│                        DRIVE:                            │
│              NEW VOLUME NAME:                            │
│  —PRESS <RET> TO ACCEPT: <ESC> TO EXIT—                  │
│                                                          │
└─────────────────────────────────────────────────────────┘
```

DO THIS
NOW!

READ VERY
CAREFULLY!

4. The display you see is not a menu. It is a series of statements. The flashing square over the number 6 is the cursor. The numbers in the parentheses are defaults. They are *defaults* because they'll be used by default unless you supply another number. You can accept the default by pressing <**RETURN**>. You can change the default by typing over it.

5. If you have two disk drives, your blank disk should be in drive 2, because your ProDOS™ is in drive 1. If you have one disk drive, take out your ProDOS™ User's Disk and insert your blank disk.

   Note: You can also insert a full disk, one that is not new. The Volume Commands on the Filers Utilities Menu can be used to format and erase a full disk that you may want to erase and reuse as a clean disk again.

6. Fill in the slot number.
   For two drives the information is:

   SLOT 6
   DRIVE 2

For one drive the information is:

   SLOT 6
   DRIVE 1

Press: <**RETURN**>.

7. When you are at New Volume Name you can either type in a name you make up for the disk you are formatting or accept the default/ BLANKXX. (XX can be a number between 00 and 99.) Example:

   NEW VOLUME NAME: STEVES

   or

   NEW VOLUME NAME:/BLANK01
   Press: <**RETURN**>.

The default/BLANKXX provides you with the option of numbering your disks in numerical order. This is useful if you are storing a lot of information and you want to use the disks in sequence.

Note: If you see

DESTROY ' XXX'? (Y/N)

bear in mind that **XXX** is the name of the disk you inserted and that it already contains some saved information.

If you Press Y, you will delete everything on that disk. If you Press N or the **<ESC>**, this will take you back to the Volume Commands menu.

9. When the disk is formatted you will receive a message:

Format COMPLETE

10. The formatted disk is now ready to save your programs.

STEP 25a: PRACTICING SAVING AND RETRIEVING PROGRAMS

1. Insert ProDOS™ User's Disk.

   Type: PR#6 or **<CONTROL> <OPEN APPLE> <RESET>**.

2. You will see the main menu.

   Press: B-Applesoft BASIC.

3. If you have two disk drives, insert your newly formatted disk into drive 2. If you have one disk drive, take out your ProDOS™ disk and insert your newly formatted disk.

4. Now you are ready to practice saving and retrieving programs.

   Type: NEW and press **<RETURN>**.

   Type: HOME and press **<RETURN>**.

Your screen is now clear. Type the following program EXACTLY as shown here.

```
10 HOME              Press <RETURN>.
20 PRINT "HI THERE!"  Press <RETURN>.
30 END               Press <RETURN>.
RUN                  Press <RETURN>.
```

5. To save your program on a disk by typing SAVE and the name of the program:

   Type: SAVE EXAMPLE, D **<RETURN>** (-1 for Drive 1, 2 for Drive 2)

   You will hear a whirring sound and your short program is saved on the disk.

6. Now type:

NEW and press <**RETURN**>.

HOME and press <**RETURN**>.

Your screen should be clear with the cursor in the upper left corner.

7. To retrieve your program:

Type: LOAD EXAMPLE, D and press <**RETURN**>.

Type: LIST and press <**RETURN**>. You will see your program listing.

Type: RUN and press <**RETURN**>. You will run the program.

STEP 26a: DISPLAYING THE CATALOG OF PROGRAMS ON A DISK (VOLUME)

1. A volume has a main listing of all of the programs on your disk.
2. Type:

CAT and press <**RETURN**>.

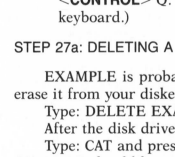

You will see a listing of all the programs stored on the disk.

(You will find it much easier to read the screen display if the screen is in the 80-column format. Check with your Apple dealer regarding this option or try typing PR#3. If you have an 80-column card, the cursor will shrink. To return to a 40-column screen, type: <**ESC**> <**CONTROL**> Q. If you have an Apple IIc, press the 80/40 key above the keyboard.)

STEP 27a: DELETING A PROGRAM FROM YOUR DISK

EXAMPLE is probably not a program you want to save for posterity. To erase it from your diskette:

Type: DELETE EXAMPLE and press <**RETURN**>.

After the disk drive stops, list the catalog.

Type: CAT and press <**RETURN**>.

EXAMPLE should be gone from the menu.

SUMMARY OF STEPS 21a TO 27a

A. About your ProDOS™ User's Disk (STEP 21a)

B. Booting your ProDOS™ User's Disk (STEP 22a)

C. Making a copy of your master disk (STEP 23a)

D. Formatting a disk (STEP 24a)

E. Saving and retrieving programs (STEP 25a)

F. Displaying a catalog of programs (STEP 26a)

G. Deleting a program from a disk (STEP 27a)

GOTO Chapter 2 to learn some elementary statements in BASIC. After completing Chapter 2, you will be ready to copy the programs in Chapter 3 (Reading/Language Arts) and Chapter 4 (Mathematics/Science).

LEARNING TO PROGRAM
AND TO COPY PROGRAMS
FOR CLASSROOM USE
ON YOUR APPLE

BEGINNING PROGRAMMING

Before beginning to copy the programs in this book, it is important to become familiar with some BASIC programming language. A simple BASIC program is made up of some fundamental BASIC statements. These statements include such words as FOR, NEXT, LET, PRINT, GOTO, INPUT, and END. These words tell the computer how to perform. They are instructions, directing the computer to logically execute a program line by line.

The instructions are like a road map to the computer. If you give the wrong instruction, the computer becomes lost and usually responds with an error message or won't run a program as intended. The instructions are very important and must be presented logically and unambiguously to the computer.

Read the next few pages and practice the simple programs presented here on your computer. Each program will demonstrate some basic instructions that will be of help while you copy the programs in this book.

You will not need to insert your initialized disk into the drive to practice these programs. After completing this chapter, you will be ready to insert the disk for saving the programs in Chapters 3 and 4.

WHAT IS A PROGRAM?

Let us examine a simple program of instructions to the computer and a command that tells the computer to carry out the instructions.

A simple BASIC program might look like this:

Do this Now.

```
10 PRINT "I LOVE TO LEARN HOW TO PROGRAM."
20 PRINT "MY STUDENTS LOVE PROGRAMMING, TOO."
30 END
```

The procedure below will help you to enter and run this program.
Turn on the computer.
Press: <**CTRL**> <**RESET**>.
Type: NEW <**RETURN**>. (NEW clears the computer's memory.)
Enter the program by typing it exactly as shown.
Press <**RETURN**> at the end of each line.
When you have finished, type RUN and press <**RETURN**>.
The computer will print on the screen:

```
I LOVE TO LEARN HOW TO PROGRAM.
MY STUDENTS LOVE PROGRAMMING, TOO.
```

Examine the program presented. Each line began with a line number. The first number was 10; the second was 20, followed by 30. The line numbers tell the computer the order to follow as instructions are given. The computer will start with the lowest number and go to the next highest number.

Each instruction to the computer must begin with a LINE NUMBER. The computer will always list the instructions in order of their line numbers.

In lines 10 and 20, the next statement after the number is PRINT. PRINT, along with words in quotation marks, tells the computer what to print on the screen. PRINT is a statement in BASIC. Statements tell the computer what to do.

Line 30 is an END statement. END tells the computer that the program has ended.

Finally, you typed in the command RUN. RUN is a system command that tells the computer to process the set of statements in the program you have just entered.

SUMMARY OF EVENTS

The statements of the program are:

```
10 PRINT "I LOVE TO LEARN HOW TO PROGRAM."
20 PRINT "MY STUDENTS LOVE PROGRAMMING, TOO."
30 END
```

The command to process the program is:

```
RUN
```

The OUTPUT of the program is:

I LOVE TO LEARN HOW TO PROGRAM.
MY STUDENTS LOVE PROGRAMMING, TOO.

Notice that RUN does not have a line number. The numbered parts of the program instruct the computer what to do. RUN is a system command that tells the computer to act immediately on the statements of the program.

USING PUNCTUATION MARKS: THE COMMA AND SEMICOLON

Try these programs:

```
10 PRINT 5 + 6
20 PRINT 28 / 4
30 PRINT 56 * 3
40 END
```

Now try:

```
10 PRINT 5 + 6,
20 PRINT 28 / 4,
30 PRINT 56 * 3,
40 END
RUN
```

Notice that the first program printed the answers in a vertical column, and the second program printed them horizontally. The comma (,) in a program will instruct the computer to print the program output separated into zones.

The output from line 10 was printed in the first zone, the output from line 20 was printed in the second zone, and the output from line 30 was printed in the third zone. A PRINT statement with commas is often used to print output in columns.

Using semicolons in a program tells the computer to do something different. A comma is used to print output in different zones. A semicolon can be used to make the printed output run together horizontally on the same line.

Try this program:

```
10 PRINT "TEACHER", "STUDENTS", "AIDES"
20 PRINT "TEACHER"; "STUDENTS"; "AIDES"
30 END
RUN
```

The output is:

```
TEACHER   STUDENTS   AIDES
TEACHERSTUDENTSAIDES
```

If you want a space between the words TEACHER, STUDENTS, and AIDES, then there must be a space inserted between the last letter of the word and the quotation marks: "TEACHER "; "STUDENTS "; "AIDES "

Now try adding a semicolon (;) after the last word "AIDES" in line 10. Just retype line 10 and put a semicolon at the end ("AIDES";). RUN the program. What happens?

CORRECTING ERRORS

Now let us consider what to do if you make an error in typing and you want to retype an instruction. No problem! If you have made an error in typing a line, either in spelling or leaving out a special instruction, just retype the line until you type it correctly. In the beginning, while learning to program, you may find yourself retyping the same line over and over again until you have typed it error (or bug) free. One nice feature about entering programs is that you can retype a line until it is entered correctly without retyping the whole program.

However, if you simply misspelled a word, you can quickly correct it before pressing <**RETURN**> by pressing your left-arrow key to skip over those letters already typed and retyping the character.

Typing a line is like thinking about something. Pressing <**RETURN**> is like saying it. Using <**RETURN**> is a commitment. Proofread the line you just typed before committing yourself by pressing <**RETURN**> and you will save yourself a lot of work.

Type the following program that has an error in line 20 and a change of instruction. Begin by typing: NEW <**RETURN**>.

```
10 PRINT "THERE IS NO ERROR IN THIS LINE."
20 PRINT "THERE IS AN ERROR IN THIS LINE."
30 END
20 PRINT "THERE IS NO BUG IN THIS LINE."
```

There are other ways to correct errors besides retyping lines. When you become more familiar with programming, you may want to consult your owner's manual for editing procedures.

USING THE "LIST" COMMAND

Notice that there is an error in line 20 in the above program. It was retyped correctly again at the end of the program without typing the RUN command. When you type the command, LIST, you will see that the computer has automatically replaced the old line 20 with the new line 20. And, if you then type RUN, it will run the correct program.

Suppose you want to add a line 15 to the above program. No problem! Just type the line below after line 20 or in any other place, and then type: LIST.

15 PRINT "THIS IS BUGLESS"

The program listing will show you what is stored in the computer's memory with replaced and inserted lines in the number order given.

ERASING THE MEMORY AND USING THE "NEW" AND "HOME" STATEMENTS

To erase any program from a computer's memory, type in the word NEW. The word NEW is a system command that tells the computer to clear its memory and make room for a new program.

Often the NEW command is followed by the first numbered line with HOME. HOME is another instruction that will clear your screen. When in doubt about clearing the screen, try typing HOME. However, HOME will not clear the memory, only the screen. Make sure you know the difference between NEW and HOME.

USING THE "FOR" AND "NEXT" STATEMENTS

Two new statements, FOR and NEXT, always appear as a pair in a program. FOR/NEXT statements instruct the computer to make a loop in the program. Every time there is a FOR there must be a NEXT. FOR/NEXT can be used as a shortcut to produce more output. Enter this program into your computer.

```
NEW
100 HOME
110 FOR R = 1 TO 5
120 PRINT "+ + + + + + + + + +"
130 NEXT R
999 END
RUN
```

The output is:

```
+ + + + + + + + + +
+ + + + + + + + + +
+ + + + + + + + + +
+ + + + + + + + + +
+ + + + + + + + + +
```

The two statements, FOR and NEXT, define a loop within a program. A loop permits the processing of data within the program in a repetitive way. The loop is executed over and over again until the given number of repetitions is reached. In the above program, the FOR/NEXT loop will be executed five times. The output is five lines of + + + + + + + + + +.

Notice the letter R in the program. R is called a variable because it represents various numbers while the program is being executed. The first time through the loop, R is 1. The second time, R is 2, and so on until the last time, R is 5. The letter R is chosen arbitrarily. It could just as well have been B, G, T, or any other letter.

NEW informed the computer that new information was being put into the memory, and told it to erase everything old in the memory. 100 HOME cleared the screen. Line 110 told the computer that the loop was to be executed five times. This was written as "FOR R = 1 TO 5".

Line 120 told the computer to print a + + + + + + + + + + pattern.

Line 130 told the computer to return to the second line and to continue with the loop. The program will return to line 110 until all five lines of the + + + + + + + + + + pattern are printed.

For the fun of it, try:

Do this Now.

```
NEW
100 HOME
110 FOR N = 2 TO 48 STEP 2
120 PRINT N,
130 NEXT N
140 END
RUN
```

HURRAY!   Retype line 120 as   120 PRINT N;   and RUN again.
Retype line 120 as   120 PRINT N ",";   and RUN again.
WASN'T THAT FUN!

I can do it. Can You?

Now try writing your own simple program using NEW, HOME, PRINT, FOR/NEXT, END, and RUN. Also include the use of punctuation marks such as the quotation mark ("), comma (,), and semicolon (;).

USING THE "INPUT" AND "GOTO" STATEMENTS/ USING "$" STRINGS

BASIC

INPUT is a statement that allows you to enter data using the keyboard while a program is running. GOTO causes the computer to branch to a different section of the program.

Examine this program.

```
NEW
5 HOME
10 PRINT "WHAT IS YOUR NAME?"
20 INPUT N$
30 PRINT
40 PRINT "HELLO " ;N$; " GLAD TO MEET YOU."
```

```
50 END
RUN
```

This program tells the computer to ask for your name. In Line 20, INPUT along with N$ tells the computer that you are going to type in a response and that your response should remain in the memory under the code of "N$". "$" (read *string*) is a symbol for a string of alphanumeric (alphabetic or numeric) characters. Every time PRINT N$ appears in the program the computer will print your name.

Line 30 in the program above contains PRINT all by itself. This instructs the computer to skip a line (or double space) when printing lines on the screen. Notice that in line 40 there is a new use of the semicolon. It permits the two messages in quotes and the N$ between them to appear as one line on the screen.

Computers can store words, groups of words, and numbers when they are instructed to do so. The symbol "$" indicates that an alphanumeric response will be typed into the computer. Numbers can be stored as strings too. They will be treated as "words," and you will not be able to do arithmetic with them.

For the fun of it, try this simple program on your computer.

TRY THIS.
IT'S FUN!

```
NEW
10 HOME
20 INPUT "WHAT IS YOUR NAME?";N$
30 PRINT N$;
40 GOTO 30
RUN
```

Notice that there is no END to this program. The GOTO statement will cause it to go on until you stop it. Programmers call this an infinite loop. When you are tired of this program, press <**CONTROL**> <**RESET**>. Pressing <**CONTROL**> <**RESET**> lets you break into a program that doesn't end by itself. Now type NEW and go on to the next program.

GOTO is another statement that can make a loop in a program.

INPUT is a statement that asks for information from the user.

Type: NEW. The command NEW will clear the memory and the screen. The command HOME will clear the screen only.

Remember: Before entering any program always type: NEW.

The next program will teach you how to program your computer so it will respond to an answer. REM represents REMARK. This is a statement used to remind the programmer what the program does. It will not be printed on the screen. Often a program will be all worked out and bug free, but you may not know what it does. REM is a way of documenting (explaining) a program. The computer ignores a line that begins with REM.

Enter this program:

Do this Now.

```
NEW
10 HOME
20 REM THIS PROGRAM ASKS THE
30 REM USER FOR TWO NUMBERS
40 REM AND THEN PRINTS OUT
50 REM THE SUM, DIFFERENCE,
60 REM PRODUCT, AND QUOTIENT
70 REM OF THE NUMBERS.
100 PRINT "GIVE ME TWO NUMBERS."
110 INPUT A,B
120 PRINT A + B
130 PRINT A − B
140 PRINT A * B
150 PRINT A/B
160 PRINT
170 GOTO 100
RUN
```

Notice that the INPUT statement, line 110, required that you respond by typing in two numbers.

BASIC

USING "IF/THEN" STATEMENTS

An IF/THEN statement tells the computer that a decision must be made. After a choice is made, a statement tells the computer how to proceed.

Read this program.

```
10 PRINT "DO YOU WANT APPLES OR BANANAS?"
20 INPUT A$
30 IF A$ = "APPLES" THEN PRINT "APPLES ARE RED."
40 IF A$ = "BANANAS" THEN PRINT "BANANAS ARE YELLOW."
50 END
```

Examine the program below and try it. It has many "$" statements asking the computer to remember responses given to it. The computer is programmed to respond to the information given. Try entering this one and running it.

THIS IS A HUMDINGER!

```
NEW
5 HOME
10 PRINT "I AM YOUR FRIENDLY ADVISOR."
15 INPUT "WHAT IS YOUR NAME?" ;N$
20 PRINT "HELLO, " ;N$;", I AM VERY HAPPY TO MEET YOU."
30 PRINT "TELL ME, " ;N$;", HAVE YOU EVER SOUGHT ADVICE?"
```

```
31 INPUT A$
40 PRINT "THAT IS VERY INTERESTING, " ;N$;"."
50 PRINT "HOW ARE YOU FEELING TODAY?"
51 INPUT F$
60 PRINT "I WOULD BE SURPRISED IF YOU NEVER FELT"
70 PRINT F$;"."
80 INPUT "HOW OLD ARE YOU?";A
90 IF A<30 THEN 150
100 IF A<60 THEN 130
110 PRINT "THE GOLDEN YEARS ARE MARVELOUS."
120 GOTO 160
130 PRINT "EXERCISE AND GOOD FOOD WILL KEEP YOU HEALTHY."
140 GOTO 160
150 PRINT "YOUTH HAS SPUNK. KEEP SMILING!"
160 PRINT "GOOD-BYE NOW, ";N$
999 END
RUN
```

The program above has many INPUT, PRINT, and GOTO statements. It also makes use of the IF/THEN statements. These two terms are always used together to instruct the computer to make decisions. IF a person responds one way, THEN the computer will go to a designated line number or follow an instruction embedded in the THEN portion of the IF/THEN statement.

Now try writing your own simple program using INPUT, GOTO, IF/THEN, and "$".

When you have worked through these simple programs, you will be familiar with some of the terminology, statements, and instructions used in BASIC programming.

USING "LET" STATEMENTS

Now try some of these programs using LET.

```
NEW
10 HOME
20 LET X = 46
30 LET Y = 5
40 PRINT X + Y, X − Y
```

```
50 PRINT X * Y, X/Y
60 END
RUN
```

The output is:

```
  51      41
230        9.2

NEW
10 HOME
20 LET S = 4
30 PRINT S
40 LET S = S + 8
50 GOTO 30
60 END
RUN
```

This program will go on printing numbers because it contains an infinite loop. The computer will automatically stop when the number becomes so large that the computer cannot handle it anymore.

LET can be omitted from a statement, but the computer will act as if it were still there. In the program below, LET is understood in lines 20 through 70.

```
NEW
10 HOME
20 P$ = "GOOD"
30 S$ = "AND"
40 T$ = "JUICY"
50 M$ = "ORANGES"
60 O = 5
70 R$ = "CENTS"
80 PRINT P$,S$,T$,M$,O,R$
90 END
RUN
```

The output is:

GOOD	AND	JUICY
ORANGES	5	CENTS

"READ/DATA" STATEMENTS

In BASIC you now know that the statement LET will assign information to a storage area, and INPUT is a way of asking for information. Both statements store information so that it can be retrieved and used within a program. Another way this can be done is by using the READ/DATA statements.

Study this program:

```
10 READ N
20 IF N = 0 THEN END
30 PRINT N
40 GOTO 10
50 DATA 2,5,4,8,4,0
60 END
```

READ THIS CAREFULLY!

Line number 10 begins with READ. READ tells the computer to go to the DATA line. If a READ statement appears in a program, the program must contain at least one DATA statement (line). Some programs contain more than one data line. It doesn't matter where the DATA line is located in the program; the READ statement will find it. The DATA line could come first, in the middle, or at the end of the program. Don't worry; the computer will locate it.

In the above program, line number 10 tells the computer to find the DATA line. It locates the first number in line 50, which is 2. Then the program tells the computer to print 2. Line 40 tells the computer to return to line 10.

The READ statement returns to the data line and locates the next number, which is 5. It prints 5. The program ends when the computer reads 0. Zero is called "dummy" data. It tells the computer when to stop.

If you are working with words, the computer needs to be told what the dummy word is in order to end the program. Remember that when alphabetical characters or a long string of numbers is used, the $ symbol is used to tell the computer that a string is in storage. Line 30 in the program below checks A$ to see if it is equal to the dummy data. That data is a special word designated by you. In the program below, it is "STOP". Try these programs using READ/DATA and $ statements.

Do this Now.

```
NEW
10 HOME
20 READ A$
30 IF A$ = "STOP" THEN 70
40 PRINT A$
50 GOTO 20
60 DATA LIONS,TIGERS,ELEPHANTS,BEARS,STOP
70 END
```

The output is:

    LIONS
    TIGERS
    ELEPHANTS
    BEARS

Did you notice that the words in line 60 did not have quotation marks around them? When strings are used in a DATA line, they do not need quotation marks around them unless they contain punctuation marks.

This summary of BASIC words will help you when entering the programs in this book. Try to remember some of the meanings, and, as you enter the program in the text, these words should guide you while you are copying a program.

INSTRUCTIONAL STEPS FOR COPYING PROGRAMS

STEP 1

Select a program from either Chapter 3 (Reading/Language Arts) or Chapter 4 (Mathematics/Science). Choose a short, easy program with which to begin.

STEP 2

Turn on your machine.

STEP 3

Press <**CONTROL**> <**RESET**>. The red light on the disk drive will turn off.

STEP 4

Insert your SYSTEM MASTER or ProDOS™ User's Disk carefully into the disk drive. Shut the door.
Apple II+ user: Type PR#6 and press <**RETURN**>.
Apple IIe and IIc user: Press <**CONTROL**> <**OPEN APPLE**> <**RESET**> or
TYPE: PR#6 and press <**RETURN**>.

After you have booted in your DOS 3.3 SYSTEM MASTER, take it out. Insert your newly formatted disk into the drive. Go to STEP 5.

If you are using the ProDOS™ User's Disk, press B Applesoft BASIC when the main menu appears on the screen. At the sign of the cursor you are ready to begin. Take out your ProDOS™ User's Disk and insert your formatted disk into the drive.

STEP 5

Select a program and copy it line by line. Be sure you type *exactly* what is printed on the page. Remember, if you make a mistake, either use your left- and right-arrow keys to retype a character or press <**RETURN**> and retype the whole line again. It would be wise to select simpler short programs at first before attempting to enter longer ones.

STEP 6

At the end of the program, after all the lines have been entered, type: SAVE (Name of program) and press <**RETURN**>.

After the word SAVE insert the name of the program. A suggested method for naming a program is to use the numbers in the Table of Contents. For example:

SAVE MATH1

MATH1 would be associated with the title listed in the Table of Contents.

You may wish to invent your own name for saving the programs, such as ALPHABETIZING. Make sure it starts with a letter. Don't use spaces or punctuation marks.

Once you type SAVE (Name of program) and press <**RETURN**>, the computer will begin to store your program on the disk. You will hear a whirring sound and the red light will come on while the computer is writing the program on the disk.

STEP 7

Check to see if you have saved the program.

Type in: LOAD (Name of program) <**RETURN**>.

The computer should load the program from the disk into memory. If the message "FILE NOT FOUND" appears on the screen, there is no problem! Your program is still in memory. Repeat STEP 6. Once you are certain the program is saved, RUN the program to see how it works.

STEP 8

If you are sure of the procedure for copying and storing programs on a disk, continue typing other programs. Begin each program by typing NEW to erase the old program from memory.

STEP 9

Select another program to copy. Repeat STEPS 5 through 9.

USING <**CTRL**> <**S**>

Frequently, when running a program that you have just typed, you will get an error message because of a typing mistake. To find the mistake, you need to look at the lines of the program. Type: LIST <**RETURN**>.

Your program listing may be too long to fit on the screen and may scroll off the screen before you can read it.

Using <**CTRL**> <**S**> will control the scrolling. Hold down the <**CTRL**> key and press <**S**>. The scrolling will stop so you can read the lines of your program. To start scrolling again, press <**CTRL**> <**S**>.

A little practice will make you proficient in this technique. You will be able to find the line that has the error in it so that you can retype it correctly.

LISTING A SINGLE LINE

Sometimes the computer will tell you in which line there is an error. When this occurs, you do not need to list the entire program to see the line in which there is an error. Simply type LIST (line number) <**RETURN**>. The line you need to retype will be displayed on the screen. For example:

    LIST 20

or

    LIST 20-40

Lines 20, 30, and 40 will appear on the screen. To delete a line, just type the line number and press <**RETURN**>.

HELPFUL HINTS

IF YOU WANT TO CHANGE DATA IN A SAVED PROGRAM

1. Insert your disk.
2. Type CATALOG to see the catalog if you don't remember the program name.
3. Type LOAD (Name of program) <**RETURN**>.
4. Type LIST to display the program lines. If you program is long, type LIST (number of line) to list only the line or lines you want to change. For example, LIST 240 or LIST 240-280.
5. To delete a line, simply type the line number and press <**RETURN**>. For example: 240 <**RETURN**>.

6. Retype the lines you wish to change.

7. While the disk is in the disk drive, type SAVE (Name of program). The new program will replace the old one.

Note: Your owner's manual contains the editing procedures for correcting lines in a program without retyping them. You may wish to learn these procedures when you become more proficient. Editing will save you time and typing.

IF ERRORS OCCUR WHILE COPYING PROGRAMS

1. Check to be sure that the disk is in the drive properly.

2. Check your screen by typing LIST to make sure you did not erase the program accidentally from memory. If that is the situation you will need to retype it.

3. Type CATALOG to see if you recorded it on the disk and it is listed in the catalog. If not, repeat STEPS 4 through 9 in the section "Instructional Steps for Copying Programs."

4. List each line to see if there are any typing errors.

WHAT TO DO IF YOUR PROGRAM DOES NOT RUN AFTER TYPING

If your program does not work after you have typed it carefully, check for the following errors that may have been made:

1. Check every line carefully to be sure you typed it exactly as shown on the program.

2. Check to make sure you did not type a ";" for a ":".

3. If you received an error message in a line that has a READ statement, the error is probably in your DATA lines. Check your DATA lines. Some computers will read the DATA lines incorrectly if you inadvertently hit the space bar before or after the comma separating the DATA items.
   INCORRECT: 210 DATA house, car, mouse , flower , bug
   CORRECT: 210 DATA house,car,mouse,flower,bug

4. Check your zeros and Os. Make sure you did not substitute a zero (0) for the letter O.

5. Check your number one (1) and letter "l". Make sure you did not substitute the alphabetical character "l" for the number one (1).

6. Check your line numbers. Make sure you did not type the alphabetical character O for a zero (0).

7. If you received an error message in a specific line, just type LIST (and the line number). Check it carefully against the program line. Make sure every parenthesis, comma, semicolon, and colon is properly entered in the line. If you find the error, retype the line and LIST the program again.

    Type: LIST (line number) <**RETURN**>.
    Type: Retype the line again to correct the error <**RETURN**>.
    Type: LIST <**RETURN**>.
    Type: RUN <**RETURN**>.

A WARNING

If you live in an area where there are frequent thunderstorms, you should unplug your system when it is not in use. There is a danger that power surges caused by lightning might damage your system severely. Also, *do not use the system during a thunderstorm.*

STOPPING A PROGRAM

If you want to stop a program, try the following five steps in the order they are presented.

1. Press <**CONTROL**> <**RESET**>. (This stops the program run. The program will still be in the memory.)

2. Press <**CONTROL**> <**RETURN**>. (This is a stronger way of getting out of some programs.)

3. Press <**OPEN-APPLE**>hold, press <**CONTROL**> <**RESET**>. (If you have an Apple IIe, this will get you out of the program, but it will also *erase* all of the current work in memory.)

4. Press <**ESC**>. (This is the easiest and quickest way. If this doesn't work try, the next method.)

5. Turn off the power. (If all else fails, take the disk out and turn off the power. You will lose your current work in the memory.)

NO CURSOR ON THE SCREEN

1. Is the monitor turned on? Is the video cable plugged in?

2. Check the brightness and contrast controls.

3. Did you turn the computer on and off and on again in succession too fast? Turn it off, wait for 15 seconds, and then turn it on again.

4. Is everything plugged into a wall outlet?

5. Press <**CONTROL**> <**RESET**>.

LIGHT WON'T GO OFF ON THE DISK DRIVE

1. Make sure the disk door is closed.
2. Press <**CONTROL**> <**RESET**>. Wait.
3. If the light is still on, press <**CONTROL**> <**RESET**> again.

DISK DRIVE IS RATTLING

1. The disk may not be set right in the disk drive. Open the door and slowly and carefully insert it again.
2. The disk may be in the wrong way. Check to make sure the oval slot enters the drive first. The label should be at the top between your fingers when you are inserting it.
3. The disk may be formatted for a different system.

SYNTAX ERROR MESSAGE

1. If you are operating an Apple IIe, make sure the <**CAPS LOCK**> key is pressed down.
2. Did you inadvertently mix control characters with command characters? Check.
3. Did you misspell any statement words?
4. Did you leave out punctuation marks?
5. Did you type *exactly* what is shown on the program line?
6. Parentheses and quotation marks always come in pairs in a program line. Check your pairs.
7. Check your owner's manual for the meaning of error messages.

chapter 3

25 PROGRAMS FOR READING AND LANGUAGE ARTS ON THE APPLE

A program is more than a set of instructions to the computer; it is also a reflection of the inner workings of a person's mind. As such, programming logic often defies understanding. Therefore, don't be discouraged when you fail to fully comprehend the significance of all the statements in the programs in this chapter. You will find yourself in good company; we, the authors, cannot always interpret the products of one another's thinking. However, we have attempted to explain ourselves as much as possible without burdensome detail. We hope that we have given you enough clues so that you can understand some of the more obscure parts of the programs, and hope that you will be able to design some programs your own.

In this chapter you will find twenty-five programs for the Apple II +, IIe or IIc microcomputer. These programs are meant to serve two purposes.

1. They provide a practical means of learning beginning programming in the BASIC language. This book is not meant to provide a complete course in programming but to introduce you to the BASIC language in an interesting and useful way.

2. The programs can serve as the beginning of your software library in that they provide short, concise exercises for specific skills in reading and language arts.

We recommend that the programs be typed in the order in which they are presented. They have been arranged in order of difficulty of programming techniques, not necessarily in order of concept difficulty. However, if you have special need for a program that appears later on, and are adventurous, please feel free to attempt the programs in any order you wish.

To assist you in understanding the purpose of the programs before typing them into your computer, each program is preceded by the following information (where applicable).

SUGGESTED FILE NAME: This is a suggested name to use when saving the program. Sometimes the program name is too long and awkward to use; a shorter file name is more desirable.

SUGGESTED GRADE RANGE: The grade levels at which a particular skill is taught and practiced.

DESCRIPTION OF THE PROGRAM: This paragraph describes the purpose of the program and some of its features.

NEW PROGRAMMING STATEMENTS: This section describes the functions of new programming statements that have not been used in a previous program.

EXPLANATION OF DATA LINES: The structure of the information in the data lines is explained in this section.

PROGRAMMING LOGIC: Here the authors attempt to explain their thinking. Program lines that might not be readily understood or that perform a special function are explained here.

HOW TO CHANGE THE DATA: It is possible to customize some of the programs to address the special needs of your students by changing data entries or certain lines of the program. The techniques needed to accomplish these changes are explained here.

A VERY IMPORTANT REMINDER

A computer line begins with the line number and ends with the last word or number before the next numbered line. *Do not press* <**RETURN**> *until you have typed the entire line.* When the cursor approaches the right side of the screen, just keep typing. Screen wraparound takes care of automatically moving the cursor down the screen.

For example, in the first program, "Flash Cards for Sight Words," line 20 will not fit on one line of the screen. Keep typing, and let screen wraparound take care of the problem. Press <**RETURN**> at the end of the word "WORDS." If you press <**RETURN**> too soon, retype the line.

1. FLASH CARDS FOR SIGHT WORDS

SUGGESTED FILE NAME: FLASH CARDS

SUGGESTED GRADE RANGE: 1–8

DESCRIPTION OF THE PROGRAM: This program provides practice in instantaneous recognition of sight words by flashing words on the screen for students to read aloud.

Note: Users of Apple IIe and Apple IIc equipment must have the <**CAPS LOCK**> key in the UP position in order for this program to run properly.

NEW PROGRAMMING STATEMENTS: An array is a list of elements. In line 10, DIM W$(100) sets aside memory space for 100 elements in the array, W$.

In line 20, HOME clears the screen; VTAB(6) positions the cursor on the sixth line from the top of the screen. PRINT TAB(7) begins printing the message in quotation marks seven spaces from the left of the screen.

READ W$(C) is the statement in line 150 that sends the computer to the data line where it reads the words to be printed on the screen. It stores them as elements of the array (list) called W$. C is used as a counter to keep track of the number of elements in the array.

GOSUB 370 appears in line 30 and directs the computer to the subroutine in line 370. Subroutines are used when the same routine is used over and over. In this case it is a FOR/NEXT loop that serves as a time delay. The computer must count to 2000 before it can proceed with the program. After executing the subroutine, RETURN returns the computer to the first statement after the GOSUB statement. In this case, line 40 is the next line executed. GOSUB/RETURN statements always appear as a pair in a program. Whenever you use GOSUB, you must also use RETURN.

In line 110, GET A$ allows the computer to accept single-character input from the keyboard without pressing <**RETURN**>.

Also in line 110, you will see ASC (A$). ASC is an abbreviation for ASCII, which means American Standard Code for Information Interchange. The ASC for keyboard characters is found in your owner's manual. For example, the ASC for "A" is 65. SC is assigned the ASC value for the keyboard character. The statement in line 120 tests to see if the key pressed is 1, 2, 3, 4, or 5. If not, then the computer is told to go to line 110 for another character.

In line 130, 48 is subtracted from SC. This number is used in line 230 to set the speed at which the words appear on the screen.

INT(C * RND(1)) + 1 appears in line 190. C is the number of items in the data list. This expression will choose a random whole number from 1 to C. For example, if there are 20 items of data, a random number from 1 to 20 will be chosen. RND(1) chooses a nine-digit decimal number between 0 and 1. Multiplying by C produces a decimal value between 0 and C. The integer function, INT, when used with positive values, drops the decimal part of the number. Thus, INT(C * RND(1)) will be a whole number from 0 to C–1. Add 1 to the expression to produce a number from 1 to C. For example, if C = 8 and RND(1) = .156938422, then C * RND(1) = 1.2555074. INT(1.2555074) + 1 = 2.

In line 270, the statement RESTORE appears. Once data is read in a program, it cannot be used again unless RESTORE is used. RESTORE tells the computer that the data is available to be read again.

EXPLANATION OF DATA LINES: Data lines 310-350 contain the words that are to appear on the screen.

PROGRAMMING LOGIC: In line 140, the counter, C, is set at zero. Lines 150 and 160 create a loop. The purpose of the loop is to read items from the data list, one at a time. The items are stored as elements of the array, W$. For example, when C=1, W$(1)=baby. When C=2, W$(2)=doll; and so on until "stop" is read. At this point, the program proceeds to line 170 and executes the remainder of the program.

The FOR/NEXT loop in lines 180-240 begins with the statement FOR X=1 TO 2 * C. The reason for the use of 2 * C is to present twice as many exercises to the student as there are words in the data list. Thus, some of the words will appear more than once, while some of them may not appear at all.

HOW TO CHANGE THE DATA: You can change or delete words in the data list. You can add words to the data list by typing new data lines between lines 310 and 360. Be very careful not to use the same line number twice, as the new line will be stored by the computer and the old line will be lost.

```
10    DIM W$(100)
20    HOME : VTAB (6): PRINT  TAB( 7);"FLASH CARDS FOR
         SIGHT WORDS"
30    GOSUB 370
40    HOME : VTAB (4): PRINT  TAB( 5);"*** FLASH SPEED
         SELECTION ***": PRINT : PRINT
50    PRINT  TAB( 15);"1) very fast": PRINT
60    PRINT  TAB( 15);"2) fast": PRINT
70    PRINT  TAB( 15);"3) medium": PRINT
80    PRINT  TAB( 15);"4) slow": PRINT
90    PRINT  TAB( 15);"5) very slow": PRINT : PRINT
100   PRINT "Press the number of your choice.";
110   GET A$:SC =  ASC (A$)
120   IF SC < 49 OR SC > 53 THEN 110
130   SC = SC - 48
140   HOME : VTAB (3): PRINT "Read to me aloud:": GOSUB
         370:C = 0
150   C = C + 1: READ W$(C): IF W$(C) = "stop" THEN C =
         C - 1: GOTO 170
160   GOTO 150
170   K = 0
180   FOR X = 1 TO 2 * C
190   J =  INT (C *  RND (1)) + 1: IF J = K THEN 190
200   K = J
210   VTAB (10): HTAB (18): PRINT "               ";
220   VTAB (10): HTAB (18): PRINT W$(J)
230   FOR I = 1 TO SC * 500: NEXT I
240   NEXT X
250   HOME : VTAB (6): PRINT "Do you want to try the
         list": PRINT : PRINT "again (Y or N)?";
260   GET A$
270   IF A$ = "Y" THEN  RESTORE : GOTO 40
```

```
280   IF A$ < > "N" THEN 260
290   HOME : VTAB (6): PRINT  TAB( 13);"Have a great
      day!!"
300   END
310   DATA  baby,doll,girl,mother,friend,car
320   DATA  feather,leaves,dog,tree,street,face
330   DATA  head,heart,kitten,yard,father,sister
340   DATA  well,house,boy,brother,bird,pet,hand
350   DATA  bike,table,chair,room,door,floor
360   DATA  stop
370   FOR T = 1 TO 2000: NEXT T: RETURN

]
```

2. ALPHABETIZING

SUGGESTED FILE NAME: ALPHABETIZING

SUGGESTED GRADE RANGE: 2–8

DESCRIPTION OF THE PROGRAM: This program will alphabetize any list of twenty words or less and show the alphabetizing process on the screen.

NEW PROGRAMMING STATEMENTS: In this program three arrays are dimensioned: C$(20), V(20), and H(20). C$ is a string array designed to store the words typed by the user. V and H are numeric arrays that position the words on the screen. When there are to be more than ten elements in an array, the array must be dimensioned.

HTAB FIRST appears in line 220. HTAB(15) moves the cursor 15 spaces from the left side of the screen.

In line 170, GOTO 70 causes the computer to return to line 70.

PROGRAMMING LOGIC: The part of the program from line 250 to 360 is the alphabetizing routine. The alphabetizing is actually done in lines 290 and 300. Lines 310-340 cause the words to be repositioned on the screen as the list is alphabetized.

As you study lines 290 and 300, you will see the sort routine called *bubble sort*. Two consecutive elements in the array, C$(1) and C$(2), are compared. If the two elements are in alphabetical order, the next pair, C$(2) and C$(3), are compared. If they are not in alphabetical order, their order is switched by line 300.

```
10   DIM C$(20),V(20),H(20)
20 CL$ = "                          "
30   HOME : VTAB (6): PRINT  TAB( 10);"*** ALPHABETIZ
     ING ***"
40   GOSUB 450
50   FOR X = 1 TO 10:V(X) = X + 5:V(X + 10) = X + 5: NEXT
     X
```

```
60    FOR X = 1 TO 10:H(X) = 1:H(X + 10) = 21: NEXT X
70    HOME : VTAB (6): PRINT "You may enter up to twen
      ty words, and": PRINT
80    PRINT "I will alphabetize them for you while": PRINT

90    PRINT "you watch me work.  Please press the": PRINT

100   PRINT "<RETURN> key after each word you type.":
      PRINT
110   PRINT "I will keep track of how many words": PRINT
      : PRINT "there are."
120   GOSUB 450
130   PRINT : PRINT : PRINT "Are you ready (Y or N)?"
      ;
140   GET A$
150   IF  ASC (A$) = 89 OR  ASC (A$) = 121 THEN 180
160   IF  ASC (A$) <  > 78 AND  ASC (A$) <  > 110 THEN
      140
170   GOTO 70
180 N = 0
190   N = N + 1: IF N > 20 THEN N = 20: GOTO 250
200   HOME : VTAB (6): PRINT "Please enter word #";N;
      " or the letter": PRINT
210   PRINT "'D' if you are done."
220   VTAB (11): HTAB (15): INPUT C$(N)
230   IF  LEN (C$(N)) = 1 AND ( ASC (C$(N)) = 68 OR  ASC
      (C$(N)) = 100) THEN N = N - 1: GOTO 250
240   GOTO 190
250   HOME : VTAB (2): PRINT "I'm alphabetizing now .
        . ."
260   FOR X = 1 TO N: VTAB (V(X)): HTAB (H(X)): PRINT
      C$(X);: NEXT X
270   FOR I = 1 TO N - 1:FL = 0
280   FOR J = 1 TO N - 1
290   IF C$(J + 1) >  = C$(J) THEN 350
300 H$ = C$(J):C$(J) = C$(J + 1):C$(J + 1) = H$:FL =
      1
310   VTAB (V(J)): HTAB (H(J)): PRINT CL$;
320   VTAB (V(J + 1)): HTAB (H(J + 1)): PRINT CL$;
330   VTAB (V(J)): HTAB (H(J)): PRINT C$(J);
340   VTAB (V(J + 1)): HTAB (H(J + 1)): PRINT C$(J +
      1);
350   FOR T = 1 TO 100: NEXT T: NEXT J
355   IF FL = 0 THEN 370
360   NEXT I
370   VTAB (2): HTAB (1): PRINT "The alphabetizing is
       complete."
380   VTAB (22): PRINT "Press 'C' to go on or 'S' to
      stop.";
390   GET A$
400   IF  ASC (A$) = 83 OR  ASC (A$) = 115 THEN 430
410   IF  ASC (A$) <  > 67 AND  ASC (A$) <  > 99 THEN
      390
420   GOTO 180
430   HOME : VTAB (6): PRINT  TAB( 12);"Have a happy,
      day!"
440   END
450   FOR T = 1 TO 2000: NEXT T: RETURN
```

3. WRITING A STORY

SUGGESTED FILE NAME: STORY

SUGGESTED GRADE RANGE: 3–8

DESCRIPTION OF THE PROGRAM: This program provides a story starter to motivate students for production writing. The program does not correct student errors or value the end product.
Note: Users of Apple IIe and Apple IIc equipment must have the <**CAPS LOCK**> key in the UP position in order for this program to run properly.

EXPLANATION OF DATA LINES: Each data line includes the information for one story. The first entry in the line is the story starter. The second entry is the title.

HOW TO CHANGE THE DATA: You can change the data items or delete them. You can add more stories to the list by adding data lines between lines 410 and 510. Do not use the same line number twice.

```
10   DIM FL$(100),T$(100)
20   HOME : VTAB (6): PRINT  TAB( 13);"WRITING A STOR
     Y"
30   FOR I = 1 TO 2000: NEXT I
40 C = 0
50 C = C + 1
60   READ FL$(C),T$(C)
70   IF FL$(C) = "stop" THEN C = C - 1: GOTO 90
80   GOTO 50
90 V =   INT (C *   RND (1)) + 1:A$ = FL$(V)
100   HOME : VTAB (3): PRINT  TAB( 5);"Please help me
      write a story.": PRINT
110   PRINT  TAB( 5);"I will start the story.": PRINT
      : PRINT
120   PRINT A$: PRINT
130   PRINT "Type in what you think happened next.": PRINT

140   INPUT B$
150   HOME : VTAB (3)
160   PRINT A$: PRINT
170   PRINT B$
180   PRINT : PRINT
190   PRINT "What happened after that?": PRINT
200   INPUT C$
210   HOME : VTAB (3)
220   PRINT A$: PRINT
230   PRINT B$: PRINT
240   PRINT C$
250   PRINT : PRINT
260   PRINT "Finish the story.": PRINT
270   INPUT D$
280   HOME : VTAB (2)
290   HTAB (20 -   INT ( LEN (T$(V)) / 2)): PRINT T$(V
      )
```

```
300   PRINT : PRINT
310   PRINT A$: PRINT
320   PRINT B$: PRINT
330   PRINT C$: PRINT
340   PRINT D$: PRINT : PRINT : PRINT
350   PRINT "Type 'C' to continue, or 'S' to stop.";
360   GET A$
370   IF A$ = "C" THEN 90
380   IF A$ < > "S" THEN 360
390   HOME : VTAB (6): PRINT "You look so nice when y
      ou smile!!"
400   END
410   DATA   "The boy had lost his homework.",The Lost
       Homework
420   DATA   "The little bird flew in the window.",The
       Bird in the House
430   DATA   "Jane won the big race yesterday.",Jane W
      ins Again
440   DATA   "Tom caught his first fish tody.",Tom's F
      irst Fish
450   DATA   "The girl fell off her bike.",The Great F
      all
460   DATA   "My teacher is very kind to me.",My Nice
      Teacher
470   DATA   "I remember my favorite birthday.",My Bes
      t Birthday
480   DATA   "It was so cloudy all day yesterday.",The
       Gray Day
490   DATA   "Mary got a kitten as a gift.",A Special
      Pet
500   DATA   "Bill's dog can do many tricks.",Bill's S
      mart Dog
510   DATA   stop,stop

]
```

4. SYNONYMS

SUGGESTED FILE NAME: SYNONYMS

SUGGESTED GRADE RANGE: 3–8

DESCRIPTION OF THE PROGRAM: This program provides practice in one type of word relationship: synonyms. Students are asked to match a given word with a synonym from the Word Bank.

Note: The number of exercises presented by the program depends on the amount of data used. If you add data to the program, the number of exercises presented will be increased. Therefore, the number of problems to be presented by this program is not printed on the screen.

Note: Users of Apple IIe and Apple IIc equipment must have the <**CAPS LOCK**> key in the UP position in order for this program to run properly.

EXPLANATION OF DATA LINES: The data is organized in pairs as each exercise requires two data items. The first entry appears on the screen. The second entry is the correct synonym from the Word Bank.

HOW TO CHANGE THE DATA: As before, you can change or delete data. You can also add new exercises by typing data lines between lines 280 and 370 if you do not use the same line numbers twice.

If you wish to change the Synonym Word Bank, retype lines 110 through 140.

```
10   DIM W$(100),S$(100)
20   HOME : VTAB (6): PRINT  TAB( 18);"SYNONYMS"
30   FOR I = 1 TO 2000: NEXT I
40 C = 0
50 C = C + 1
60   READ W$(C),S$(C)
70   IF W$(C) = "stop" THEN C = C - 1: GOTO 90
80   GOTO 50
90   FOR V = 1 TO C
100   HOME : VTAB (3): PRINT "SYNONYM WORD BANK:": PRINT

110   PRINT "    glad      shine     little    pull"
120   PRINT "    odd       run       also      cost"
130   PRINT "    wet       cool      hot       nice"
140   PRINT "    fast      sea       cup       spoil"
150   FOR I = 1 TO 40: PRINT "-";: NEXT I
160   VTAB (11): PRINT "The word is:   >>>   ";W$(V);"
        <<<": PRINT : PRINT
170   PRINT "Type a synonym from the word bank.": PRINT

180   HTAB (17): INPUT X$
190   IF X$ = S$(V) THEN  PRINT : PRINT : PRINT  TAB(
        15);"Very good!": GOTO 230
200   PRINT : PRINT : PRINT  TAB( 7);"Try again.  Typ
      e carefully."
210   FOR I = 1 TO 2000: NEXT I
220   GOTO 100
230   VTAB (22): PRINT "Press the <space bar> to cont
      inue . . .";
240   GET A$: IF A$ < > " " THEN 240
250   NEXT V
260   HOME : VTAB (6): PRINT "I'm glad we could be to
      gether today!"
270   END
280   DATA  happy,glad,unusual,odd,small,little
290   DATA  dash,run,glow,shine,drag,pull
300   DATA  too,also,charge,cost,gay,glad
310   DATA  strange,odd,mug,cup,damp,wet
320   DATA  kind,nice,rot,spoil,quick,fast
330   DATA  ocean,sea,warm,hot,cold,cool
340   DATA  rapid,fast,glass,cup,ruin,spoil
350   DATA  chilly,cool,moist,wet,trot,run
360   DATA  peculiar,odd,tiny,little,price,cost
370   DATA  stop,stop

]
```

5. USING CONTEXT CLUES

SUGGESTED FILE NAME: CONTEXT

SUGGESTED GRADE RANGE: 2–8

DESCRIPTION OF THE PROGRAM: This program promotes reading comprehension at the sentence level by requiring students to use the meaning of a sentence starter to determine if the ending makes sense. A partial sentence is shown on the screen; then several (usually ten) sentence endings are given to the student. The student must answer whether or not the ending makes a proper sentence.

EXPLANATION OF DATA LINES: Data lines 410, 450, 490, 550, 610, 650, and 690 contain the sentence starters. The data lines in between contain the possible correct endings. Notice that the lines with the sentence starters also have numbers that indicate the quantity of possible endings. Each possible ending contains the correct answer (Y or N) that states whether or not the ending is correct.

PROGRAMMING LOGIC: Lines 50 through 110 read the data into the computer's memory. In line 90, you will see what are called *double subscripted variables*. This term means there are two numbers that help identify a particular element in an array (list of items).

Here is an example to explain the process. The first time through the loop in lines 50 through 110, C=1. In line 60, the computer will read "A bird can" as R$(1) and "10" as N(1). Next, the computer will go through a FOR/NEXT loop (lines 80–100) which reads the data entries in lines 420 through 440. The arrays, W$ and A$, are double subscripted to help the computer find the proper entries when printing them on the screen and checking answers.

W$(1,1)="fly." A$(1,1)="Y." W$(1,2)="smile." A$(1,2)="N." This process continues until W$(1,10)="sing" and A$(1,10)="Y." The elements of these double subscripted arrays are used in lines 130 through 180.

HOW TO CHANGE THE DATA: The data can be changed or deleted if you are very careful. The best way to alter the program is simply to retype the data entry by entry. If you decide to add more exercises, you can add data lines between lines 410 and 730. *Remember:* Do not use the same line number twice. Be sure that the number following the sentence starter is exactly the same as the quantity of endings you type.

```
10   DIM R$(20),N(20),W$(20,20),A$(20,20)
20   HOME : VTAB (6): PRINT  TAB( 10);"USING CONTEXT
     CLUES"
30   FOR I = 1 TO 2000: NEXT I
40   C = 0
```

```
50  C = C + 1
60   READ R$(C),N(C)
70   IF R$(C) = "stop" THEN C = C - 1: GOTO 120
80   FOR X = 1 TO N(C)
90   READ W$(C,X),A$(C,X)
100   NEXT X
110   GOTO 50
120 H = 0
130 V =  INT (C *  RND (1)) + 1: IF V = H THEN 130
140 H = V
150  FOR X = 1 TO N(V)
160  HOME : VTAB (4): PRINT R$(V);" ......";
170  VTAB (7): HTAB (15): PRINT W$(V,X)
180 C$ = A$(V,X)
190 LN = 9: GOSUB 740: PRINT "Does this word fit in
      the": PRINT : PRINT "sentence (Y or N)?"
200  GET A$
210  IF C$ = "Y" AND A$ = "Y" THEN 260
220  IF C$ = "N" AND A$ = "N" THEN 260
230  IF A$ <  > "Y" AND A$ <  > "N" THEN 200
240  VTAB (14): HTAB (1): PRINT "Think about it and
      try again.": FOR T = 1 TO 2000: NEXT T
250  GOTO 190
260 LN = 6: GOSUB 740
270  VTAB (4): HTAB ( LEN (R$(V)) + 1): PRINT "
          ";
280  IF C$ = "N" THEN 310
290  VTAB (4): HTAB ( LEN (R$(V)) + 2): PRINT W$(V,X
      );"."
300  GOTO 320
310  VTAB (4): HTAB ( LEN (R$(V)) + 2): PRINT "not "
      ;W$(V,X);"."
320 LN = 22: GOSUB 740: PRINT "Press the <space bar>
      to continue . . .";
330  GET A$: IF A$ <  > " " THEN 330
340  NEXT X
350  HOME : VTAB (6): PRINT "Press 'C' to continue,
      or 'S' to stop.";
360  GET A$
370  IF A$ = "C" THEN 130
380  IF A$ <  > "S" THEN 360
390  HOME : VTAB (6): PRINT "You seem to be a really
      nice person!"
400  END
410  DATA  A bird can,10
420  DATA   fly,Y,smile,N,run,Y,eat,Y
430  DATA   read,N,learn,Y,drive,N
440  DATA   hop,Y,work,N,sing,Y
450  DATA   A dog can,10
460  DATA   run,Y,sleep,Y,talk,N,swim,Y
470  DATA   jump,Y,sit,Y,bake,N,bark,Y
480  DATA   yawn,Y,write,N
490  DATA   A boy can,20
500  DATA   swim,Y,cook,Y,read,Y,dance,Y
510  DATA   draw,Y,sing,Y,sew,Y,play,Y
520  DATA   run,Y,dig,Y,hop,Y,slide,Y
```

```
530  DATA   sweep,Y,throw,Y,sleep,Y,sit,Y
540  DATA   teach,Y,learn,Y,smile,Y,cry,Y
550  DATA   A girl can,20
560  DATA   hop,Y,dig,Y,slide,Y,learn,Y
570  DATA   sweep,Y,throw,Y,smile,Y,teach,Y
580  DATA   swim,Y,cook,Y,sit,Y,read,Y
590  DATA   dance,Y,draw,Y,sew,Y,run,Y
600  DATA   sing,Y,play,Y,sleep,Y,cry,Y
610  DATA   A fish can,10
620  DATA   run,N,dance,N,eat,Y,drive,N
630  DATA   swim,Y,read,N,breathe,N,smile,N
640  DATA   draw,N,bark,N
650  DATA   A cat can,10
660  DATA   bark,N,run,Y,jump,Y,purr,Y
670  DATA   climb,Y,read,N,eat,Y,scratch,Y
680  DATA   cook,N,sleep,Y
690  DATA   A teacher can,10
700  DATA   smile,Y,learn,Y,cry,Y,sit,Y
710  DATA   sing,Y,draw,Y,read,Y,sleep,Y
720  DATA   cook,Y,throw,Y
730  DATA   stop,0
740  POKE 34,LN: HOME : POKE 34,0: VTAB (LN + 1): RETURN
```

]

6. ALPHABETICAL ORDER

SUGGESTED FILE NAME: ORDER

SUGGESTED GRADE RANGE: 1–3

DESCRIPTION OF THE PROGRAM: Four consecutive letters of the alphabet appear on the screen. The student is instructed to type the next letter of the alphabet. This program provides practice in alphabetical order. The use of a score adds the aspect of a game which provides motivation for a routine task. The program provides some teaching as it gives the correct answer after three trials. This program also provides practice in lower case letter recognition.
Note: Users of Apple IIe and Apple IIc equipment must have the <**CAPS LOCK**> key in the UP position in order for this program to run properly.

PROGRAMMING LOGIC: In line 30, AL$ is the alphabet in lower case letters. In line 40, a loop is initiated which will execute fifty times. This means that there will be fifty problems given to the student. In line 50, P is randomly assigned a number from 1 to 22. MID$(AL$,P,4) tells the computer to look in the "middle" of AL$ at the four characters beginning with the Pth character from the left. For example, if P=15, then MID$(AL$,P,4)="opqr."
This explains why, in line 50, the random number is multiplied by 22. The greatest value for P must be 22, so that, when looking at AL$, the last four letters chosen begin with "v" and the answer that the student must type is "z."

N$ (in line 60) is the correct answer. It is MID$(AL$,P+4,1). In the example above, opqr, MID$(AL$,P+4,1) is "s."

The scoring routine in this program is composed of lines 95, 190, and 220. In line 95, TI, the variable used to store the value of the correct response, is initially set at 2000 for each new exercise. If the student answers correctly on the first attempt, he or she will get 2000 points for the answer. Line 190 will be executed if an incorrect answer is given, reducing the value of the correct answer by 800 points. If the first answer is incorrect, the second attempt, if correct, will earn 1200 (2000 − 800) points for the student. This means that if the first two attempts are incorrect for a particular exercise, the value of the correct answer will be reduced to 2000 − 800 − 800 = 400 points. After a third incorrect attempt the answer is given, and no points are awarded for the correct response.

Line 220 contains the statement S = S + TI, which instructs the computer to add to S (the variable used to keep track of the total score at any given time) the value of the correct response just entered. Line 220 will be executed only if the response is correct because of the IF/THEN statement found in line 130. This is a fairly typical method of scoring for use in simple game-oriented programs.

```
10   HOME : VTAB (6): PRINT  TAB( 11);"ALPHABETICAL O
     RDER"
20   FOR I = 1 TO 2000: NEXT I
30  AL$ = "abcdefghijklmnopqrstuvwxyz"
40   FOR X = 1 TO 50
50  P =   INT (22 *  RND (1)) + 1:L$ =   MID$ (AL$,P,4)

60  N$ =  MID$ (AL$,P + 4,1)
70  N = 0:LN = 2: GOSUB 280: PRINT "Letter #";X
80   VTAB (6): PRINT  TAB( 11);"ALPHABETICAL ORDER:"
90   VTAB (9): PRINT  TAB( 17);L$
95  TI = 2000
100 LN = 11: GOSUB 280: PRINT "Type the next letter
     in the alphabet.";
120  GET X$
130  IF X$ = N$ THEN 220
140 N = N + 1
150  IF N < 3 THEN 190
160  PRINT : PRINT "The next letter is:    ";N$
170  VTAB (22): PRINT "Press the <space bar> to cont
     inue . . .";
180  GET A$: IF A$ <  > " " THEN 180
190 TI = TI - 800: IF TI < 0 THEN TI = 0
195  IF N  > = 3 THEN 100
200  PRINT : PRINT "Try again.": FOR I = 1 TO 1000: NEXT
     I: GOTO 100
220 S = S + TI
230  VTAB (2): HTAB (25): PRINT "SCORE: ";S
240  NEXT X
250  HOME : VTAB (6): PRINT "Your final score is ";S
     ;" points."
260  VTAB (9): PRINT "Keep up the good work!"
```

```
270   END
280   POKE 34,LN: HOME : POKE 34,0: VTAB (LN + 1): RETURN
```

]

7. PRONOUNS

SUGGESTED FILE NAME: PRONOUNS

SUGGESTED GRADE RANGE: 3–8

DESCRIPTION OF THE PROGRAM: This program provides guided practice in substituting pronouns for words or phrases for people or things. A word or phrase appears on the screen. The student must type a pronoun to replace it. Students are required to know how to spell pronoun words or to have a master list available.

Note: The number of exercises presented by this program depends on the amount of data used. If you add data to the program, the number of exercises presented will be increased. Therefore, the number of problems to be presented by this program is not printed on the screen.

Note: Users of Apple IIe and Apple IIc equipment must have the <**CAPS LOCK**> key in the UP position in order for this program to run properly.

EXPLANATION OF DATA LINES: Each exercise requires three data entries. Therefore, the data items are typed in groups of three. The first item is the word or phrase that appears on the screen. The second and third items are the correct answers. The student can type either one of them and his answer will be accepted as correct.

Notice that some of the data entries are "". This occurs when there is only one correct answer. The "" serves to hold that place so that the data entries do not get "out of sync" with one another.

HOW TO CHANGE THE DATA: The best way to change data is to retype the lines, replacing items one by one. You can add exercises to this program by typing data lines between lines 360 and 450. Do not use the same line number twice.

```
10   DIM P$(100),A1$(100),A2$(100)
20   HOME : VTAB (6): PRINT  TAB( 16);"PRONOUNS"
30   FOR I = 1 TO 2000: NEXT I
40 C = 0
50 C = C + 1
60   READ P$(C),A1$(C),A2$(C)
```

```
70    IF P$(C) = "stop" THEN C = C - 1: GOTO 90
80    GOTO 50
90    FOR X = 1 TO C
100   HOME : VTAB (2): PRINT  TAB( 16);"PRONOUNS"
110   VTAB (3): PRINT  TAB( 12);"*******************"
120  LN = 6: GOSUB 460: PRINT  TAB( 20 -  INT ( LEN (
      P$(X)) / 2));P$(X)
130   VTAB (10): PRINT "Type one pronoun to replace t
      his word": PRINT : PRINT "or phrase."
140   VTAB (14): HTAB (17): INPUT X$
150   IF A2$(X) <  > "" THEN 180
160   IF X$ = A1$(X) THEN 290
170   GOTO 190
180   IF X$ = A1$(X) OR X$ = A2$(X) THEN 290
190  N = N + 1
200   IF N <  > 3 THEN 270
210   IF A2$(X) = "" THEN 240
220   VTAB (17): PRINT "The pronouns are: ";A1$(X);"
      and ";A2$(X)
230   GOTO 250
240   VTAB (17): PRINT "The pronoun is: ";A1$(X)
250  N = 0
260   GOSUB 330: GOTO 300
270   PRINT : PRINT  TAB( 15);"Try again.": FOR I = 1
       TO 1200: NEXT I
280   GOTO 120
290   PRINT : PRINT  TAB( 15);"Very good!": GOSUB 330

300   NEXT X
310   HOME : VTAB (6): PRINT "I hope to see you again
       very soon!"
320   END
330   VTAB (22): PRINT "Press the <space bar> to cont
      inue . . .";
340   GET A$: IF A$ <  > " " THEN 340
350   RETURN
360   DATA  John and Mary,they,them,mother,she,her
370   DATA  the boy,he,him,books,they,them,the girls,
      they,them
380   DATA  you and I,we,"",animals,they,them,food,it
      ,""
390   DATA  the pencil,it,"",many people,they,them
400   DATA  sand,it,"",the birds,they,them,the chair,
      it,""
410   DATA  you and me,us,"",Tim and his dog,they,the
      m
420   DATA  the car,it,"",teachers,they,them
430   DATA  the sky,it,"",three fish,they,them
440   DATA  the cat and the mouse,they,them,a rock,it
      ,""
450   DATA  stop,stop,stop
460   POKE 34,LN: HOME : POKE 34,0: VTAB (LN + 1): RETURN
```

]

8. GUESSING LETTERS

SUGGESTED FILE NAME: LETTERS

SUGGESTED GRADE RANGE: 2–6

DESCRIPTION OF THE PROGRAM: This program provides practice in determining the placement of letters in the alphabet. It develops skills necessary to
rapidly find reference materials that are alphabetically arranged. The program
requires the computer to randomly choose a letter. The student must guess the
letter in as few guesses as possible. The game format motivates students to
perform a routine task.

Note: Users of Apple IIe and Apple IIc equipment must have the <**CAPS
LOCK**> key in the DOWN position in order for this program to function
properly.

```
10   HOME : VTAB (6): PRINT  TAB( 13);"GUESSING LETTE
     RS"
20   FOR I = 1 TO 2000: NEXT I
30   HOME : VTAB (2): PRINT  TAB( 8);"Guess my letter
     (A-Z)."
40   VTAB (4): PRINT "Letters used:": PRINT
50 L = 66 +  INT (26 *  RND (1))
60 G = 0
70 LN = 9: GOSUB 240
80   GET L$
90   IF  ASC (L$) < 65 OR  ASC (L$) > 90 THEN 80
100 G = G + 1
110   IF  ASC (L$) = L THEN 170
120   IF  ASC (L$) > L THEN 150
130 LN = 7: GOSUB 240: PRINT "Too low in the alphabe
     t.  Try again."
140   VTAB (6): HTAB (2 * G - 1): PRINT L$;: GOTO 70
150 LN = 7: GOSUB 240: PRINT "Too high in the alphab
     et.  Try again."
160   VTAB (6): HTAB (2 * G - 1): PRINT L$;: GOTO 70
170 LN = 7: GOSUB 240: PRINT "You guessed with ";G;"
      guesses.": PRINT
180   VTAB (22): PRINT "Do you want to play again (Y
     or N)?";
190   GET Y$
200   IF Y$ = "Y" THEN 30
210   IF Y$ <  > "N" THEN 190
220   HOME : VTAB (6): PRINT  TAB( 7);"I like the way
      you smile!!"
230   END
240   POKE 34,LN: HOME : POKE 34,0: VTAB (LN + 1): RETURN
```

]

9. MATCHING THE CHARACTERS

SUGGESTED FILE NAME: MATCH UP

SUGGESTED GRADE RANGE: 1–5

DESCRIPTION OF THE PROGRAM: The computer randomly chooses a character on the keyboard. The student presses the key that types the character.

PROGRAMMING LOGIC: This program contains a scoring routine that calculates the percent of correct key strokes. This scoring routine appears in both line 230 and line 250 as INT(T / N * 100 + .5). T is the number of correct answers. N is the number of tries. T/N (T divided by N) calculates the fractional part T is of N in decimal form. Multiplying by 100 changes it to a percent. Adding .5 will round the value to the next whole number when the integer (INT) part of the number is used and the decimal part is dropped. For example, if T = 8 and N = 9, then T/N = .8888888. Multiplying by 100 changes the number to 88.88888. INT(88.88888 + .5) = INT(89.38888) = 89.

```
10   HOME : VTAB (6): PRINT  TAB( 9);"MATCHING THE CH
     ARACTERS": VTAB (10): HTAB (1): PRINT "** Fifty
     exercises will be presented. **"
20   FOR I = 1 TO 3000: NEXT I
30   T = 0:N = 0
40   FOR W = 1 TO 50
50   C = 33 +  INT (58 *  RND (1))
60   HOME
70   VTAB (6): HTAB (19): PRINT  CHR$ (C)
80   VTAB (10): PRINT  TAB( 3);"Type the character sh
     own above.";
90   GET A$
100  T = T + 1
110   IF  ASC (A$) = C THEN 160
120  VTAB (14): HTAB (3): PRINT "Please try again."
130  GOSUB 250
140  FOR I = 1 TO 2000: NEXT I
150  GOTO 60
160  VTAB (14): HTAB (3): PRINT "Very good!!!"
170 N = N + 1
180  GOSUB 250
190  FOR I = 1 TO 2000: NEXT I
200  NEXT W
210  HOME : VTAB (6): PRINT  TAB( 3);"You and I seem
     to be a good match!!"
220 N = 13
230  VTAB (10): PRINT  TAB( 7);"Your final score was
     "; INT (T / N * 100 + .5);"%."
240  END
250  VTAB (18): PRINT  TAB( 10);"Your score is "; INT
     (N / T * 100 + .5);"%.": RETURN
```

]

10. SUFFIXES

SUGGESTED FILE NAME: SUFFIXES

SUGGESTED GRADE RANGE: 3–8

DESCRIPTION OF THE PROGRAM: This program provides students with a Root Word Bank to use in deciding if a root word can be combined with a suffix. The program also illustrates the joining of a root to its suffix with movement on the screen. A suffix is printed on the screen. The student types a word from the Word Bank that can be used with the suffix to make an adjective. There are five suffixes that are used four times, making a total of twenty exercises.
Note: Users of Apple IIe and Apple IIc equipment must have the <**CAPS LOCK**> key in the UP position in order for this program to run properly.

EXPLANATION OF DATA LINES: The first entry in each data line is the suffix. The remaining entries are the root words from the Word Bank that can be used with that suffix.

HOW TO CHANGE THE DATA: If you want to change the data in this program, you must also change the Root Word Bank. You can add exercises by typing more data lines using line numbers between 370 and 420. Each data line must end with the word: stop. Be sure to use line numbers that have not been used before.

```
10   DIM S$(20),R$(20,20),N(20),U(20,20)
20   HOME : VTAB (6): PRINT  TAB( 17);"SUFFIXES": VTAB
     (10): HTAB (1): PRINT "* practice with root wor
     ds & suffixes *"
30   FOR I = 1 TO 3500: NEXT I
40 C = 0
50 D = 0:C = C + 1
60   READ S$(C)
70   IF S$(C) = "stop" THEN C = C - 1: GOTO 120
80 D = D + 1
90   READ R$(C,D)
100   IF R$(C,D) = "stop" THEN D = D - 1:N(C) = D: GOTO
      50
110   GOTO 80
120   FOR N = 1 TO 4
130   HOME : VTAB (2): PRINT "ROOT WORD BANK:"
140   PRINT "care      help      work      child"
150   PRINT "wonder    kind      teach     life"
160   PRINT "same      thought   hour      read"
170   PRINT "like      time      mind      play"
180   FOR X = 1 TO 40: PRINT "-";: NEXT X
190   FOR W = 1 TO C
200 LN = 8: GOSUB 430: HTAB (20): PRINT S$(W)
210 LN = 10: GOSUB 430: PRINT "Please type a root wo
    rd to use with": PRINT
```

```
220   PRINT "this suffix.    ";: INPUT RR$
230   FOR X = 1 TO N(W)
240   IF RR$ = R$(W,X) THEN 280
250   NEXT X
260  LN = 14: GOSUB 430: PRINT "Please try again."
270   GOSUB 440: IF FL = 0 THEN 200
275   GOTO 480
280   FOR Q = 2 TO 20 -  LEN (RR$)
290  LN = 8: GOSUB 430: HTAB (Q): PRINT RR$; TAB( 20)
      ;S$(W);
300   FOR I = 1 TO 30: NEXT I
310   NEXT Q
320   GOSUB 440: IF FL = 1 THEN 480
330   NEXT W
340   NEXT N
350   HOME : VTAB (6): PRINT  TAB( 5);"You are fun to
       work with!!!"
360   END
370   DATA   less,care,help,child,life,thought,time,mi
      nd,stop
380   DATA   able,work,teach,read,like,time,play,stop
390   DATA   ful,care,help,wonder,thought,mind,play,st
      op
400   DATA   ness,kind,same,like,stop
410   DATA   ly,kind,hour,like,time,stop
420   DATA   stop
430   POKE 34,LN: HOME : POKE 34,0: VTAB (LN + 1): RETURN

440  LN = 21: GOSUB 430: PRINT "Press C to continue,
      or S to stop . . .";
450   GET A$: IF A$ < > "c" AND A$ < > "s" THEN 450

460   IF A$ = "c" THEN FL = 0: RETURN
470   IF A$ = "s" THEN FL = 1: RETURN
480   HOME : PRINT "It is likely that we will meet again.": END
```

11. PRACTICING FASTER READING

SUGGESTED FILE NAME: SPEED READ

SUGGESTED GRADE RANGE: 1–8

DESCRIPTION OF THE PROGRAM: This program presents phrases at one of five speeds selected by the student for instant sight reading.

Note: The number of exercises presented by this program depends on the amount of data used. If you add data to the program, the number of exercises presented will be increased. Therefore, the number of problems to be presented by this program is not printed on the screen.

EXPLANATION OF DATA LINES: The data lines contain the phrases that appear on the screen to be read by the student.

PROGRAMMING LOGIC: Line 220 contains a circumflex. This is used to indicate to the computer to calculate 2 to the S power and assign it to S. Thus, if in line 180, S = 3, in line 220, S would be given the value 8, which is 2 to the S power. S varies from 1 to 5 as it is calculated by subtracting 48 from the ASC values of 1, 2, 3, 4, and 5. For example, if the student chooses #3, medium speed, then S = ASC(3) − 48 = 3.

In line 230, S is used to set the length of time that each phrase stays on the screen. The greater the value of S, the longer it stays on the screen. If S = 3, then N = 200 + (3 * 90) = 570. In line 280, the time delay would make the computer count to 570 before it could proceed to print the next phrase on the screen.

The statement in line 240 chooses the number of exercises that will be presented to the student. C is the number of data entries. If there are twenty phrases, the program will print phrases randomly chosen on the screen forty times before ending.

HOW TO CHANGE THE DATA: You can change data items by replacing them one for one. You can also add more phrases by typing data lines numbered between 380 and 520 if you do not use a line number that has already been used.

```
10    DIM T$(100)
20    HOME : VTAB (6): PRINT  TAB( 8);"PRACTICING FAST
      ER READING"
30    FOR I = 1 TO 2000: NEXT I
40  C = 0
50  C = C + 1
60    READ T$(C)
70    IF T$(C) = "stop" THEN C = C - 1: GOTO 90
80    GOTO 50
90    HOME : VTAB (3): PRINT  TAB( 6);"How fast do you
       want to read?": PRINT
100    PRINT  TAB( 14);"1) very fast": PRINT
110    PRINT  TAB( 14);"2) fast": PRINT
120    PRINT  TAB( 14);"3) medium speed": PRINT
130    PRINT  TAB( 14);"4) slow": PRINT
140    PRINT  TAB( 14);"5) very slow": PRINT : PRINT
150    PRINT "Press the number of your choice (1-5).";

160    GET A$
170    IF  ASC (A$) < 49 OR  ASC (A$) > 53 THEN 160
180  S =   ASC (A$) - 48
190    VTAB (22):: HTAB (1): PRINT "Press the <space b
      ar> to continue . . .";
200    GET A$: IF A$ <  > " " THEN 200
210    HOME : FOR I = 1 TO 2000: NEXT I
220  S = 2 ^ S
230  N = 200 + S * 90
240    FOR Z = 1 TO 2 * C
250  Q =   INT (C *  RND (1)) + 1: IF Q = L THEN 250
260  L = Q
270    VTAB (8): HTAB (20 -  INT ( LEN (T$(Q)) / 2)): PRINT
      T$(Q)
```

```
280   FOR I = 1 TO N: NEXT I
290   HOME
300   FOR T = 1 TO 200: NEXT T
310   NEXT Z
320   VTAB (22): PRINT "Do you want to try again (Y o
      r N)?";
330   GET Y$
340   IF Y$ = "Y" THEN 90
350   IF Y$ < > "N" THEN 330
360   HOME : VTAB (6): PRINT  TAB( 3);"I hope this is
       a great day for you!!"
370   END
380   DATA   in the house,on the boat
390   DATA   under the tree,at home
400   DATA   next to me,behind the wall
410   DATA   by my side,over my head
420   DATA   inside the box,in front of the room
430   DATA   behind the fence,around the corner
440   DATA   after the game,before the rain
450   DATA   under the desk,over the roof
460   DATA   with my friend,in the room
470   DATA   after my lunch,on the table
480   DATA   with our dog,around the room
490   DATA   before morning,during the night
500   DATA   behind the house,in the yard
510   DATA   behind your back,over your shoulder
520   DATA   stop
```

]

12. SPELLING AND TYPING

SUGGESTED FILE NAME: TYPE IT

GRADE RANGE: 3–8

DESCRIPTION OF THE PROGRAM: This program provides practice for the student in spelling skills. Five words are chosen at random from the word list in the data lines and displayed on the screen. The student can study them at leisure. When ready, the student presses the space bar and a countdown begins. One of the words flashes on the screen. The student must type that word. The program presents twenty exercises each time it is run.
Note: Users of Apple IIe and Apple IIc equipment must have the <**CAPS LOCK**> key in the UP position in order for this program to run properly.

EXPLANATION OF DATA LINES: The data lines contain the words from which the spelling exercises are randomly chosen, five words at a time. You may change words, delete words, or add words by typing new data lines that have line numbers between 540 and 550.

PROGRAMMING LOGIC: If the student types the word incorrectly, lines 380 through 410 contain a routine that prints the letters of the word one at a time beginning with the left-most letter. For example, if the word should have been "light," then line 380 becomes FOR Y = 1 to 5 (5 is the LENgth of W$). The first time through the loop, line 400 prints MID$(W$,1,1), which tells the computer to begin at the left end of "light," look at the second character, and print it. The second time through the loop, line 400, prints MID$(W$,2,1) which tells the computer to begin at the left end of "light," look at the second character, and print it. This process continues until the computer prints the fifth character in "light."

Line 390 is a time delay. The computer must count to 700 each time it prints a letter. This slows down the printing process so that each letter prints separately on the screen.

HOW TO CHANGE THE DATA:
You may wish to put your own list of spelling or reading vocabulary words in this program. Simply retype the data lines replacing the words already in the program with your words one for one. Be sure to separate entries with commas, and do not use spaces between entries.

You can also add more words to the program by typing data lines that have line numbers between 460 and 550 as long as you don't use a line number that has already been used.

```
10    DIM W$(200)
20    HOME : VTAB (6): PRINT  TAB( 10);"SPELLING AND T
      YPING": VTAB (10): HTAB (1): PRINT "** Twenty e
      xercises will be presented.**"
30    FOR I = 1 TO 3000: NEXT I
40    C = 0
50    C = C + 1
60    READ W$(C)
70    IF W$(C) = "stop" THEN C = C - 1: GOTO 90
80    GOTO 50
90    FOR X = 1 TO 20
100    FOR Y = 1 TO 5
110    W(Y) =  INT (C *  RND (1)) + 1: IF Y = 1 THEN 15
       0
120    FOR Z = Y - 1 TO 1 STEP  - 1
130    IF W(Y) = W(Z) THEN 110
140    NEXT Z
150    NEXT Y
160    HOME : VTAB (3): PRINT "You will be asked to ty
       pe a word from": PRINT
170    PRINT "the list below.  Study the list until": PRINT

180    PRINT "you feel you are ready.": PRINT
190    FOR Y = 1 TO 5
200    PRINT  TAB( 17);W$(W(Y)): PRINT
210    NEXT Y
220    GOSUB 560
```

```
230   HOME : VTAB (8): PRINT "Here comes the word:
      ";
240   FOR Y = 5 TO 1 STEP  - 1
250   VTAB (8): HTAB (24): PRINT Y;: FOR T = 1 TO 600
      : NEXT T
260   NEXT Y
270   W =  INT (5 *  RND (1)) + 1:W$ = W$(W(W))
280   VTAB (8): HTAB (24): PRINT W$
290   FOR T = 1 TO 250: NEXT T
300   HOME : VTAB (4): PRINT "Type the word you just
      saw"
310   VTAB (9): PRINT  TAB( 12);"====>   ";
320   INPUT AN$
330   IF AN$ <  > W$ THEN 360
340   VTAB (14): PRINT  TAB( 12);"Very good work!"
350   GOSUB 560: GOTO 430
360   HOME : VTAB (4): PRINT "The word you were to ty
      pe was"
370   VTAB (9): PRINT  TAB( 12);"====>   ";
380   FOR Y = 1 TO  LEN (W$)
390   FOR T = 1 TO 700: NEXT T
400   PRINT  MID$ (W$,Y,1);
410   NEXT Y
420   GOSUB 560
430   NEXT X
440   HOME : VTAB (6): PRINT "I hope you had as much
      fun as I did!"
450   END
460   DATA   cat,happy,dog,sad,funny,ball,tree,house,m
      other
470   DATA   father,sister,brother,book,chair,table,ca
      r
480   DATA   jump,play,game,friend,work,hear,see,feel,
      touch
490   DATA   smell,taste,shirt,shoe,sock,hat,coat,fish
      ,goat
500   DATA   animal,mouse,horse,sand,dirt,mud,rain,sun
      ,cloud
510   DATA   water,milk,soda,cream,butter,meat,meal,ni
      ce,kind
520   DATA   mean,soft,hard,smooth,rough,heavy,light,l
      oud,quiet
530   DATA   pretty,love,smile,hair,clean,dry,wet,carr
      y,load
540   DATA   stand,sit,lean,fall,push,pull,drag,sky,ea
      rth
550   DATA   stop
560   VTAB (22): HTAB (1): PRINT "Press the <space ba
      r> to continue . . .";
570   GET A$: IF A$ <  > " " THEN 570
580   RETURN

]
```

13. PLURALS

SUGGESTED FILE NAME: PLURALS

SUGGESTED GRADE RANGE: 2–8

DESCRIPTION OF THE PROGRAM: This program provides guided practice in forming regular plurals using -s and -es endings. Words are presented randomly.

EXPLANATION OF DATA LINES: The data lines contain the words that will be changed to plural form and the choices of correct answers. The choice for the ending "s" is "1"; the choice for the ending "es" is "2."

HOW TO CHANGE THE DATA: You may change or delete data. You may add data by typing data lines numbered between 380 and 490. Do not use numbers that have previously been used.

```
10   DIM W$(200),P(200)
20   HOME : VTAB (6): PRINT  TAB( 18);"PLURALS": VTAB
     (10): HTAB (1): PRINT "Twenty-five exercises wi
     ll be presented."
30   FOR I = 1 TO 3000: NEXT I
40   C = 0
50   C = C + 1
60   READ W$(C),P(C)
70   IF P(C) = 99 THEN C = C - 1: GOTO 90
80   GOTO 50
90 L = 0
100   FOR W = 1 TO 25
110 N =   INT (C *  RND (1)) + 1: IF N = L THEN 110
120 L = N
130   HOME : VTAB (4): PRINT "The word is ===>  ";W$(
     L)
140   VTAB (8): PRINT "Choose the plural ending:"
150   VTAB (11): PRINT  TAB( 15);"1) add 's'"
160   VTAB (13): PRINT  TAB( 15);"2) add 'es'"
170   LN = 15: GOSUB 500: PRINT  TAB( 15);"Type 1 or 2
     .";
180   GET A$
190   IF A$ <  > "1" AND A$ <  > "2" THEN 180
200 X =   VAL (A$)
210   IF X = P(L) THEN 240
220 LN = 15: GOSUB 500: PRINT  TAB( 16);"Try again."

230   FOR T = 1 TO 1200: NEXT T: GOTO 170
240 LN = 7: GOSUB 500
250   IF A$ = "1" THEN P$ = "s"
260   IF A$ = "2" THEN P$ = "es"
270   FOR Q = 39 TO 19 +  LEN (W$(L)) STEP  - 1
280 LN = 3: GOSUB 500
290   PRINT "The word is ===>   ";W$(L); TAB( Q);P$
300   FOR I = 1 TO 50: NEXT I
```

```
310   NEXT Q
320 LN = 22: GOSUB 500
330   PRINT "Press the <space bar> to continue . . ."
      ;
340   GET R$: IF R$ < > " " THEN 340
350   NEXT W
360   HOME : VTAB (6): PRINT "Seeing you is one of my
      favorite things."
370   END
380   DATA   house,1,car,1,box,2,bus,2,clock,1
390   DATA   dress,2,egg,1,flower,1,class,2,head,1
400   DATA   boy,1,tree,1,kiss,2,hug,1,toe,1,guess,2,h
      and,1
410   DATA   girl,1,mess,2,toss,2,pet,1,cup,1,paper,1,
      eye,1
420   DATA   finger,1,friend,1,dog,1,cat,1,ear,1,word,
      1,test,1
430   DATA   miss,2,pass,2,loss,2,moss,2,sea,1,beach,2
      ,touch,2
440   DATA   plate,1,fork,1,spoon,1,meal,1,table,1,cha
      ir,1,lamp,1
450   DATA   ditch,2,paint,1,color,1,pencil,1,duck,1,c
      ow,1,horse,1
460   DATA   scratch,2,match,2,catch,2,batch,2,hatch,2
      ,latch,2
470   DATA   cut,1,dent,1,drip,1,watch,2,bat,1,zoo,1,z
      ebra,1
480   DATA   sip,1,pitch,2,hit,1,glove,1,hour,1,minute
      ,1,boss,2
490   DATA   99,99
500   POKE 34,LN: HOME : POKE 34,0: VTAB (LN + 1): RETURN
```

14. SIGNAL WORDS

SUGGESTED FILE NAME: SIGNAL

SUGGESTED GRADE RANGE: 2–8

DESCRIPTION OF THE PROGRAM: This program provides guided practice in identifying signal words (connectives, adjectives, prepositions, adverbs) that signal information about time, place, order, comparison, contrast, negative information, amount, and so forth. This is an important inferential comprehension skill.

Note: The number of exercises presented by this program depends on the amount of data used. If you add data to the program, the number of exercises presented will be increased. Therefore, the number of problems to be presented by this program is not printed on the screen.

Note: Users of Apple IIe and Apple IIc equipment must have the <**CAPS LOCK**> key in the UP position in order for this program to run properly.

EXPLANATION OF DATA LINES: Each data line contains information required for one exercise. The first data entry is the sentence, the second is the correct answer, and the third entry is the signal word.

HOW TO CHANGE THE DATA: You may change or delete data. You may add data by typing new data lines numbered between 330 and 490 as long as your line numbers have not already been used.

```
10    DIM S$(100),A$(100),B$(100)
20    HOME : VTAB (6): PRINT  TAB( 15);"SIGNAL WORDS"
30    FOR I = 1 TO 2000: NEXT I
40 C = 0
50 C = C + 1
60    READ S$(C),A$(C),B$(C)
70    IF S$(C) = "stop" THEN C = C - 1: GOTO 90
80    GOTO 50
90    FOR W = 1 TO C
100   HOME : VTAB (2): PRINT  TAB( 14);"SIGNAL WORDS"

110   PRINT  TAB( 14);"============"
120   VTAB (5): PRINT "The sentence:"
130   VTAB (8): PRINT S$(W)
140   VTAB (11): PRINT "Type one word from the senten
      ce"
150   VTAB (13): PRINT "that signals ";B$(W);"."
160 LN = 15: GOSUB 500: HTAB (15): INPUT X$
170   IF X$ = "" THEN 150
180   IF  RIGHT$ (X$,1) = " " THEN X$ =  LEFT$ (X$, LEN
      (X$) - 1): GOTO 180
190   IF  LEFT$ (X$,1) = " " THEN X$ =  MID$ (X$,2)
200   IF X$ = A$(W) THEN  VTAB (18): HTAB (15): PRINT
      "Very good!": GOTO 290
210 N = N + 1
220   IF N <  > 3 THEN 260
230 LN = 15: GOSUB 500
240   PRINT "The ";B$(W);" signal is: ";A$(W)
250   GOTO 290
260   VTAB (18): HTAB (7): PRINT "Try again.  Type ca
      refully."
270   FOR I = 1 TO 1500: NEXT I
280   GOTO 160
290 N = 0: GOSUB 510
300   NEXT W
310   HOME : VTAB (6): PRINT "You are the best in my
      memory chips!!"
320   END
330   DATA  "Let's go to the movies tomorrow.",tomorr
      ow,time
340   DATA  "Put the book underneath the table.",unde
      rneath,place
350   DATA  "I like the movies but you like T.V.",but
      ,contrast
```

```
360   DATA   "He looks like his mother.",like,comparis
      on
370   DATA   "We never eat raw meat.",never,a negative

380   DATA   "The book is very funny.",very,how much
390   DATA   "Write your name last.",last,order
400   DATA   "Give him a piece too.",too,addition
410   DATA   "Do it immediately.",immediately,when
420   DATA   "Sit opposite John.",opposite,place
430   DATA   "The ball went over the house.",over,plac
      e
440   DATA   "Sit in the front row.",front,order
450   DATA   "He can sing very well.",very,much
460   DATA   "Please bring it now.",now,when
470   DATA   "My dog does not swim.",not,a negative
480   DATA   "The game was yesterday.",yesterday,time
490   DATA   stop,stop,stop
500   POKE 34,LN: HOME : POKE 34,0: VTAB (LN + 1): RETURN

510   LN = 22: GOSUB 500: PRINT "Press the <space bar>
          to continue . . .";
520   GET A$: IF A$ < > " " THEN 520
530   RETURN
```

15. VISUAL MEMORY

SUGGESTED FILE NAME: VISUAL MEM

SUGGESTED GRADE RANGE: 1–8

DESCRIPTION OF THE PROGRAM: This program assists students in developing short-term visual memory for words. It is not a spelling task because students are not required to retrieve the word from long-term memory without a clue. However, it is a subskill necessary for spelling. It is an important skill for primary students to develop and will assist older students in the intermediate steps of learning their spelling words.

The student is shown a word, then asked to type it from memory. Twenty-five words are given each time the program is run.

Note: Users of Apple IIe and Apple IIc equipment must have the <**CAPS LOCK**> key in the UP position in order for this program to run properly.

EXPLANATION OF DATA LINES: The data lines contain the words that appear on the screen for the student to remember and type. Each time the program is run, twenty-five of the words are chosen randomly. Words may appear more than once.

HOW TO CHANGE THE DATA: You may change or delete data. You can add new data by typing data lines numbered between 400 and 480 as long as your line numbers are used only once.

```
10   DIM W$(200)
20   HOME : VTAB (6): PRINT  TAB( 15);"VISUAL MEMORY"
     : VTAB (10): HTAB (1): PRINT "Twenty-five exerc
     ises will be presented."
30   FOR I = 1 TO 3000: NEXT I
40   C = 0
50   C = C + 1
60   READ W$(C)
70   IF W$(C) = "stop" THEN C = C - 1: GOTO 90
80   GOTO 50
90   L = 0
100   FOR X = 1 TO 25
110   W =  INT (C *  RND (1)) + 1: IF W = L THEN 110
120   L = W
130   HOME : VTAB (3): PRINT  TAB( 13);"Watch careful
      ly."
140   VTAB (5): PRINT "You will be asked to remember
      the word."
150   IF X = 1 THEN  GOSUB 500
160 LN = 6: GOSUB 490: GOTO 180
170   FOR I = 1 TO 1000: NEXT I
180 LN = 8: GOSUB 490: PRINT  TAB( 20 -  INT ( LEN (
    W$(W)) / 2));W$(W)
190   FOR I = 1 TO 1500: NEXT I
200 LN = 8: GOSUB 490
210   FOR I = 1 TO 1000: NEXT I
220   VTAB (12): PRINT  TAB( 7);"Type the word from m
      emory."
230   VTAB (14): HTAB (18): INPUT Y$
240   IF Y$ = "" THEN 230
250   IF  LEFT$ (Y$,1) = " " THEN Y$ =  MID$ (Y$,2)
260   IF  RIGHT$ (Y$,1) = " " THEN Y$ =  LEFT$ (Y$, LEN
      (Y$) - 1): GOTO 260
270   IF Y$ = W$(W) THEN  PRINT : PRINT : PRINT  TAB(
      16);"Very good": GOTO 350
280 N = N + 1: IF N <  > 3 THEN 320
290 LN = 11: GOSUB 490
300   PRINT "The word is ====>  ";W$(W)
310   GOSUB 500: GOTO 360
320 LN = 11: GOSUB 490: PRINT  TAB( 15);"Try again."
330   FOR I = 1 TO 1000: NEXT I
340   GOTO 180
350   GOSUB 500
360 N = 0
370   NEXT X
380   HOME : VTAB (6): PRINT "I love your mind - you
      use it well!!"
390   END
400   DATA  boy,house,car,doll,toy,truck,green,blue,r
      ed,sun
410   DATA  dog,cat,bread,boat,girl,walk,play,jump,ho
      p,run,skip
420   DATA  friend,nice,happy,mother,father,sister,br
      other
```

```
430   DATA   smile,ball,toss,food,milk,water,soda,moon
      ,earth
440   DATA   hair,ear,mouth,chin,nose,eye,hand,foot,le
      g,arm,neck
450   DATA   chair,table,floor,wall,light,dress,shirt,
      sock,pants
460   DATA   cry,loud,soft,kind,one,two,three,four,fiv
      e,six,seven
470   DATA   eight,nine,ten,more,less,even,same,like,o
      ver,under
480   DATA   stop
490   POKE 34,LN: HOME : POKE 34,0: VTAB (LN + 1): RETURN

500 LN = 22: GOSUB 490: PRINT "Press the <space bar>
       to continue . . .";
510   GET A$: IF A$ < > " " THEN 510
520   RETURN

]
```

16. MULTIPLE MEANINGS

SUGGESTED FILE NAME: MULTIPLE

SUGGESTED GRADE RANGE: 3–8

DESCRIPTION OF THE PROGRAM: This program provides practice in using entries for words with multiple meanings. A sentence provides the context for which the student selects the correct meaning. Because approximately 75 percent of the words in a basic vocabulary have multiple meanings, the ability to use the sentence context is an important inferential skill.

A dictionary of meanings for the word "run" is shown on the screen. A sentence is then shown using a variation of that word. The student must choose the dictionary meaning of the word based on its context.

Note: The number of exercises presented by this program depends on the amount of data used. If you add data to the program, the number of exercises presented will be increased. Therefore, the number of problems to be presented by this program is not printed on the screen.

EXPLANATION OF DATA LINES: The two entries in each data line contain a question for which the answer is found in the dictionary meanings for "run" and the correct choice from the dictionary.

HOW TO CHANGE THE DATA: You can change or delete data. You can add data by typing new data lines numbered between 410 and 540 as long as you use numbers that have not already been used.

```
10   DIM ST$(50),XX(50)
20   HOME : VTAB (6): PRINT  TAB( 13);"MULTIPLE MEANI
     NGS"
30   FOR I = 1 TO 2000: NEXT I
40   C = 0
50   C = C + 1
60   READ ST$(C),XX(C)
70   IF XX(C) = 99 THEN C = C - 1: GOTO 90
80   GOTO 50
90   HOME : VTAB (2)
100  PRINT "DICTIONARY MEANING:": PRINT
110  PRINT "run V. 1. to move fast on the ground"
120  PRINT "        2. to follow a course of action"
130  PRINT "        3. to drive"
140  PRINT "        4. to stab"
150  PRINT "run N. 5. a complete circuit of bases"
160  FOR X = 1 TO 40: PRINT "=";: NEXT X
170  FOR W = 1 TO C
180  LN = 10: GOSUB 550: PRINT ST$(W)
190  LN = 13: GOSUB 550
200  PRINT "Which meaning is correct in the sentence
     ": PRINT "above (1-5)?"
210  VTAB (16): HTAB (19)
220  GET X$
230  IF  ASC (X$) < 49 OR  ASC (X$) > 53 THEN 220
240  VTAB (16): HTAB (19): PRINT X$
250  IF  VAL (X$) = XX(W) THEN 350
260  N = N + 1
270  IF N <  > 3 THEN 320
280  LN = 17: GOSUB 550
290  PRINT "The correct meaning is number:  ";XX(W)
300  GOSUB 560
310  GOTO 370
320  LN = 17: GOSUB 550
330  PRINT "Read the sentence carefully.": PRINT : PRINT
     "Think about it, then try again."
340  GOSUB 560: GOTO 190
350  LN = 17: GOSUB 550: PRINT  TAB( 13);"Good for yo
     u!!"
360  GOSUB 560
370  N = 0
380  NEXT W
390  HOME : VTAB (6): PRINT  TAB( 5);"Say a kind wor
     d to someone today."
400  END
410  DATA  "Does he know how to run a train?",3
420  DATA  "Who runs faster, Mary or Tammy?",1
430  DATA  "Run through your lines for the play.",2
440  DATA  "He ran him through with the sword.",4
450  DATA  "Run the wire along the ground.",2
460  DATA  "Patty hit a home run.",5
470  DATA  "The race was run on grass.",1
480  DATA  "The clock ran down.",2
490  DATA  "Run the seam up on your sewing machine."
     ,2
500  DATA  "John ran toward the house.",1
```

```
510   DATA  "Can you run this tractor?",3
520   DATA  "We ran through the rain yesterday.",1
530   DATA  "Our team scored the first run today.",5
540   DATA  99,99
550   POKE 34,LN: HOME : POKE 34,0: VTAB (LN + 1): RETURN
560 LN = 22: GOSUB 550: PRINT "Press the <space bar>
         to continue . . .";
570   GET A$: IF A$ < > " " THEN 570
580   RETURN
```

17. ANTONYMS

SUGGESTED FILE NAME: ANTONYMS

SUGGESTED GRADE RANGE: 2–8

DESCRIPTION OF THE PROGRAM: This program provides practice in identifying antonyms in the context of a sentence. This is another important word relationship skill and helps develop vocabulary.

Note: The number of exercises presented by this program depends on the amount of data used. If you add data to the program, the number of exercises presented will be increased. Therefore, the number of problems to be presented by this program is not printed on the screen.

Note: Users of Apple IIe and Apple IIc equipment must have the <**CAPS LOCK**> key in the UP position in order for this program to run properly.

EXPLANATION OF DATA LINES: Each data line contains the information for one exercise. The first entry is the sentence. The second entry is the antonym of the underlined word. The third entry tells the computer how far from the left of the screen to begin underlining. The fourth entry tells the computer how many dashes to use in underlining.

PROGRAMMING LOGIC: Notice that in line 60 there is an array: L(C). There is also a variable called "L" in line 110. These two uses of "L" are different. "L(C)" stores the lengths of the words. "L" refers to the last sentence used.

In line 100, a number is chosen randomly from one (1) to C (the number of words in the data list). That number is compared to L so that the last sentence shown is not used again. Then, in line 110, L is assigned the value of W so that the next time around the same checking routine can be executed. That is, the next sentence will not be the same as the present one.

HOW TO CHANGE THE DATA: You can change or delete data. You can add data by typing new data lines using line numbers between 290 and 490 as long as they have not already been used.

In composing new data lines, determine the third data entry by counting the characters (including spaces) from the left of your sentence to the first letter in the word to be underlined. The fourth data entry is the number of letters in the word to be underlined.

```
10   DIM S$(50),AN$(50),S(50),L(50)
20   HOME : VTAB (6): PRINT  TAB( 17);"ANTONYMS"
30   FOR I = 1 TO 2000: NEXT I
40   C = 0:L = 0
50   C = C + 1
60   READ S$(C),AN$(C),S(C),L(C)
70   IF S(C) = 99 THEN C = C - 1: GOTO 90
80   GOTO 50
90   FOR Y = 1 TO 2 * C
100  W =  INT (C *  RND (1)) + 1: IF W = L THEN 100
110  L = W
120   HOME : VTAB (4): PRINT S$(W)
130   FOR X = 0 TO L(W) - 1
140   PRINT  TAB( S(W) + X);"-";
150   NEXT X
160   PRINT
170  LN = 9: GOSUB 500: PRINT "Look at the underlined
       word.": PRINT
180   PRINT "Type the word that means the opposite."
190   VTAB (15): HTAB (17): INPUT X$
200   IF X$ = "" THEN 170
210   IF X$ = AN$(W) THEN  PRINT : PRINT  TAB( 16);"V
     ery good!": GOTO 240
220   PRINT : PRINT  TAB( 7);"Try again.  Type carefu
     lly."
230   GOSUB 510: GOTO 170
240   GOSUB 510
250   NEXT Y
260   HOME : VTAB (6): PRINT "Try to do your very bes
     t at everything"
270   PRINT : PRINT "you do."
280   END
290   DATA  "The big boy stood by the little girl.",l
     ittle,5,3
300   DATA  "The tap has hot and cold water.",hot,21,
     4
310   DATA  "She runs up and down the stairs.",up,17,
     4
320   DATA  "Shut the screen when you go in and out."
     ,out,29,2
330   DATA  "Look over the top and then under it.",un
     der,6,4
340   DATA  "The ground was very hard and rocky.",sof
     t,21,4
350   DATA  "My cat had climbed high in the tree.",lo
     w,20,4
360   DATA  "Loud music hurts my dog's ears.",soft,1,
     4
370   DATA  "Mary is playing outside.",inside,17,7
380   DATA  "Small insects are hard to see.",large,1,
     5
```

```
390   DATA   "Be a good sport when you play ball.",bad
             ,6,4
400   DATA   "Harry is shorter than I am.",taller,10,7

410   DATA   "My best friend is Walter.",worst,4,4
420   DATA   "I can ride very fast on my bike.",slow,1
             7,4
430   DATA   "It is easy to be nice to people.",hard,7
             ,4
440   DATA   "My old house had lots of rooms.",new,4,3

450   DATA   "Running is good for your health.",bad,12
             ,4
460   DATA   "Smooth floors are fun to walk on.",rough
             ,1,6
470   DATA   "The front of our house is made of brick.
             ",back,5,5
480   DATA   "I draw best with my right hand.",left,21
             ,5
490   DATA   99,99,99,99
500   POKE 34,LN: HOME : POKE 34,0: VTAB (LN + 1): RETURN

510 LN = 22: GOSUB 500: PRINT "Press the <space bar>
         to continue . . .";
520   GET A$: IF A$ <  > " " THEN 520
530   RETURN

]
```

18. CONTRACTIONS

SUGGESTED FILE NAME: CONTRACTIONS

SUGGESTED GRADE RANGE: 3–6

DESCRIPTION OF THE PROGRAM: This program provides practice in forming contractions with not. The program illustrates the replacement of the "o" in not with the apostrophe and the joining of the verb and "n't" into one word by physical movement visible on the screen. This reinforces the word-building aspects of contractions for students.

Note: The number of exercises presented by this program depends on the amount of data used. If you add data to the program, the number of exercises presented will be increased. Therefore, the number of problems to be presented by this program is not printed on the screen.

Note: Users of Apple IIe and Apple IIc equipment must have the <**CAPS LOCK**> key in the UP position in order for this program to run properly.

EXPLANATION OF DATA LINES: Each data line contains the information necessary for one problem. The sentence in the exercise is broken into three parts so that the parts can be moved on the screen.

PROGRAMMING LOGIC: Lines 170 through 300 accomplish the animation on the screen using FOR/NEXT loops.

HOW TO CHANGE THE DATA: You can change or delete data. You can add data by typing new data lines numbered between 440 and 640. Do not use the same line numbers twice.

```
10   HOME : VTAB (6): PRINT  TAB( 15);"CONTRACTIONS"
20   GOSUB 660
30 C = 0
40 C = C + 1
50   READ S1$,V$,S2$
60   IF S1$ = "stop" THEN C = C - 1: GOTO 80
70   GOTO 40
80   RESTORE
90   FOR Q = 1 TO C
100   READ S1$,V$,S2$: IF  RIGHT$ (V$,1) <  > "n" THEN
      CT$ = V$ + "n't": GOTO 120
110 CT$ = V$ + "'t"
120   HOME : VTAB (2): PRINT S1$ + V$;" not ";S2$
130   VTAB (8): PRINT  TAB( 20 -  LEN (V$));V$;
140 V = 21
150   PRINT  TAB( 21);"not";
160   GOSUB 670
170   FOR W = 8 TO 3 STEP  - 1
180   VTAB (W): HTAB (22): PRINT "o";
190   FOR I = 1 TO 200: NEXT I
200   VTAB (W): HTAB (22): PRINT " ";
210   NEXT W
220   GOSUB 670
230   FOR W = 3 TO 8
240   VTAB (W): HTAB (22): PRINT "'";
250   FOR I = 1 TO 100: NEXT I
260   VTAB (W): HTAB (22): PRINT " ";
270   NEXT W
280   VTAB (8): HTAB (21): PRINT "n't";
290   GOSUB 670
300   VTAB (8): HTAB (21): PRINT "   ";
310 LN = 7: GOSUB 650: PRINT  TAB( 20 -  LEN (V$));C
    T$
320   GOSUB 660
330   VTAB (12): PRINT S1$ + CT$;" ";S2$
340 LN = 15: GOSUB 650: PRINT "Type the contraction
    carefully.": PRINT
350   INPUT C$
360   IF C$ = CT$ THEN 390
370   PRINT : PRINT  TAB( 7);"Try again.  Type carefu
    lly."
380   GOSUB 660: GOTO 340
390   PRINT : PRINT  TAB( 15);"Good work!"
400   GOSUB 660
410   NEXT Q
420   HOME : VTAB (6): PRINT "I couldn't have enjoyed
     myself more."
```

```
430    END
440    DATA    "The man ","could","work by himself."
450    DATA    "People ","should","overeat."
460    DATA    "The children ","were","in the house."
470    DATA    "Mary ","did","meet her parents there."
480    DATA    "I ","have","enough crayons."
490    DATA    "I ","do","want to play now."
500    DATA    "My mother ","has","left for the store."
510    DATA    "You ","did","do your chores today."
520    DATA    "They ","have","ever been to the circus."

530    DATA    "We ","are","supposed to run in the halls
       ."
540    DATA    "What if we ","can","go to the movie?"
550    DATA    "He said he ","does","know how to swim."
560    DATA    "Maybe she ","has","told you yet."
570    DATA    "You ","should","worry about it."
580    DATA    "Tom ","was","able to go with us."
590    DATA    "We ","were","at the front of the line."
600    DATA    "People ","should","drive so fast."
610    DATA    "Pets ","can","tell us where it hurts."
620    DATA    "Children ","should","walk in the road."
630    DATA    "It ","has","rained much lately."
640    DATA    stop,stop,stop
650    POKE 34,LN: HOME : POKE 34,0: VTAB (LN + 1): RETURN

660    FOR I = 1 TO 2000: NEXT I: RETURN
670    FOR I = 1 TO 1000: NEXT I: RETURN

]
```

19. MAKING COMPARISONS

SUGGESTED FILE NAME: COMPARISONS

SUGGESTED GRADE RANGE: 2–8

DESCRIPTION OF THE PROGRAM: This program requires students to identify two words that are compared in a sentence. Both similes and metaphors are used. The program provides the attribute in which they are comparable. This skill aids inferential comprehension by helping students notice and interpret similes and metaphors in reading.

Note: The number of exercises presented by this program depends on the amount of data used. If you add data to the program, the number of exercises presented will be increased. Therefore, the number of problems to be presented by this program is not printed on the screen.

Note: Users of Apple IIe and Apple IIc equipment must have the <**CAPS LOCK**> key in the UP position in order for this program to run properly.

EXPLANATION OF DATA LINES: Each data line contains the information necessary for one exercise. The first entry is the sentence containing the two words that are compared. The second and third entries are the things being compared. The fourth entry is the attribute in which they are comparable.

HOW TO CHANGE THE DATA: You may change or delete data. You can add data by typing new data lines numbered between 440 and 590. Do not use the same line number twice.

```
10   HOME : VTAB (6): PRINT  TAB( 12);"MAKING COMPARI
     SONS"
20   FOR I = 1 TO 2000: NEXT I
30 C = 0
40 C = C + 1
50   READ ST$,S1$,S2$,CP$
60   IF ST$ = "stop" THEN C = C - 1: GOTO 80
70   GOTO 40
80   RESTORE
90   FOR Q = 1 TO C
100   READ ST$,S1$,S2$,CP$
110   HOME : VTAB (2): PRINT "The sentence is:"
120   VTAB (6): HTAB (21 - LEN (ST$) / 2): PRINT ST$
      : GOSUB 610
130 LN = 8: GOSUB 600: PRINT "Type one of the two th
     ings being"
140   PRINT : PRINT "compared.  ";: INPUT X$
150   IF X$ = S1$ OR X$ = S2$ THEN 220
160   IF  LEFT$ (X$,4) <  >  LEFT$ (S1$,4) THEN 190
170 X$ = S1$
180   GOTO 150
190   IF  LEFT$ (X$,4) =  LEFT$ (S2$,4) THEN 210
200   GOSUB 620: GOSUB 610: GOTO 130
210 X$ = S2$
220 LN = 8: GOSUB 600: PRINT "Type the other of the
     two things being"
230   PRINT : PRINT "compared.  ";: INPUT Y$
240   IF X$ = Y$ THEN 220
250   IF Y$ = S1$ OR Y$ = S2$ THEN 320
260   IF  LEFT$ (Y$,4) <  >  LEFT$ (S1$,4) THEN 290
270 Y$ = S1$
280   GOTO 250
290   IF  LEFT$ (Y$,4) =  LEFT$ (S2$,4) THEN 310
300   GOSUB 620: GOSUB 610: GOTO 220
310 Y$ = S2$
320 LN = 8: GOSUB 600
330   FOR X = 1 TO 40
340   VTAB (9): HTAB (X): PRINT "=";
350   VTAB (11): HTAB (X): PRINT "=";
360   NEXT X
370   PRINT
380   VTAB (10): HTAB (18 - (15 + LEN (S1$ + S2$)) /
      2): PRINT S1$;" and ";S2$;" are both ";CP$
390 LN = 22: GOSUB 600: PRINT "Press the <space bar>
      to continue . . .";
400   GET A$: IF A$ <  > " " THEN 400
```

```
410   NEXT Q
420   HOME : VTAB (6): PRINT  TAB( 7);"Make this a wo
      nderful day!"
430   END
440   DATA  "A snake is like a shiny twig.",snake,twi
      g,shiny
450   DATA  "Her eyes were like blue lakes.",eyes,lak
      es,blue
460   DATA  "The icing was as white as snow.",icing,s
      now,white
470   DATA  "The sun felt like fire on her skin.",sun
      ,fire,hot
480   DATA  "The ice was as hard as a rock.",ice,rock
      ,hard
490   DATA  "His shirt was a soft as silk.",shirt,sil
      k,soft
500   DATA  "The sound was like an explosion.",sound,
      explosion,loud
510   DATA  "Her voice was as harsh as sandpaper.",vo
      ice,sandpaper,harsh
520   DATA  "This computer is as fast as lightning.",
      computer,lightning,fast
530   DATA  "The turtle moved as slow as a snail.",tu
      rtle,snail,slow
540   DATA  "The son was as strong as his father.",so
      n,father,strong
550   DATA  "The earth is like a ball in space.",eart
      h,ball,round
560   DATA  "The building was like a box with doors."
      ,building,box,square
570   DATA  "The paper was as light as a feather.",pa
      per,feather,light
580   DATA  "The daughter is as nice as her mother.",
      daughter,mother,nice
590   DATA  stop,stop,stop,stop
600   POKE 34,LN: HOME : POKE 34,0: VTAB (LN + 1): RETURN

610   FOR T = 1 TO 1000: NEXT T: RETURN
620   PRINT : PRINT "Please try again.": GOSUB 610: RETURN
```

]

20. ANALOGIES

SUGGESTED FILE NAME: ANALOGIES

SUGGESTED GRADE RANGE: 4–8

DESCRIPTION OF THE PROGRAM: This program provides students with the name of the analogy and three words in the analogy. The student identifies the missing word from the Word Bank. This is a thinking skill activity that involves the five most common word relationships found in analogies.

Note: The number of exercises presented by this program depends on the amount of data used. If you add data to the program, the number of exercises presented will be increased. Therefore, the number of problems to be presented by this program is not printed on the screen.

Note: Users of Apple IIe and Apple IIc equipment must have the <**CAPS LOCK**> key in the UP position in order for this program to run properly.

EXPLANATION OF DATA LINES: The words in lines 280, 350, and 420 make up the Word Bank to be used in completing the analogies. Each line makes one word bank which is used with the analogies following the particular line number.

The data lines between each word bank line and "stop,stop,stop,stop,stop" contain the types of analogies and the words that make up the analogies. The fourth word in the analogy is the correct answer and is left out of the exercise on the screen.

HOW TO CHANGE THE DATA: You may change or delete data. You may add data by typing new data lines numbered between 280 and 480. Be sure that you do not use the same line number twice. Also, in this program, be especially careful that you group your data lines correctly. Your first data line should contain the five word bank items. The remaining data lines should contain the analogies as well as the types of analogies.

```
10   HOME : VTAB (6): PRINT  TAB( 16);"ANALOGIES"
20   FOR T = 1 TO 2000: NEXT T
30   FOR X = 1 TO 5: READ X$(X): NEXT X
40   IF X$(1) = "stop" THEN 260
50   READ T$,A1$,A2$,A3$,A4$
60   IF T$ = "stop" THEN 30
70   HOME : PRINT "WORD BANK:": PRINT
80   FOR Z = 1 TO 5: PRINT "  ";X$(Z);: NEXT Z: PRINT

90   FOR Z = 1 TO 40: PRINT "-";: NEXT Z: PRINT
100  VTAB (6): PRINT "This is a(n) ";T$;" analogy:"
110  VTAB (8): PRINT  TAB( 5);A1$; TAB( 18);"is to";
     TAB( 28);A2$
120  PRINT  TAB( 18);"=====": PRINT
130  PRINT  TAB( 20);"as"
140  VTAB (13): PRINT  TAB( 5);A3$; TAB( 18);"is to"
     ; TAB( 28);"?"
150  PRINT  TAB( 18);"====="
160 LN = 16: GOSUB 500: PRINT "Type a word from the
     word bank to": PRINT
170  PRINT "complete this analogy.  ";: INPUT X$
180  IF X$ = A4$ THEN 220
190 LN = 21: GOSUB 500: PRINT "Try again.  Look in t
     he word bank."
200  FOR T = 1 TO 1500: NEXT T
210  GOTO 160
220  VTAB (13): HTAB (28): PRINT A4$
```

```
230 LN = 16: GOSUB 500: PRINT "Press the <space bar>
     to continue . . .";
240  GET A$: IF A$ < > " " THEN 240
250  GOTO 50
260  HOME : VTAB (6): PRINT "I hope you are having a
     terrific day!!"
270  END
280  DATA  hot,egg,hungry,unclear,supper
290  DATA  synonym,huge,large,muddy,unclear
300  DATA  cause and effect,running,tired,fasting,hu
     ngry
310  DATA  antonym,winter,summer,cold,hot
320  DATA  part/whole,fin,fish,salad,supper
330  DATA  action/object,bake,bread,boil,egg
340  DATA  stop,stop,stop,stop,stop
350  DATA  find,bat,arm,fall,wise
360  DATA  antonym,up,down,rise,fall
370  DATA  action/object,hit,ball,swing,bat
380  DATA  synonym,swift,fast,smart,wise
390  DATA  cause and effect,study,learn,seek,find
400  DATA  part/whole,foot,leg,hand,arm
410  DATA  stop,stop,stop,stop,stop
420  DATA  flour,tree,hear,draw,soft
430  DATA  cause and effect,try,succeed,listen,hear
440  DATA  part/whole,room,house,leaf,tree
450  DATA  synonym,speak,talk,sketch,draw
460  DATA  action/object,pour,water,sift,flour
470  DATA  antonym,win,lose,hard,soft
480  DATA  stop,stop,stop,stop,stop
490  DATA  stop,stop,stop,stop,stop
500  POKE 34,LN: HOME : POKE 34,0: VTAB (LN + 1): RETURN
```

]

21. SHOWING POSSESSION

SUGGESTED FILE NAME: POSSESSION

SUGGESTED GRADE RANGE: 3–8

DESCRIPTION OF THE PROGRAM: This program provides practice in forming possessives with 's, and '. The visible formation of the possessive on the screen reinforces the word-building aspects of this program and aids in vocabulary development.

Note: The number of exercises presented by this program depends on the amount of data used. If you add data to the program, the number of exercises presented will be increased. Therefore, the number of problems to be presented by this program is not printed on the screen.

EXPLANATION OF DATA LINES: Each group of three entries in the data lines determines one exercise. The first and third items make up the sentence that may or may not have words that need to be in possessive form. The second data entry is the correct choice in the "possession menu."

PROGRAMMING LOGIC: Lines 250 through 390 contain the routines for reprinting the letters on the screen to show possession.

HOW TO CHANGE THE DATA: You can change, delete, or add data. Be very careful to structure your exercises correctly.

```
10    HOME : VTAB (6): PRINT  TAB( 12);"SHOWING POSSES
      SION": VTAB (10): HTAB (1): PRINT "* Thirty  ex
      ercises will be presented. *"
20    GOSUB 240: GOSUB 240
30    READ W$,RR,P$
40    IF W$ = "99" THEN 220
50    HOME : VTAB (3): PRINT "The sentence:"
60    VTAB (8): PRINT "It is ";W$;" ";P$;"."
70    VTAB (12): PRINT "We show that the ";P$
80    VTAB (14): PRINT "belongs to < ";W$;" >"
90    VTAB (16): PRINT  TAB( 10);"1. by adding 's"
100   PRINT  TAB( 10);"2. by adding '"
110   PRINT  TAB( 10);"3. not possession"
120   LN = 19: GOSUB 490: PRINT "Pick an answer (1-3)"
      ;
130   GET R$
140   IF  VAL (R$) > 0 AND  VAL (R$) < 4 THEN R =  VAL
      (R$): GOTO 160
150   GOTO 130
160   IF R = 3 AND RR = 3 THEN 30
170   IF R = RR THEN 200
180   LN = 19: GOSUB 490: PRINT  TAB( 11);"Please try
      again."
190   GOSUB 240: GOTO 120
200   ON R GOSUB 250,330
210   GOTO 30
220   HOME : VTAB (6): PRINT "It's been great to work
       for you!!!"
230   END
240   FOR T = 1 TO 1500: NEXT T: RETURN
250   LN = 11: GOSUB 490: VTAB (8): HTAB (7 +  LEN (W$
      )): PRINT "   ";P$;"."
260   FOR V = 4 TO 8
270   VTAB (V): HTAB (7 +  LEN (W$)): PRINT "'s";
280   FOR TI = 1 TO 100: NEXT TI
290   VTAB (V): HTAB (7 +  LEN (W$)): PRINT "  ";
300   NEXT V
310   VTAB (8): HTAB (7 +  LEN (W$)): PRINT "'s";
320   GOSUB 240: GOSUB 240: RETURN
330   LN = 11: GOSUB 490: VTAB (8): HTAB (7 +  LEN (W$
      )): PRINT "   ";P$;"."
340   FOR V = 4 TO 8
350   VTAB (V): HTAB (7 +  LEN (W$)): PRINT "'";
360   FOR TI = 1 TO 100: NEXT TI
370   VTAB (V): HTAB (7 +  LEN (W$)): PRINT " ";
```

```
380    NEXT V
390    VTAB (8): HTAB (7 +  LEN (W$)): PRINT "'";
400    GOSUB 240: GOSUB 240: RETURN
410    DATA   John,1,book,the girls,2,ball,a new,3,toy,
       a blue,3,bike,the boy,1,glove
420    DATA   father,1,chair,the students,2,song,a larg
       e,3,boat,Roger,1,hat,the last,3,meeting
430    DATA   mother,1,ring,Bill,1,radio,the boss,2,son
       ,the first,3,page,Mary,1,paper
440    DATA   the last,3,day,the teachers,2,lounge,the
       pilot,1,plane,Bess,2,sister
450    DATA   Harry,1,friend,the best,3,one,the green,3
       ,car,Jess,2,record
460    DATA   Jane,1,desk,the man,1,house,the warm,3,fi
       re,Tess,2,coat
470    DATA   the softest,3,fur,the pretty,3,picture,th
       e ladies,2,club
480    DATA   99,99,99
490    POKE 34,LN: HOME : POKE 34,0: VTAB (LN + 1): RETURN
```

22. PLAYING CONCENTRATION

SUGGESTED FILE NAME: CONCENTRATION

SUGGESTED GRADE RANGE: 2–8

DESCRIPTION OF THE PROGRAM: This program builds short-term visual memory and attention span in students. It is a subskill of learning to spell and is especially valuable for students who are impulsive rather than reflective. A score is used to increase the desire to concentrate.

Five words are presented on the screen for varying lengths of time and are then erased. The student must remember in which position one of the words was shown.

Note: The number of exercises presented by this program depends on the amount of data used. If you add data to the program, the number of exercises presented will be increased. Therefore, the number of problems to be presented by this program is not printed on the screen.

EXPLANATION OF DATA LINES: Each data line contains the set of five words that are printed on the screen.

HOW TO CHANGE THE DATA: You may change or delete data. You may add data simply by typing new data lines numbered between 460 and 620. Do not use the same line number twice.

```
10    DIM W$(100,5):UL$ = "------":BL$ = "         "
20    HOME : VTAB (6): PRINT  TAB( 12);"PLAYING CONCEN
      TRATION"
30    FOR I = 1 TO 1000: NEXT I
40    C = 0:SC = 0
50    C = C + 1
```

```
60    FOR X = 1 TO 5
70    READ W$(C,X)
80    NEXT X
90    IF W$(C,1) < > "stop" THEN 50
100   FOR X = 1 TO 5:W$(C,X) = "": NEXT X:C = C - 1
110   FOR W = 1 TO 2 * C
120   T = 5
130   N =  INT (C *  RND (1)) + 1
140   HOME : PRINT  TAB( 15);"CONCENTRATE!!"
150   PRINT : PRINT  TAB( 15);"Score is:";SC
160   PRINT : PRINT "You will need to remember where
      all the"
170   PRINT : PRINT "words are in the list."
180   FOR I = 1 TO 40: PRINT "=";: NEXT I
190 LN = 22: GOSUB 630: PRINT "Press the <space bar>
       to continue . . .";
200 A =  INT (5 *  RND (1)) + 1:AN$ = W$(N,A)
210   GET A$: IF A$ < > " " THEN 210
220 LN = 10: GOSUB 630: HTAB (1)
230   FOR X = 0 TO 4: PRINT  TAB( X * 8 + 2);W$(N,X +
      1);: NEXT X
240   PRINT
250   FOR X = 0 TO 4: PRINT  TAB( X * 8 + 2);UL$;: NEXT
      X
260   PRINT
270   FOR X = 0 TO 4: PRINT  TAB( X * 8 + 4);X + 1;: NEXT
      X
280   FOR I = 1 TO 5000 - 500 * T: NEXT I
290   VTAB (10): FOR X = 0 TO 4: PRINT  TAB( X * 8 +
      2);BL$;: NEXT X
300   VTAB (15): HTAB (1): PRINT  TAB( 10);"Where was
       ";AN$;" (1-5)? ";
310   GET A$
320   IF  VAL (A$) > 0 AND  VAL (A$) < 6 THEN X =  VAL
      (A$): GOTO 340
330   GOTO 310
340   IF X = (A) THEN 390
350 LN = 14: GOSUB 630: PRINT  TAB( 15);"Try again."
      :T = T - 1: IF T < 0 THEN T = 0
360   FOR I = 1 TO 1000: NEXT I
370 LN = 14: GOSUB 630
380   GOTO 190
390 LN = 14: GOSUB 630: PRINT "Good for you - ";AN$;
      " was in space ";A;"."
400   GOSUB 640
410 SC = SC + 1000 * T
420   NEXT W
430   HOME : VTAB (6): PRINT "Concentrate on doing yo
      ur best each day.": PRINT : PRINT
440   PRINT "Your final score was ";SC;" points."
450   END
460   DATA  green,yellow,blue,black,red
470   DATA  bird,bear,pig,cow,goose
480   DATA  truck,car,plane,boat,sled
490   DATA  bread,milk,meat,apple,soup
500   DATA  shoe,glove,dress,coat,skirt
```

```
510   DATA   over,under,above,on,in
520   DATA   pretty,silly,funny,happy,sleepy
530   DATA   they,she,we,he,you
540   DATA   arm,leg,head,foot,eye
550   DATA   bed,clock,chair,table,desk
560   DATA   fast,slow,quick,move,jump
570   DATA   high,tree,bush,low,ball
580   DATA   Mary,Don,Susan,Dave,Bill
590   DATA   hair,nose,tow,toe,finger
600   DATA   roof,door,floor,wall,window
610   DATA   dad,glad,mad,sad,bad
620   DATA   stop,stop,stop,stop,stop
630   POKE 34,LN: HOME : POKE 34,0: VTAB (LN + 1): RETURN

640 LN = 22: GOSUB 630: PRINT "Press the <space bar>
      to continue . . .";
650   GET A$: IF A$ <  > " " THEN 650
660   RETURN

]
```

23. WRITING POEMS

SUGGESTED FILE NAME: POEMS

SUGGESTED GRADE RANGE: 4–8

DESCRIPTION OF THE PROGRAM: In this program, the computer produces a poem by selecting words at random from four dictionaries. Students are asked to critically analyze the poem produced, edit it, and copy their own version for later use in group activities. This program requires students to use critical reading skills, encourages poetry writing by providing a poetry starter, and improves editing skills.

EXPLANATION OF DATA LINES: Each group of five data lines contains the information from which the computer selects the words to make a poem. The first line in the group is the title of the poem. The computer selects three of the words in the second line, three words from the third line, one word from the fourth line, and one word from the fifth line, to make a poem. These selections are done in lines 250 through 270.

PROGRAMMING LOGIC: Lines 190 through 240 choose random numbers to be used to select the data used in the poem. Lines 250 through 270 print the poem on the screen.

HOW TO CHANGE THE DATA: You may change or delete data. You may also add data by typing new data lines numbered between 470 and 670. The data must be entered in groups of five lines. Each of the four lines of words used to make the poem must contain exactly five entries.

```
10    DIM T$(10),A$(10,5),N$(10,5),V$(10,5),P$(10,5)
20    HOME : VTAB (6): PRINT  TAB( 15);"WRITING POEMS"

30    FOR I = 1 TO 2000: NEXT I
40  CN = 0
50  CN = CN + 1
60    READ T$(CN)
70    IF T$(CN) = "stop" THEN T$(CN) = "":CN = CN - 1:
      GOTO 130
80    FOR X = 1 TO 5: READ A$(CN,X): NEXT X
90    FOR X = 1 TO 5: READ N$(CN,X): NEXT X
100   FOR X = 1 TO 5: READ V$(CN,X): NEXT X
110   FOR X = 1 TO 5: READ P$(CN,X): NEXT X
120   GOTO 50
130 PN =  INT (CN *  RND (1)) + 1: IF CN = 1 THEN PN
      = 1
140   HOME : VTAB (8): PRINT  TAB( 12);"I can write a
      poem."
150   GOSUB 430
160   HOME : VTAB (2): PRINT  TAB( 16);T$(PN)
170   VTAB (4): PRINT  TAB( 14);"by the COMPUTER"
180   PRINT : PRINT
190 C =  INT (5 *  RND (1)) + 1:D =  INT (5 *  RND (
      1)) + 1
200 E =  INT (5 *  RND (1)) + 1:F =  INT (5 *  RND (
      1)) + 1
210 G =  INT (5 *  RND (1)) + 1: IF G = C THEN 210
220 H =  INT (5 *  RND (1)) + 1: IF H = D THEN 220
230 I =  INT (5 *  RND (1)) + 1: IF I = C OR I = G THEN
      230
240 J =  INT (5 *  RND (1)) + 1: IF J = D OR J = H THEN
      240
250   PRINT  TAB( 10);"The ";A$(PN,C);" ";N$(PN,D);"
      ";V$(PN,E): PRINT
260   PRINT  TAB( 10);P$(PN,F);" the ";A$(PN,G);" ";N
      $(PN,H);".": PRINT
270   PRINT  TAB( 10);"See the ";A$(PN,I);" ";N$(PN,J
      );".": PRINT
280   PRINT : PRINT "Do you want to change my poem to
      make": PRINT
290   PRINT "it better (Y or N)?";
300   GET Z$
310   IF Z$ = "Y" THEN 340
320   IF Z$ <  > "N" THEN 300
330   GOTO 360
340 LN = 17: GOSUB 460: PRINT "Rewrite my poem on yo
      ur paper."
350   GOSUB 430
360 LN = 19: GOSUB 460: PRINT "Do you want another p
      oem (Y or N)?";
370   GET Y$
380   IF Y$ = "Y" THEN 130
390   IF Y$ <  > "N" THEN 370
400   HOME : VTAB (6): PRINT "You and I could make be
      autiful poetry": PRINT
410   PRINT "together!"
```

```
420   END
430 LN = 22: GOSUB 460: PRINT "Press the <space bar>
      to continue . . .";
440   GET A$: IF A$ <  > " " THEN 440
450   RETURN
460   POKE 34.LN: HOME : POKE 34.0: VTAB (LN + 1): RETURN
470   DATA   THE DESERT
480   DATA   dry,yellow,powdery,acrid,sandy
490   DATA   rock,plateau,sand,view,plain
500   DATA   drifts,spreads,lies,blows,heats
510   DATA   on,in,over,under,near
520   DATA   THE SWAMP
530   DATA   moist,damp,humid,wet,slimy
540   DATA   soil,air,clearing,muck,foliage
550   DATA   steams,smells,grows,shifts,sinks
560   DATA   around,beside,under,on,in
570   DATA   THE OCEAN
580   DATA   smooth,raging,calm,fierce,cold
590   DATA   surface,wave,tide,flow,current
600   DATA   slides,rolls,leaps,crests,flows
610   DATA   over,around,onto,through,into
620   DATA   THE STORM
630   DATA   gusting,blowing,soaking,cruel,tropical
640   DATA   wind,rain,sleet,hail,lightning
650   DATA   pushes,gushes,blows,heaves,strikes
660   DATA   into,toward,at,onto,on
670   DATA   stop

]
```

24. VERB TENSES

SUGGESTED FILE NAME: TENSES

SUGGESTED GRADE RANGE: 2–8

DESCRIPTION OF THE PROGRAM: In this program, students identify the correct verb tense for a variety of verbs to use within a variety of sentence contexts. This is both a literal comprehension and a grammatical skill.

EXPLANATION OF DATA LINES: The information needed to print the problems on the screen is organized in groups of six data lines. The first line in the group contains the three verbs. The remaining five lines contain the sentences or phrases for which the student must choose verbs that correctly complete the sentences or phrases. The numbers in the data lines are the correct choices.

HOW TO CHANGE THE DATA: You may change or delete groups of data lines. You may add data by typing it in groups of six lines following the same pattern established by the current data lines. Use line numbers between 410 and 650. Do not use the same line number twice.

```
10   DIM VT$(20,3),VF$(20,5),CA(20,5)
20   HOME : VTAB (6): PRINT  TAB( 16);"VERB TENSES": VTAB
     (10): HTAB (1): PRINT "Twenty-five questions wi
     ll be presented."
30   FOR T = 1 TO 3000: NEXT T
40   C = 0
50   C = C + 1
60   FOR X = 1 TO 3: READ VT$(C,X): NEXT X
70   IF VT$(C,1) = "stop" THEN C = C - 1: GOTO 90
80   FOR X = 1 TO 5: READ VF$(C,X),CA(C,X): NEXT X: GOTO
     50
90  NL = 0:LS = 0
100  FOR X = 1 TO 25
110 N =  INT (C *  RND (1)) + 1:S =  INT (5 *  RND (
    1)) + 1
120  IF N = NL AND S = LS THEN 110
130 NL = N:LS = S:R = CA(N,S)
140  HOME : VTAB (2): PRINT  TAB( 18);"VERB TENSES"
150  VTAB (5): PRINT VF$(N,S)
160  VTAB (8): PRINT  TAB( 15);"1. ";VT$(N,1);"."
170  VTAB (10): PRINT  TAB( 15);"2. ";VT$(N,2);"."
180  VTAB (12): PRINT  TAB( 15);"3. ";VT$(N,3);"."
190 LN = 14: GOSUB 400: PRINT  TAB( 6);"Which tense
     is correct (1-3)?";
200  GET R$
210  IF  ASC (R$) < 49 OR  ASC (R$) > 51 THEN 200
220 AN =  VAL (R$)
230  IF AN = R THEN LN = 7: GOSUB 400: GOTO 260
240 LN = 14: GOSUB 400: PRINT  TAB( 13);"Please try
     again!"
250  FOR T = 1 TO 2000: NEXT T: GOTO 190
260  FOR Q = 39 -  LEN (VT$(N,R)) TO 2 +  LEN (VF$(N
    ,S)) STEP  - 1
270  VTAB (5): HTAB (Q + 1)
280  FOR Y = 1 TO  LEN (VT$(N,R)): PRINT " ";: NEXT
    Y
290  VTAB (5): HTAB (Q): PRINT VT$(N,R);
300  FOR I = 1 TO 50: NEXT I
310  NEXT Q
320  VTAB (5): HTAB ( LEN (VT$(N,R)) +  LEN (VF$(N,S
    )) + 2): PRINT "."
330  GOSUB 370
340  NEXT X
350  HOME : VTAB (6): PRINT "Be a special friend to
     someone today."
360  END
370 LN = 22: GOSUB 400: PRINT "Press the <space bar>
     to continue . . . .";
380  GET A$: IF A$ <  > " " THEN 380
390  RETURN
400  POKE 34,LN: HOME : POKE 34,0: VTAB (LN + 1): RETURN

410  DATA   run,ran,will run
420  DATA   Yesterday he,2
430  DATA   Tomorrow he,3
```

```
440   DATA   My legs get stronger when I,1
450   DATA   They were chased so they,2
460   DATA   Next week Jane,3
470   DATA   eat,eaten,will eat
480   DATA   The dogs have,2
490   DATA   In two hours I,3
500   DATA   Not until after we have,2
510   DATA   Tom has decided what he,3
520   DATA   Wash your hands before you,1
530   DATA   help,helped,will help
540   DATA   Mother said you can,1
550   DATA   Next week I,3
560   DATA   It couldn't be,2
570   DATA   I wish I could,1
580   DATA   I'm glad you were,2
590   DATA   pick,picked,will pick
600   DATA   The flowers are there to be,2
610   DATA   I hope that Rob is,2
620   DATA   Which one should she,1
630   DATA   Tomorrow is when he,3
640   DATA   It's time for them to,1
650   DATA   stop,stop,stop

    ]
```

25. SENTENCE TRANSFORMATION

SUGGESTED FILE NAME: TRANSFORM

SUGGESTED GRADE RANGE: 3–8

DESCRIPTION OF THE PROGRAM: A sentence is printed on the screen and the student is asked to type a question for which that sentence is an answer. Five sentences are presented, one at a time, in the same order each time the program is run. There are two correct answers given for each sentence.

Note: Users of Apple IIe and Apple IIc equipment must have the <**CAPS LOCK**> key in the UP position in order for this program to run properly.

EXPLANATION OF DATA LINES: Every three data lines contain the information for one exercise. The first line is the sentence, and the next two lines are the possible questions that the student could type as his or her response.

HOW TO CHANGE THE DATA: Data can be changed simply by replacing sentences one for one. No third alternative responses can be added. However, additional exercises can be added simply by adding three data lines for each exercise beginning with line 420. If you choose to add exercises, line 30 must also be changed. For example, if you add three exercises (nine data lines), line 30 must be changed to read 30 FOR W=1 TO 8.

```
10   HOME : VTAB (6): PRINT  TAB( 10);"SENTENCE TRANS
     FORMATION": VTAB (10): HTAB (1): PRINT "** Five
     problems will be presented. **"
20   FOR I = 1 TO 3000: NEXT I
30   FOR W = 1 TO 5
40   READ S$,Q1$,Q2$
50   HOME : VTAB (4): PRINT "Type a sentence as a que
     stion for which": PRINT
60   PRINT "the sentence below is an answer.  Be": PRINT

70   PRINT "sure you put a ? at the end.": PRINT
80   PRINT : PRINT S$
90 N = 0
100   PRINT
110 LN = 13: GOSUB 410: INPUT X$
120   IF X$ = Q1$ OR X$ = Q2$ THEN 230
130 N = N + 1
140   IF N = 3 THEN 180
150   PRINT : PRINT "Try again.  Type carefully.": PRINT

160   PRINT "Put a ? at the end."
170   FOR I = 1 TO 2000: NEXT I: GOTO 110
180 LN = 13: GOSUB 410
190   PRINT Q1$: PRINT
200   PRINT Q2$: PRINT
210   PRINT "Press the <space bar> to go on . . .";
220   GET A$: IF A$ <  > " " THEN 220
230   NEXT W
240   HOME : VTAB (6): PRINT  TAB( 10);"I like you ve
     ry much!!"
250   END
260   DATA  "The man is my father."
270   DATA  "Who is the man?"
280   DATA  "Who is my father?"
290   DATA  "My pencils are in my pocket."
300   DATA  "Where are my pencils?"
310   DATA  "What is in my pocket?"
320   DATA  "Birds fly well."
330   DATA  "What do birds do well?"
340   DATA  "How do birds fly?"
350   DATA  "He swims like a fish."
360   DATA  "How does he swim?"
370   DATA  "Who swims like a fish?"
380   DATA  "She went home yesterday."
390   DATA  "When did she go home?"
400   DATA  "What did she do yesterday?"
410   POKE 34,LN: HOME : POKE 34,0: VTAB (LN + 1): RETURN

]
```

chapter 4

25 PROGRAMS FOR MATHEMATICS AND SCIENCE ON THE APPLE

A program is more than a set of instructions to the computer; it is also a reflection of the inner workings of a person's mind. As such, programming logic often defies understanding. Therefore, don't be discouraged when you fail to fully comprehend the significance of all the statements in the programs in this chapter. You will find yourself in good company; we, the authors, cannot always interpret the products of one another's thinking. However, we have attempted to explain ourselves as much as possible without burdensome detail. We hope that we have given you enough clues so that you can understand some of the more obscure parts of the programs, and we hope that you will be able to design some programs of your own.

In this chapter you will find twenty-five programs for the Apple II +, IIe, or IIc microcomputer. These programs are meant to serve two purposes.

1. They provide a practical means of learning beginning programming in the BASIC language. This book is not meant to provide a complete course in programming, but to introduce you to the BASIC language in an interesting and useful way.

2. The programs can serve as the beginning of your software library in that they provide short, concise exercises for specific skills in mathematics and science.

We recommend that the programs be typed in the order in which they are presented. They have been arranged in order of difficulty of programming techniques, not necessarily in order of concept difficulty. However, if you have a special need for a program that appears later on and are adventurous, please feel free to attempt the programs in any order you wish.

To assist you in understanding the purpose of the programs before typing them into your computer, each program is preceded by the following information (where applicable).

SUGGESTED FILE NAME: This is a suggested name to use when saving the program. Sometimes the program name is too long and awkward to use; a shorter file name is more desirable.

SUGGESTED GRADE RANGE: The grade levels at which a particular skill is taught and practiced.

DESCRIPTION OF THE PROGRAM: This paragraph describes the purpose of the program and some of its features.

NEW PROGRAMMING STATEMENTS: This section describes the functions of new programming statements that have not been used in a previous program.

EXPLANATION OF DATA LINES: The structure of the information in the data lines is explained in this section.

PROGRAMMING LOGIC: Here the authors attempt to explain their thinking. Program lines that might not be readily understood or that perform a special function are explained here.

HOW TO CHANGE THE DATA: It is possible to customize some of the programs to address the special needs of your students by changing data entries or certain lines of the program. The techniques needed to accomplish these changes are explained here.

A VERY IMPORTANT REMINDER

A computer line begins with the line number and ends with the last word or number before the next numbered line. *Do not press <**RETURN**> until you have typed the entire line.* When the cursor approaches the right side of the screen, just keep typing. Screen wraparound takes care of automatically moving the cursor down the screen.

For example, in the first program, "Guess the Mystery Number," line 10 will not fit on one line of the screen. Keep typing, and let screen wraparound take care of the problem. Press <**RETURN**> at the end of the expression "NEXT TI." If you press <**RETURN**> too soon, retype the line.

1. GUESS THE MYSTERY NUMBER

SUGGESTED FILE NAME: GUESS

SUGGESTED GRADE RANGE: 2–5

DESCRIPTION OF THE PROGRAM: This program provides practice in formulating a systematic method for solving a problem. The computer randomly chooses a number between 1 and 100. The student must guess it in the least number of tries. We hope that the student will discover that halving differences is the most efficient way to "guess."

NEW PROGRAMMING STATEMENTS: HOME clears the screen. VTAB (6) moves the cursor six lines vertically from the top of the screen. PRINT TAB(8) moves the cursor in eight spaces where the printing will begin. Thus, the title will be printed six lines from the top and eight spaces from the left of the screen. The FOR/NEXT loop in line 10 is called a time delay. It makes the computer count to 2000 before proceeding with the program.

$M = INT (100 * RND (1)) + 1$ is a statement which assigns the variable, M, an integer value from one (1) to one hundred (100). RND (1) chooses a nine-digit decimal number. It is then multiplied by 100. The INT part of the statement lops off the decimal part of the number and keeps only the integer part. Adding one (1) assures that the final value for M will not be zero and that, possibly, M could be 100. For example, suppose $RND(1) = .326678571$. Multiplying by 100 results in the number, 32.6678571. The integer part of this number is 32; adding one makes it 33. Therefore, $M = 33$.

The colon (:) separates one statement from the next. Theoretically, each BASIC statement should be on a separate line. However, several statements can be placed on the same line when separated by colons.

I is a counter that counts the number of attempts by the user to guess the mystery number. In line 40, I is set at zero. After each guess, line 50, the counter is increased by 1, line 60.

If a guess is equal to the mystery number, the computer prints that the user guessed the number and how many guesses were required. If the guess is less than the number, line 80, then the computer prints "TOO LOW." If the guess is neither the mystery number nor less than the mystery number, it must be greater than the mystery number. This possibility is addressed by line 90.

Lines 100 through 130 give the student the chance to play the game again. Line 140 is a goodbye message.

HOW TO CHANGE THE DATA: You may want to adjust the program to use smaller numbers or larger ones. If so, change lines 20 and 40. For example, if you want the mystery number to be between 1 and 1000, change the lines to read

```
20 M = INT (1000 * RND (1)) + 1
40 PRINT : PRINT "FROM 1 TO 1000.": PRINT :I = 0
```

Be aware of the need to distinguish between the numeral zero and the letter O. The program listing does not have slashes through the zeros. Nevertheless, if 0 is in the context of a number, use the number, zero.

```
10    HOME : VTAB (6): PRINT  TAB( 8);"GUESS THE MYSTE
      RY NUMBER": FOR TI = 1 TO 2000: NEXT TI
20 M =   INT (100 *  RND (1)) + 1
30    HOME : PRINT : PRINT "I'M THINKING OF A MYSTERY
      NUMBER"
40   PRINT : PRINT "FROM 1 TO 100.": PRINT :I = 0
50   INPUT "GUESS  ";G
60 I = I + 1
70   IF G = M THEN  PRINT "YOU HIT THE NUMBER IN ";I;
     " GUESSES.": GOTO 100
80   IF G < M THEN  PRINT "TOO LOW": GOTO 50
90   PRINT "TOO HIGH": GOTO 50
100   PRINT : PRINT "DO YOU WANT TO PLAY AGAIN (Y OR
      N)";
110   INPUT Z$
120   IF Z$ = "Y" THEN 20
130   IF Z$ <  > "N" THEN  PRINT "PLEASE TYPE Y OR N.
      ";: GOTO 110
140   PRINT : PRINT "THAT'S ALL FOR NOW. BYE-BYE."
150   END

]
```

2. SOME—MORE OR LESS

SUGGESTED FILE NAME: SOMEMORE

SUGGESTED GRADE RANGE: 3–4

DESCRIPTION OF THE PROGRAM: The program gives students practice in adding to or subtracting from a given number when given the word "more" or "less." The number added or subtracted will be chosen by the user.

NEW PROGRAMMING STATEMENTS: GET A$ allows the computer to accept a number without requiring that <**RETURN**> be pressed. The number is stored as an alphanumeric value in A$ and no arithmetic can be done with it. In order to use the number as a number, it must be stored as a numeric value. VAL(A$) accomplishes this. N = VAL(A$) assigns to N the numeric value of A$.

```
10    HOME : VTAB (6): HTAB (9): PRINT "SOME --- MORE
      OR LESS": FOR TI = 1 TO 2000: NEXT TI
20    HOME : VTAB (3): PRINT "PROBLEMS OF THE FORM:": PRINT
      : PRINT "<NUMBER> MORE/LESS THAN A GIVEN NUMBER
      ."
30   PRINT : PRINT "TYPE THE <NUMBER> TO BE USED IN T
     HIS": PRINT : PRINT "PROGRAM.";
40 A$ = "": GET A$
50   IF  VAL (A$) = 0 THEN 40
60 N =   VAL (A$)
70 O =   INT (2 *  RND (1) + 1: IF O = 2 THEN O$ = "
     LESS": GOTO 90
80 O$ = "MORE"
90 V =   INT (10 * N *  RND (1)) + N + 9
```

```
100   IF O = 2 THEN CA = V - N: GOTO 120
110 CA = V + N
120   HOME : VTAB (4)
130   PRINT "FIND THE NUMBER WHICH IS": PRINT : PRINT
      : PRINT  TAB( 5);A$;"  ";O$;" THAN  "V
140   FOR TI = 1 TO 400: NEXT TI
150   PRINT : PRINT : PRINT "PLEASE TYPE YOUR ANSWER
      AND PRESS THE": PRINT : PRINT "<RETURN> KEY.";
160   INPUT A
170   IF A = (CA) THEN  PRINT : PRINT "GOOD!!!": GOTO
      190
180   PRINT : PRINT : PRINT "SORRY, THE NUMBER IS ";C
      A;"."
190   PRINT : PRINT "PRESS C TO CONTINUE, OR S TO STO
      P . . .";
200   GET R$
210   IF R$ < > "C" AND R$ < > "S" THEN 200
220   IF R$ = "C" THEN 70
230   HOME : VTAB (6): HTAB (1): PRINT "I HOPE TO SEE
      YOU MORE IN THE FUTURE!!"
240   END

]
```

3. GREATER THAN–LESS THAN SYMBOLS

SUGGESTED FILE NAME: GRTRTHAN

SUGGESTED GRADE RANGE: 3–5

DESCRIPTION OF THE PROGRAM: This program gives the student practice using the greater than (>) and less than (<) symbols. The student chooses the largest number that he or she wishes to use in these exercises. The computer then displays two randomly selected numbers that are less than that largest number and asks the student to choose the symbol less than (<) or greater than (>) that correctly compares the two numbers.

NEW PROGRAMMING STATEMENTS: SC = INT (NC / T * 100 + .5) is an arithmetic statement that calculates the student's score. NC represents the "number correct." Each time the student answers correctly, NC is increased by 1 (line 120). T is the total number of times the student answers. Each time the student types an answer, T is increased by 1 (line 110). In line 140, the quotient of the number of correct answers and the total number of answers is multiplied by 100 to get the student's score. To round the score to the nearest whole number percent, .5 is added. Finally, INT assigns the integer value of the score to SC and the decimal number is dropped.

For example, if NC = 8 and T = 11, then NC/T = .727272. Multiplying by 100 results in 72.727272. Adding .5 rounds the number to the nearest whole number percent when the integer value is assigned to SC, the score. Therefore, INT(72.727272 + .5) = INT(73.227272) = 73.

PROGRAMMING LOGIC: Notice in the score computation—INT(NC / T * 100 + .5)—that .5 is added to the score before the decimal part is dropped. In effect, adding .5 rounds the number to the nearest ones place. For example, in rounding 88.7 to the nearest ones place, the computer calculates 88.7 + .5, then drops the decimal. Therefore, INT(88.7 + .5) = INT(89.2) = 89.

```
10    HOME : VTAB (5)
20    PRINT  TAB( 5);"GREATER THAN - LESS THAN SYMBOLS
      ": FOR TI = 1 TO 2000: NEXT TI
30    PRINT : PRINT : PRINT  TAB( 4);"WHAT IS THE LARG
      EST NUMBER YOU WISH": PRINT  TAB( 4);"TO USE";
40    INPUT N: IF N < 2 THEN 10
50 N1 =  INT (N *  RND (1)) + 1:N2 =  INT (N *  RND
      (1)) + 1
60    IF N1 = N2 THEN 50
70    IF N1 > N2 THEN CA$ = ">": GOTO 80
75 CA$ = "<"
80    HOME : PRINT : PRINT  TAB( 13);N1;"            ";N
      2
85    PRINT  TAB( 18);"----"
90    PRINT : PRINT "TYPE THE CORRECT SYMBOL, > (GREAT
      ER": PRINT : PRINT "THAN), OR < (LESS THAN) TO
      FILL IN THE": PRINT : PRINT "BLANK, AND PRESS <
      RETURN>";
100   INPUT AN$
110 T = T + 1
120   IF AN$ = CA$ THEN  PRINT : PRINT "CORRECT.":NC =
      NC + 1: GOTO 140
130   PRINT : PRINT "SORRY, NOT CORRECT."
140 SC =  INT (NC / T * 100 + .5)
150   PRINT : PRINT "YOUR SCORE IS ";SC;"."
160   PRINT : PRINT "PRESS C TO CONTINUE, OR S TO STO
      P . . .";
170   GET R$
180   IF R$ < > "C" AND R$ < > "S" THEN 170
190   IF R$ = "C" THEN 50
200   HOME : VTAB (6): HTAB (1): PRINT "MAKE THIS A G
      REAT DAY FOR YOURSELF!!!": END

]
```

4. MORE THAN–FEWER THAN

SUGGESTED FILE NAME: MOREFEW

SUGGESTED GRADE RANGE: 3–5

DESCRIPTION OF THE PROGRAM: The student has the opportunity to practice the mathematical meaning of "more than" and "fewer than" in a counting context. The computer randomly chooses two letters and prints different amounts of the letters on the screen. The student then types the letter of which there are "more" or "fewer."

NEW PROGRAMMING STATEMENTS: Sometimes it is convenient to enter values into the computer as lists (called arrays) that use the same variable. In this program there are four arrays: Q$, L, N, and L$. Each of these arrays has only two values in it. Each value is denoted by its numbered place in the list. For example, MORE is the first value in Q$ and is denoted Q$(1). The second value in array L is a random number between 1 and 26 added to 64.

In line 40, INT(26 * RND(1))+65 is used to pick a letter of the alphabet randomly. Each character that can be typed into the computer from the keyboard is given a decimal code. These codes are found in the Appendix of your owner's manual. The decimal codes for letters of the alphabet begin with 65 and end with 90.

In lines 90 and 100, the values in array L$ are obtained from taking the Character Code of the values in array L. For example, if L(1)=82, then L$(1)=CHR$(82)=R.

PROGRAMMING LOGIC: In line 60 the computer is told to choose how many of each of the two letters to print on the screen. Line 80 tells the computer that if the two values chosen are the same, to go back to line 60 and choose again. The routine in lines 120-170 is to print the correct number of each of the two letters on the screen in random order. This loop of instructions will be executed over and over until all of the required letters appear on the screen.

```
10 T = 0
20  HOME : VTAB (6): HTAB (9): PRINT "MORE THAN - FE
    WER THAN": FOR TI = 1 TO 2000: NEXT TI
30  HOME :Q$(1) = "MORE":Q$(2) = "FEWER"
40 L(1) =  INT (26 *  RND (1)) + 65:L(2) =  INT (26 *
    RND (1)) + 65
50  IF L(1) = L(2) THEN 40
60 N1 =  INT (8 *  RND (1)) + 1:N2 =  INT (8 *  RND
    (1)) + 1
70 N(1) = N1:N(2) = N2
80  IF N(1) = N(2) THEN 60
90 L$(1) =  CHR$ (L(1))
100 L$(2) =  CHR$ (L(2))
110  PRINT : PRINT
120 LC =  INT (2 *  RND (1)) + 1
130 N(LC) = N(LC) - 1
140  IF N(1) < 0 AND N(2) < 0 THEN 180
150  IF N(LC) < 0 THEN 120
160  PRINT L$(LC);" ";
170  GOTO 120
180 Q =  INT (2 *  RND (1)) + 1
190  PRINT : PRINT : PRINT
200  PRINT "TYPE THE LETTER OF WHICH THERE ARE"
210  PRINT : PRINT Q$(Q);" ABOVE AND PRESS <RETURN>.
    "
220  INPUT AN$
230 T = T + 1
240  IF Q = 1 AND N1 > N2 THEN CA$ = L$(1): GOTO 260
```

```
250   IF Q = 1 AND N2 > N1 THEN CA$ = L$(2)
260   IF Q = 2 AND N1 < N2 THEN CA$ = L$(1): GOTO 280

270   IF Q = 2 AND N2 < N1 THEN CA$ = L$(2)
280   IF AN$ = CA$ THEN  PRINT : PRINT "CORRECT.":NR =
      NR + 1: GOTO 300
290   PRINT : PRINT "SORRY, NOT CORRECT."
300 SC =  INT (NR / T * 100 + .5)
310   PRINT : PRINT "YOUR SCORE IS ";SC;"."
320   PRINT : PRINT "PRESS C TO CONTINUE, OR S TO STO
      P . . .";
330   GET R$
340   IF R$ < > "C" AND R$ < > "S" THEN 330
350   IF R$ = "C" THEN  HOME : GOTO 40
360   HOME : VTAB (6): HTAB (1): PRINT "TRY TO MAKE T
      HE MOST OF EVERY DAY!!!": END

]
```

5. CHOOSE THE LARGEST NUMBER

SUGGESTED FILE NAME: LARGEST

SUGGESTED GRADE RANGE: 3–8

DESCRIPTION OF THE PROGRAM: The object of this program is to choose the largest number from three numbers shown on the screen.

NEW PROGRAMMING STATEMENTS: Notice the subroutine in line 240. Sometimes a routine in a program must be executed several times. A subroutine is used to shorten a program and make it more readable. It relieves the programmer of having to retype the same lines over in a program several times. The computer is sent to the subroutine by the statement GOSUB. Whenever there is a GOSUB, there must be a RETURN statement. RETURN is found at the end of the subroutine. RETURN returns the computer to that statement in the program which directly follows the GOSUB. Remember, GOSUB/RETURN are statements that must both appear in a program; one may not appear without the other.

EXPLANATION OF DATA LINES: The two data lines contain a total of twenty numbers. The numbers are read into the computer; then three of them are chosen randomly to appear on the screen.

HOW TO CHANGE THE DATA: The numbers in the data lines may be too difficult for your students. You can change the numbers simply by retyping the data lines. *You must be careful to use exactly ten numbers per data line and to separate each number from the next by a comma.*

```
10    DIM A(20):R = 0:T = 0:N = 0
20    HOME : VTAB (6): PRINT   TAB( 8);"CHOOSE THE LARG
      EST NUMBER": FOR TI = 1 TO 2000: NEXT TI
30    FOR I = 1 TO 20: READ A(I): NEXT I
40    HOME : INPUT "WHAT IS YOUR NAME?   ";N$
50    PRINT : PRINT "HAPPY TO MEET YOU, ";N$;".": FOR
      TI = 1 TO 2000: NEXT TI
60 N = N + 1: HOME
70 B =   INT (20 *   RND (1)) + 1:C =   INT (20 *   RND
      (1)) + 1:D =   INT (20 *   RND (1)) + 1
80    IF B = C OR C = D OR B = D THEN 70
90    PRINT "#";N: PRINT : PRINT : PRINT "WHICH OF THE
      NUMBERS BELOW IS LARGEST?"
100   PRINT : PRINT : PRINT A(B),A(C),A(D)
110   PRINT : PRINT : PRINT "TYPE YOUR CHOICE, ";N$;"
      .": PRINT : PRINT
120   INPUT X:T = T + 1
130   IF X < > A(B) AND X < > A(C) AND X < > A(D) THEN
       PRINT : PRINT "PLEASE TYPE ONE OF THE NUMBERS
      ABOVE.": FOR TI = 1 TO 2000: NEXT TI:LN = 12: GOSUB
      240: GOTO 120
140   IF X > = A(B) AND X > = A(C) AND X > = A(D) THEN
      160
150   PRINT : PRINT "PLEASE TRY AGAIN.": FOR TI = 1 TO
      2000: NEXT TI:LN = 12: GOSUB 240: GOTO 120
160 R = R + 1: PRINT : PRINT "YOU ARE CORRECT, ";N$;
      "!!!": PRINT : PRINT "YOUR SCORE IS "; INT (R /
      T * 100 + .5): PRINT : PRINT "DO YOU WANT ANOTH
      ER PROBLEM (Y OR N)"
170   INPUT Z$
180   IF Z$ = "Y" THEN 60
190   IF Z$ = "N" THEN 210
200   PRINT "PLEASE TYPE Y OR N, ";N$;".": FOR TI = 1
      TO 2000: NEXT TI:LN = 19: GOSUB 240: GOTO 170
210   PRINT : PRINT "GOOD-BYE FOR NOW, ";N$;".": END

220   DATA   -3,.5,13,0,-7,.44,.444,1.2,1.02,11
230   DATA   -1.1,-1.11,.05,.112,.11,6,-4,-1,9,-8,7.2
240   POKE 34,LN: HOME : POKE 34,0: VTAB (LN + 1): RETURN
```

]

6. UNDERSTANDING MULTIPLICATION
(ROWS AND COLUMNS)

SUGGESTED FILE NAME: UNDMULT

SUGGESTED GRADE RANGE: 3–5

DESCRIPTION OF THE PROGRAM: This program shows the connection between a rectangular display of rows and columns, and multiplication. The computer prints a rectangular array of squares on the screen. The student must count the rows of squares, count the columns, then count the squares. The student then multiplies the number of rows by the number of columns. The student should realize that multiplication of rows by columns is the efficient way to count items in a rectangular array.

NEW PROGRAMMING STATEMENTS: In line 50 are the statements that put the Apple into low resolution graphics mode. TEXT puts the computer into text mode, that allows printing to appear on the entire screen. HOME clears the screen. GR changes to low resolution graphics mode. (HGR is the statement for high resolution graphics.) When in graphics mode, four lines are set aside at the bottom of the screen for text.

The next line sets the color for the graphics. COLOR = INT(14 * RND(1)) + 1 randomly chooses a value from 1 to 14. This value will set different colors on the screen as the program is run.

PLOT J,I plots a square on the screen at the location J,I. Look at the Apple Video Display Worksheet in the Appendix of this book. It is a picture of the locations on the screen of your monitor. There are numbers across the top and down the sides of the sheet. These numbers are used to locate graphics on the screen. PLOT J,I means to print a square at the location which is determined by J at the top and I at the side. For example, PLOT 25,13 would print a square 25 spaces from the left and 13 spaces down the screen.

PROGRAMMING LOGIC: The number of rows (NR) and the number of columns (NC) are chosen at random. Lines 80 through 140 draw the rows and columns on the screen. STEP 3 makes the rows and columns print three spaces apart. This is done so that the squares show up individually on the screen and the student can count them.

```
10   TEXT : HOME : VTAB (6): PRINT  TAB( 7);"UNDERSTA
     NDING MULTIPLICATION"
20   VTAB (8): PRINT  TAB( 12);"(ROWS AND COLUMNS)": GOSUB
      380: GOSUB 380: HOME : GR
30  N = 0:T = 0
40  NR = 0:NC = 0
50   TEXT : HOME : GR
60   COLOR=  INT (14 *  RND (1)) + 1
70  R =   INT (36 *  RND (1)) + 1:C =  INT (36 *  RND
     (1)) + 1
80   FOR I = 1 TO R STEP 3
90  NR = NR + 1
100   FOR J = 1 TO C STEP 3
110 NC = NC + 1
120   PLOT J,I
130   NEXT J
140   NEXT I
150   HOME
160   PRINT "HOW MANY ROWS";:T = T + 1: INPUT RN
170   IF RN = NR THEN 190
```

```
180   HOME : PRINT "COUNT THE ROWS AGAIN.": GOSUB 380
      : HOME : GOTO 160
190 N = N + 1: HOME
200   PRINT "HOW MANY COLUMNS";:T = T + 1: INPUT CN
210   IF CN = NC / NR THEN 230
220   HOME : PRINT "COUNT THE COLUMNS AGAIN.": GOSUB
      380: HOME : GOTO 200
230 N = N + 1
240   HOME : PRINT RN;"   X   ";CN;"  =  ";:T = T + 1: INPUT
      P
250   IF P = CN * RN THEN 270
260   HOME : PRINT "NOT CORRECT - TRY AGAIN.": GOSUB
      380: HOME : GOTO 240
270 N = N + 1
280   HOME : PRINT "HOW MANY SQUARES";:T = T + 1: INPUT
      NS
290   IF NS = CN * RN THEN 310
300   HOME : PRINT "NOT CORRECT - TRY AGAIN.": GOSUB
      380: HOME : GOTO 280
310 N = N + 1
320   HOME : PRINT "THAT'S RIGHT!!!": GOSUB 380
330   HOME : PRINT "YOUR SCORE IS " INT (N / T * 100 +
      .5);"%.": GOSUB 380: GOSUB 380
340   HOME : PRINT "HOW ABOUT ANOTHER PROBLEM (Y/N)";
      : INPUT Z$: IF Z$ = "Y" THEN 40
350   IF Z$ = "N" THEN  TEXT : HOME : VTAB (6): PRINT
      TAB( 10);"HAVE A SUPER DAY!!!": END
360   HOME : PRINT "PLEASE TYPE Y OR N.": GOSUB 380: GOTO
      340
370   END
380   FOR TI = 1 TO 1500: NEXT TI: RETURN

]
```

7. UNDERSTANDING DIVISION

SUGGESTED FILE NAME: UNDDIV

SUGGESTED GRADE RANGE: 4–8

DESCRIPTION OF THE PROGRAM: This program shows the relationship between division and multiplication. A two-digit number is randomly chosen as the divisor. The products of the divisor and the digits, one through nine, are shown across the top of the screen. A division problem with the two-digit divisor is shown at the center of the screen. The student uses the products at the top of the screen to find the quotient.

PROGRAMMING LOGIC: Lines 160 and 170 draw the division symbol in the division problem. CHR$(95) is the code for the underline symbol. The expression "PRINT CHR$(95);" appears in a FOR/NEXT loop in line 160. This group of statements causes the computer to print six consecutive underline symbols to form the top line of the division symbol. The semicolon (;) prevents the computer from erasing the next line.

```
10 S = 0
20  HOME : VTAB (6): PRINT  TAB( 10);"UNDERSTANDING
    DIVISION": FOR TI = 1 TO 2000: NEXT TI
30 X =  INT (89 *  RND (1)) + 11
40  HOME : VTAB (2): FOR I = 1 TO 9: PRINT  TAB( 2 +
    4 * (I - 1));X;: NEXT I
50  VTAB (3): HTAB (1): FOR I = 1 TO 9: PRINT  TAB(
    1 + 4 * (I - 1));"X ";I;: NEXT I
60  VTAB (4): HTAB (1): FOR I = 1 TO 9: PRINT  TAB(
    1 + 4 * (I - 1));"---";: NEXT I
70  FOR I = 1 TO 9
80 P$(I) =  STR$ (I * X)
90  IF  LEN (P$(I)) = 2 THEN P$(I) = " " + P$(I)
100   NEXT I
110   VTAB (5): HTAB (1): FOR I = 1 TO 9: PRINT  TAB(
    1 + 4 * (I - 1));P$(I);: NEXT I
120 Y =  INT (9 *  RND (1)) + 1
130 Z =  INT (Y *  RND (1))
140 D$ =  STR$ (Y * X + Z): IF  LEN (D$) = 2 THEN D$
    = " " + D$
150   VTAB (9): HTAB (13): PRINT X;: HTAB (18): PRINT
    D$
160   VTAB (8): HTAB (16): FOR I = 1 TO 6: PRINT  CHR$
    (95);: NEXT I
170   VTAB (9): HTAB (16): PRINT ")";
180 LN = 17: GOSUB 460: PRINT "TYPE THE PRODUCT NEAR
    EST ";(Y * X) + Z;" WITHOUT": PRINT
190   PRINT "GOING OVER ";(Y * X) + Z;".";: INPUT P
200   IF P <  > Y * X AND S = 1 THEN LN = 17: GOSUB 4
    60: PRINT "THE PRODUCT IS ";Y * X;".": FOR I =
    1 TO 2000: NEXT I:S = 0: GOTO 180
210   IF P = Y * X THEN 230
220 LN = 17: GOSUB 460: PRINT "NOT CORRECT -- CHECK
    THE ANSWERS AT THE": PRINT : PRINT "TOP OF THE
    SCREEN.": FOR I = 1 TO 2000: NEXT I:S = 1: GOTO
    180
230 LN = 17: GOSUB 460: PRINT "THAT'S CORRECT!!":S =
    0
240 PP$ =  STR$ (Y * X): IF  LEN (PP$) = 2 THEN PP$ =
    " " + PP$
250   VTAB (10): HTAB (18): PRINT PP$;" = ";Y;" X ";X

260   VTAB (11): HTAB (17): PRINT "-----"
270   FOR I = 1 TO 1200: NEXT I
280 LN = 17: GOSUB 460: PRINT "TYPE THE QUOTIENT."
290   VTAB (7): HTAB (19): INPUT Q
300   IF Q <  > Y AND S = 1 THEN LN = 17: GOSUB 460: PRINT
    "THE QUOTIENT IS ";Y;".": FOR I = 1 TO 1200: NEXT
    I: VTAB (7): HTAB (19): PRINT "     ";:S = 0: GOTO
    280
310   IF Q = Y THEN 330
320 LN = 17: GOSUB 460: PRINT "NOT CORRECT -- LOOK A
```

```
        GAIN.": FOR I = 1 TO 1200: NEXT I: VTAB (7): HTAB
        (19): PRINT "     ";:S = 1: GOTO 280
330     VTAB (7): HTAB (19): PRINT " ";Y;:LN = 17: GOSUB
        460: PRINT "THAT'S RIGHT!!":S = 0
340     FOR I = 1 TO 1200: NEXT I
350     LN = 17: GOSUB 460: PRINT "WHAT IS THE REMAINDER
        ?"
360     VTAB (12): HTAB (19): INPUT R
370     IF R = Z THEN 390
380     LN = 17: GOSUB 460: PRINT "NOT CORRECT -- SUBTRA
        CT AGAIN.": FOR I = 1 TO 1500: NEXT I: VTAB (12
        ): HTAB (19): PRINT "     ";: GOTO 350
390     VTAB (12): HTAB (19): PRINT " ";Z;:LN = 17: GOSUB
        460: PRINT "CORRECT!!     ";(Y * X + Z);" = (";Y
        ;" X ";X;") + ";Z: FOR I = 1 TO 2000: NEXT I
400     PRINT : PRINT "DO YOU WANT ANOTHER PROBLEM (Y O
        R N)";: INPUT W$
410     IF W$ = "Y" THEN 30
420     IF W$ = "N" THEN 440
430     LN = 19: GOSUB 460: PRINT "PLEASE TYPE EITHER Y
        OR N.": FOR I = 1 TO 1200: NEXT I:LN = 19: GOSUB
        460: GOTO 400
440     HOME : VTAB (8): PRINT "I HOPE THIS IS A GREAT
        DAY FOR YOU!!!"
450     END
460     POKE 34,LN: HOME : POKE 34,0: VTAB (LN + 1): RETURN
```

]

8. FUN WITH DECIMALS

SUGGESTED FILE NAME: DECFUN

SUGGESTED GRADE RANGE: 5–8

DESCRIPTION OF THE PROGRAM: This program provides practice in decimal arithmetic using three-digit numbers with one decimal place.

PROGRAMMING LOGIC: In line 120, ASC is used in a different way from the previous program. Here the input for A$ is a letter. In line 110, 64 is subtracted from the ASC for A$; then line 120 checks to see if the value of the code is from 1 through 5. In your manual, you will find that the decimal codes for A, B, C, D, and E begin with 65 and end with 69. Subtracting 64 from the appropriate code leaves a number from 1 to 5.

If choice E is selected from the menu, the computer is directed to line 350. In line 350 a random whole number from 1 to 4 is selected. This value determines which operation is to be used in the next exercise. Depending on the value (1 to 4) selected, the computer is directed to go to line 310, 320, 330, or 340. For example, if the value chosen and stored in the variable O is 2, the operation indicated is subtraction and the computer is told to go to the subtraction routine beginning in line 320. This routine is rather complicated; don't feel bad if you can't follow it completely the first few times through.

```
10    HOME : VTAB (6): HTAB (12): PRINT "FUN WITH DECI
      MALS": FOR TI = 1 TO 2000: NEXT TI
20    HOME : VTAB (3): HTAB (12): PRINT "** PROGRAM ME
      NU **"
30    PRINT : PRINT  TAB( 8);"A) ADDITION OF DECIMALS"

40    PRINT  TAB( 8);"B) SUBTRACTION OF DECIMALS"
50    PRINT  TAB( 8);"C) MULTIPLICATION OF DECIMALS"
60    PRINT  TAB( 8);"D) DIVISION OF DECIMALS"
70    PRINT  TAB( 8);"E) ALL OF THE ABOVE"
80    PRINT : PRINT : PRINT "PRESS THE LETTER OF YOUR
      CHOICE."
100   GET A$
110   A =  ASC (A$) - 64
120   IF A < 1 OR A > 5 THEN 100
130   ON A GOSUB 310,320,330,340,350
140   N1 =  INT (999 *  RND (1)) * .1:N2 =  INT (999 *
      RND (1)) * .1
150   IF O = 2 AND N1 < N2 THEN 140
160   IF O = 4 AND N1 < N2 THEN 140
170   ON O GOSUB 360,370,380,390
180   HOME : VTAB (3): PRINT  TAB( 4);O$: PRINT : PRINT
       TAB( 4);N1;"   ";OP$;"   ";N2;" = ?"
190   PRINT : PRINT : PRINT  TAB( 4);"PLEASE TYPE YOU
      R ANSWER AND PRESS": PRINT : PRINT  TAB( 4);"TH
      E <RETURN> KEY."
200   PRINT : PRINT  TAB( 10);" ";: INPUT AV: PRINT
210   IF  ABS (AV - AN) < .00005 THEN CA = 1:NC = NC +
      1: GOTO 230
220   CA = 0
230   T = T + 1
240   SC =  INT (NC / T * 100 + .5)
250   IF CA = 1 THEN  PRINT  TAB( 11);"CORRECT!"
260   IF CA = 0 THEN  PRINT  TAB( 7);"SORRY, ANSWER I
      S ";AN
270   PRINT : PRINT  TAB( 7);"YOUR SCORE IS ";SC
280   PRINT : PRINT "PRESS C TO CONTINUE, OR S TO STO
      P . . .";
285   GET R$: IF R$ <  > "C" AND R$ <  > "S" THEN 285

290   IF R$ = "C" THEN 130
300   HOME : VTAB (6): HTAB (1): PRINT "WORK TO MAKE
      THIS A TERRIFIC DAY!!!": END
310   O = 1:O$ = "ADD":OP$ = "+": RETURN
320   O = 2:O$ = "SUBTRACT":OP$ = "-": RETURN
330   O = 3:O$ = "MULTIPLY":OP$ = "X": RETURN
340   O = 4:O$ = "DIVIDE":OP$ = "/": RETURN
350   O =  INT (4 *  RND (1)) + 1: ON O GOSUB 310,320,
      330,340: RETURN
360   AN = N1 + N2: RETURN
370   AN = N1 - N2: RETURN
```

```
380 AN = N1 * N2: RETURN
390 AN = N1:N1 = N1 * N2: RETURN

]
```

9. PERIMETER AND AREA OF RECTANGLES

SUGGESTED FILE NAME: RECTANGLES

SUGGESTED GRADE RANGE: 6–8

DESCRIPTION OF THE PROGRAM: A rectangle is printed on the screen, and the student is asked to calculate the perimeter of the rectangle, then to calculate its area.

NEW PROGRAMMING STATEMENTS: VLIN and HLIN appear in lines 50 through 80. These two statements may be used only when the Apple is in the low resolution graphics mode. The computer was put in the appropriate mode by line 40. VLIN instructs the computer to draw a vertical line. HLIN instructs it to draw a horizontal line. VLIN 1,W at 1 will result in a line drawn from vertical position 1 to vertical position W (value stored in variable W) at horizontal position 1. See your owner's manual for the low resolution graphics screen positions. For example, if W=15, VLIN 1,15 at 1 will result in a line from vertical position 1 to vertical position 15 at horizontal position 1.

Similarly, HLIN 1,L at W will draw a horizontal line from position 1 to position L at vertical position W. For example, if L=8 and W=15, HLIN 1,8 at 15 will result in a horizontal line from position 1 to position 8 at vertical position 15.

```
10   HOME : TEXT : VTAB (6): PRINT  TAB( 12);"PERIMET
     ER AND AREA": VTAB (8): PRINT  TAB( 14);"OF REC
     TANGLES": FOR TI = 1 TO 2000: NEXT TI
20   L =  INT (39 *  RND (1)) + 1:W =  INT (39 *  RND
     (1)) + 1
30   P = 2 * (L + W):A = L * W
40   GR : HOME : COLOR=  INT (14 *  RND (1)) + 1
50   VLIN 1,W AT 1
60   VLIN 1,W AT L
70   HLIN 1,L AT 1
80   HLIN 1,L AT W
90   GOSUB 310
100   PRINT "WHAT IS THE PERIMETER";: INPUT PG
110   IF PG > P THEN  HOME : PRINT "YOUR ANSWER IS TO
      O LARGE.": GOSUB 290: GOSUB 300: GOTO 90
120   IF PG < P THEN  HOME : PRINT "YOUR ANSWER IS TO
      O SMALL.": GOSUB 290: GOSUB 300: GOTO 90
130   HOME : PRINT "VERY GOOD!!!  THAT IS CORRECT.": GOSUB
      250
140   GOSUB 310
```

```
150   PRINT "WHAT IS THE AREA";: INPUT AG
160   IF AG > (A) THEN   HOME : PRINT "YOUR ANSWER IS
      TOO LARGE.": GOSUB 290: GOSUB 300: GOTO 140
170   IF AG < (A) THEN   HOME : PRINT "YOUR ANSWER IS
      TOO SMALL.": GOSUB 290: GOSUB 300: GOTO 140
180   HOME : PRINT "EXCELLENT!!  YOU FOUND BOTH THE":
       PRINT "PERIMETER AND THE AREA CORRECTLY.": GOSUB
      290
190   PRINT "DO YOU WANT ANOTHER RECTANGLE (Y OR N)";

200   GET A$
210   IF A$ = "Y" THEN 20
220   IF A$ < > "N" THEN 200
230   TEXT : HOME : VTAB (8): PRINT  TAB( 10);"HAVE A
       HAPPY DAY!!"
240   END
250   PRINT "PRESS THE <SPACE BAR> TO CONTINUE . . ."

260   GET A$
270   IF A$ < > " " THEN 260
280   RETURN
290   FOR T = 1 TO 1200: NEXT T: RETURN
300   PRINT "PLEASE TRY AGAIN.": GOSUB 250: RETURN
310   HOME : PRINT "THIS IS A ";L;" BY ";W;" RECTANGL
      E.": RETURN

]
```

10. COMPUTER ROUNDING AID

SUGGESTED FILE NAME: ROUNDING

SUGGESTED GRADE RANGE: 5–8

DESCRIPTION OF THE PROGRAM: This program is a tool for the student to use when rounding numbers. The student types in a decimal number from 1 to 10,000 and the computer rounds the number to the place value selected by the student.

NEW PROGRAMMING STATEMENTS: Line 140 contains an arithmetic calculation using the symbol for exponent ($\wedge$). In the arithmetic statement:
$$N * 10 \wedge X - INT((N + .000001) * 10 \wedge X) > = .049$$
First, 10 is raised to the X power. That number is then multiplied by N. Finally, the INT value is taken of the rest of the expression.

PROGRAMMING LOGIC: The calculations in line 210 perform the rounding of the number given to the place desired. First, the number entered is multiplied by a power of ten to move the decimal point to the desired position. Then, .5 is added to the result. When the INT function is applied to this value, the result is a whole number with the correct digits for the answer. Finally, the whole number result is divided by a power of ten to reposition the decimal point in the proper place.

HOW TO CHANGE THE DATA: This program should not be changed.

```
10   HOME : VTAB (6): PRINT  TAB( 6);">>> COMPUTER RO
     UNDING AID <<<": FOR TI = 1 TO 2000: NEXT TI
20   FOR X = 1 TO 7: READ RP$(X): NEXT X
30   DATA  THOUSAND,HUNDRED,TEN,UNIT,TENTH,HUNDREDTH,
     THOUSANDTH
40   HOME : VTAB (2): PRINT  TAB( 11);"*** INSTRUCTIO
     NS ***": PRINT
50   PRINT  TAB( 5);"I WILL GLADLY ROUND ANY WHOLE OR
     ": PRINT : PRINT "DECIMAL NUMBER FOR YOU WHICH
     IS BETWEEN": PRINT
60   PRINT "0 AND 10000.  BE SURE WHEN YOU TYPE THE":
      PRINT : PRINT "NUMERAL THAT YOU DO NOT INCLUDE
     A COMMA."
70   PRINT "FOR EXAMPLE, PLEASE TYPE ONE THOUSAND AS"
     : PRINT "1000 AND NOT AS 1,000.  BE SURE TO": PRINT

80   PRINT "INCLUDE THE DECIMAL POINT IF THERE": PRINT
     : PRINT "SHOULD BE ONE IN THE NUMERAL."
90   GOSUB 300
100   HOME : VTAB (3): PRINT "WHAT IS THE NUMBER YOU
     WOULD LIKE ME": PRINT : PRINT "TO ROUND";: INPUT
     N
110   IF N <  = 0 THEN LN = 16: GOSUB 290: PRINT "THE
      NUMBER MUST BE GREATER THAN 0.": GOSUB 260: GOTO
     100
120   IF N >  = 10000 THEN LN = 16: GOSUB 290: PRINT
     "THE NUMBER MUST BE LESS THAN 10000.": GOSUB 26
     0: GOTO 100
130   IF N =  INT (N) THEN P = 0: GOTO 160
140   FOR X = 0 TO 3: IF N * 10 ^ X -  INT ((N + .000
     001) * 10 ^ X) >  = .049 THEN P = X + 1
150   NEXT X
160   HOME : VTAB (2): PRINT "I CAN ROUND < ";N;" >":
      PRINT : PRINT "TO THE NEAREST:"
170   FOR X = 1 TO 3 + P: VTAB (5 + X * 2): HTAB (12)
     : PRINT X;") ";RP$(X);: NEXT X
180   LN = 22: GOSUB 290: PRINT "PLEASE PRESS THE NUMB
     ER OF YOUR CHOICE.";: GET A$
190   IF  ASC (A$) < 49 OR  ASC (A$) > 51 + P THEN 18
     0
200   RP =  VAL (A$)
210   RV =  INT (N * 10 ^ (RP - 4) + .5) / 10 ^ (RP -
     4):CH = RV
220   HOME : VTAB (3): PRINT "THE VALUE OF < ";N;" >"

230   VTAB (7): HTAB (1): PRINT "ROUNDED TO THE NEARE
     ST ";RP$(RP);" IS"
240   VTAB (11): HTAB (16): PRINT "< ";CH;" >."
250   LN = 22: GOSUB 290: PRINT "PRESS C TO CONTINUE,
     OR S TO STOP . . .";
```

```
260   GET A$: IF A$ < > "C" AND A$ < > "S" THEN 260

270   IF A$ = "C" THEN 100
280   HOME : VTAB (6): PRINT "MAKE A FRIEND SMILE TOD
      AY!!!": END
290   POKE 34,LN: HOME : POKE 34,0: VTAB (LN + 1): RETURN

300   LN = 22: GOSUB 290: PRINT "PRESS THE <SPACE BAR>
         TO CONTINUE . . .";
310   GET A$: IF A$ < > " " THEN 310
320   RETURN
```

11. THE LCM CHALLENGE

SUGGESTED FILE NAME: LEASTCOM

SUGGESTED GRADE RANGE: 5–8

DESCRIPTION OF THE PROGRAM: The LCM Challenge gives students practice in determining the least common multiple of two numbers. The program is written in a game format in which the student tries to achieve the best score given twenty-five exercises. The range of the numbers varies with the success the student has as the game is played. If the student gets the first five problems right, then the problems that follow may contain larger numbers and will be worth more points. If the student makes errors as the game is played, the range of the numbers and the point values of the questions will be reduced.

PROGRAMMING LOGIC: There are four levels of difficulty and point values used in this program. Level one, the least difficult, is found in lines 30-130; level two in lines 140-250; level three in lines 260-380; and level four in lines 390-480.

The first line in each of these routines sets the point value of the questions and stores that value in variable PV. The variable N is used to keep track of the total number of questions asked. The variables C1, C2, C3, and C4 are used to store the number of questions asked at each of levels 1-4.

The IF/THEN statements found in each of these routines determine whether the program should stay at the same level, move to the next higher level, or return to the previous level, based on the student's success rate. The last line in each of these program segments will send the computer to line 490 after twenty-five questions have been asked.

HOW TO CHANGE THE DATA: This program should not be changed.

```
10   HOME : VTAB (6): PRINT  TAB( 8);"<<< THE LCM CHA
        LLENGE >>>": FOR TI = 1 TO 2000: NEXT TI
20   C = 0:SC = 0: HOME
30   PV = 100:N = 0:C1 = 0
40   C = C + 1:C1 = C1 + 1
```

```
50   IF C = 26 THEN 490
60  FV =  INT (8 *  RND (1)) + 1:SV =  INT (8 *  RND
     (1)) + 1: IF FV = SV THEN 60
70   GOSUB 600: GOSUB 510
80   IF AN = LC THEN  GOSUB 530: GOTO 100
90   GOSUB 550
100  IF C1 = 5 AND N = 5 THEN 140
110  IF C1 = 10 AND N > 7 THEN 140
120  IF C < 25 THEN 40
130  GOTO 490
140 PV = 300:N = 0:C2 = 0
150 C = C + 1:C2 = C2 + 1
160  IF C = 26 THEN 490
170 FV =  INT (15 *  RND (1)) + 1:SV =  INT (15 *  RND
     (1)) + 1: IF FV = SV THEN 170
180  GOSUB 600: GOSUB 510
190  IF AN = LC THEN  GOSUB 530: GOTO 210
200  GOSUB 550
210  IF C2 = 5 AND N = 5 THEN 260
220  IF C2 = 10 AND N > 7 THEN 260
230  IF C2 = 10 AND N < 4 THEN 30
240  IF C < 25 THEN 150
250  GOTO 490
260 PV = 700:N = 0:C3 = 0
270 C = C + 1:C3 = C3 + 1
280  IF C = 26 THEN 490
290 FV =  INT (25 *  RND (1)) + 1:SV =  INT (25 *  RND
     (1)) + 1
300  IF FV = SV OR FV / SV =  INT (FV / SV) OR SV /
     FV =  INT (SV / FV) THEN 290
310  GOSUB 600: GOSUB 510
320  IF AN = LC THEN  GOSUB 530: GOTO 340
330  GOSUB 550
340  IF C3 = 5 AND N = 5 THEN 390
350  IF C3 = 10 AND N > 7 THEN 390
360  IF C3 = 10 AND N < 4 THEN 140
370  IF C < 25 THEN 270
380  GOTO 490
390 PV = 1200:N = 0:C4 = 0
400 C = C + 1:C4 = C4 + 1
410  IF C = 26 THEN 490
420 FV =  INT (50 *  RND (1)) + 1:SV =  INT (50 *  RND
     (1)) + 1
430  IF FV = SV OR FV / SV =  INT (FV / SV) OR SV /
     FV =  INT (SV / FV) THEN 420
440  GOSUB 600: GOSUB 510
450  IF AN = LC THEN  GOSUB 530: GOTO 470
460  GOSUB 550
470  IF C4 = 5 AND N < 4 THEN 260
480  IF C < 25 THEN 400
490  HOME : VTAB (4): PRINT "THE << LCM CHALLENGE >>
     IS OVER.": PRINT : PRINT "YOUR SCORE IS ";SC;"
     POINTS.": PRINT : PRINT "A PERFECT SCORE IS 17
     500 POINTS."
500  END
510 LN = 10: GOSUB 680: PRINT "ENTER THE LEAST COMMO
```

```
         N MULTIPLE OF": PRINT : PRINT : PRINT  TAB( 15)
         ;FV;" AND ";SV;
520   INPUT AN: RETURN
530 SC = SC + PV:N = N + 1
540   GOSUB 570: RETURN
550 SC = SC - PV * .5: IF SC < 0 THEN SC = 0
560   GOSUB 570: RETURN
570   VTAB (2): HTAB (24): PRINT "            ";: HTAB
         (24): PRINT "SCORE = ";SC;
580   VTAB (3): HTAB (24): PRINT "             ";: HTAB
         (24): PRINT "TURNS LEFT = ";25 - C;
590   RETURN
600 V1 = FV:V2 = SV
610   IF V1 < V2 THEN TV = V1: GOTO 630
620 TV = V2
630 LC = FV * SV
640   FOR X = TV TO 2 STEP  - 1
650   IF V1 / X =  INT (V1 / X) AND V2 / X =  INT (V2
         / X) THEN V1 = V1 / X:V2 = V2 / X:LC = LC / X
660   NEXT X
670   RETURN
680   POKE 34,LN: HOME : POKE 34,0: VTAB (LN + 1): RETURN
```
]

12. BASIC NUMBER FACTS

SUGGESTED FILE NAME: NUMFACTS

SUGGESTED GRADE RANGE: 3–5

DESCRIPTION OF THE PROGRAM: This program provides practice in addition and multiplication facts. The student chooses either addition or multiplication. Numbers are presented randomly in a table with four numbers across the top and four down the side. The student fills in the body of the table.

PROGRAMMING LOGIC: The data lines are used to print the addends (or factors) horizontally and vertically on the screen. See lines 200 and 210.

There are two loops, lines 240-290 and lines 300-350, which illustrate how to choose numbers randomly so that no number is chosen twice. Each number that is chosen is checked against all numbers previously chosen to make sure it has not already been selected. If it has already been selected, the program cycles back to choose another number.

This routine is used several times, notably in the two programs: "Twenty Science Questions" and "Abbreviations for Elements."

EXPLANATION OF DATA LINES: The data lines are used to print the factors (or addends) at the four horizontal or vertical locations in the table.

HOW TO CHANGE THE DATA: The data should not be changed.

```
10    DIM HP(16),VP(16):PS$ = "<?>"
20    HOME : VTAB (6): PRINT  TAB( 12);"BASIC NUMBER F
      ACTS": VTAB (12): HTAB (8): PRINT "PRACTICE WIT
      H ADDITION AND": PRINT  TAB( 11);"MULTIPLICATIO
      N FACTS": FOR TI = 1 TO 3000: NEXT TI
30    FOR X = 1 TO 16: READ VP(X): NEXT X
40    FOR X = 1 TO 16: READ HP(X): NEXT X
50    HOME : VTAB (2): PRINT  TAB( 12);"** PROGRAM MEN
      U **"
60    VTAB (5): PRINT  TAB( 10);"A) ADDITION FACTS"
70    VTAB (7): PRINT  TAB( 10);"B) MULTIPLICATION FAC
      TS"
80    VTAB (9): PRINT  TAB( 10);"C) END THE PROGRAM"
90    VTAB (12): PRINT "TYPE THE LETTER OF YOUR CHOICE
      .";
100   GET A$
110   IF A$ = "A" THEN 150
120   IF A$ = "B" THEN 170
130   IF A$ = "C" THEN 190
140   GOTO 100
150   O$ = "+":OF = 1:P = 0:T = 0: GOSUB 230: GOSUB 43
      0: GOSUB 500
160   GOSUB 600: GOTO 50
170   O$ = "X":OF = 2:P = 0:T = 0: GOSUB 230: GOSUB 43
      0: GOSUB 500
180   GOSUB 600: GOTO 50
190   HOME : VTAB (8): PRINT  TAB( 8);"YOU ARE A FINE
      PERSON!!!": END
200   DATA  3,1,2,4,1,2,3,2,1,4,4,2,4,3,3,1
210   DATA  2,3,1,4,2,4,1,3,1,3,1,2,2,4,3,4
220   REM  * SUBROUTINES FOLLOW
230   H(1) = INT (9 * RND (1)) + 1:V(1) = INT (9 *
      RND (1)) + 1
240   FOR X = 2 TO 4
250   H(X) = INT (9 * RND (1)) + 1
260   FOR Y = 1 TO X - 1
270   IF H(X) = H(Y) THEN 250
280   NEXT Y
290   NEXT X
300   FOR X = 2 TO 4
310   V(X) = INT (9 * RND (1)) + 1
320   FOR Y = 1 TO X - 1
330   IF V(X) = V(Y) THEN 310
340   NEXT Y
350   NEXT X
360   FOR X = 1 TO 4
370   FOR Y = 1 TO 4
380   IF OF = 1 THEN N(X,Y) = H(Y) + V(X): GOTO 400
390   N(X,Y) = H(Y) * V(X)
400   NEXT Y
410   NEXT X
420   RETURN
430   HOME
```

```
440   FOR X = 3 TO 17: VTAB (X): PRINT   TAB( 12);"*":
      NEXT X
450   VTAB (5): FOR X = 9 TO 32: PRINT   TAB( X);"*";:
      NEXT X
460   VTAB (3): HTAB (9): PRINT O$
470   VTAB (3): FOR X = 1 TO 4: HTAB (10 + 5 * X): PRINT
      H(X);: NEXT X
480   FOR Y = 1 TO 4: HTAB (10): VTAB (4 + 3 * Y): PRINT
      V(Y);: NEXT Y
490   RETURN
500 P = P + 1: IF P = 17 THEN  RETURN
510 R = VP(P):C = HP(P)
520   VTAB (4 + 3 * R): HTAB (9 + 5 * C): PRINT PS$;
530 LN = 18: GOSUB 710: PRINT "ENTER THE NUMBER THAT
      BELONGS IN THE": PRINT : PRINT "SPACE SHOWN.";

540   INPUT AN:T = T + 1
550   IF AN = N(R,C) THEN LN = 18: GOSUB 710: PRINT "
      VERY GOOD!!!!";: GOSUB 570: GOSUB 670: GOTO 500

560 LN = 18: GOSUB 710: PRINT "THINK CAREFULLY, THEN
      TRY AGAIN.";: GOSUB 670: GOTO 530
570   VTAB (4 + 3 * R): HTAB (9 + 5 * C): PRINT "   "
      ;
580   VTAB (4 + 3 * R): HTAB (10 + 5 * C): PRINT AN;
590   RETURN
600   HOME : VTAB (4): PRINT "YOU TOOK ";T;" TRIES TO
      ANSWER": PRINT
610   PRINT "THE SIXTEEN (16) PROBLEMS.": PRINT
620   PRINT "YOUR SCORE IS "; INT (16 / T * 100 + .5)
      ;"%.": PRINT : PRINT : PRINT
630   PRINT "PRESS THE <SPACE BAR> TO CONTINUE...";
640   GET A$
650   IF A$ <  > " " THEN 640
660   RETURN
670 LN = 20: GOSUB 710: PRINT "PRESS THE <SPACE BAR>
      TO CONTINUE...";
680   GET A$
690   IF A$ <  > " " THEN 680
700   RETURN
710   POKE 34,LN: HOME : POKE 34,0: VTAB (LN + 1): RETURN

]
```

13. REDUCING FRACTIONS

SUGGESTED FILE NAME: REDFRAC

SUGGESTED GRADE RANGE: 5–8

DESCRIPTION OF THE PROGRAM: This program contains twenty-nine exercises in reducing fractions. The student is given a fraction and asked to type it in its reduced form.

EXPLANATION OF DATA LINES: Each problem consists of three data items. The first two items are the numerator and denominator, respectively, of the fraction to be reduced. The third data entry is the answer. For example, in line 30, 3,6,1/2 defines the problem, three-sixths; 1/2 is the reduced form of the fraction.

HOW TO CHANGE THE DATA: You may substitute any fractions and their reduced form for those appearing in the data lines; just make sure you enter them in the correct order: numerator, denominator, answer.

Remember to keep the same number of data entries in each line and to separate them with commas.

You may decide that twenty-nine problems are too many for your students. You can change the number of problems presented in each run of the program by changing line 100. For example, you may want each program run to contain only twenty problems. In that case, change line 100 to read:

```
100 FOR X = 1 TO 20
```

```
10   DIM N$(29),D$(29),LT$(29)
20   HOME : VTAB (6): HTAB (11): PRINT "REDUCING FRAC
     TIONS": VTAB (12): HTAB (1): PRINT "TWENTY-NINE
      PROBLEMS WILL BE PRESENTED": FOR TI = 1 TO 300
     0: NEXT TI
30   DATA  3,6,1/2,8,10,4/5,12,14,6/7,6,9,2/3,12,15,4
     /5
40   DATA  21,30,7/10,15,20,3/4,25,35,5/7,45,50,9/10
50   DATA  8,12,2/3,20,24,5/6,40,44,10/11,18,24,3/4
60   DATA  30,36,5/6,12,15,4/5,24,30,4/5,80,90,8/9
70   DATA  49,70,7/10,28,30,14/15,20,45,4/9,12,28,3/7

80   DATA  6,48,1/8,24,60,2/5,7,42,1/6,24,64,3/8
90   DATA  50,90,5/9,42,66,7/11,28,98,2/7,105,120,7/8

100  FOR X = 1 TO 29
110  READ N$(X),D$(X),LT$(X)
120  NEXT X
130  HOME : VTAB (3): PRINT "IN THIS PROGRAM YOU WIL
     L BE ASKED TO": PRINT : PRINT "REDUCE EACH FRAC
     TION GIVEN TO LOWEST": PRINT : PRINT "TERMS.   F
     OR EXAMPLE:"
140  PRINT : PRINT  TAB( 25);"6"
150  PRINT "EXPRESS THE FRACTION   ----   IN LOWEST"
160  PRINT  TAB( 24);"10": PRINT "TERMS."
170  PRINT : PRINT "YOU SHOULD TYPE YOUR ANSWER AS 3
     /5 AND": PRINT : PRINT "PRESS <RETURN>."
180  PRINT : PRINT : PRINT "PRESS <RETURN> TO CONTIN
     UE.";: INPUT D$
190  FOR X = 1 TO 29
```

```
200   HOME : PRINT "# ";X: VTAB (3): PRINT  TAB( 24);
      N$(X): PRINT "EXPRESS THE FRACTION ----- IN LOW
      EST"
210   PRINT  TAB( 24);D$(X): PRINT "TERMS.": PRINT : PRINT
220   PRINT "TYPE YOUR ANSWER IN THE FORM N/D AND": PRINT
      : PRINT "PRESS <RETURN>."
230   PRINT : PRINT " ";: INPUT AN$: PRINT
240   IF AN$ = LT$(X) THEN CA = 1:NC = NC + 1: GOTO 2
      60
250 CA = 0
260 T = T + 1
270   IF CA = 1 THEN  PRINT "THAT IS CORRECT!!!": GOTO
      300
280   PRINT "SORRY, THAT IS NOT CORRECT.": PRINT
290   PRINT "THE CORRECT ANSWER IS ";LT$(X);"."
300   VTAB (23): PRINT "PRESS <RETURN> TO CONTINUE.";
      : INPUT D$
310   NEXT X
320   HOME : VTAB (10): PRINT "THIS IS THE END OF THE
       PROGRAM . . ."
330   END

]
```

14. ADDITION OF INTEGERS

SUGGESTED FILE NAME: ADDINT

SUGGESTED GRADE RANGE: 5–8

DESCRIPTION OF THE PROGRAM: This program provides practice in the six forms of adding integers.

1. Both integers are positive or zero. For example, 13 + 28.
2. The first integer is positive and the second is negative. The absolute value of the first is greater than the absolute value of the second. For example, 28+(−13).
3. The first integer is positive (or zero) and the second is negative. The absolute value of the second is greater than the absolute value of the first. For example, 13+(−28).
4. The first integer is negative and the second is positive (or zero). The absolute value of the first is greater than the absolute value of the second. For example, (−28)+13.
5. The first integer is negative and the second is positive. The absolute value of the second is greater than the absolute value of the first. For example, (−13)+28.
6. Both integers are negative.

PROGRAMMING LOGIC: In line 50, J and K represent the two integers to be added. Each one is assigned a random number from 0 to 29 and then 15 is subtracted from the number. This results in the addends being integers from −15 to 14.

HOW TO CHANGE THE DATA: This program can be changed in several ways. Suppose you want your students to use values less than −15 and greater than 15. Change line 50. For example, if you want to use integers from −50 to 49, change line 50 to read:

```
50 J = INT(100 * RND(1)) − 50 :
   K = INT(100 * RND(1)) − 50
```

Another change you may wish to make is to use decimal numbers for addends. In that case, change line 50 to read:

```
50 J = INT(1000 * RND(1))/100 :
   K = INT(1000 * RND(1))/10
```

You will get two decimal numbers: J, having two decimal places, and K, having one decimal place.

If you change the program to decimal values, be sure to change the title to something appropriate like "ADDING POSITIVE AND NEGATIVE DECIMAL NUMBERS."

```
10 N = 0:X = 0
20  HOME : VTAB (6): PRINT  TAB( 11)"ADDITION OF INT
    EGERS": FOR TI = 1 TO 2000: NEXT TI
40  HOME :N = N + 1
50 J =  INT (30 *  RND (1)) − 15:K =  INT (30 *  RND
   (1)) − 15
60  IF J >  = 0 AND K >  = 0 THEN 130
70  IF J >  = 0 AND K < 0 AND ( − 1) * K < J THEN 15
    0
80  IF J >  = 0 AND K < 0 THEN 170
90  IF J < 0 AND K >  = 0 AND ( − 1) * J > K THEN 19
    0
100  IF J < 0 AND K >  = 0 THEN 210
110  PRINT : PRINT "(";J;") + (";K;") = −(";  − J;" +
     ";  − K;") = ";: INPUT T: GOSUB 230: ON FL GOTO
     40,320
120  HOME : GOTO 110
130  PRINT : PRINT J;" + ";K;" = ";: INPUT T: GOSUB
     230: ON FL GOTO 40,320
140  HOME : GOTO 130
150  PRINT : PRINT J;" + (";K;") = ";J;" − ";  − K;"
     = ";: INPUT T: GOSUB 230: ON FL GOTO 40,320
160  HOME : GOTO 150
170  PRINT : PRINT J;" + (";K;") = ";J;" − ";  − K;"
     = −(";  − K;" − ";J;") = ";: INPUT T: GOSUB 230:
     ON FL GOTO 40,320
```

```
180   HOME : GOTO 170
190   PRINT : PRINT J;" + ";K;" = ";K;" + (";J;") = "
      ;K;" - "; - J;" =": PRINT : PRINT "- ("; - J;"
      - ";K;") ";: INPUT T: GOSUB 230: ON FL GOTO 40
      ,320
200   HOME : GOTO 190
210   PRINT : PRINT J;" + ";K;" = ";K;" + (";J;") = "
      ;K;" - "; - J;" = ";: INPUT T: GOSUB 230: ON FL
       GOTO 40,320
220   HOME : GOTO 210
230   PRINT : IF T = J + K THEN 250
240   PRINT "NOT CORRECT.   TRY AGAIN.":N = N + 1: FOR
      TI = 1 TO 1400: NEXT TI:FL = 0: RETURN
250   PRINT : PRINT "THAT'S RIGHT!!!":X = X + 1
260   PRINT : PRINT  INT (X / N * 100 + .5);"% OF YOU
      R ANSWERS HAVE BEEN CORRECT.": PRINT
270   PRINT
280   PRINT "DO YOU WANT ANOTHER PROBLEM (Y OR N)?": INPUT
      W$
290   IF W$ = "Y" THEN FL = 1: RETURN
300   IF W$ = "N" THEN FL = 2: RETURN
310   PRINT "TYPE Y FOR 'YES' OR N FOR 'NO'.";: INPUT
      W$: PRINT : GOTO 290
320   HOME : VTAB (6): PRINT "IT'S BEEN A PLEASURE AD
      DING INTEGERS": PRINT
330   PRINT "WITH YOU.   SO LONG FOR NOW."
340   END

]
```

15. SUBTRACTION OF INTEGERS

SUGGESTED FILE NAME: SUBTINT

SUGGESTED GRADE RANGE: 6–8

DESCRIPTION OF THE PROGRAM: In this program, subtraction of integers is defined in terms of addition of integers. The student is given one addend, B, and the sum, C, and asked to fill in the missing addend, A. The problem is then restated as the sum, C, minus the addend, B, equals the difference, A. For example:

WHAT INTEGER ADDED TO -13 EQUALS 15?	Answer: 28
THEN $15-(-13)=?$	Answer: 28

PROGRAMMING LOGIC: The numbers used for the programs are -15 through 14. In the loop in line 30, I runs from -15 to 14. The array numbers will be 1, 2, 3, and so on. The values assigned to the array elements will be -15, -14, -13, and so on until 14 is assigned. For example, $A(1) = -15$, $A(2) = -14$, $A(3) = -13, \ldots A(30) = 14$.

The elements of array A are chosen randomly in line 40 to be used in the problems presented by this program.

```
10   DIM A(30):W = 0:N = 0
20   HOME : VTAB (6): PRINT  TAB( 9);"SUBTRACTION OF
     INTEGERS": FOR TI = 1 TO 2000: NEXT TI
30   FOR I =  - 15 TO 14:A(I + 16) = I: NEXT I
40   HOME :J =  INT (30 *  RND (1)) + 1:K =  INT (30 *
     RND (1)) + 1
50   Y = A(K) - A(J)
60   VTAB (3): PRINT "WHAT INTEGER ADDED TO ";A(J);"
     EQUALS ";A(K);"?"
70   PRINT : INPUT X:N = N + 1: IF Y = X THEN 90
80   PRINT "TRY AGAIN": GOTO 70
90 W = W + 1
100   PRINT : PRINT "THEN ";A(K);" - (";A(J);") = ";:
      INPUT T:N = N + 1
110   PRINT : IF Y = T THEN 130
120   PRINT "TRY AGAIN": GOTO 100
130 W = W + 1: PRINT : PRINT "THAT'S RIGHT!!!"
140   PRINT : PRINT "YOUR SCORE IS NOW "; INT (W / N *
      100 + .5);"%."
150   PRINT : PRINT "DO YOU WANT ANOTHER PROBLEM (Y O
      R N)?"
160   INPUT M$
170   IF M$ = "Y" THEN 40
180   IF M$ = "N" THEN 200
190   PRINT "PLEASE TYPE Y OR N.";: INPUT M$: GOTO 17
      0
200   HOME : VTAB (6): PRINT  TAB( 12);"GOOD-BYE FOR
      NOW.": END
]
```

16. MULTIPLICATION OF INTEGERS

SUGGESTED FILE NAME: MULTINT

SUGGESTED GRADE RANGE: 6–8

DESCRIPTION OF THE PROGRAM: This program provides practice in multiplying integers. There are four forms of integer multiplication addressed by the program.

    1. Both integers are positive or zero.

        $(9)(13) = ?$ Answer: 117

    2. The first integer is positive or zero and the second is negative or zero.

        $(10)(-4) = -(10)(4) = ?$ Answer: -40

    3. The first integer is negative or zero and the second is positive or zero.

        $(-5)(12) = -(5)(12) = ?$ Answer: -60

    4. Both integers are negative or zero.

        $(-11)(-2) = (11)(2) = ?$ Answer: 22

```
10  R = 0:S = 0
20   HOME : VTAB (6): PRINT  TAB( 7);"MULTIPLICATION
     OF INTEGERS": FOR TI = 1 TO 2000: NEXT TI
30   HOME : VTAB (2)
40  X =  INT (30 *  RND (1)) - 15:Y =  INT (30 *  RND
     (1)) - 15
50   PRINT "(";X;")(";Y;") =";
60   IF X >  = 0 AND Y >  = 0 THEN 100
70   IF X >  = 0 AND Y <  = 0 THEN 110
80   IF X <  = 0 AND Y >  = 0 THEN 120
90   IF X <  = 0 AND Y <  = 0 THEN 130
100  INPUT T: GOTO 140
110  PRINT "-(";X;")(";  - Y;") =";: INPUT T: GOTO 14
     0
120  PRINT "-(";  - X;")(";Y;") =";: INPUT T: GOTO 14
     0
130  PRINT "(";  - X;")(";  - Y;") =";: INPUT T
140 S = S + 1: IF T = X * Y THEN 160
150  PRINT : PRINT "NOT CORRECT.   TRY AGAIN.": INPUT
     T: GOTO 140
160 R = R + 1: PRINT : PRINT "THAT'S RIGHT!!"
170  PRINT : PRINT "YOUR SCORE IS "; INT (R / S * 10
     0 + .5);"%."
180  PRINT : PRINT "DO YOU WANT ANOTHER PROBLEM (Y O
     R N)";
190  INPUT Z$
200  IF Z$ = "Y" THEN 30
210  IF Z$ = "N" THEN 230
220  PRINT "PLEASE TYPE Y OR N.": GOTO 190
230  HOME : VTAB (6): PRINT  TAB( 8);"PRACTICE MAKES
      PERFECT!!!"
240  END

]
```

17. DIVISION OF INTEGERS

SUGGESTED FILE NAME: DIVINT

SUGGESTED GRADE RANGE: 6–8

DESCRIPTION OF THE PROGRAM: This program gives students practice in division of integers.

PROGRAMMING LOGIC: The integers in this program are chosen randomly and no data lines are used. Line 30 shows two variables, X and Y, the values for which are chosen randomly by the expression: INT(41 * RND(1)) − 20. This statement chooses a number from 1 to 40, then subtracts 20 from the number. In effect, this assigns values from −20 to 20.

HOW TO CHANGE THE PROGRAM: You may wish to modify the program to include division of integers by decimals or decimals by integers. You can accomplish this by changing one or both of the statements in line 30. For example, if you wish to divide a number in tenths by an integer, change line 30 to read:

30 . . . Y = (INT(41 * RND(1)) – 20)/10

This will change the value for Y to a decimal number in tenths.

Also, change the title to something appropriate such as "Division of Decimal Numbers."

```
10    DIM A(40):R = 0:T = 0
20    HOME : VTAB (6): PRINT  TAB( 11);"DIVISION OF IN
      TEGERS": FOR TI = 1 TO 2000: NEXT TI
30    HOME :X =   INT (41 *  RND (1)) – 20:Y =   INT (41
      *  RND (1)) – 20: IF X = 0 THEN 30
40 P = X * Y: PRINT
50    PRINT P;" DIVIDED BY ";X;" = ";:T = T + 1: INPUT
      Q: PRINT
60    IF Q = Y THEN 80
70    PRINT "NOT CORRECT -- TRY AGAIN.": FOR I = 1 TO
      1200: NEXT I: HOME : PRINT : GOTO 50
80 R = R + 1: PRINT "THAT'S RIGHT!!": PRINT : PRINT
       INT (R / T * 100 + .5);"% OF YOUR ANSWERS ARE
      CORRECT.": PRINT
90    PRINT "DO YOU WANT ANOTHER PROBLEM (Y OR N)";: INPUT
      Z$
100   IF Z$ = "Y" THEN 30
110   IF Z$ = "N" THEN 130
120   PRINT "PLEASE TYPE Y OR N.": PRINT : GOTO 90
130   HOME : PRINT : PRINT "YOUR FINAL SCORE IS " INT
      (R / T * 100 + .5);"%.": PRINT : PRINT "BYE-BYE
      ."
140   END

]
```

18. THE CONCEPT OF PERCENT

SUGGESTED FILE NAME: PERCENT

SUGGESTED GRADE RANGE: 6–8

DESCRIPTION OF THE PROGRAM: The concept of percent is explained in terms of a set of items, each having a value that is a fractional part of one hundred. For example, in a set of twenty items, each item has a value of five which is interpreted as 5% of the set.

EXPLANATION OF DATA LINES: In this program, three problems are based on the same set of items. Each data line contains entries for three problems. The set of items contains stars that are printed across the top of the screen.

Line 30 reads all the data items in one line. The data entries are as follows.

1. The number of stars to appear at the top of the screen: L
2. First question: Q$(1)
3. Value of one star in the set: V(1)
4. The quantity of squares in the question: N(1). This number prints as the numerator of a fraction later on in the program.
5. The second question to the student: Q$(2)
6. The value of a second quantity of squares in the set: V(2)
7. The quantity of squares in the second question: N(2). This number prints as the numerator of a fraction later on.
8. The third question to the student: Q$(3)
9. The value of the stars in the third question: V(3)
10. The quantity of stars in the third question: N(3). This number prints as the numerator of a fraction later on in the program.

PROGRAMMING LOGIC: In lines 190 and 200, the program checks to see if the value of a square is less than ten or is a decimal number. If it is less than ten, a zero is inserted between the value of the square and the decimal point. If it is a decimal number, it is multiplied by ten. This is done so that the percent has the decimal point in the right location.

```
10 T = 0
20  HOME : VTAB (6): PRINT  TAB( 9);"THE CONCEPT OF
       PERCENT": VTAB (10): HTAB (1): PRINT "* EIGHTEE
       N PROBLEMS WILL BE PRESENTED *": FOR TI = 1 TO
       3000: NEXT TI
30  READ L,Q$(1),V(1),N(1),Q$(2),V(2),N(2),Q$(3),V(3
       ),N(3)
40 S = L: HOME : VTAB (2)
50  PRINT "PERCENT IS A WAY TO COMPARE NUMBERS": PRINT
       : PRINT "BASED ON 100."
60  PRINT : PRINT : FOR X = 1 TO L: PRINT "* ";: NEXT
       X: PRINT
70 LN = 9: GOSUB 400: PRINT "HOW MANY STARS IN THE S
       ET";: INPUT A
80  IF A = S THEN 100
90 LN = 9: GOSUB 400: PRINT "PLEASE COUNT THE STARS
       AGAIN.": GOSUB 410: GOTO 70
100 LN = 11: GOSUB 400: PRINT "100 DIVIDED BY ";S;"
       = ";: INPUT B
110  IF B = 100 / S THEN 130
120 LN = 11: GOSUB 400: PRINT "PLEASE DIVIDE AGAIN."
       : GOSUB 410: GOTO 100
130 K = 1
140 LN = 13: GOSUB 400: PRINT Q$(K);: INPUT D
```

```
150   IF D = V(K) THEN 170
160 LN = 13: GOSUB 400: PRINT "LOOK AGAIN.": GOSUB 4
    10: GOTO 140
170   IF V(K) <  >  INT (V(K)) THEN LN = 15: GOSUB 40
    0: PRINT  TAB( 10);N(K); TAB( 17);V(K): GOTO 19
    0
180 LN = 15: GOSUB 400: PRINT  TAB( 10);N(K); TAB( 1
    8);V(K)
190   IF V(K) < 10 THEN V$ = "0" +  STR$ (V(K)): GOTO
    220
200   IF V(K) <  >  INT (V(K)) THEN V$ =  STR$ (V(K) *
    10): GOTO 230
210 V$ =  STR$ (V(K))
220 LN = 16: GOSUB 400: PRINT  TAB( 9);"--- = ---
    = .";V$;" = ";V$;"%": GOTO 240
230 LN = 16: GOSUB 400: PRINT  TAB( 9);"--- = ---
    = .";V$;" = ";V(K);"%"
240 LN = 17: GOSUB 400: PRINT  TAB( 10);S; TAB( 17);
    "100"
250 T = T + 1:LN = 22: GOSUB 400: PRINT "PRESS <SPAC
    E BAR> TO CONTINUE . . .";
260   GET A$
270   IF A$ <  > " " THEN 260
280   IF T = 18 THEN 310
290 K = K + 1: IF K = 4 THEN 30
300   GOTO 140
310   HOME : VTAB (8): PRINT "YOU HAVE FINISHED ALL T
    HE PROBLEMS IN": PRINT : PRINT "THIS EXERCISE."
    : PRINT : PRINT : PRINT
320   PRINT  TAB( 15);"GOOD WORK!!"
330   END
340   DATA  5,WHAT IS ONE STAR WORTH,20,1,WHAT ARE TW
    O STARS WORTH,40,2,WHAT ARE FOUR STARS WORTH,80
    ,4
350   DATA  10,WHAT IS ONE STAR WORTH,10,1,WHAT ARE T
    HREE STARS WORTH,30,3,WHAT ARE SEVEN STARS WORT
    H,70,7
360   DATA  4,WHAT IS ONE STAR WORTH,25,1,WHAT ARE TW
    O STARS WORTH,50,2,WHAT ARE THREE STARS WORTH,7
    5,3
370   DATA  20,WHAT IS ONE STAR WORTH,5,1,WHAT ARE NI
    NE STARS WORTH,45,9,WHAT ARE FOURTEEN STARS WOR
    TH,70,14
380   DATA  25,WHAT IS ONE STAR WORTH,4,1,WHAT ARE FI
    FTEEN STARS WORTH,60,15,WHAT ARE TWENTY STARS W
    ORTH,80,20
390   DATA  8,WHAT IS ONE STAR WORTH,12.5,1,WHAT ARE
    THREE STARS WORTH,37.5,3,WHAT ARE SIX STARS WOR
    TH,75,6
400   POKE 34,LN: HOME : POKE 34,0: VTAB (LN + 1): RETURN

410   FOR I = 1 TO 1200: NEXT I: RETURN

]
```

19. COMPUTER CHALLENGE

SUGGESTED FILE NAME: GESSGAME

SUGGESTED GRADE RANGE: 4–8

DESCRIPTION OF THE PROGRAM: In this challenge game, the student chooses a number for the computer to guess and the computer chooses a number for the student to guess. The challenge is that the student must guess the computer's number in fewer guesses than it takes the computer to guess the student's number.

```
10   DIM G(11),S(11),R$(11)
20   DATA  5000,4000,3000,2000,1500,1200,1000,750,500
     ,250,0
30   FOR X = 1 TO 11: READ S(X): NEXT X
40   FOR X = 1 TO 30: VTAB (8): PRINT  TAB( 7);"***
     COMPUTER CHALLENGE ***": FOR T = 1 TO 50: NEXT
     T: HOME : NEXT X
50   VTAB (2): PRINT  TAB( 5);"YOU AND I ARE ABOUT TO
      TAKE PART": PRINT : PRINT "IN A MENTAL CHALLEN
     GE.  YOU AND I WILL": PRINT
60   PRINT "TAKES TURNS.  EACH OF US WILL CHOOSE A": PRINT
     : PRINT "NUMBER AND THE OTHER WILL HAVE ONLY TE
     N": PRINT
70   PRINT "CHANCES TO GUESS THAT NUMBER.  THE": PRINT
     : PRINT "NUMBER MAY BE ANY INTEGER FROM 1 TO 20
     0."
80   PRINT "THE SCORE WILL BE BASED ON THE NUMBER OF"
     : PRINT "GUESSES IT TAKES TO GET THE NUMBER.": PRINT

90   GOSUB 740
100   HOME : VTAB (4): PRINT  TAB( 5);"THE ONE OF US
      WITH THE HIGHEST": PRINT : PRINT "SCORE AFTER F
      IVE TURNS EACH IS THE": PRINT
110   PRINT "GREAT WIZARD OF THE MENTAL NUMBER": PRINT
      : PRINT "GUESSING WORLD!!!": GOSUB 740
120  Y = 0:M = 0:YS = 0:MS = 0
130   HOME : VTAB (4): PRINT "DO YOU WANT TO CHOOSE T
      HE FIRST NUMBER?": PRINT : PRINT "PLEASE TYPE E
      ITHER Y OR N.";
140   GET A$
150   IF A$ = "N" THEN 440
160   IF A$ <  > "Y" THEN 140
170  C = 0: HOME : VTAB (2): PRINT "PLEASE ENTER YOUR
      NUMBER FROM 1 TO 200.": PRINT : PRINT "I PROMI
     SE NOT TO PEEK.";
180   INPUT N
190   HOME : VTAB (2): IF N < 1 OR N > 200 OR  INT (N
     ) <  > N THEN  PRINT "YOUR NUMBER MUST BE AN IN
```

```
          TEGER": PRINT : PRINT "FROM 1 TO 200.": GOSUB 7
          10: GOTO 170
200   C = C + 1: IF C > 10 THEN 380
210    IF C = 1 THEN G(1) =   INT (200 *   RND (1)) + 1:
       GOTO 340
220    IF HF = 1 AND C = 2 THEN G(C) =   INT ((G(1) - 1
       ) / 2): GOTO 340
230    IF HF = 0 AND C = 2 THEN G(C) = G(1) +   INT ((2
       00 - G(1)) / 2): GOTO 340
240    IF HF = 1 AND C < 10 THEN G(C) = G(C - 1) -   INT
       (( ABS (G(C - 1) - G(C - 2))) / 2 + .5): GOTO 2
       60
250    GOTO 280
260    IF G(C) < 1 THEN G(C) = 1
270    GOTO 340
280    IF HF = 0 AND C < 10 THEN G(C) = G(C - 1) +   INT
       (( ABS (G(C - 1) - G(C - 2))) / 2 + .5): GOTO 3
       00
290    GOTO 320
300    IF G(C) > 200 THEN G(C) = 200
310    GOTO 340
320    IF HF = 1 THEN G(C) = 1: GOTO 340
330  G(C) = 200
340    PRINT "MY GUESS # ";C;" IS ";G(C);".": TAB( 21)
       ;" ";
350    IF G(C) > N THEN  PRINT "TOO HIGH!":HF = 1: GOTO
       200
360    IF G(C) < N THEN  PRINT "TOO LOW!":HF = 0: GOTO
       200
370    PRINT "JUST RIGHT!!!!"
380  MS = MS + S(C)
390    PRINT : PRINT "I JUST EARNED ";S(C);" POINTS.":
       PRINT
400    PRINT "MY TOTAL SCORE IS NOW ";MS;" POINTS."
410  M = M + 1: GOSUB 720
420    IF DF = 1 THEN  GOSUB 740: GOTO 600
430    GOSUB 740
440  C = 0: HOME : VTAB (2):N =   INT (200 *   RND (1))
       + 1
450    PRINT "I HAVE CHOSEN MY SECRET NUMBER.": PRINT
       : PRINT "GOOD LUCK!!!": GOSUB 740
460  C = C + 1: IF C = 11 THEN 530
470    HOME : VTAB (2): PRINT "PLEASE ENTER YOUR GUESS
       ";: INPUT G(C)
480    IF G(C) > N THEN R$(C) = "TOO HIGH!": GOTO 510
490    IF G(C) < N THEN R$(C) = "TOO LOW!": GOTO 510
500  R$(C) = "JUST RIGHT!!!"
510    HOME : VTAB (2): FOR X = 1 TO C: PRINT "YOUR GU
       ESS # ";X;" WAS ";G(X);".": TAB( 23);R$(X): NEXT
       X
520    IF G(C) < > N THEN  GOSUB 740: GOTO 460
530    IF C = 11 THEN C = 10
540    HOME : VTAB (2): FOR X = 1 TO C: PRINT "YOUR GU
       ESS # ";X;" WAS ";G(X);".": TAB( 23);R$(X): NEXT
       X:YS = YS + S(C)
```

```
550    PRINT : PRINT "YOU JUST EARNED ";S(C);" POINTS.
       "
560    PRINT : PRINT "YOUR TOTAL SCORE IS NOW ";YS;" P
       OINTS."
570 Y = Y + 1: GOSUB 720
580    IF DF = 1 THEN  GOSUB 740: GOTO 600
590    GOSUB 740: GOTO 170
600    HOME : VTAB (2): PRINT "YOUR TOTAL SCORE IS ";Y
       S;" POINTS.": PRINT
610    PRINT "MY TOTAL SCORE IS ";MS;" POINTS.": PRINT
       : PRINT
620    IF MS > YS THEN  PRINT "I AM THE VICTOR, THE WI
       NNER,": PRINT : PRINT  TAB( 12);"THE CONQUEROR!
       !!!!!": GOTO 650
630    IF YS > MS THEN  PRINT "SOMEHOW YOU MANAGED TO
       BEAT ME.": PRINT : PRINT "I'LL GET YOU NEXT TIM
       E!!!": GOTO 650
640    PRINT "IT'S A TIE.  I THOUGHT SURE I HAD YOU!!"

650    GOSUB 740: HOME : VTAB (6): PRINT "WOULD YOU LI
       KE TO PLAY AGAIN?": PRINT : PRINT "PLEASE TYPE
       EITHER Y OR N.";
660    GET A$
670    IF A$ = "Y" THEN 120
680    IF A$ < > "N" THEN 660
690    HOME : VTAB (6): PRINT "YOU'RE VERY SMART FOR A
        MERE HUMAN!!"
700    END
710    FOR T = 1 TO 2000: NEXT T: RETURN
720    IF Y = 5 AND M = 5 THEN DF = 1: RETURN
730 DF = 0: RETURN
740 LN = 19: GOSUB 780: PRINT "PRESS THE <SPACE BAR>
        TO CONTINUE . . .";
750    GET A$
760    IF A$ < > " " THEN 750
770    RETURN
780    POKE 34,LN: HOME : POKE 34,0: VTAB (LN + 1): RETURN

790 LN = 19: GOSUB 780: PRINT "PRESS THE <SPACE BAR>
        TO CONTINUE . . .";
800    GET A$
810    IF A$ < > " " THEN 800
820    RETURN

]
```

20. READING A SCALE

SUGGESTED FILE NAME: SCALE

SUGGESTED GRADE RANGE: 6–8

DESCRIPTION OF THE PROGRAM: This activity is designed to give students practice in determining coordinates that correspond to points on a vertical scale. There are a total of thirty problems. A vertical scale is shown on which there are six coordinates; two of the coordinates are missing. The student must type the missing coordinates.

EXPLANATION OF DATA LINES: Each data line contains sufficient information for two problems on the same scale. In the data lines, −1 and −2 denote the missing coordinates. The first entry in each line is the coordinate that replaces −1. The next six entries are the coordinates that first appear on the scale. Remember, the spaces where −1 and −2 appear will be blank on the screen. The eighth entry is the other missing coordinate. It will replace −1 in the next six entries.

HOW TO CHANGE THE DATA: The data in this program includes decimal as well as integer data. You may wish to change it so that all numbers are whole numbers. The data in this program can be changed by replacing items one for one.

You can also change the program so that fewer than thirty problems are given to your students. To do this, in line 70 change the value with which P is compared. For example, if you want your students to do only twenty problems, change line 70 to:

```
70 HOME : P = P + 1 : IF P > 20 THEN 230
```

```
10   HOME : VTAB (6): PRINT  TAB( 5);"-+--+- READING
     A SCALE -+--+-": FOR TI = 1 TO 2000: NEXT TI
20   HOME : VTAB (7)
30   PRINT  TAB( 4);"THIS PROGRAM CONSISTS OF THIRTY"
     : PRINT
40   PRINT  TAB( 4);"EXERCISES ON READING A SCALE."
50   GOSUB 260
60 P = 0
70   HOME :P = P + 1: IF P > 30 THEN 230
80   FOR X = 2 TO 17: HTAB (17): VTAB (X): PRINT "!";
     : NEXT X
90   FOR X = 2 TO 17 STEP 3: HTAB (17): VTAB (X): PRINT
     "+";: NEXT X
100  HTAB (1): VTAB (3): PRINT "# ";P;
110  READ A: FOR X = 1 TO 6: READ V$(X): NEXT X
120  FOR X = 1 TO 6: IF V$(X) = "-1" THEN V$(X) = "
        <----":VP = X
130  IF V$(X) = "-2" THEN V$(X) = ""
140  NEXT X
150  FOR X = 17 TO 2 STEP  - 3: HTAB (20): VTAB (X):
        PRINT V$( INT ((20 - X) / 3));: NEXT X
160 LN = 18: GOSUB 250: PRINT "WHAT VALUE CORRESPOND
     S TO THIS POINT";: INPUT V
170  IF V = (A) THEN 200
180  IF W = 1 THEN LN = 18: GOSUB 250: PRINT "THE CO
     ORDINATE IS ";A;".": FOR I = 1 TO 1200: NEXT I:
     W = 0: GOTO 160
```

```
190 LN = 18: GOSUB 250: PRINT "TRY AGAIN.": FOR I =
    1 TO 1200: NEXT I:W = 1: GOTO 160
200 LN = 18: GOSUB 250: PRINT "THAT'S RIGHT!!":W = 0

210  HTAB (20): VTAB (20 - VP * 3): PRINT "
        ";: HTAB (20): VTAB (20 - VP * 3): PRINT A: GOSUB
     260
220  GOTO 70
230  HOME : VTAB (6): PRINT "YOU'RE DEFINITELY A 10
     ON MY SCALE!!!"
240  END
250  POKE 34,LN: HOME : POKE 34,0: VTAB (LN + 1): RETURN

260 LN = 23: GOSUB 250: PRINT "PRESS THE <SPACE BAR>
        TO CONTINUE . . .";
270  GET A$: IF A$ < > " " THEN 270
280  RETURN
290  DATA    1,0,-1,2,3,4,-2,5,0,1,2,3,4,-1
300  DATA   20,0,10,-1,30,-2,50,40,0,10,20,30,-1,50
310  DATA  100,0,-1,200,-2,400,500,300,0,100,200,-1,
     400,500
320  DATA   10,0,5,-1,15,20,-2,25,0,5,10,15,20,-1
330  DATA    2,0,-1,4,6,-2,10,8,0,2,4,6,-1,10
340  DATA    0,-1,50,-2,150,200,250,100,0,50,-1,150,2
     00,250
350  DATA   75,0,25,50,-1,100,-2,125,0,25,50,75,100,-
     1
360  DATA   20,0,-1,40,60,-2,100,80,0,20,40,60,-1,100

370  DATA   24,20,22,-1,26,-2,30,28,20,22,24,26,-1,30

380  DATA .2,0,.1,-1,-2,.4,.5,.3,0,.1,.2,-1,.4,.5
390  DATA .2,0,-1,.4,-2,.8,1.0,.6,0,.2,.4,-1,.8,1.0

400  DATA  .42,.40,-1,.44,.46,.48,-2,.5,.40,.42,.44,
     .46,.48,-1
410  DATA  2.1,-1,2.2,2.3,-2,2.5,2.6,2.4,2.1,2.2,2.3
     ,-1,2.5,2.6
420  DATA  1,0,.5,-1,1.5,2.0,-2,2.5,0,.5,1.0,1.5,2.0
     ,-1
430  DATA  250,0,-1,500,750,-2,1250,1000,0,250,500,7
     50,-1,1250

    ]
```

21. FEET PER SECOND AND MILES PER HOUR

SUGGESTED FILE NAME: FPS

SUGGESTED GRADE RANGE: 7–8

DESCRIPTION OF THE PROGRAM: This program is a simulation of a car (shown as a moving asterisk) traveling 1000 feet in periods of time measured in seconds. The student is asked to calculate its rate of speed in feet per second by dividing 1000 by the number of seconds. The student is then instructed to convert the rate in feet per second to miles per hour by using the fact that 88 feet per second is approximately 60 miles per hour. A calculator helps in this one.

PROGRAMMING LOGIC: To accomplish the animation of the asterisk, a PRINT statement (see line 250) is used inside a FOR/NEXT loop (lines 190-270.) The value of the variable D increases by one with each pass through the loop. In line 250, the value of D is used to determine how far from the left margin the printing should begin. The PRINT statement in line 250 causes a blank space and an asterisk to be printed one after the other. The first time through the loop, the space is printed at the left margin and the asterisk in the second position on that line of the display. The second time through the loop, the space is printed in the second position, wiping out the asterisk that was there, and the asterisk appears in position three. By erasing the asterisk printed the time before, and by printing the new asterisk one position to the right each time, the illusion of one asterisk moving from left to right is created.

```
10   HOME : VTAB (6): PRINT  TAB( 13);"FEET PER SECON
     D": PRINT : PRINT  TAB( 20);"&": PRINT : PRINT
      TAB( 13);"MILES PER HOUR"
20   FOR TI = 1 TO 2000: NEXT TI
30   HOME : VTAB (2): PRINT "<< FEET PER SECOND & MIL
     ES PER HOUR >>"
40   PRINT : PRINT "IN THESE EXERCISES, A CAR IS TIME
     D AS": PRINT : PRINT "IT TRAVELS 1000 FEET.  YO
     U WILL BE ASKED"
50   PRINT "TO DETERMINE THE SPEED OF THE CAR IN": PRINT
     : PRINT "FEET PER SECOND.  USING THE FACT THAT"
     : PRINT
60   PRINT "60 MILES PER HOUR IS APPROXIMATELY": PRINT
     : PRINT "88 FEET PER SECOND, YOU WILL BE ASKED
     TO"
70   PRINT "CONVERT THE CAR'S SPEED IN FEET PER": PRINT
     : PRINT "SECOND TO MILES PER HOUR.  A CALCULATO
     R": PRINT
80    PRINT "WILL BE A BIG HELP TO YOU."
90 LN = 22: GOSUB 480: PRINT "PRESS THE <SPACE BAR>
     TO CONTINUE . . .";
100   GET A$: IF A$ < > " " THEN 100
110   HOME : VTAB (5): HTAB (1)
120   FOR X = 1 TO 4
130   PRINT "+";
140   FOR Y = 1 TO 8: PRINT "-";: NEXT Y
150   NEXT X: PRINT "+"
160   PRINT "0"; TAB( 9);"250"; TAB( 18);"500"; TAB(
     27);"750"; TAB( 35);"1000"
170   VTAB (2): PRINT  TAB( 26);"SECONDS:";
180 K = 1:T = 0
```

```
190   FOR I = 0 TO 35 STEP K
200 X =   INT (9 *   RND (1)) + 1
210 Y =   INT (2 *   RND (1)) + 1
220  IF X < 6 THEN 240
230 T = T + Y: VTAB (2): HTAB (36): PRINT T;
240 D = I + K
250  VTAB (4): HTAB (D): PRINT " *";
260  FOR J = 1 TO 35: NEXT J
270  NEXT I
280 LN = 7: GOSUB 480: PRINT "HOW MANY FEET PER SECO
     ND TO THE NEAREST": PRINT : PRINT "TENTH";: INPUT
     FPS
290  IF  ABS (FPS - (1000 / T)) < .05 THEN 320
300  IF W = 1 THEN LN = 7: GOSUB 480: PRINT "DIVIDE
     1000 BY ";T;".": FOR I = 1 TO 1200: NEXT I:W =
     0: GOTO 280
310 LN = 7: GOSUB 480: PRINT "TRY AGAIN.";: FOR I =
     1 TO 1200: NEXT I:W = 1: GOTO 280
320 LN = 11: GOSUB 480: PRINT "WAY TO GO!!!": FOR I =
     1 TO 1200: NEXT I:W = 0
330 LN = 11: GOSUB 480: PRINT FPS;" FEET PER SECOND
     IS HOW MANY MILES": PRINT : PRINT "PER HOUR?"
340 LN = 15: GOSUB 480: PRINT "SOLVE THIS PROPORTION
     :";
350 LN = 17: GOSUB 480: PRINT  TAB( 10);"60 MPH"; TAB(
     21);"?    MPH"
360  PRINT  TAB( 10);"------  =  ---------"
370  PRINT  TAB( 10);"88 FPS      ";FPS;" FPS";
380 LN = 21: GOSUB 480: PRINT "MPH  =  ";: INPUT S
390  IF  ABS (S - (FPS * 60 / 88)) < .05 THEN 410
400 LN = 21: GOSUB 480: PRINT "MULTIPLY ";FPS;" BY 6
     0 AND DIVIDE BY 88.": FOR I = 1 TO 2000: NEXT I
     : GOTO 380
410  VTAB (18): HTAB (21): PRINT S;
420 LN = 21: GOSUB 480: PRINT "THAT'S RIGHT!!    ";FP
     S;" FPS IS ";S;" MPH."
430 LN = 23: GOSUB 480: PRINT "PRESS <SPACE BAR> TO
     GO ON, 'Q' TO QUIT";
440  GET A$: IF A$ <  > " " AND A$ <  > "Q" THEN 440

450  IF A$ = " " THEN 110
460 HOME : VTAB (4): PRINT "REMEMBER THAT THE SPEED
     LIMIT IS 55 MPH.";
470 END
480 POKE 34,LN: HOME : POKE 34,0: VTAB (LN + 1): RETURN
```

]

22. ABBREVIATIONS FOR ELEMENTS

SUGGESTED FILE NAME: ELEMENTS

SUGGESTED GRADE RANGE: 7–8

DESCRIPTION OF THE PROGRAM: A self-challenging game format is used in this program to help students learn the abbreviations for chemical elements. Each time the game is played, twenty elements are chosen randomly from a list of fifty. The maximum number of points a student can earn in one game is 10,000 (500 per element name). The faster and more accurately the student types abbreviations for the elements, the higher the score.

EXPLANATION OF DATA LINES: Each group of four data entries defines one problem. The first entry in the group is the element name; the second is the first letter in the abbreviation. The third data entry is the second letter in the abbreviation; if there is no second letter, 999 is used to fill that spot and clue the computer that there is no second letter. The fourth data entry is the second letter, if any, in lower case.

The program must be run in upper case. The student does not use upper/lower case and the <**RETURN**> key. In this program, GET$ is used. Therefore, the second letter in the abbreviation is given twice in the data. The first time, it is checked against the student's response; the second time, it is in lower case to be printed on the screen.

PROGRAMMING LOGIC: The loop in lines 90 through 140 chooses twenty different random integers from one through fifty. These numbers are used to choose which elements will appear in the exercises in a game. In line 100, a number is chosen. Lines 110 through 130 check to see that the number has not already been chosen. If it has been, the program returns to line 100 to choose a different number.

The scoring technique is shown in line 380. Each time the student answers correctly, the program directs the computer to line 380 and 500 is added to SS, the variable used to keep the score. SS is printed on the screen each time the student gives an answer. Of course, if the student gets a MISS!!, then the score remains the same as before.

```
10   DIM A$(50),B$(50),C$(50),D$(50),A(50)
20   HOME : VTAB (6): PRINT  TAB( 8);"ABBREVIATIONS F
     OR ELEMENTS"
30   FOR X = 1 TO 2000: NEXT X
40   VTAB (12): PRINT "The more careful and accurate
     you are": PRINT
50   PRINT "in typing the abbreviatios, the higher": PRINT

60   PRINT "your score will be.  Good luck!!"
70   FOR J = 1 TO 50: READ A$(J),B$(J),C$(J),D$(J): NEXT
     J
80   A(1) =  INT (50 *  RND (1)) + 1
90   FOR Y = 2 TO 20
100  A(Y) =  INT (50 *  RND (1)) + 1
110   FOR X = Y - 1 TO 1 STEP  - 1
120   IF A(Y) = A(X) THEN 100
```

```
130   NEXT X
140   NEXT Y
150   VTAB (22): PRINT "Press the <SPACE BAR> to cont
      inue . . .";
160   GET Z$: IF Z$ < > " " THEN 160
170   HOME : VTAB (3): PRINT "Type the abbreviation f
      or this element:"
180   VTAB (6): FOR X = 11 TO 31: PRINT  TAB( X);"=";
      : NEXT X: PRINT
190   VTAB (11): FOR X = 11 TO 31: PRINT  TAB( X);"="
      ;: NEXT X: PRINT
200   VTAB (15): PRINT  TAB( 10);"PERFECT SCORE:   10
      000"
210   VTAB (17): PRINT  TAB( 13);"YOUR SCORE:    ";SS
220   FOR T = 1 TO 20
230   VTAB (1): HTAB (1): PRINT "# ";T
240   Z = A(T)
250   VTAB (8): HTAB (21 -  LEN (A$(Z)) / 2): PRINT A
      $(Z)
260   VTAB (9): HTAB (21 -  LEN (A$(Z)) / 2)
270   X$ = ""
280   GET X$: PRINT X$;
290   IF X$ = B$(Z) THEN 310
300   VTAB (13): HTAB (15): PRINT "M I S S ! !": GOTO
      380
310   IF C$(Z) = "999" THEN 350
320   GET Y$
330   IF Y$ = C$(Z) THEN 350
340   VTAB (13): HTAB (15): PRINT "M I S S ! !": GOTO
      380
350   SS = SS + 500
360   VTAB (13): HTAB (15): PRINT "H I T ! ! !"
370   VTAB (17): HTAB (27): PRINT SS;
380   IF C$(Z) = "999" THEN  VTAB (9): HTAB (21 -  LEN
      (A$(Z)) / 2): PRINT B$(Z);: GOTO 400
390   VTAB (9): HTAB (21 -  LEN (A$(Z)) / 2): PRINT B
      $(Z);D$(Z);
400   FOR I = 1 TO 1200: NEXT I
410   FOR I = 11 TO 31
420   VTAB (8): HTAB (I): PRINT " ";
430   VTAB (9): HTAB (I): PRINT " ";
440   NEXT I
450   VTAB (13): HTAB (15): PRINT "            ";
460   NEXT T
470   FOR I = 1 TO 3000: NEXT I
480   HOME : VTAB (6): PRINT "To play another game, t
      ype RUN and press": PRINT
490   PRINT "the <RETURN> key."
500   END
510   DATA  Hydrogen,H,999,999,Magnesium,M,G,g,Alumin
      um,A,L,l
520   DATA  Lithium,L,I,i,Silicon,S,I,i,Phosphorus,P,
      999,999
530   DATA  Berylium,B,E,e,Sulfur,S,999,999,Chlorine,
      C,L,l
```

```
540   DATA   Helium,H,E,e,Argon,A,R,r,Potassium,K,999,
             999
550   DATA   Carbon,C,999,999,Calcium,C,A,a,Titanium,T
             ,I,i
560   DATA   Nitrogen,N,999,999,Chromium,C,R,r,Mangane
             se,M,N,n
570   DATA   Oxygen,O,999,999,Iron,F,E,e,Cobalt,C,O,o
580   DATA   Fluorine,F,999,999,Nickel,N,I,i,Copper,C,
             U,u
590   DATA   Neon,N,E,e,Uranium,U,999,999,Zinc,Z,N,n
600   DATA   Sodium,N,A,a,Arsenic,A,S,s,Selenium,S,E,e

610   DATA   Bromine,B,R,r,Krypton,K,R,r,Strontium,S,R
             ,r
620   DATA   Zirconium,Z,R,r,Molybdenum,M,O,o,Rhodium,
             R,H,h
630   DATA   Silver,A,G,g,Cadmium,C,D,d,Tin,S,N,n
640   DATA   Antimony,S,B,b,Iodine,I,999,999,Barium,B,
             A,a
650   DATA   Tungsten,W,999,999,Platinum,P,T,t,Gold,A,
             U,u
660   DATA   Mercury,H,G,g,Lead,P,B,b,Bismuth,B,I,i
670   DATA   Radium,R,A,a,Plutonium,P,U,u

]
```

23. SOLVING PROPORTIONS

SUGGESTED FILE NAME: SIMILAR

SUGGESTED GRADE RANGE: 6–8

DESCRIPTION OF THE PROGRAM: Two similar rectangles are drawn on the screen to scale (more or less). The lengths of the sides of one rectangle can be multiplied by some number to obtain the lengths of the sides of the other rectangle. Three of the dimensions are given. The student must type the missing dimension.

EXPLANATION OF DATA LINES: Each data line contains the information for one problem. There are nine entries in each data line. Each entry performs the function described below.

1. A, the answer, is the length of the fourth side.
2. X1$ is the length of the base of the first rectangle.
3. Y1$ is the length of the height of the first rectangle.
4. X2$ is the length of the base of the second rectangle.
5. Y2$ is the length of the height of the second rectangle.
6. B1 is the number used to draw the bases of the first rectangle.

7. H1 is the number used to draw the heights of the first rectangle.

8. B2 is the number used to draw the bases of the second rectangle.

9. H2 is the number used to draw the heights of the second rectangle.

```
10    HOME : VTAB (6): PRINT  TAB( 12);"SOLVING PROPOR
      TIONS": VTAB (10): HTAB (1): PRINT "* TWENTY EX
      ERCISES WILL BE PRESENTED *": FOR TI = 1 TO 300
      0: NEXT TI
20    HOME : VTAB (2): PRINT "THE RECTANGLES WHICH YOU
       WILL SEE ON": PRINT : PRINT "THE SCREEN ARE IN
       PROPORTION.  THAT IS,": PRINT
30    PRINT "THE LENGTHS OF THE SIDES OF ONE": PRINT :
       PRINT "RECTANGLE CAN BE MULTIPLIED BY SOME": PRINT

40    PRINT "NUMBER TO OBTAIN THE LENGTHS OF THE": PRINT
       : PRINT "CORRESPONDING SIDES OF THE OTHER": PRINT

50    PRINT "RECTANGLE.  OF THE FOUR DIMENSIONS OF": PRINT
       : PRINT "THE RECTANGLES, THREE OF THEM ARE GIVE
      N."
60    PRINT "YOU MUST FIND THE MISSING LENGTH."
70 LN = 22: GOSUB 290
80    HOME : VTAB (2):Z = 0
90 N = 0
100 N = N + 1: IF N > 20 THEN 260
110   HOME
120   READ A,X1$,Y1$,X2$,Y2$,B1,H1,B2,H2
130 LN = 19: GOSUB 280: PRINT "# ";N;"   THE SIDES OF
       THESE TWO": PRINT "RECTANGLES ARE IN PROPORTIO
      N."
140   FOR I = 1 TO B1: HTAB (I): VTAB (2): PRINT "*";
      : HTAB (I):: VTAB (2 + H1): PRINT "*";: NEXT I
150   FOR I = 2 TO H1: HTAB (1): VTAB (I + 1): PRINT
      "*";: HTAB (B1): VTAB (I + 1): PRINT "*";: NEXT
      I
160   FOR I = 1 TO B2: HTAB (I + 20): VTAB (2): PRINT
      "*";: HTAB (I + 20): VTAB (2 + H2): PRINT "*";:
       NEXT I
170   FOR I = 2 TO H2: HTAB (21): VTAB (I + 1): PRINT
      "*";: HTAB (20 + B2): VTAB (I + 1): PRINT "*";:
       NEXT I
180   VTAB (1): HTAB (4): PRINT X1$;: VTAB (4): HTAB
      (2): PRINT Y1$;: VTAB (1): HTAB (24): PRINT X2$
      ;: VTAB (4): HTAB (22): PRINT Y2$;
190   GOSUB 290
200 LN = 19: GOSUB 280: PRINT "LENGTH OF THE MISSING
       SIDE  ";: INPUT S
210   IF S = (A) THEN 250
220   IF Z = 0 THEN LN = 19: GOSUB 280: PRINT "NOT CO
      RRECT -- TRY AGAIN.": FOR I = 1 TO 1200: NEXT I
      :Z = 1: GOTO 200
230   IF Z = 2 THEN LN = 19: GOSUB 280: PRINT "THE AN
      SWER IS ";A;".": FOR I = 1 TO 1200: NEXT I:Z =
      0: GOTO 200
```

```
240   IF Z = 1 THEN  GOSUB 320: GOTO 200
250 LN = 21: GOSUB 280: PRINT "THAT'S RIGHT!!";: FOR
      I = 1 TO 1200: NEXT I:Z = 0: GOSUB 290: GOTO 10
      0
260   HOME : VTAB (4): PRINT "YOU HAVE ANSWERED ALL T
      WENTY PROBLEMS.": PRINT : PRINT "HAVE A TERRIFI
      C DAY!!!"
270   END
280   POKE 34,LN: HOME : POKE 34,0: VTAB (LN + 1): RETURN

290 LN = 23: GOSUB 280: PRINT "PRESS THE <SPACE BAR>
       TO CONTINUE . . .";
300   GET A$: IF A$ <  > " " THEN 300
310   RETURN
320 Z = 2:LN = 19: GOSUB 280: PRINT  TAB( 25);X1$; TAB(
      34);X2$
330   PRINT "SOLVE THE PROPORTION:"; TAB( 24);"----
      = ----"
340   PRINT  TAB( 25);Y1$; TAB( 34);Y2$;
350   GOSUB 290: RETURN
360   DATA  8,4,2,?,4,8,3,16,5
370   DATA  9,?,12,27,36,6,5,18,15
380   DATA   30,5,10,15,?,5,7,13,16
390   DATA   4,7,?,35,20,6,3,19,9
400   DATA  32,20,?,5,8,14,17,4,5
410   DATA  45,20,15,60,?,6,3,18,9
420   DATA  8,?,12,24,36,4,5,12,15
430   DATA  30,20,10,?,15,10,3,15,5
440   DATA  28,11,7,44,?,6,3,19,10
450   DATA  15,12,?,8,10,12,10,8,6
460   DATA  9,36,36,9,?,16,11,5,3
470   DATA  35,14,14,35,?,8,5,18,13
480   DATA   60,18,?,27,90,6,12,9,15
490   DATA  30,?,12,40,16,14,5,17,6
500   DATA  20,?,8,15,6,16,5,12,4
510   DATA  18,21,?,28,24,12,6,16,8
520   DATA  45,35,49,?,63,8,8,10,10
530   DATA  60,120,80,90,?,16,8,12,6
540   DATA  1.6,3.2,2,?,1,16,6,8,3
550   DATA  2.7,1.8,1.2,?,1.8,10,5,15,8
```

]

24. ESTIMATING MEASUREMENTS

SUGGESTED FILE NAME: ESTIMATE

SUGGESTED GRADE RANGE: 5–8

DESCRIPTION OF THE PROGRAM: Thirty exercises are presented in estimating measurements in one dimension. The exercises compare two horizontal lines. The length and unit of measure of the first line is given. The student uses this measurement to estimate the length of the second line.

EXPLANATION OF DATA LINES: Each data line defines one exercise. The explanations for the five data items in each line are as follows:

1. The unit of measure: U$
2. The number which is used to draw the first line: C1
3. The length of the first line: L1
4. The number which is used to draw the second line: C2
5. The length of the second line (the correct answer): L2

HOW TO CHANGE THE DATA: You may wish to present fewer than thirty problems to your students. To do this, change line 140. For example, if you want your students to do only ten problems, change line 140 to read:

```
140 ... IF N > 10 THEN 270
```

```
10   HOME : VTAB (6): PRINT  TAB( 9);"ESTIMATING MEAS
     UREMENTS": FOR TI = 1 TO 2000: NEXT TI
20   HOME : VTAB (4): PRINT "PLEASE TYPE YOUR FIRST N
     AME AND PRESS": PRINT : PRINT "THE <RETURN> KEY
     .  ";: INPUT N$
30   VTAB (10): PRINT "I'M HAPPY TO MEET YOU ";N$;"."
     : FOR I = 1 TO 1500: NEXT I
40   R = 0:T = 0: HOME : VTAB (2): PRINT "YOU WILL BE
     SHOWN A LINE AND ASKED TO": PRINT : PRINT "ESTI
     MATE ITS LENGTH WHEN COMPARED TO": PRINT
50   PRINT "ANOTHER LINE.": PRINT : PRINT "HERE IS AN
     EXAMPLE, ";N$;"."
60   VTAB (11): FOR I = 1 TO 20: PRINT "-";: NEXT I: PRINT

70   PRINT "12 INCHES"
80   VTAB (15): FOR I = 1 TO 30: PRINT "-";: NEXT I: PRINT

90   PRINT "HOW MANY INCHES LONG?": PRINT : PRINT : PRINT

100  PRINT "YOUR ESTIMATE SHOULD BE ABOUT 18."
110  VTAB (22): PRINT "PRESS THE <SPACE BAR> TO CONT
     INUE . . .";
120  GET A$: IF A$ <  > " " THEN 120
130 N = 0
140 N = N + 1: IF N > 30 THEN 270
150  READ U$,C1,L1,C2,L2
160  HOME : VTAB (2): PRINT "# ";N
170  VTAB (5): FOR X = 1 TO C1: PRINT "-";: NEXT X: PRINT

180  PRINT L1;" ";U$: PRINT : PRINT
190  FOR X = 1 TO C2: PRINT "-";: NEXT X: PRINT
200  PRINT "HOW MANY ";U$;" LONG";
210  INPUT E:T = T + 1
220  IF  ABS (E - L2) < 3 THEN 250
230  IF E - L2 > 0 THEN LN = 12: GOSUB 310: PRINT "T
     OO HIGH -- ESTIMATE AGAIN.": FOR I = 1 TO 1200:
     NEXT I: GOTO 160
```

```
240 LN = 14: GOSUB 310: PRINT "TOO LOW -- ESTIMATE A
    GAIN.": FOR I = 1 TO 1200: NEXT I: GOTO 160
250 LN = 14: GOSUB 310: PRINT "THAT'S A GOOD ESTIMAT
    E, ";N$;"!!":R = R + 1: PRINT
260 PRINT "YOUR SCORE IS " INT (R / T * 100 + .5);"
    %.": FOR I = 1 TO 1600: NEXT I: GOTO 140
270 HOME : VTAB (5): PRINT "YOU HAVE ESTIMATED ALL
    THE MEASUREMENTS": PRINT : PRINT "IN THIS PROGR
    AM.": PRINT : PRINT
280 PRINT "YOUR FINAL SCORE IS "; INT (R / T * 100 +
    .5);"%.": PRINT : PRINT
290 PRINT "GO OUT AND MAKE THIS A TERRIFIC DAY!!"
300 END
310 POKE 34,LN: HOME : POKE 34,0: VTAB (LN + 1): RETURN

320 DATA    INCHES,15,20,30,40
330 DATA    FEET,30,12,25,10
340 DATA    MILES,10,5,30,15
350 DATA    YARDS,25,100,15,60
360 DATA    METERS,16,40,24,60
370 DATA    KILOMETERS,20,80,12,48
380 DATA    CENTIMETERS,16,8,20,10
390 DATA    FEET,20,4,25,5
400 DATA    YARDS,36,9,24,6
410 DATA    METERS,20,5,28,7
420 DATA    INCHES,36,9,16,4
430 DATA    KILOMETERS,24,100,36,150
440 DATA    MILES,30,300,10,100
450 DATA    CENTIMETERS,4,7,20,35
460 DATA    MILES,25,40,15,24
470 DATA    INCHES,30,10,12,4
480 DATA    YARDS,7,6,21,18
490 DATA    METERS,28,600,14,300
500 DATA    KILOMETERS,10,13,20,26
510 DATA    FEET,30,15,34,17
520 DATA    CENTIMETERS,35,70,20,40
530 DATA    MILES,16,60,12,45
540 DATA    YARDS,16,12,12,9
550 DATA    INCHES,15,9,10,6
560 DATA    METERS,16,8,36,18
570 DATA    KILOMETERS,32,32,28,28
580 DATA    FEET,14,28,30,60
590 DATA    MILES,10,14,25,35
600 DATA    YARDS,36,80,27,60
610 DATA    METERS,8,12,30,45
```

]

25. TWENTY SCIENCE QUESTIONS

SUGGESTED FILE NAME: SCIENCE

SUGGESTED GRADE RANGE: 6–8

DESCRIPTION OF THE PROGRAM: This activity presents science facts in a game format. Twenty exercises are chosen at random from a set of forty-nine questions. The questions are to be answered "T" for true or "F" for false. As the program runs, a random amount of money is chosen for each question. As the student answers the questions correctly, his "jackpot" increases. Also, extra information is provided for most questions.

EXPLANATION OF DATA LINES: Each data line contains three entries that determine one science question. There are forty-nine data lines. You will see words running together in the data lines. You will also see some large spaces between words. These two features have to do with printing the lines on the screen so that they are spaced correctly. Be sure to type the spacing as it appears in the data lines.

HOW TO CHANGE THE DATA: You may change data by simply retyping data lines and substituting your questions for the ones that are currently in the program.

```
10  SUM = 0:C = 1
20  DIM R(20),Q$(150)
30  HOME : VTAB (6): PRINT  TAB( 8);"TWENTY SCIENCE
      QUESTIONS": FOR TI = 1 TO 2000: NEXT TI
40  FOR J = 1 TO 147: READ Q$(J): NEXT J
50  R(0) =  INT (48 *  RND (1)) + 1:R(1) =  INT (48 *
      RND (1)) + 1
60  IF R(0) = R(1) THEN 50
70  FOR X = 2 TO 19
80  R(X) =  INT (48 *  RND (1)) + 1
90  FOR Y = X - 1 TO 0 STEP  - 1
100   IF R(X) = R(Y) THEN 80
110   NEXT Y
120   NEXT X
130   FOR T = 1 TO 20
140   HOME : VTAB (2): PRINT "QUESTION VALUE:   ";
150   FOR I = 1 TO 10: VTAB (2): HTAB (18): PRINT "
        ";:M =  INT (1000 *  RND (1)) + 1: VTAB (2)
      : HTAB (18): PRINT "$";M;: FOR J = 1 TO 60: NEXT
      J: NEXT I
160   VTAB (5): HTAB (10): PRINT "ANSWER <T>RUE OR <F
      >ALSE."
170 A = 3 * R(T) + 1: PRINT : PRINT Q$(A)
180   VTAB (11): HTAB (19)
190   GET A$: IF A$ <  > "F" AND A$ <  > "T" THEN 190

200   PRINT A$
210   IF A$ <  > Q$(A + 1) THEN 240
220   PRINT "THAT'S RIGHT!!": PRINT : PRINT Q$(A + 2)
      :SUM = SUM + M
230   PRINT : PRINT "YOU WIN $";M;" => TOTAL WINNINGS
       = $";SUM: GOTO 260
240   PRINT "YOUR ANSWER IS NOT CORRECT.": PRINT : PRINT
      Q$(A + 2):SUM = SUM - M
250   PRINT : PRINT "YOU LOSE $";M;" => TOTAL WINNING
      S = $";SUM
```

```
260   VTAB (22): HTAB (1): PRINT "PRESS THE <SPACE BA
      R> TO CONTINUE . . .";
270   GET A$: IF A$ <  > " " THEN 270
280   NEXT T
290   HOME : VTAB (6): PRINT  TAB( 12);"THIS GAME IS
      OVER.": PRINT : PRINT
300   PRINT  TAB( 12);"YOU HAVE WON $";SUM;".": PRINT
      : PRINT
310   PRINT "YOU HAVE PROVEN YOURSELF TO BE A WORTHY"
      : PRINT : PRINT "OPPONENT AND I SALUTE YOU!!"
320   END
330   DATA  "A MUZZLE SETTING OF 45 DEGREES WILL GIVE
      A CANNON ITS MAXIMUM RANGE.",T,""
340   DATA  "MANHOLES AND MANHOLE COVERS ARE CIRCULAR
      BECAUSE IT IS EASIER TO DIG CIRCULAR    HOLES T
      HAN RECTANGULAR ONES.",F,"THEY ARE MADE IN THE
      SHAPE OF A CIRCLE  SO THAT THE COVERS WILL NOT
      FALL THROUGH"
350   DATA  "THE EARTH IS SAID TO BE AN OBLATE
      SPHEROID.",T,"IT IS AN OBLATE SPHEROID, A SPHER
      E WHICHIS FLATTENED AT THE POLES."
360   DATA  "THE DIAMETER OF THE MOON IS 2160 MILES."
      ,T,"IT IS 2160 MILES, THE DISTANCE FROM    SAN
      FRANCISCO TO CLEVELAND."
370   DATA  "THE AVERAGE DISTANCE OF THE MOON FROM
      THE EARTH IS 238,856 MILES.",T,"AT IS FARTHEST
      POINT, IT IS 251,968    MILES FROM THE EARTH,
      AT ITS CLOSEST    POINT, 225,742 MILES."
380   DATA  "THE MOON GIVES OFF NO LIGHT OF ITS OWN.",
      T,"IT REFLECTS LIGHT RECEIVED FROM THE SUN."
390   DATA  "ON THE MOON YOU WOULD WEIGH SIX TIMES AS
      MUCH AS YOU WEIGH ON EARTH.",F,"YOU WOULD WEIGH
      ONE-SIXTH AS MUCH AS YOUWEIGH ON EARTH."
400   DATA  "THERE ARE STORMS ON THE MOON.",F,"THE MO
      ON HAS NO WEATHER BECAUSE IT HAS  NO ATMOSPHERE
      ."
410   DATA  "AN ECLIPSE OF THE MOON OCCURS WHEN THE
      SUN IS DIRECTLY BETWEEN THE EARTH AND  THE MOO
      N.",F,"AN ECLIPSE OF THE MOON OCCURS WHEN THE
      EARTH IS DIRECTLY BETWEEN THE MOON AND  THE SUN
      ."
420   DATA  "(1543) COPERNICUS THEORIZED THAT THE
      PLANETS AND THE SUN REVOLVE AROUND THE  EARTH."
      ,F,"COPERNICUS THEORIZED THAT THE EARTH AND THE
      PLANETS REVOLVE AROUND THE SUN."
430   DATA  "(1774)JOSEPH PRIESTLEY DISCOVERED OXYGEN
      .",T,""
440   DATA  "(1858) CHARLES DARWIN ADVANCED HIS
      THEORY OF EVOLUTION OF PLANTS AND        ANIMALS
      .",T,""
450   DATA  "(1876) LOUIS PASTEUR DISCOVERED THAT
      VIRUSES CAUSE DISEASE.",F,"PASTEUR FOUND THAT M
      ICROORGANISMS CAUSE DISEASE."
460   DATA  "(1950) WILLIAM ROENTGEN DISCOVERED
      X RAYS.",F,"ROENTGEN DISCOVERED X RAYS IN 1895.
      "
470   DATA  "(1900) PAUL EHRLICH ORIGINATED
```

```
      CHEMOTHERAPY, THE TREATMENT OF DISEASE  WITH CH
      EMICALS.",T,""
480   DATA  "(1905) ALBERT EINSTEIN PRESENTED HIS
      SPECIAL THEORY OF RELATIVITY.",T,""
490   DATA  "(1960) ALEXANDER FLEMING DISCOVERED
      PENICILLIN.",F,"FLEMING DISCOVERED PENICILLIN I
      N 1926."
500   DATA  "(1942) ENRICO FERMI ACHIEVED THE FIRST
      SUCCESSFUL NUCLEAR CHAIN REACTION.",T,""
510   DATA  "(1953) FRANKLIN ROOSEVELT PRODUCED THE
      FIRST EFFECTIVE VACCINE AGAINST POLIO.",F,"JONA
      S SALK INVENTED THE FIRST POLIO     VACCINE."
520   DATA  "FRANCE LAUNCHED THE FIRST ARTIFICIAL
      SATELLITE.",F,"THE FIRST ARTIFICIAL SATELLITE W
      AS       LAUNCHED BY RUSSIA."
530   DATA  "(1980) ARTHUR KORNBERG GREW DNA, THE
      BASE CHEMICAL OF THE GENE, IN A TEST    TUBE.",
      F,"KORNBERG GREW DNA IN 1957."
540   DATA  "MICKEY ROONEY AND LORNA DOONE (1961)
      BECAME THE FIRST HUMANS TO FLY IN SPACE.",F,"TH
      E FIRST HUMANS TO FLY IN SPACE WERE   YURI GAGA
      RIN AND ALAN SHEPARD."
550   DATA  "NEIL ARMSTRONG (1969) BECAME THE FIRST
      PERSON TO WALK ON THE MOON.",T,"HE SAID: ONE SM
      ALL STEP FOR A MAN; ONE  GIANT LEAP FOR MANKIND
      ."
560   DATA  "LIGHT TRAVELS AT 186,000 MILES PER HOUR.
      ",F,"LIGHT TRAVELS AT 186,000 MILES PER      SE
      COND."
570   DATA  "ENIAC, THE FIRST ALL-ELECTRONIC DIGITAL
      COMPUTER, WAS BUILT IN 1975.",F,"THE ELECTRONIC
       NUMERICAL INTEGRATOR AND AUTOMATIC COMPUTER WA
      S BUILT IN 1946."
580   DATA  "SOUND TRAVELS 1,100 FEET PER SECOND IN
      AIR.",T,"IT TRAVELS 1,100 FPS IN AIR BUT NOT AT
       ALL IN A VACUUM."
590   DATA  "THE STARS ARE SUNS, VERY HOT MASSES OF
      GAS.",T,""
600   DATA  "OUR SUN IS ABOUT 93 BILLION MILES FROM
      THE EARTH.",F,"IT IS ABOUT 93 MILLION MILES FRO
      M EARTH."
610   DATA  "A MACH NUMBER IS A MEASURE OF SPEED.",T,
      "MACH 1 IS THE SPEED OF SOUND; MACH 2 IS TWICE
      THE SPEED OF SOUND, ETC.  MACH IS NAMED FOR ERN
      ST MACH (1838-1916)."
620   DATA  "THREE SIMPLE MACHINES ARE: LEVER,
      PULLEY, WHEEL AND AXLE.",T,"THE SIX SIMPLE MACH
      INES ARE: LEVER,     PULLEY, WHEEL AND AXLE, IN
      CLINED PLANE, WEDGE, AND SCREW."
630   DATA  "(1862) RICHARD GATLING INVENTED THE
      GATLING GUN.",T,""
640   DATA  "IRA GERSHWIN (1763) INVENTED THE STEAM
      ENGINE.",F,"JAMES WATT INVENTED THE STEAM ENGIN
      E."
```

```
650 DATA   "THOMAS A. EDISON (1847-1931) PATENTED
    ONLY A FEW INVENTIONS.",F,"EDISON PATENTED MORE
    THAN 1,100        INVENTIONS IN 60 YEARS."
660 DATA   "ALEXANDER GRAHAM BELL INVENTED THE
    TELEPHONE IN 1874.",T,""
670 DATA   "THE SIZE OF AN ATOM IS ABOUT ONE-FIFTH
    ITS NUCLEUS.",F,"THE SIZE OF AN ATOM IS ABOUT 5
    0,000      TIMES THAT OF ITS NUCLEUS."
680 DATA   "THE EARTH IS ABOUT 4.5 BILLION YEARS
    OLD.",T,""
690 DATA   "THE EQUATORIAL DIAMETER OF THE EARTH IS
    7,926 MILES.",T,""
700 DATA   "THE EQUATORIAL CIRCUMFERENCE OF THE
    EARTH IS 24,901 MILES.",T,""
710 DATA   "50% OF THE EARTH'S ATMOSPHERE IS LESS
    THAN 100 MILES ABOVE THE EARTH'S        SURFACE
    .",F,"99% OF THE EARTH'S ATMOSPHERE IS LESS    T
    HAN 100 MILES ABOVE THE EARTH'S         SURFACE.
    "
720 DATA   "THE EARTH TRAVELS 595 MILLION MILES
    AROUND THE SUN IN 365 DAYS, 6 HOURS,     9 MINUT
    ES, AND 9.54 SECONDS.",T,"THAT'S TRUE.   ALSO, I
    TS SPEED IS        APPROXIMATELY 66,000 MILES P
    ER HOUR."
730 DATA   "SCIENTISTS ESTIMATE THE TEMPERATURE AT
    THE CENTER OF THE EARTH TO BE AS HIGH AS9,000 D
    EGREES FAHRENHEIT.",T,""
740 DATA   "DINOSAURS LIVED ABOUT 10 MILLION YEARS
    AGO.",F,"THEY LIVED ABOUT 180 MILLION YEARS AGO
    ."
750 DATA   "THE FIRST REGULARLY SCHEDULED TELEVISION
    BROADCASTS BEGAN IN 1928.",T,"THAT'S TRUE.   ALS
    O, NBC BEGAN TV        BROADCASTS IN 1930 AND C
    BS IN 1931."
760 DATA   "THOMAS A. EDISON INVENTED THE PHONOGRAPH
    IN 1870 AND THE ELECTRIC LIGHT BULB IN  1879.",
    T,"HE INVENTED BOTH OF THOSE AND, IN 1889, MOTI
    ON PICTURES AS WELL."
770 DATA   "ONE NAUTICAL MILE IS 1.151 STATUTE MILES
    OR 6,076 FEET.",T,""
780 DATA   "ACCELERATION DUE TO GRAVITY AT SEA LEVEL
    IS 32.17 FEET PER SECOND PER SECOND.",T,""
790 DATA   "ONE KNOT IS 1.152 MILES PER HOUR.",T,""
800 DATA   "OUR SOLAR SYSTEM AND THE EARTH REVOLVE
    AROUND THE CENTER OF THE MILKY WAY       GALAXY
    AT A SPEED OF 43,000 MILES PER   HOUR.",T,""
810 DATA   "THE INTEGRATED CIRCUITRY ON A SILICON
    CHIP WAS INVENTED IN 1958.",T,"IT'S INVENTION I
    N 1958 IS CREDITED TO   JACK KELLY OF TEXAS INS
    TRUMENTS."

]
```

section TWO

LEARNING TO OPERATE AND PROGRAM YOUR TRS-80™

chapter 5

HOW TO OPERATE
A TRS-80™ MODEL III
AND MODEL IV

OPERATING THE KEYBOARD

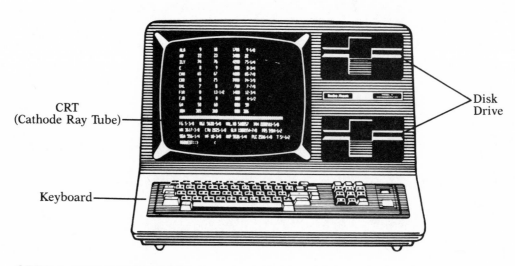

CRT
(Cathode Ray Tube)

Disk
Drive

Keyboard

STEP 1: THE EQUIPMENT

Examine your equipment. The illustration above shows a TRS-80™ micro-computer.[1] The microcomputer has three main parts. The first and most important part is the *central processing unit* (CPU). It is the piece that does all the work. The CPU itself is hidden from view inside the case of the machine. It is made up of chips and circuitry. The CPU is accessed by typing on the keyboard.

---

[1]From *TRS-80 Model III Operations and BASIC Language Reference Manual.* Radio Shack, A Division of Tandy Corporation, Fort Worth, Texas 1980.

Attached to the computer is a *screen* or *CRT*. The CRT shows the output. The CRT is like a television screen. CRTs for some computers are in color. The CRT for the TRS-80™ Model III or Model IV is black and white, or green phosphor.

The third piece of equipment, the little rectangular black box to the right of the CRT, is called a *disk drive*. Your machine may have one or two drives. The disk drive is the device that reads and writes data on a disk. The disk drive is the piece of hardware into which the diskette or "floppy" is inserted. The diskette looks like a little square flat plastic record. It is inserted into the disk drive so that the message the user is placing into the computer's memory can be saved.

The CPU, the CRT, and the disk drives are all called the *hardware* of the system.

The information on the diskette, this book, and any paper on which you scribble ideas while learning to use the computer are called the *software* of the system.

STEP 2: TURNING THE COMPUTER ON

Turn on your computer by pressing the rocker switch located at the front right underside of the keyboard. The red light will turn off automatically. Run your hand along the underside of the left edge, and you will find two dials to adjust clarity and brightness.

STEP 3: RED LIGHT ON THE DISK DRIVE

Check the red light on the bottom disk drive (drive 0). It should be off. If it is on, push the orange <**RESET**> button on the right of the keyboard and wait a few seconds.

STEP 4: GETTING STARTED

Hold down the <**BREAK**> key while pressing the orange <**RESET**> button. The screen will display

CASS?

Now press the <**ENTER**> key twice.

STEP 5: THE CURSOR

The screen will display

READY
>

Whenever you see a ">" on the screen, you know that the computer is waiting for you to type something into it. The ">" is called a *prompt*. You will also see a blinking small square to the right of the ">". The square is called a *cursor*, and it tells you where you are on the screen. It is a position indicator.

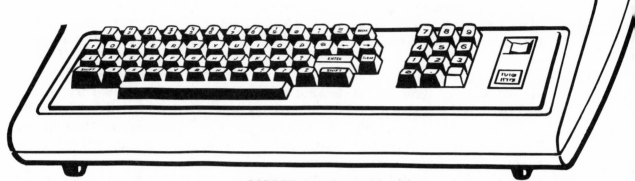

MODEL III KEYBOARD²

MODEL IV KEYBOARD²

STEP 6: LEARNING THE KEYBOARD

Study the keyboard for the computer you are using. One difference between the Model III and Model IV is that the Model IV has more special keys. Both are similar to a standard typewriter keyboard. The first thing you notice about your keyboard is that there are no lower case letters shown on the keys. The <**SHIFT**> key is used in the same way it is used on a typewriter. Press it down to type the upper characters on the keys in the top row of the keyboard. Release the <**SHIFT**> key to type the main characters shown on the keys. That is all you need to do to communicate with the machine.

Now, type a few letters. Type your name. Don't worry about spacing or lines. Just keep typing. *Do not push the* <**ENTER**> *key until you are instructed to do so.*

STEP 7: SCREEN WRAPAROUND

Now type: "The quick red fox jumped over the lazy brown dog" and "the cow jumped over the moon."

---

²From *TRS-80 Model III Operations and BASIC Language Reference Manual.* Radio Shack, A Division of Tandy Corporation, Fort Worth, Texas 1980.

Notice that when you get to the right side of the screen, the computer will automatically go to the next line. This is called *screen wraparound*.

Make a mistake. Spell the word *dog* as "doh." You can correct the error by pressing the ← key. Press the left-arrow key to erase the incorrect letter. Try it. Now press g, the correct letter. It's amazing! You don't need any white liquid on this machine to correct errors.

STEP 8: LEFT- AND RIGHT-ARROW KEYS

Now try: <**SHIFT**> ←. Hold down the <**SHIFT**> key while pressing the left-arrow key. The cursor is positioned at the beginning of a new line. Try it.

STEP 9: MOVING THE CURSOR

Hold down →. The cursor should move rapidly to the right. To move the cursor back to the beginning of a line, press <**SHIFT**> ←.

STEP 10: CLEARING THE SCREEN

Try typing in your name, address, phone number, and whatever you like. The screen should be filled with a lot of information. To clear the screen, press the <**CLEAR**> key.

STEP 11: DIFFERENCES BETWEEN O AND 0, L AND 1

Press the L key. An upper case "L" appears. It cannot be used as the number 1. The number 1 is the first key in the set of numeral keys at the top of the keyboard. The same is true of 0. An upper case O cannot be used for zero. Press both keys to study the difference in characters. Press 0 and press O. Remember that the alphabetic symbols on the keyboard are different from the numerical symbols in the top row of the keyboard. You cannot interchange them just because they might look the same.

STEP 12: CHANGING FROM UPPER CASE LETTERS TO LOWER CASE LETTERS

You can change from upper case to lower case letters on the TRS-80™ microcomputer. Hold down the <**SHIFT**> key and press the zero key (0). Now type the alphabet. The letters should be lower case. Type your name and capitalize the first letter. The process is the same as on a typewriter. Hold down the <**SHIFT**> key to type the first letter; release it to type the remaining letters. To return to upper case, press <**SHIFT**> 0.

Important Note: All statements and comands to the computer must be in upper case. The statement, print "Hello", will result in a syntax error. The correct way to give this command is: PRINT "Hello".

STEP 13: TALKING WITH THE COMPUTER

Now let's talk with the computer. To begin, press <**BREAK**>.

<**BREAK**> interrupts the computer and tells it to get ready to receive new instructions. After you press <**BREAK**> the screen shows:

    READY
    >

STEP 14: PRACTICING A PRINT STATEMENT

Type in this statement exactly as shown:

    PRINT "THIS IS FUN!"

Note that quotation marks (" ") are used around the message you want printed. Now press the <**ENTER**> key . The computer will print:

    THIS IS FUN!

Remember: At the end of every command or statement, press the <**ENTER**> key.

From this point on, no mention of pushing the <**ENTER**> key after every statement or command will be made. The <**ENTER**> key always tells the computer when you have completed a statement, command, or instruction.

PRINT was the statement. "THIS IS FUN!" was the message. Pressing the <**ENTER**> key told the computer that that was the end of the statement.

    >
    PRINT "THIS IS FUN!"
    THIS IS FUN!
    Ready
    >

STEP 15: PRACTICING STATEMENTS

Try some other statements. Type:

```
PRINT   "ROSES ARE RED
        VIOLETS ARE BLUE
        COMPUTERS ARE FUN
        AND THIS ONE IS, TOO."
```

Press: <**ENTER**>.

Hint: After you have typed the first line, press the space bar until the cursor wraps around and is underneath the R. Follow the same procedure for the third and fourth lines of the poem before you press <**ENTER**>.

```
PRINT "ROSES ARE RED,
       VIOLETS ARE BLUE,
       COMPUTERS ARE FUN,
       AND THIS ONE IS TOO."
ROSES ARE RED,
VIOLETS ARE BLUE,
COMPUTERS ARE FUN,
AND THIS ONE IS TOO.
Ready
>
```

STEP 16: PRINTING NUMBERS

Tell the computer to:

PRINT 43297 <**ENTER**>.

Notice that you did not use the quotation marks. The computer will print numbers without quotation marks. Also, commas are not used in numbers when working with the computer.

STEP 17: THE TRS-80™ CALCULATOR

The computer can be used as a simple calculator. The basic operation symbols are:

```
        addition:  +
     subtraction:  −
  multiplication:  *
        division:  /
```

Study these. Now try the statements below. Don't forget to press <**ENTER**>.

```
PRINT 3 + 4
PRINT 16 − 10
```

```
PRINT 439 * 48
PRINT 45/6
PRINT 972 / 4 + 18 − 306 * 31
```

A "[" can be used to multiply a number by itself any given number of times. This symbol is obtained by typing the up-arrow key.

```
PRINT 2 * 2 * 2 * 2 * 2 * 2 * 2
```

can be written

```
PRINT 2 [ 7
```

Remember: Use the ↑ to type the "[".
Now try:

```
PRINT " 8 + 9 "
PRINT 8 + 9
```

Notice the difference between the two.

STEP 18: IF YOU MAKE AN ERROR

If you misspelled **PRINT** or omitted a quotation mark (") around a message, an error will occur. You might receive a syntax error message.

```
? SN ERROR
```

Try:

```
PRNIT "I LOVE YOU"
```

You receive:

```
? SN ERROR.
```

Now correct the word **PRNIT** to **PRINT**. Just retype the line correctly.
? SN is the most common error message you will receive on the screen. It means that you made an error in punctuation or spelling when typing a command or statement. Correct the error before pressing <**ENTER**> or retype the line correctly.

There are some mathematical calculations that the computer cannot handle. The computer will notify you of a problem by printing an error message. Among the problems that can result are:
Division by zero
 Type: PRINT 25/0 <**ENTER**>
Overflow (value too large)
 Type: PRINT 10   100
Consult your owner's manual for the meaning of any error messages that appear on the screen.

STEP 19: PRACTICE SUMMARY OF KEY FUNCTIONS

DO IT OVER AND
OVER AGAIN
UNTIL YOU
GET IT RIGHT!

Practice this summary of the Key Functions before you go to STEP 20.

1. Turn your computer on. Hold <**BREAK**>, and press the orange <**RESET**> button.
2. Type your name, address, and a short message.
3. Correct your errors using the ← and → keys.
4. Clear the screen. Press <**CLEAR**>.
5. Type 0, O, L and 1.
6. Type a PRINT statement.
7. Type a PRINT statement with an error. Correct it.
8. Type a PRINT statement using numbers.
9. Use the TRS-80™ calculator.

Remember:
<**CLEAR**> erases the display from the screen but not from the memory.
<**BREAK**> interrupts the computer and readies it for new instructions.
<**ENTER**> must be pressed after every statement or command.

YOU DID
A
MARVELOUS
JOB!

INITIALIZING A DISK

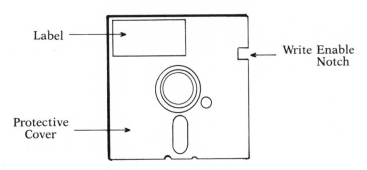

Label

Write Enable
Notch

Protective
Cover

STEP 20: LEARNING ABOUT DISKETTES

Inside the square cover is a thin, floppy circular disk, about the size of a 45-rpm record, on which information is stored by a magnetizing process. A diskette is reliable and should last for years. However, it is also vulnerable and subject to damage. These rules should be followed in the care of your diskettes.

1. Never write on the diskette with a ball point pen or pencil. Doing this may make an indentation on the diskette that will prevent it from running. If you must write on it, use a felt tip pen. It is much safer to write on a label and then affix the label to the diskette.
2. Keep diskettes away from magnets and magnetic fields such as the screen of your monitor or a TV set.
3. Do not bend the diskette. Any creases in the diskette will prevent it from running.
4. Keep fingers off the shiny exposed parts of the diskette.
5. Protect the diskette from extreme heat or cold.
6. Protect the diskette from dust by keeping it in its jacket when it is not being used.
7. Never insert or remove a diskette when the red disk drive light is on.

You need to purchase a blank diskette in order to proceed efficiently with this chapter. Blank 5 1/4-inch single-sided double density diskettes cost less than $4.00 each from any computer store. Once in a while you will run across a faulty diskette. Your computer will not write on it, and you will get an error message on the screen. Take the faulty diskette back to the dealer and exchange it for a good one.

At this point, begin from scratch. Turn off your computer.

Model III user: A manual and disk were delivered to you along with your computer. You need to find this disk. It is called the "Model III TRSDOS Disk Operating System and Basic Interpreter." It should be inside the "Disk System Owner's Manual."

Model IV user: You must use a Model III TRSDOS disk (Cat. #26-0312) available from Radio Shack.

STEP 21: BOOTING THE DISKETTE

The procedure described in this step is called *booting* the diskette.

1. Turn the computer on.
2. The red light on the disk drive will go out, and the whirring sound will stop in a few seconds.
3. Open the disk drive door and, holding the diskette so that your thumb is over the label, gently slide the TRSDOS diskette into drive 0 (the bottom drive) horizontally, label up and oval slot to the back of the drive.
4. Close the door.
5. Press the orange <**RESET**> button.

The red light will come on, the drive will whir, and, in a few seconds, you will see a message on the screen. If you have trouble or the procedure hasn't worked, take the disk out, press <**RESET**>, and begin again.

STEP 22: THE DIRECTORY OF PROGRAMS

Type the date using two numerals for the month, then a slash, two numerals for the day, then another slash, and two numerals for the year. For example, September 3, 1985 would be typed in as 09/03/85. Press the <**ENTER**> key.

Next, you will be asked to type in the time. Simply press the <**ENTER**> key to skip this chore.

You will now see "TRSDOS Ready" and, underneath, a dotted line. TRSDOS stands for Tandy Radio Shack Disk Operating System.

Your computer is now at your command.

Type: DIR <**ENTER**>.

What you see on the screen is a directory of the programs on your disk. The programs that are on your TRSDOS disk at this time allow the computer to use disks for a storage medium and much more. You will want to read your "Disk System Owner's Manual" to discover all that TRSDOS can do for you.

STEP 23: MAKING A BACKUP COPY OF YOUR TRSDOS DISK

A backup copy needs to be made of your TRSDOS disk if you are going to save programs on it. You need a blank disk as well as your TRSDOS disk. The TRSDOS disk will be the "source" disk. The blank disk will be the "destination" disk.

If you have two disk drives, the TRSDOS disk should be in drive 0 (the bottom drive) and the blank disk in drive 1 (the top drive). If you have one disk drive, the TRSDOS disk should be in drive 0. With one disk drive, you will have to switch diskettes several times as the copy is being made. However, all the directions you need will be given on the screen as you run the program.

TRSDOS Ready should be across the bottom of your screen. If it is not, press the orange <**RESET**> button.

Type: BACKUP and press <**ENTER**>.

Now give the information requested on the screen. For two drives, the information to the computer is:

SOURCE DRIVE: 0
DESTINATION DRIVE: 1

For one drive, the information to the computer is:

SOURCE DRIVE: 0
DESTINATION DRIVE: 0

Unless otherwise specified, the password for your TRSDOS diskette is PASSWORD. When asked for the password, type PASSWORD and press <**ENTER**>. Now wait until you see the message:

BACKUP COMPLETE

You will want to refer to the TRSDOS manual for more information about making backup copies of diskettes. The new disk you just made will be the disk on which you will save programs from Chapters 7 and 8. Preparing a disk for saving programs is often referred to as initializing a disk.

STEP 24: PREPARING THE DISK TO STORE PROGRAMS

Put your original TRSDOS diskette away in your manual and save it to make other backup copies to use when you need disks to save programs.

On the disk you just made, write TRSDOS on a label. (Do not write on the diskette itself.) Affix the label to your new copy. You will use your new TRSDOS diskette in the next step. If you have two drives, move your new TRSDOS diskette to drive 0.

You cannot store programs on a blank diskette. The diskette must have the operating system on it in order to use it to store and retrieve programs.

STEP 25: SAVING PROGRAMS

In this step you will write a short practice program to illustrate how to store and retrieve your programs.

Your new TRSDOS diskette should be in disk drive 0. Boot it up by pressing the orange <**RESET**> button. This enters the disk operating system into the computer's memory so that you can store programs on the diskette.

At: TRSDOS Ready, type BASIC and press <**ENTER**>. This tells the computer that you are going to use the BASIC language.

At: How many files? press <**ENTER**>.

At: Memory size? press <**ENTER**>.

At this point you will see on the screen:

```
READY
>
```

Now, after the above message appears, type:

NEW and press <**ENTER**>.

This command clears the memory and prepares the computer to receive new instructions. The new instructions will be in the form of a program. Continue by typing the following lines. Notice that each line is numbered so that the computer will execute the lines in the sequence determined by the order of the numbers.

```
10 LS                        (CLS clears the screen)
20 PRINT "HELLO";            (The ; makes HELLO repeat
                              horizontally.)

30 GOTO 20
```

Type: RUN and press <**ENTER**>.

The program will run until you stop it.

To stop the program: Press <**BREAK**>. <**BREAK**> will break into the program.

To save the program on your diskette, you must give it a name no longer than eight characters. For example, name it EXAMPLE.

Type: SAVE "EXAMPLE" and press <**ENTER**>. Be sure to type the quotation marks.

The red light and the whirring sound mean that the program is being written on your diskette. When this process ends, you will see a blinking cursor on the screen, and the red light will go out.

Press the orange <**RESET**> button.

At: TRSDOS Ready

Type: DIR and press <**ENTER**>.

EXAMPLE should appear on the directory for your diskette.

STEP 26: LOADING PROGRAMS

At this point, the EXAMPLE program is no longer in the memory of the computer. To load it into memory:

At: TRSDOS Ready

Type: BASIC and press <**ENTER**>.

Now: Press <**ENTER**> twice to skip the questions on files and memory.

At: Ready

Type: LOAD "EXAMPLE" and press <**ENTER**>.

Then type: RUN and press <**ENTER**>.

You can see that your program is back in the computer. Stop the program by pressing <**BREAK**>.

Type: LIST and press <**ENTER**>.

You should get a listing of the program. The lines you typed in from STEP 25 should appear in the program listing.

Now try this little exercise. Under the program listing, type line 25 like this:

    25 PRINT "(your first name)"

Run the program by typing RUN and pressing <**ENTER**>. What do you see? Is the computer saying "Hello" to you on the screen?

Stop the program and list it. Remember how?

Press <**BREAK**> to stop the program.

Type: LIST and press <**ENTER**> to see listing. You should see line 25 between lines 20 and 30.

STEP 27: ERASING A PROGRAM FROM A DISK

EXAMPLE is probably not a program you want to save for posterity. To erase it from your diskette, type:

KILL "EXAMPLE" and press <**ENTER**>.

After the disk drive turns off, press the orange <**RESET**> button.

    At: TRSDOS Ready

    Type: DIR and press <**ENTER**>.

EXAMPLE should be gone from the directory.

The following is a summary of booting your diskette and running a program.

1. Turn on the computer.

2. Enter the date.

3. Press <**ENTER**> to skip the time.

4. At TRSDOS Ready, type BASIC.

5. At How many files? press <**ENTER**>.

6. At Memory size? press <**ENTER**>.

7. At Ready, type LOAD "Program Name" and press <**ENTER**>.

8. Type RUN.

SUMMARY OF STEPS 20 THROUGH 27

    A.   Booting a diskette (STEP 21)

    B.   How to list the directory of programs (STEP 22)

    C.   How to make a backup diskette (STEP 23)

    D.   How to prepare your disk for storing programs (STEP 24)

    E.   How to save a program (STEP 25)

    F.   How to name a program (STEP 25)

    G.   How to load and list a program (STEP 26)

    H.   How to kill a program (STEP 27)

You should be familiar with your computer and ready to learn some elementary BASIC statements and commands that will help you while you are copying the programs in this book. Please read Chapter 6 ("Learning to Program and to Copy Programs for Classroom Use on Your TRS-80™"). After completing Chapter 6 you should be ready to select programs to save on your disk from Chapter 7 (Reading/Language Arts) and Chapter 8 (Mathematics/Science).

chapter 6

LEARNING TO PROGRAM AND TO COPY PROGRAMS FOR CLASSROOM USE ON YOUR TRS-80™

BEGINNING PROGRAMMING

Before beginning to copy the programs in this book, it is important to become familiar with some BASIC programming language. A simple BASIC program is made up of some fundamental BASIC statements. These statements include such words as FOR, NEXT, LET, PRINT, GOTO, INPUT, and END. These words tell the computer how to perform. They are instructions directing the computer to logically execute a program line by line.

The instructions are like a road map to the computer. If you give the wrong instruction, the computer becomes lost and usually responds with an error message or won't run a program as intended. The instructions are very important and must be presented logically and unambiguously to the computer.

Read the next few pages and practice the simple programs presented here on your computer. The programs will demonstrate some basic instructions that will be of help while you copy the programs in this book.

You will not need to insert your initialized disk into the drive to practice these programs. After completing this chapter, you will be ready to insert the disk for saving the programs in Chapters 7 and 8.

WHAT IS A PROGRAM?

Let us examine a simple program of instructions to the computer and a command that tells the computer to carry out the instructions.

A simple BASIC program might look like this:

```
10 PRINT "I LOVE TO LEARN HOW TO PROGRAM."
20 PRINT "MY STUDENTS LOVE PROGRAMMING, TOO."
30 END
```

Do this Now. The procedure below will help you to enter and run this program.

Turn on the computer.

Hold <**BREAK**> while you press the orange <**RESET**> button.

Press <**ENTER**> twice.

Type: NEW <**ENTER**>.

Enter the program above by typing it exactly as shown.

Press <**ENTER**> at the end of each line.

When you have finished, type RUN and press <**ENTER**>.

The computer will print on the screen:

> I LOVE TO LEARN HOW TO PROGRAM.
>
> MY STUDENTS LOVE PROGRAMMING, TOO.

Examine the program presented. Each line began with a line number. The first number was 10; the second was 20, followed by 30. The line numbers tell the computer the order to follow as instructions are given. The computer will start with the lowest number and go to the next highest number.

Each instruction to the computer must begin with a LINE NUMBER. The computer will always list the instructions in order of their line numbers.

In lines 10 and 20, the statement after the number is the word PRINT. PRINT, along with words in quotation marks, tells the computer what to print on the screen. PRINT is a statement in BASIC. Statements tell the computer what to do.

Line 30 is an END statement. END tells the computer that the program has ended.

Finally, you typed in the command RUN. RUN is a system command that tells the computer to process the set of statements in the program you have just entered.

SUMMARY OF EVENTS

The statements of the program are:

> 10 PRINT "I LOVE TO LEARN HOW TO PROGRAM."
> 20 PRINT "MY STUDENTS LOVE PROGRAMMING, TOO."
> 30 END

The command to process the progam is:

> RUN

The OUTPUT of the program is:

> I LOVE TO LEARN HOW TO PROGRAM.
> MY STUDENTS LOVE PROGRAMMING, TOO.

Notice that RUN does not have a line number. The numbered parts of the program instruct the computer what to do. RUN is a system command that tells the computer to act immediately on the statements of the program.

USING PUNCTUATION MARKS: THE COMMA AND SEMICOLON

Try these programs:

```
10 PRINT 5 + 6
20 PRINT 28 / 4
30 PRINT 56 * 3
40 END
```

Now try

```
10 PRINT 5 + 6,
20 PRINT 28 / 4,
30 PRINT 56 * 3,
40 END
RUN
```

YOU HAVE iT!

Notice that the first program printed the answers in a vertical column, and the second program printed them horizontally. The comma (,) in a program will instruct the computer to print the program output separated into zones.

The output from line 10 was printed in the first zone, the output from line 20 was printed in the second zone, and the output from line 30 was printed in the third zone. A PRINT statement with commas is often used to print output in columns.

Using semicolons in a program tells the computer to do something different. A comma is used to print output in different zones. A semicolon can be used to make the printed output run together horizontally on the same line.

Try this program:

```
10 PRINT "TEACHER", "STUDENTS", "AIDES"
20 PRINT "TEACHER"; "STUDENTS"; "AIDES"
30 END
RUN
```

The output is:

HURRAY!

```
TEACHER    STUDENTS    AIDES
TEACHERSTUDENTSAIDES
```

If you want a space between the words TEACHER, STUDENTS, and AIDES, then there must be a space inserted between the last letter of the word and the quotation marks: "TEACHER "; "STUDENTS "; "AIDES "

Now try adding a semicolon (;) after the last word "AIDES" in line 10. Just retype line 10 and put a semicolon at the end ("AIDES";). RUN the program. What happens?

CORRECTING ERRORS

Now let us consider what to do if you make an error in typing and you want to retype an instruction. No problem! If you have made an error in typing a line either in spelling or leaving out a special instruction, just retype the line until you type it correctly. In the beginning while learning to program, you may find yourself retyping the same line over and over again until you have typed it error (or bug) free. One nice feature about entering programs is that you can retype a line until it is entered correctly without retyping the whole program.

However, if you simply misspelled a word, you can quickly correct it before pressing <**ENTER**> by pressing your left-arrow key to return to your error and retyping the character. When you use your left-arrow key, it automatically erases the text on the screen.

Typing a line is like thinking about something. Pressing <**ENTER**> is like saying it. Using <**ENTER**> is a commitment. Proofread the line you just typed before committing yourself by pressing <**ENTER**> and you will save yourself a lot of work.

Type the following program that has an error in line 20 and a change of instruction. Begin by typing: NEW <**ENTER**>.

```
10 PRINT "THERE IS NO ERROR IN THIS LINE."
20 PRINT THERE IS AN ERROR IN THIS LINE."
30 END
20 PRINT "THERE IS NO BUG IN THIS LINE."
```

There are other ways to correct errors besides retyping lines. When you become more familiar with programming, you may want to consult your owner's manual for editing procedures.

USING THE "LIST" COMMAND

Notice that there is an error in line 20 in the above program. It was retyped correctly again at the end of the program without typing the RUN command. When you type the command, LIST, you will see that the computer has automatically replaced the old line 20 with the new line 20. And, if you then type RUN, it will run the correct program.

Suppose you want to add a line 15 to the above program. No problem! Just type the line below after line 20 or in any other place, and then type: LIST.

```
15 PRINT "THIS IS BUGLESS"
```

The program listing will show you what is stored in the computer's memory with replaced and inserted lines in the number order given.

ERASING THE MEMORY AND USING "NEW" AND "CLS"

To erase any program from a computer's memory, type in the word NEW. The word NEW is a system command that tells the computer to clear its memory and make room for a new program.

Often the NEW command is followed by the first numbered line with CLS. CLS is another instruction that will clear your screen. When in doubt about clearing the screen, try typing CLS. However, CLS will not clear the memory, only the screen. Make sure you know the difference between NEW and CLS.

USING THE "FOR" and "NEXT" STATEMENTS

Two new statements, FOR and NEXT, always appear as a pair in a program. FOR/NEXT statements instruct the computer to make a loop in the program. Every time there is a FOR there must be a NEXT. FOR/NEXT can be used as a shortcut to produce more output. Enter this program into your computer.

```
NEW
100 CLS
110 FOR R = 1 TO 5
120 PRINT " + + + + + + + + + + "
130 NEXT R
999 END
RUN
```

The output is:

```
+ + + + + + + + + +
+ + + + + + + + + +
+ + + + + + + + + +
+ + + + + + + + + +
+ + + + + + + + + +
```

The two statements, FOR and NEXT, define a loop within a program. A loop permits the processing of data within the program in a repetitive way. The loop is executed over and over again until the given number of repetitions is reached. In the above program, the FOR/NEXT loop will be executed five times. The output is five lines of + + + + + + + + + +.

Notice the letter R in the program. R is called a variable because it represents various numbers while the program is being executed. The first time through the loop, R is 1. The second time R is 2 and so on until the last time, R is 5. The letter R is chosen arbitrarily. It could just as well have been B, G, T, or any other letter.

NEW informed the computer that new information was being put into the memory and told it to erase everything old in the memory. 100 CLS cleared the screen. Line 110 told the computer that the loop was to be executed five times. This was written as "FOR R = 1 TO 5".

Line 120 told the computer to print a + + + + + + + + + + pattern.

Line 130 told the computer to return to the second line and to continue with the loop. The program will return to line 110 until all five lines of the + + + + + + + + + + pattern are printed.

For the fun of it, try:

```
NEW
100 CLS
110 FOR N = 2 TO 48 STEP 2
120 PRINT N,
130 NEXT N
140 END
RUN
```

Retype line 120 as   120 PRINT N,   and RUN again.
Retype line 120 as   120 PRINT N; ",";   and RUN again.
                      WASN'T THAT FUN!

Now try writing your own simple program using NEW, PRINT, FOR/ NEXT, END, and RUN. Also include the use of punctuation marks such as the quotation mark ("), comma (,), and semicolon (;).

USING THE "INPUT" AND "GOTO" STATEMENTS/ USING "$" STRINGS

INPUT is a statement that allows you to enter data using the keyboard while a program is running. GOTO causes the computer to branch to a different section of the program.

Examine this program.

```
NEW
5 CLS
10 PRINT "WHAT IS YOUR NAME?"
20 INPUT N$
30 PRINT
40 PRINT "HELLO" ;N$; "GLAD TO MEET YOU."
50 END
RUN
```

This program tells the computer to ask for your name. In line 20 INPUT along with N$ tells the computer that you are going to type in a word and your response should remain in the memory under the code of "N$". "$" (read *string*) is a symbol for a string of alphanumeric (alphabetic or numeric) characters. Every time PRINT N$ appears in the program the computer will print your name.

Line 30 in the program above contains PRINT all by itself. This instructs the computer to skip a line (or double space) when printing lines on the screen. Notice that in line 40 there is a new use of the semicolon. It permits the two messages in quotes and the N$ in between them to appear as one line on the screen.

Computers can store words, groups of words, and numbers when they are instructed to do so. The symbol "$" indicates that an alphanumeric response will be typed into the computer. Numbers can be stored as strings, too. They will be treated as "words," and you will not be able to do arithmetic with them.

For the fun of it, try this simple program on your computer.

TRY THIS.
IT'S FUN!

```
NEW
10 CLS
20 INPUT "WHAT IS YOUR NAME?" ;N$
30 PRINT N$;
40 GOTO 30
RUN
```

Notice that there is no END to this program. The GOTO statement will cause it to go on until you stop it. Programmers call this an infinite loop. When you are tired of this program, press <**BREAK**>. Pressing <**BREAK**> lets you break into a program that doesn't end by itself. Now type NEW and go on to the next program.

GOTO is another statement that can make a loop in a program.

INPUT is a statement that asks for information from the user.

Type: NEW. The command NEW will clear the memory and the screen. The command CLS will clear the screen only.

Remember: Before entering any program always type: NEW.

The next program will teach you how to program your computer so it will respond to an answer. REM represents REMARK. This is a statement used to remind the programmer what the program does. It will not be printed on the screen. Often a program will be all worked out and bug free, but you may not know what it does. REM is a way of documenting (explaining) a program. The computer ignores a line that begins with REM.

Enter this program:

Do this Now.

```
NEW
10 CLS
20 REM THIS PROGRAM ASKS THE
30 REM USER FOR TWO NUMBERS
40 REM AND THEN PRINTS OUT
50 REM THE SUM, DIFFERENCE,
```

```
60 REM PRODUCT, AND QUOTIENT
70 REM OF THE NUMBERS
100 PRINT "GIVE ME TWO NUMBERS."
110 INPUT A,B
120 PRINT A + B
130 PRINT A − B
140 PRINT A * B
150 PRINT A/B
160 PRINT
170 GOTO 100
RUN
```

Notice that the INPUT statement, line 110, required that you respond by typing in two numbers.

USING "IF/THEN" STATEMENTS

An IF/THEN statement tells the computer that a decision must be made. After a choice is made, a statement tells the computer how to proceed.
Read this program.

```
10 PRINT "DO YOU WANT APPLES OR BANANAS?"
20 INPUT A$
30 IF A$ = "APPLES" THEN PRINT "APPLES ARE RED."
40 IF A$ = "BANANAS" THEN PRINT "BANANAS ARE YELLOW."
50 END
```

Examine the program below and try it. It has many "$" statements asking the computer to remember responses given to it. The computer is programmed to respond to the information given. Try entering this one and running it.

```
NEW
5 CLS
10 PRINT "I AM YOUR FRIENDLY ADVISOR."
15 INPUT "WHAT IS YOUR NAME?" ;N$
20 PRINT "HELLO, " ;N$;", I AM VERY HAPPY TO MEET YOU."
30 PRINT "TELL ME, " ;N$;", HAVE YOU EVER SOUGHT ADVICE?"
31 INPUT A$
40 PRINT "THAT IS VERY INTERESTING, " ;N$;"."
50 PRINT "HOW ARE YOU FEELING TODAY?"
51 INPUT F$
60 PRINT "I WOULD BE SURPRISED IF YOU NEVER FELT"
70 PRINT F$; "."
80 INPUT "HOW OLD ARE YOU?";A
```

```
90 IF A<30 THEN 150
100 IF A<60 THEN 130
110 PRINT "THE GOLDEN YEARS ARE MARVELOUS."
120 GOTO 160
130 PRINT "EXERCISE AND GOOD FOOD WILL KEEP YOU HEALTHY."
140 GOTO 160
150 PRINT "YOUTH HAS SPUNK. KEEP SMILING!"
160 PRINT "GOOD-BYE NOW, ";N$
999 END
RUN
```

The program above has many INPUT, PRINT, and GOTO statements. It also makes use of the IF/THEN statements. These two terms are always used together to instruct the computer to make decisions. IF a person responds one way, THEN the computer will go to a designated line number or follow an instruction embedded in the THEN portion of the IF/THEN statement.

Now try writing your own simple program using INPUT, GOTO, IF/THEN, and "$".

When you have worked through these simple programs, you will be familiar with some of the terminology, statements, and instructions used in BASIC programming.

USING "LET" STATEMENTS

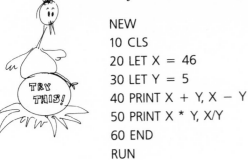

Now try some of these programs using LET.

```
NEW
10 CLS
20 LET X = 46
30 LET Y = 5
40 PRINT X + Y, X - Y
50 PRINT X * Y, X/Y
60 END
RUN
```

The output is:

```
  51      41
 230       9.2
```

```
NEW
10 CLS
20 LET S = 4
30 PRINT S
```

```
40 LET S = S + 8
50 GOTO 30
60 END
RUN
```

YOU HAVE IT!

This program will go on printing numbers because it contains an infinite loop. The computer will automatically stop when the number becomes so large that the computer cannot handle it anymore.

LET can be omitted from a statement, but the computer will act as if it were still there. In the program below, LET is understood in lines 20 through 70.

```
NEW
10 CLS
20 P$ = "GOOD"
30 S$ = "AND"
40 T$ = "JUICY"
50 M$ = "ORANGES"
60 O = 5
70 R$ = "CENTS"
80 PRINT P$,S$,T$,M$,O,R$
90 END
RUN
```

The output is:

GOOD	AND	JUICY	ORANGES
5	CENTS		

DON'T TRY TO DO TOO MUCH AT ONCE!

"READ/DATA" STATEMENTS

In BASIC you now know that the statement LET will assign information to a storage area, and INPUT is a way of asking for information. Both statements store information so that it can be retrieved and used within a program. Another way this can be done is by using the READ/DATA statements.

Study this program:

```
10 READ N
20 IF N = 0 THEN 60
30 PRINT N
40 GOTO 10
50 DATA 2,5,4,8,4,0
60 END
```

READ THIS CAREFULLY!

Line number 10 begins with READ. READ tells the computer to go to the DATA line. If a READ statement appears in a program, then the program must contain at least one DATA statement (line). Some programs contain more than one data line. It doesn't matter where the DATA line is located in the program; the READ statement will find it. The DATA line could come first, in the middle, or at the end of the program. Don't worry; the computer will locate it.

In the above program, line number 10 tells the computer to find the DATA line. It locates the first number in line 50, which is 2. Then the program tells the computer to print 2. Line 40 tells the computer to return to line 10.

The READ statement returns to the data line and locates the next number, which is 5. It prints 5. The program ends when the computer reads 0. Zero is called "dummy" data. It tells the computer when to stop.

If you are working with words, the computer needs to be told what the dummy word is in order to end the program. Remember that when alphabetical characters or a long string of numbers is used, the $ symbol is used to tell the computer that a string is in storage. Line 30 in the program below checks A$ to see if it is equal to the dummy data. That data is a special word designated by you. In the program below, it is "STOP". Try these programs using **READ/DATA** and $ statements.

```
NEW
10 CLS
20 READ A$
30 IF A$ = "STOP" THEN 70
40 PRINT A$
50 GOTO 20
60 DATA LIONS,TIGERS,ELEPHANTS,BEARS,STOP
70 END
```

The output is:

```
LIONS
TIGERS
ELEPHANTS
BEARS
```

Did you notice that the words in line 60 did not have quotation marks around them? When strings are used in a DATA line they do not need quotation marks around them unless they contain punctuation marks.

This summary of **BASIC** words will help you when entering the programs in this book. Try to remember some of the meanings, and, as you enter the programs in the text, these words should guide you while you are copying a program.

INSTRUCTIONAL STEPS FOR COPYING PROGRAMS

STEP 1

Select a program from either Chapter 7 (Reading/Language Arts) or Chapter 8 (Mathematics/Science). Choose a short, easy program with which to begin.

STEP 2

Turn on your machine. Press the orange <**RESET**> button. The red light on the disk drive will turn off automatically.

STEP 3

Insert your initialized disk carefully into the disk drive. Shut the door. Press <**RESET**>. Type in the date. Press <**ENTER**> when asked for the time.

STEP 4

At TRSDOS Ready, type BASIC and press <**ENTER**>. Press <**ENTER**> twice to skip the questions on memory and files.

STEP 5

Select a program and copy it line by line. Be sure you type *exactly* what is printed on the page. Remember, if you make a mistake, either use your left-arrow key to retype a character or press <**ENTER**> and retype the whole line again. LIST will show any corrected line in sequence. It would be wise to select simpler short programs at first before attempting to enter longer ones.

STEP 6

At the end of the program, after all the lines have been entered, type: SAVE "(Name of program)" and press <**ENTER**>.

After the word SAVE insert the name of the program between quotation marks. A suggested method for naming a program is to use the numbers in the Table of Contents. For example:

SAVE "MATH1"

MATH1 would be associated with the title listed in the Table of Contents. You may wish to invent your own name for saving the programs. For example, SAVE "ALPHABET". Make sure it has eight or fewer characters and starts with a letter. Remember not to use punctuation marks in the name.

Once you type SAVE "(Name of program)" and press <**ENTER**>, the computer will begin to store your program on the disk. You will hear a whirring sound, and the red light will come on while the computer is saving the program on the disk.

STEP 7

Check to see if you have saved the program.
Type: LOAD "(Name of program)" press <**ENTER**>.
The computer should load the program from the disk into memory. If the message "FILE NOT FOUND" appears on the screen, there is no problem! Your program is still in memory. Repeat STEP 6. Once you are certain the program is SAVED, RUN the program to see how it works.

STEP 8

If you are sure of the procedure for copying and storing programs on a disk, continue typing other programs. Begin each program by typing NEW to erase the old program from memory. Type: NEW press <**ENTER**>.

STEP 9

Select another program to copy. Repeat STEPS 5 through 9.

USING <**SHIFT**> @

Frequently, when running a program that you have just typed, you will get an error message because of a typing mistake. To find the mistake, you need to look at the lines of the program. Type: LIST <**ENTER**>. Your program listing may be too long to fit on the screen and may scroll off the screen before you can read it.
Using <**SHIFT**> @ will control the scrolling. Hold down the <**SHIFT**> key and press @. The scrolling will stop so you can read the lines of your program. To start scrolling again press <**SHIFT**> @.
A little practice will make you proficient in this technique. You will be able to find the line that has the error in it so you can retype it correctly.
Another way to list program lines is to list one line (Type: LIST [line number] <**ENTER**>) and then to use the up-arrow or down-arrow. This will list lines that precede or follow the given line, one at a time.

HELPFUL HINTS

IF YOU WANT TO CHANGE DATA IN A SAVED PROGRAM

1. Insert your disk.
2. Type DIR to see the directory if you don't remember the program name.
3. Type LOAD "(Name of program)" <**ENTER**>.
4. Type LIST to display the program lines. If your program is long, type LIST (number of line) to list only the line you want to change. For example, LIST 240.

5. To delete a line, simply type the line number and press <**ENTER**>.

6. Retype the lines you wish to change.

7. Type LIST again to check your new line.

8. While the disk is in the disk drive, type SAVE "(Name of program)". The new program will replace the old one.

Note: Your owner's manual contains the editing procedures for correcting lines in a program without retyping them. You may wish to learn these procedures when you become more proficient. Editing will save you time and typing.

IF ERRORS OCCUR WHILE COPYING PROGRAMS

1. Check to be sure that the disk is in the drive properly.

2. Check your screen by typing LIST to make sure you did not erase the program accidentally from memory. If that is the situation you will need to retype it.

3. At TRSDOS Ready, type DIR to see if you recorded it on the disk and it is listed in the directory. If not, repeat STEPS 4 through 7 in the section "Instructional Steps for Copying Programs."

4. List each line to see if there are any typing errors.

WHAT TO DO IF YOUR PROGRAM DOES NOT RUN AFTER TYPING

If your program does not work after you have typed it carefully, check for the following errors that may have been made:

1. Check every line carefully to be sure you typed it *exactly* as shown on the program.

2. Check to make sure you did not type a ";" for a ":".

3. If you received an error message in a line that has a READ statement, the error is probably in your DATA lines. Check your DATA lines. Some computers will read the DATA lines incorrectly if you inadvertently hit the space bar before or after the comma separating the DATA items.

   INCORRECT: 210 DATA house, car, mouse , flower , bug

   CORRECT: 210 DATA house,car,mouse,flower,bug

4. Check your zeros and Os. Make sure you did not substitute a zero (0) for the letter O.

5. Check your number one (1) and letter "l". Make sure you did not substitute the alphabetical character "l" for the number one (1).

6. Check your line numbers. Make sure you did not type the alphabetical character O for a zero (0).

7. If you received an error message in a specific line, just type LIST (and the line number). Check it carefully against the program line. Make sure every parenthesis, comma, semicolon, and colon is properly entered in the line. If you find the error, retype the line and LIST the program again.

   Type: LIST (line number) <**ENTER**>.
   Type: Retype the line again to correct the error <**ENTER**>.
   Type: LIST <**ENTER**>.
   Type: RUN <**ENTER**>.

A WARNING

If you live in an area where there are frequent thunderstorms, you should unplug our system when it is not in use. A power surge caused by lightning might damage your system severely. Also, *do not use the system during a thunderstorm.*

STOPPING A PROGRAM

If you want to stop a program, try the following three steps in the order they are presented.

1. Press <**BREAK**>. (This stops the program run. The program will still be in the memory.)
2. Press the orange <**RESET**> button. (This stops the program and ERASES the memory.)
3. RUN THE PROGRAM TO CONCLUSION. (Some programs will not allow you out until they are completed.)

NO CURSOR ON THE SCREEN

1. Is the monitor turned on?
2. Check the brightness and contrast controls.
3. Did you turn the computer on and off and on again in succession too fast? Turn it on again and wait for a few moments.
4. Is everything plugged into a wall outlet?
5. Press orange <**RESET**>.

LIGHT WON'T GO OFF ON THE DISK DRIVE

1. Make sure the disk drive door is closed.
2. Press the orange <**RESET**> button. Wait.
3. If the light is still on, press the orange <**RESET**> button again.

DISK DRIVE IS RATTLING

1. The disk may not be set right in the disk drive. Open the door slowly and carefully insert it again.
2. The disk may be in the wrong way. Check to make sure the oval slot enters the drive first. The label should be at the top between your fingers when you are inserting it.
3. The disk may be formatted for a different system.

SYNTAX ERROR MESSAGE

1. Did you inadvertently mix control characters with command characters? Check.
2. Did you misspell any statement words such as PRINT or INPUT?
3. Did you leave out punctuation marks?
4. Did you type *exactly* what is shown on the program line?
5. Parentheses and quotation marks always come in pairs in a program line. Check your pairs.
6. Check your owner's manual for the meaning of error messages.

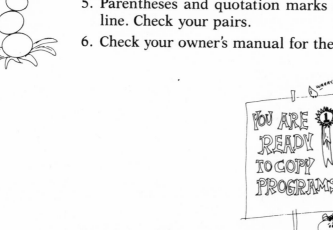

chapter 7

25 PROGRAMS FOR READING AND LANGUAGE ARTS ON THE TRS-80™

In this chapter you will find twenty-five microcomputer programs for the TRS-80™ III/IV. These programs will serve two purposes.

1. They are models for you to use as you refine your programming skills.
2. They are small programs to assist you in teaching reading and language arts in your classroom.

We recommend that the program models be typed in the order in which they are presented. They have been arranged in order of difficulty of programming techniques. However, if you have special need for an instructional program that appears later on, and are adventurous, you may change the order in which you use the programs. If you are unsure of program statements, refer back to the earlier book section on programming or to earlier programs in the set.

To assist you, each program is accompanied by a cover sheet that contains the following information (where applicable).

TITLE: A name for the program that describes the program.

SUGGESTED FILE NAME: As the TRS-80™ III/IV only accepts disk file names of eight characters or less, the program title usually cannot be used. You may use any program title or file name you wish.

SUGGESTED GRADE RANGE: These are the grade levels at which most students will perform satisfactorily in the program and at which most teachers teach these skills. You will use some programs with students at an earlier grade than suggested, or conversely, use some programs with older students later on as remedial programs. You should be the final judge of the appropriate programs to use with your students.

DESCRIPTION OF THE PROGRAM: This describes the program from an instructional point of view and provides some insights into its use.

NEW PROGRAMMING STATEMENTS: Any new programming statements that have not already been explained in earlier sections of the book are explained as they are introduced.

EXPLANATION OF DATA LINES: Many variables are used in the programs. To determine which variable is meant at any given point in a program execution, the variable is given a unique "name." This explanation assists you in understanding the meaning and function of each variable used in a program.

PROGRAMMING LOGIC: This section explains the logic used in the program design by the author of the program and refers to specific line numbers in the program for unusual programming techniques.

HOW TO CHANGE THE DATA: In reading and language arts programs, many skills are taught at a large number of grades (vocabulary extension, for example). The difference is in the readability or syntactical complexity of the material. A number of suggestions for changing the data or content of the programs have been made to make these programs useful to teachers at a wide range of grade levels. These programs have a number of instructional characteristics to assist you in teaching.

1. Language is presented with appropriate upper/lower case use to reinforce your classroom instruction.
2. Students are always supplied with the correct answer before being allowed to proceed. In some cases the student is allowed three trials to arrive at the correct answer before help is given.
3. These programs are not suitable for initial instruction. They are drill and practice, or guided practice activities.
4. Some of the programs are interactive, in that the computer and the student appear to be engaged interactively in language production. As you know, motivational experiences improve students' language production.
5. Some programs provide opportunities for you to use them in conjunction with later group activities. Most microcomputer programs are ineffective if they are isolated from the rest of the instruction provided in your classroom.
6. In most cases, students pace themselves through the programs to make allowances for a variety of reading and working speeds.

7. In many programs, students type in a response. Although this may take students with poor keyboard skills longer to complete the program, the reinforcement for serial order of letters and careful spelling compensates for the extra time involved.

8. None of these programs is suitable for testing or assessment of mastery of a skill. They are designed to assist in the intermediate stage of acquiring a skill.

TWO VERY IMPORTANT REMINDERS:

1. A computer line begins with the line number and ends with the last word or number before the next numbered line. *Do not press* <**ENTER**> *until you have typed the entire line.* When your cursor approaches the right side of the screen, keep typing. Screen wraparound will automaticallly take care of moving the cursor down the screen.

2. MODEL IV USER: You must use a Model III TRSDOS disk (Cat. #26-0312) available from Radio Shack.

1. FLASH CARDS FOR SIGHT WORDS

SUGGESTED FILE NAME: FLASH

SUGGESTED GRADE RANGE: 1–8

DESCRIPTION OF THE PROGRAM: This program provides practice in instantaneous recognition of sight words by flashing words on the screen for students to read aloud in pairs.

NEW PROGRAMMING STATEMENTS:

```
20 CLEAR 1000
```

Clears room in the computer's memory for 1000 characters, that is 1000 letters, spaces, or punctuation marks.

```
30 PRINT @276, "..."
```

Prints the material between quotes starting at location 276 on the screen. A Video Display Worksheet is in the Appendix for your use.

```
40 PRINT TAB (20) "..."
```

Prints the material between quotes starting at space 20 in from the left-hand side of the screen. It functions like a typewriter tab; it does not move down the lines as PRINT @ does.

   50 FOR I = 1 to 1000 :NEXT I

This loop performs no work. It delays the action on the screen for approximately three seconds to make the screen display more comfortable for students.

   60 RESTORE

Restores all the words in the DATA statements to use so the program can be run more than once.

   140 PRINT @345, CHR$(200)

Prints eight blank spaces; CHR$ is read as character string. A Video Display Worksheet is in the Appendix for your use.

   190 Y$ = LEFT$ (Y$,1)

The computer will look at the first letter only of string Y$ starting at the left. This allows all variations of yes and no to be accepted, e.g.: Yes, YES, Y, y, yes.

   200 IF . . . . OR . . . . THEN . . . . ELSE

A logic statement that tells the program to go to the line following THEN if the information following IF or the information following OR is correct. If neither is correct (ELSE), the program goes to the line that follows ELSE.

EXPLANATION OF DATA LINES: W$ – sight words displayed on screen

PROGRAMMING LOGIC: The loop in lines 100-150 presents one sight word at a time. Line 130 determines the speed at which words are presented by delaying 1 1/2 seconds between each word. Line 100 tells how many words will be presented (12).

HOW TO CHANGE THE DATA:
1. Change the words in lines 230-260.
2. Change the speed of presentation in line 120; the higher the number (500), the slower the speed.
3. Change the number of words presented in line 100.
4. Change the difficulty of the words used.

```
10 CLS
20 CLEAR 1000
30 PRINT @273, "FLASH CARDS FOR SIGHT WORDS"
40 PRINT TAB(18) "by Gloria Kuchinskas Ed.D."
50 FOR I=1 TO 1000 :NEXT I
51 CLS
52 PRINT @266, "In this program you will have 12 words "
53 PRINT TAB(20) "to try to read aloud."
54 FOR I=1 TO 2000 :NEXT I
60 RESTORE
70 CLS
80 PRINT "Read to me aloud:"
90 FOR I=1 TO 500   :NEXT I
100 FOR W=1 TO 12
110 READ W$
120 PRINT @345, W$
130 FOR I=1 TO 500 :NEXT I
140 PRINT @345, CHR$(200)
150 NEXT W
160 PRINT
170 PRINT TAB(8) "Do you want to try the list again (Y/N) ";
180 INPUT Y$
190 Y$=LEFT$(Y$,1)
200 IF Y$="Y" OR Y$="y" THEN 60    ELSE 210
210 IF Y$="N" OR Y$="n" THEN 220    ELSE 180
220 END
230 DATA baby,doll,girl
240 DATA feather,leaves,dog
250 DATA head,heart,kitten
260 DATA well,house,boy
```

2. ALPHABETIZING

SUGGESTED FILE NAME: ALPHABET

SUGGESTED GRADE RANGE: 2–8

DESCRIPTION OF THE PROGRAM: This program will alphabetize any list of twenty words or less and provide either a screen display or a printed copy. This allows teachers and students to alphabetize lists automatically as a utility or allows students to check their own work after they have alphabetized a list independently.

NEW PROGRAMMING STATEMENTS:

    30 DIM N(20),W$(20)

This tells the program the dimensions (DIM) of the two variables, N and W$; e.g., there will be up to twenty words. Without a DIM statement, only eleven will be accepted.

130 LINEINPUT W$(I)

accepts any input up to 256 characters including commas.

380 LPRINT W$(I)

tells the program to print this on the printer.

EXPLANATION OF DATA LINES: N   – number of words to be typed in

W$ – words typed in

PROGRAMMING LOGIC: Lines 180-260 form two loops, one inside the other. The I loop (lines 180-260) looks at each word in the list. The J loop (lines 190-250) looks at each pair of words. Line 220 decides if Y$ (the second word in the pair) is higher in the alphabet (>) than X$ (the first word in the pair). If the order of the pair of words is correct, the program goes to line 250. If the order is incorrect, the program reverses the order (lines 230-240). If the first letter of Y$ is the same as the first letter of X$ (=), the program looks at the second letter (line 250) and so on.

HOW TO CHANGE THE DATA: 1. Change the number of words in lines 30 and 80.

2. Change the words typed in.

3. Type in phrases, names, addresses, etc. instead of words.

```
10 CLS
20 CLEAR 500
30 DIM N(20),W$(20)
40 PRINT a278, "ALPHABETIZING"
50 PRINT TAB(16) "by Gloria Kuchinskas Ed.D."
60 FOR I=1 TO 1000 :NEXT I
70 CLS
80 PRINT TAB(5) "How many words to you want to alphabetize (1-
20) ";
90 INPUT N
100 PRINT :PRINT "Type one word at a time."
110 PRINT "Press ENTER after each word."
120 FOR I=1 TO N
130 LINEINPUT W$(I)
140 NEXT I
150 CLS
160 PRINT TAB(10)"Please wait."
170 PRINT TAB(10) "I'm alphabetizing your list:"
180 FOR I=1 TO N-1
190    FOR J=1 TO N-1
200       X$=W$(J)
210       Y$=W$(J+1)
220       IF Y$>=X$ THEN 250
230       W$(J)=Y$
```

```
240        W$(J+1)=X$
250    NEXT J
260 NEXT I
270 PRINT TAB(10) "Do you want a printed copy (Y/N) ";
280 INPUT Y$
290 Y$=LEFT$(Y$,1)
300 IF Y$="N" OR Y$="n" THEN 360
310 IF Y$="Y" OR Y$="y" THEN 320  ELSE 280
320 PRINT TAB(10)"Is your printer ready (Y/N) ";
330 INPUT YY$
340 YY$=LEFT$(YY$,1)
350 IF YY$="Y" OR YY$="y" THEN 360  ELSE 330
360 FOR I=1 TO N
370 IF Y$="Y" OR Y$="y" THEN 380  ELSE 390
380 LPRINT W$(I)
390 PRINT TAB(20) W$(I)
400 FOR Q=1 TO 100 :NEXT Q
410 NEXT I
420 PRINT :PRINT "Do you want to alphabetize another list (Y/N
) ";
430 INPUT YZ$ :YZ$=LEFT$(YZ$,1)
440 IF YZ$="Y" OR YZ$="y" THEN CLEAR :GOTO 70
450 IF YZ$="N" OR YZ$="n" THEN 460 ELSE 430
460 CLS :PRINT @346, "GOOD-BY !!!" :END
```

3. WRITING A STORY

SUGGESTED FILE NAME: STORY

SUGGESTED GRADE RANGE: 3–8

DESCRIPTION OF THE PROGRAM: This program provides a story starter to motivate students for production writing. The program does not correct student errors or value the end product. Instead, the program instructs students to copy their stories for group work in the classroom at the teacher's convenience.

EXPLANATION OF DATA LINES: A\$ – the story starter

T\$ – the story title

B\$ – the first response typed in by the student

C\$, D\$ – the rest of the responses typed in

PROGRAMMING LOGIC: No new structures

HOW TO CHANGE THE DATA: 1. Change the story starters (lines 450-540).

2. Change the number of story starters (line 70).

3. Raise the grade level of the story starters.

```
10 CLS : POKE 16409,0
20 CLEAR 2000
30 PRINT @280, "WRITING A STORY"
40 PRINT TAB(19) "by Gloria Kuchinskas Ed.D."
50 FOR I=1 TO 1000 :NEXT I
60 CLS
70 FOR I=1 TO 10
80 READ A$,T$
90 PRINT TAB(10) "Help me write a story."
100 PRINT TAB(10) "I will start the story."
110 PRINT
120 PRINT A$
130 PRINT
140 PRINT "Type what you think happened next."
150 LINEINPUT B$
160 CLS
170 PRINT A$
180 PRINT B$
190 PRINT
200 PRINT "What happened after that ?"
210 LINEINPUT C$
220 CLS
230 PRINT A$
240 PRINT B$
250 PRINT C$
260 PRINT
270 PRINT "Finish the story."
280 LINEINPUT D$
290 CLS
300 PRINT TAB(10) T$
310 PRINT
320 PRINT A$
330 PRINT B$
340 PRINT C$
350 PRINT D$
360 PRINT
370 PRINT "Copy your story on paper and show it to your teache
r later."
380 PRINT "Do you want to write another story (Y/N) ";
390 INPUT Y$
400 Y$=LEFT$(Y$,1)
410 IF Y$="N" OR Y$="n" THEN 440   ELSE 420
420 IF Y$="Y" OR Y$="y" THEN 430 ELSE 390
430 CLS :NEXT I
440 CLS :PRINT @346, "GOOD-BY !!!" : POKE 16409,1 : END
450 DATA "Johnny lost his homework.","The Lost Homework"
460 DATA "The little bird flew in the window.","The Bird In Th
e House"
470 DATA "Jane won the big race yesterday.","Jane's Big race"
480 DATA "Tom caught his first fish yesterday.","Tom's Fish"
490 DATA "Sue had a birthday yesterday.","Sue's Birthday"
500 DATA "It rained all day yesterday.","A Rainy day"
510 DATA "Mother gave Mary a kitten.","The Kitten"
520 DATA "Bill's dog did a trick for us.","A Smart Dog"
530 DATA "We went to the circus yesterday.","The Circus"
540 DATA "Our class took a train ride.","The Train Ride"
```

4. PARTS OF SPEECH

SUGGESTED FILE NAME: PARTS

SUGGESTED GRADE RANGE: 3–8

DESCRIPTION OF THE PROGRAM: This program provides guided practice in identifying parts of speech—nouns, pronouns, adjectives, adverbs, and verbs. The parts of speech are presented in a sentence context.

NEW PROGRAMMING STATEMENTS:

    210 X = INSTR(1,ST$,WD$)

This line tells the computer where to underline a word in the sentence. X is equal to the length of the sentence (ST$) from the first letter in the sentence to the first letter in the word (WD$).

    220 PRINT @256, + X − 1, ...

256 is the space for the first letter in the sentence. X is the length of the sentence including the first letter in the word to be underlined. −1 starts the underlining at the first letter of the word.

    220 . . . . STRING$(LEN(WD$),131)

A string of bars, CHR$(131), is printed. The length of the string is equal to the LENgth of the word (WD$).

    400 IK$ = INKEY$ . . . .

Any response is acceptable.

    400 . . . . . : IF K$ = "" THEN 400 ELSE RETURN

If no answer is given, wait. When an answer is given, RETURN to the program.

EXPLANATION OF DATA LINES:

ST$	–	sentence
WD$	–	the word or words to be underlined
PT$	–	the part of speech
X	–	the place to start underlining
W	–	the error counter
RP$	–	the correct response
AS$	–	the student's answer

PROGRAMMING LOGIC: Lines 160-360 present each sentence in turn.

HOW TO CHANGE THE DATA:
1. Change the sentences in lines 410-600.
2. Change the difficulty of the sentences.
3. Change the parts of speech asked for.
4. Add additional parts of speech (article, preposition, conjunction).

```
10 CLEAR 1000
20 CLS
30 PRINT @87, "PARTS OF SPEECH"
40 PRINT TAB(19)"by GLORIA KUCHINSKAS Ed.D."
50 PRINT :PRINT TAB(9)"In this program, you will practice iden
tifying"
60 PRINT TAB(9) "parts of speech. You will have 20 sentences"
70 PRINT TAB(9) "to practice.      Type: N for noun"
80 PRINT TAB(20) "            P for pronoun"
90 PRINT TAB(20) "            A for adjective"
100 PRINT TAB(20) "            AD for adverb"
110 PRINT TAB(20) "             V for verb"
120 GOSUB 390
130 CLS
140 PRINT TAB(5) "(N)oun    (P)ronoun    (A)djective    (AD)verb
   (V)erb"
150 PRINT STRING$(63,"*")
160 FOR I=1 TO 10
170 W=0
180 READ ST$,WD$,PT$,RP$
190 POKE 16916,2
200 PRINT @192, ST$
210 X=INSTR(1,ST$,WD$)
220 PRINT @256+X-1, STRING$(LEN(WD$),131)
230 PRINT @394, "What part of speech is the underlined word(s)
   ?"
240 POKE 16409,1
250 PRINT CHR$(220); :LINEINPUT AS$
260 IF AS$=RP$ THEN 350   ELSE 270
270 W=W+1 :IF W=2 THEN 310   ELSE 280
280 PRINT :PRINT TAB(10) "Try again."
290 FOR Q=1 TO 500 :NEXT Q
300 PRINT @512, CHR$(31) :GOTO 230
310 PRINT @512, CHR$(31)
320 PRINT TAB(10) "The part of speech is:   ";PT$
330 GOSUB 390
340 PRINT @512, CHR$(31) :GOTO 230
350 PRINT :PRINT TAB(10) "Good for you !"
360 GOSUB 390   :CLS :NEXT I
370 PRINT :PRINT TAB(25) "GOOD-BY !!!"
380 POKE 16916,0 :END
390 PRINT :PRINT TAB(20) "Press any key to go on."
400 IK$=INKEY$ :IF IK$="" THEN 400   ELSE RETURN
410 DATA "Give the books to John and Mary.",books,noun,N
420 DATA "Susan is a good girl.",is,verb,V
```

```
430 DATA "The teacher gave a red pencil to Jill.",red,adjectiv
e,A
440 DATA "The bicycle belongs to you and me.",me,pronoun,P
450 DATA "Mary always does her work carefully.",always,adverb,
AD
460 DATA "Why can't you come out to play with me ?",you,pronou
n,P
470 DATA "The magic show was so exciting.",exciting,adjective,
A
480 DATA "Seashells come in many sizes and colors.",colors,nou
n,N
490 DATA "You can't write with a broken pencil point.","can't"
,verb,V
500 DATA "Susan was very sorry she lost her book.",very,adverb
,AD
510 DATA "Typing is a good skill to know.",to know,verb,V
520 DATA "The dragon breathed fire through his nose.",dragon,n
oun,N
530 DATA "The coach wants her to try out for the team.",her,pr
onoun,P
540 DATA "The water trickled slowly over the dam.",slowly,adve
rb,AD
550 DATA "The volcano shot fiery lava into the air.",fiery,adj
ective,A
560 DATA "A newspaper contains both facts and opinions.",facts
,noun,N
570 DATA "John likes stories about far-away lands.","far-away"
,adjective,A
580 DATA "The store sells shoes for men and women.",sells,verb
,V
590 DATA "Don't throw away that good dress.",away,adverb,AD
600 DATA "Give him a chance to finish his work.",him,pronoun,P
```

5. SYNONYMS

SUGGESTED FILE NAME: SYNONYM

SUGGESTED GRADE RANGE: 3–8

DESCRIPTION OF THE PROGRAM: This program provides practice in one type of word relationship: synonyms. Students are asked to match a given word with a synonym from the Word Bank.

EXPLANATION OF DATA LINES: W$ — the word presented

S$ — its synonym

X$ — the student's answer

HOW TO CHANGE THE DATA: 1. Change the words in the Word Bank in lines 80-90.

2. Change the number of words in lines 120 and 260.

3. Change the words in lines 310-340.

4. Increase the difficulty of the words.

5. Use content area words.

```
10 CLS
20 CLEAR 1000
30 PRINT @282, "SYNONYMS"
40 PRINT TAB(18) "by Gloria Kuchinskas Ed.D."
50 FOR I=1 TO 1000 :NEXT I
51 CLS
52 PRINT @266, "The words:   BIG   and   LARGE    are synonyms."
53 PRINT TAB(15) "They mean the same thing."
54 PRINT :PRINT TAB(15) "In this program, you will try to"
55 PRINT TAB(15) "find 10 sets of synonyms."
56 GOSUB 301
60 CLS:POKE 16409,0
70 PRINT "SYNONYM WORD BANK:"
80 PRINT "    glad       shine     little     pull"
90 PRINT "    odd        run       also       cost
100 PRINT STRING$(63,"*")
110 POKE 16916,5
120 FOR W=1 TO 10
130 READ W$,S$
140 PRINT @404, W$;
150 PRINT @522, "Type a synonym from the word bank."
160 PRINT CHR$(212);
170 LINEINPUT X$
180 IF X$=S$ THEN 210   ELSE 181
181 WR=WR+1
182 IF WR=2 THEN 183 ELSE 190
183 WR=0 :PRINT @394, S$
184 PRINT @448, CHR$(31)
185 FOR I=1 TO 500 :NEXT I
186 GOTO 230
190 PRINT TAB(10) "Try again. Type carefully."
200 GOTO 160
210 PRINT @576, CHR$(31)
220 PRINT @394, X$
230 GOSUB 301
260 IF W=10 THEN 290
270 CLS
280 NEXT W
290 POKE 16916,0
300 CLS :PRINT @346, "GOOD-BY !!!" : POKE 16409,1 : END
301 PRINT @783, "Press any key to go on."
302 A$=INKEY$
303 IF A$="" THEN 302 ELSE RETURN
310 DATA happy,glad,unusual,odd,small,little
320 DATA dash,run,glow,shine,drag,pull
330 DATA too,also,charge,cost,gay,glad
340 DATA strange,odd
```

6. USING CONTEXT CLUES

SUGGESTED FILE NAME: CONTEXT

SUGGESTED GRADE RANGE: 2–8

DESCRIPTION OF THE PROGRAM: This program promotes reading comprehension at the sentence level by requiring students to use the meaning of a sentence starter to determine if the ending makes sense.

NEW PROGRAMMING STATEMENTS:

150 IF...OR ...AND ...THEN ...ELSE

A logic statement that includes IF, OR, and AND, as well as THEN and ELSE. If the information following IF, or the information following OR is true, the program will look at the information following AND. If this information is also true, the program will go to the line after THEN. If the information following IF or OR is not correct, or if the information following AND is not correct, the program will go to the line after ELSE.

EXPLANATION OF DATA LINES: W$ – the sentence ending

                               Y$ – either yes or no, depending upon whether the ending makes sense in the context or not

HOW TO CHANGE THE DATA: 1. Change the sentence starter in line 90.

                                        2. Change the sentence endings in lines 350-370.

                                        3. Increase the difficulty of the vocabulary.

                                        4. Change the number of endings in line 70.

```
10 CLS
20 CLEAR
30 PRINT @275, "USING THE CONTEXT"
40 PRINT TAB(15) "by Gloria Kuchinskas Ed.D."
50 FOR I=1 TO 1000 :NEXT I
51 CLS
52 PRINT @74, "Read these sentences:"
53 PRINT TAB(15) "1. A boy can read."
54 PRINT TAB(15) "2. A cat can read."
55 PRINT :PRINT TAB(10) "Sentence 1 makes sense."
56 PRINT TAB(10) "Sentence 2 does not make sense."
57 PRINT :PRINT TAB(10) "In this program, you will decide if"
58 PRINT TAB(15) "10 words make sense in a sentence."
59 GOSUB 341
```

```
60 CLS
70 FOR W=1 TO 10
80 READ W$,Y$
90 PRINT @330, "A bird can .........";
100 PRINT @478, W$
110 PRINT
120 PRINT TAB(10) "Does this word fit in the sentence (Y/N) "
130 PRINT CHR$(222);
140 INPUT Z$
150 Z$=LEFT$(Z$,1)
160 IF Z$=Y$ OR Z$="y" AND Y$="Y" THEN 220  ELSE 170
170 IF Z$="Y" OR Z$="y" AND Y$="N" THEN 200  ELSE 180
180 IF Z$="N" OR Z$="n" AND Y$="N" THEN 220  ELSE 190
190 IF Z$="N" OR Z$="n" AND Y$="Y" THEN 200  ELSE 140
200 PRINT TAB(20) "Try again."
210 GOTO 130
220 PRINT @448, CHR$(31)
230 PRINT @340, CHR$(203)
240 IF Y$="Y" THEN 250  ELSE 270
250 PRINT @330, "A bird can ";W$;"."
260 GOTO 280
270 PRINT @330, "A bird can not ";W$;"."
280 GOSUB 341
310 IF W=10 THEN 340  ELSE 320
320 CLS
330 NEXT W
340 CLS :PRINT @346, "GOOD-BY !!!" :END
341 PRINT @783, "Press any key to go on."
342 A$=INKEY$
343 IF A$="" THEN 342 ELSE RETURN
350 DATA fly,Y,swim,Y,run,Y,eat,Y
360 DATA read,N,learn,Y,drive,N
370 DATA hop,Y,type,N,sing,Y
```

7. MAKING SENTENCES

SUGGESTED FILE NAME: SENTENCE

SUGGESTED GRADE RANGE: 4–8

DESCRIPTION OF THE PROGRAM: The student types in five nouns, verbs, adjectives, and adverbs to form four sets of dictionaries for the computer. The computer selects one word from each dictionary to form a sentence. The student is asked to judge whether the sentences make sense. Nonsense is often produced as the computer selects by random choice. This program helps students who have difficulty understanding that sentences must make sense when they are read. Students are encouraged to edit sentences and copy them for later use with small groups. This improves sentence writing skills.

EXPLANATION OF DATA LINES: N$ – nouns typed in

                                     V$ – verbs typed in

AJ$ – adjectives typed in

AV$ – adverbs typed in

N – random number from 1-5 for nouns

V – random number from 1-5 for verbs

AJ – random number from 1-5 for adjectives

AV – random number from 1-5 for adverbs

PROGRAMMING LOGIC: Line 420 determines the sentence structure. It also provides for spaces between the words, a period at the end of the sentence, and an "s" on the end of the verb as the nouns are singular. Lines 380-410 tell the program which of the five selections for each word type will be used in the sentence.

HOW TO CHANGE THE DATA:

1. Have students type in plural nouns. To do this, change "singular" to "plural" in line 70 and delete: "s"; from line 420.

2. Change the number of words of each type. To do this, change "five" in lines 70, 150, 220, 290.

3. Have students type in adverbial phrases instead of adverbs to make the program harder; change line 290.

4. Omit lines 280-340, 410 and ;AV$(AV) in line 420 to eliminate the adverbs and make the program easier.

```
10 CLS
20 CLEAR 1000
30 PRINT @278, "MAKING SENTENCES"
40 PRINT TAB(17) "by Gloria Kuchinskas Ed.D."
50 FOR I=1 TO 1000 :NEXT I
51 CLS
52 PRINT @74, "In this program, the computer will make sentenc
es."
53 PRINT TAB(10) "you will type in 5 nouns,"
54 PRINT TAB(10) "                5 adjectives,"
55 PRINT TAB(10) "                5 verbs,"
56 PRINT TAB(10) "            and 5 adverbs."
57 PRINT :PRINT TAB(10) "You will be able to help the computer
"
58 PRINT TAB(10) "rewrite the sentences, if they are not good"
59 PRINT TAB(25) "sentences."
60 GOSUB 581
61 CLS
70 PRINT TAB(10) "Type in five singular nouns. (car)"
80 PRINT TAB(10) "Press ENTER after each noun."
```

```
90 POKE 16409,0
100 FOR W=1 TO 5
110 PRINT CHR$(214);
120 LINEINPUT N$(W)
130 NEXT W
140 CLS
150 PRINT TAB(10) "Type in five verbs. (run)"
160 PRINT TAB(10) "Press ENTER after each verb."
170 FOR W=1 TO 5
180 PRINT CHR$(214);
190 LINEINPUT V$(W)
200 NEXT W
210 CLS
220 PRINT TAB(10) "Type in five adjectives. (happy)"
230 PRINT TAB(10) "Press ENTER after each adjective."
240 FOR W=1 TO 5
250 PRINT CHR$(214);
260 LINEINPUT AJ$(W)
270 NEXT W
280 CLS
290 PRINT TAB(10) "Type in five adverbs. (slowly)"
300 PRINT TAB(10) "Press ENTER after each adverb."
310 FOR W=1 TO 5
320 PRINT CHR$(214);
330 LINEINPUT AV$(W)
340 NEXT W
350 CLS
360 PRINT TAB(10)"I will use your words to make a sentence."
370 FOR I=1 TO 500 :NEXT I
380 N=RND(5)
390 V=RND(5)
400 AJ=RND(5)
410 AV=RND(5)
420 PRINT @335, "The ";AJ$(AJ);" ";N$(N);" ";V$(V);"s ";AV$(AV
);"."
430 PRINT
440 PRINT TAB(10) "Does my sentence make sense (Y/N) ";
450 INPUT Z$
460 Z$=LEFT$(Z$,1)
470 IF Z$="Y" OR Z$="y" THEN 530  ELSE 480
480 IF Z$="N" OR Z$="n" THEN 490  ELSE 450
490 PRINT TAB(10) "Rewrite my sentence on your paper."
491 GOSUB 581
530 PRINT TAB(10) "Do you want another sentence (Y/N) ";
540 INPUT Y$
550 Y$=LEFT$(Y$,1)
560 IF Y$="Y" OR Y$="y" THEN 590  ELSE 570
570 IF Y$="N" OR Y$="n" THEN 580  ELSE 540
580 POKE 16409,1 : END
581 PRINT :PRINT TAB(20) "Press any key to go on."
582 A$=INKEY$
583 IF A$="" THEN 582 ELSE RETURN
590 RESTORE
600 PRINT @320, CHR$(31)
610 GOTO 380
```

8. PRONOUNS

SUGGESTED FILE NAME: PRONOUN

SUGGESTED GRADE RANGE: 3–8

DESCRIPTION OF THE PROGRAM: This program provides guided practice in substituting pronouns for words or phrases for people or things. Students are required to know how to spell pronoun words or to have a master list available.

NEW PROGRAMMING STATEMENTS:

260 IF ASC(X$)<91 AND ASC(X$)>65 THEN 270 ELSE 310

ASC(X$) looks at the decimal code number of the first letter in X$. If that number is between 64 and 90, it is a capital letter. The program then goes to line 270. If ASC(X$) is any other number, the program goes to line 310.

530 DATA you and I,we,"", ...

The phrase, you and I, has only one pronoun as a possible answer, we. Most of the other items, such as mother, have two (she, her). To help the computer count two pronouns for each phrase, "" preserves the count but leaves the space blank.

EXPLANATION OF DATA LINES:
P$	–	a word or phrase
A1$	–	the first pronoun as a possible answer
A2$	–	the second pronoun
X$	–	the student's answer
WR	–	the error counter

HOW TO CHANGE THE DATA:
1. Change the phrases and pronouns in lines 500-540.
2. Change the number of items in line 100.

```
10 CLEAR 1000
20 CLS
30 PRINT @345,"PRONOUNS"
40 PRINT :PRINT TAB(17)"by GLORIA KUCHINSKAS Ed.D."
50 FOR I=1 TO 1000 :NEXT I
60 CLS
70 PRINT TAB(10)  "The sentence:          John loves to swim
."
80 PRINT TAB(10) "could be written as :   He loves to swim."
90 PRINT :PRINT TAB(19) "'He' is a pronoun."
100 PRINT TAB(19) "It replaces the word 'John'."
```

```
110 PRINT TAB(19) "It means the same as John."
120 PRINT :PRINT TAB(12) "In this program, you will practice"
130 PRINT TAB(12) "replacing 10 nouns with pronouns."
140 GOSUB 480
150 CLS
160 PRINT TAB(24)"TYPE THE PRONOUN"
170 PRINT STRING$(63,"*")
180 FOR W=1 TO 10
190 READ P$,A1$,A2$
200 POKE 16916,2
210 PRINT @284, P$
220 PRINT @399, "Type one pronoun to replace this."
230 POKE 16409,0
240 X$=""
250 PRINT CHR$(220); :LINEINPUT X$
260 IF ASC(X$)<91 AND ASC(X$)>65 THEN 270   ELSE 310
270 PRINT TAB(16) "Don't use a capital letter."
280 FOR I=1 TO 500 :NEXT I
290 PRINT @399, CHR$(31)
300 GOTO 220
310 IF X$=A1$ OR X$=A2$ THEN 420   ELSE 320
320 WR=WR+1 :IF WR=2 THEN 370   ELSE 330
330 PRINT :PRINT TAB(25) "Try again."
340 FOR Q=1 TO 500 :NEXT Q
350 PRINT @384, CHR$(31)
360 GOTO 220
370 PRINT @384, CHR$(31)
380 PRINT TAB(18) "The pronoun is: ";A1$
390 GOSUB 480
400 WR=0
410 PRINT @384, CHR$(31) :GOTO 220
420 PRINT :PRINT TAB(20) "Good for you !"
430 GOSUB 480
440 PRINT @256, CHR$(31)
450 NEXT W
460 POKE 16916,0
470 CLS :PRINT @346, "GOOD-BY !" :END
480 PRINT :PRINT TAB(19) "Press any key to go on."
490 A$=INKEY$ :IF A$="" THEN 490   ELSE RETURN
500 CLS :PRINT @346, "GOOD-BY !" : POKE 16409,1 : END
510 DATA mother,she,her,John and Mary,they,them
520 DATA the boy,he,him,books,they,them,the girls,they,them
530 DATA you and I,we,"",animals,they,them,food,it,""
540 DATA the pencil,it,"",many people,they,them
```

9. COMPOUND WORDS

SUGGESTED FILE NAME: COMPOUND

SUGGESTED GRADE RANGE: 2–8

DESCRIPTION OF THE PROGRAM: This program provides students with a bank of words that can be combined to produce compound words.

EXPLANATION OF DATA LINES:
    X$ –   student's compound word
    CP$ –   possible compound words
    N   –   item counter

PROGRAMMING LOGIC: Lines 300-330 compare the student's answer with all possible answers. Line 290 restores all the possible answers each time.

HOW TO CHANGE THE DATA:
1. Change the words in the word bank (lines 80-100) and possible answers in lines 380-420. (*Note:* if the number of possible answers changes, you must change the number in line 300.)
2. Increase the difficulty of the words.
3. Use words from content areas.

```
10 CLEAR 1000
20 CLS
30 PRINT @278, "COMPOUND WORDS"
40 PRINT TAB(17) "by Gloria Kuchinskas Ed.D."
41 FOR I=1 TO 1000 :NEXT I
50 CLS
51 PRINT @74, "Watch carefully:"
52 FOR Q=256 TO 283
53 PRINT @Q, "class" :FOR I=1 TO 50 :NEXT I
54 PRINT @Q, "     " :NEXT Q :PRINT @283, "class"
55 FOR Q=315 TO 288 STEP −1
56 PRINT @Q, "room" :FOR I=1 TO 50 :NEXT I
57 PRINT @Q, "    " :NEXT Q :PRINT @288, "room"
58 PRINT :PRINT "This is a compound word. It is made up of two
   words:"
59 PRINT TAB(20) "class     room"
60 PRINT :PRINT "In this program, you will practice making com
pound words."
61 GOSUB 350
69 CLS :POKE 16409,0
70 PRINT "COMPOUND WORDS"
80 PRINT "         bed        time        road        boat"
90 PRINT "         house      side        work        sick"
100 PRINT "         rail       sea         home        wall"
110 PRINT STRING$(63,"*")
120 POKE 16916,5
130 PRINT @397, "Type 999 when you want to stop."
140 PRINT @453, "Use two words from the list to type a compoun
d word."
150 PRINT CHR$(217);
160 LINEINPUT X$
170 IF X$="999" THEN 270
180 GOSUB 290
190 PRINT TAB(17) "That is not a word. Try again."
200 FOR I=1 TO 500 :NEXT I
210 PRINT @448, CHR$(31)
```

```
220 GOTO 130
230 PRINT TAB(22) "Good for you !"
240 GOSUB 350
250 CLS
260 GOTO 130
270 POKE 16916,0
280 CLS :PRINT @346, "GOOD-BY !" :END
290 RESTORE
300 FOR W=1 TO 21
310 READ W$
320 IF X$=W$ THEN 230
330 NEXT W
340 RETURN
350 PRINT @716, "Press any key when you are ready to go on."
360 A$=INKEY$
370 IF A$="" THEN 360  ELSE RETURN
380 DATA workhouse,seabed,roadbed,railroad,bedtime
390 DATA houseboat,seaside,seawall,homework
400 DATA seasick,homesick,bedside,boathouse
410 DATA roadside,housework,roadbed,sickbed
420 DATA roadhouse,sidewall,seabed,roadwork
```

10. GUESSING LETTERS

SUGGESTED FILE NAME: LETTER

SUGGESTED GRADE RANGE: 2–6

DESCRIPTION OF THE PROGRAM: This program provides practice in determining the placement of letters in the alphabet. It develops skills necessary to rapidly find reference materials that are alphabetically arranged. The game format motivates students to perform a routine task.

NEW PROGRAMMING STATEMENTS:

    110 L = 96 + RND(26)

L is the decimal code number of the letter selected at random. The program selects a random number between 1 and 26. Adding 96 ensures that the number will fall between 97 and 122, the decimal code numbers for lower case letters.

    210 PRINT @(208 + 2*G), L$

This location places each letter attempted two spaces to the right of each other.

EXPLANATION OF DATA LINES: G – a counter for letters tried

L – decimal code number for letter selected at random

L$ – letter guessed by student

HOW TO CHANGE THE DATA: As the letters of the alphabet are fixed, no content changes are possible. Change lower case letters to upper case letters by changing lines:

```
100 PRINT @84, "Guess my letter (A-Z)."
110 L= 64+RND(26)
120 POKE 16409,1
```

```
10 CLS : POKE 16409,0
20 CLEAR 500
30 PRINT @280, "GUESSING LETTERS"
40 PRINT TAB(20) "by Gloria Kuchinskas Ed.D."
60 FOR I=1 TO 1000 :NEXT I
70 CLS
80 G=0
90 RESTORE
100 PRINT @84, "Guess my letter (a-z) ."
110 L=96+RND(26)
130 PRINT @206, CHR$(194)
140 PRINT @192, "Letters used: ";
150 LINEINPUT L$
160 PRINT @206, CHR$(194)
170 G=G+1
180 IF ASC(L$)=L THEN 290 ELSE 190
190 IF ASC(L$)>L THEN 250 ELSE 200
200 IF ASC(L$)<L THEN 210 ELSE 150
210 PRINT @(208+2*G), L$
220 PRINT @330, CHR$(31)
230 PRINT @330, "Too low in the alphabet. Try a higher letter.
"
240 GOTO 150
250 PRINT @(208+2*G),L$
260 PRINT @330, CHR$(31)
270 PRINT @330, "Too high in the alphabet. Try a lower letter.
"
280 GOTO 150
290 IF G=1 THEN 300 ELSE 340
300 PRINT @(208+2*G), L$
320 PRINT :PRINT "You guessed it !"
330 GOTO 370
340 PRINT @(208+2*G),L$
360 PRINT :PRINT "You guessed with";G;"guesses."
370 PRINT :PRINT "Do you want to try another letter (Y/N) ";
380 INPUT Y$
390 Y$=LEFT$(Y$,1)
400 IF Y$="Y" OR Y$="y" THEN 70 ELSE 410
410 IF Y$="N" OR Y$="n" THEN 420 ELSE 380
420 CLS :PRINT @346, "GOOD-BY !!" : POKE 16409,1 : END
```

11. SUFFIXES

SUGGESTED FILE NAME: SUFFIX

SUGGESTED GRADE RANGE: 3–8

DESCRIPTION OF THE PROGRAM: This program provides students with a Root Word Bank to use in deciding if a root word can be combined with a suffix. The program also illustrates the joining of a root to its suffix with movement on the screen.

NEW PROGRAMMING STATEMENTS:

```
400 FOR Q = 320 to 340
410 PRINT @Q, RR$
420 FOR I = 1 to 50 :NEXT I
430 PRINT @Q, CHR$(192 + LEN(RR$))
440 NEXT Q
```

This set of lines moves the root word (RR$) twenty spaces from position 320 to position 340 to join the root word. Line 410 prints the root each time at a new location. Line 420 delays the action so the root can be seen. Line 430 prints two blanks CHR$(192) plus enough blanks to match the length of the root LEN(RR$). This causes the word to disappear in one location and appear in the next one. The root word appears to move across the screen because the action is fast.

```
450 PRINT @350-LEN(RR$), RR$ + S$
```

prints both the root (RR$) and the suffix (S$) at location 350 less the length of the root, LEN(RR$).

EXPLANATION OF DATA LINES:

S$ – the suffix

R1$ – one of the roots that can be used with that suffix

R2$,R3$,R4$ – the other possible roots

RR$ – the student's choice of root

PROGRAMMING LOGIC: Physically moving the root word to the suffix reinforces the word-building aspect of suffixes.

HOW TO CHANGE THE DATA:

1. Change root words in bank in lines 240-250 and in lines 570-610.
2. Change suffixes in lines 570-610.
3. Increase the difficulty of suffixes and/or roots.

```
10 CLS
20 CLEAR 1000
30 PRINT @283, "SUFFIXES"
40 PRINT TAB(19) "by Gloria Kuchinskas Ed.D."
50 FOR I=1 TO 1000 :NEXT I
60 CLS
```

```
70 PRINT @202, "In this program, you add root words to"
80 PRINT TAB(10) "suffixes. You will use 5 suffixes:"
90 FOR I=1 TO 1000 :NEXT I
100 PRINT TAB(10) "-less   -able   -ful   -ness   -like"
110 FOR I=1 TO 1000 :NEXT I
120 PRINT TAB(10) "For example:"
130 PRINT :PRINT @483, "ful";
140 FOR Q=450 TO 479
150 PRINT @Q, "help"
160 FOR I=1 TO 50 :NEXT I
170 PRINT @Q, "    "
180 NEXT Q :PRINT @479, "helpful"
190 PRINT :PRINT TAB(10) "The root 'help' makes a word with "
200 PRINT TAB(20) "the suffix '-ful'."
210 GOSUB 540
220 CLS :POKE 16409,0
230 PRINT "ROOT WORD BANK:"
240 PRINT "         care      help      work      child
"
250 PRINT "         wonder    kind      teach     life"
260 PRINT STRING$(63,"*")
270 FOR W=1 TO 5
280 READ S$,R1$,R2$,R3$,R4$
290 PRINT @350, S$
300 PRINT
310 PRINT TAB(10) "Type a root word to use with this suffix."
320 PRINT CHR$(217);
330 LINEINPUT RR$
340 IF RR$=R1$ OR RR$=R2$ OR RR$=R3$ OR RR$=R4$ THEN 390  ELSE
    350
350 PRINT TAB(20) "Try again."
360 FOR I=1 TO 500 :NEXT I
370 PRINT @512, CHR$(31)
380 GOTO 320
390 PRINT @384, CHR$(31)
400 FOR Q=320 TO 340
410 PRINT @Q, RR$
420 FOR I=1 TO 50 :NEXT I
430 PRINT @Q, CHR$(192+LEN(RR$))
440 NEXT Q
450 PRINT @350-LEN(RR$), RR$+S$
460 PRINT TAB(20) "Read your new word."
470 FOR I=1 TO 500 :NEXT I
480 GOSUB 540
490 POKE 16916,5
500 CLS
510 NEXT W
520 POKE 16916,0
530 CLS :PRINT @346, "GOOD-BY !" : POKE 16409,1 : END
540 PRINT @724, "Press any key to go on."
550 A$=INKEY$
560 IF A$="" THEN 550  ELSE RETURN
570 DATA less,care,help,child,life
580 DATA able,work,teach,"",""
590 DATA ful,care,help,wonder,""
600 DATA ness,kind,"","",""
610 DATA like,child,life,"",""
```

12. PRACTICING FASTER READING

SUGGESTED FILE NAME: SPEED

SUGGESTED GRADE RANGE: 1–8

DESCRIPTION OF THE PROGRAM: This program presents phrases at one of five speeds selected by the student for instant sight reading.

NEW PROGRAMMING STATEMENTS:

```
210 ON S GOTO 220, 240, 260, 280, 300
```

If the student picks speed 1 (S), the program goes to the first line in the list, 220; if the student picks speed 3, the program goes to the third line, 260; and so on.

```
320 PRINT @335, CHR$(191)+STRING$(33,131)+CHR$(191);
```

prints graphic characters across the screen to form the top of a box.

```
330 FOR W=399 to 527 STEP 64
340 PRINT @W, CHR$(191)+STRING$(33,32)+CHR$(191);
350 NEXT W
```

This set of lines prints bars forming the left and right sides of the box (CHR$(191) with 33 blank spaces between (STRING$(33,32); STEP 64 is a row. The semicolons at the ends of lines 340 and 360 must be there so words put in the box by line 400 do not erase parts of the box.

EXPLANATION OF DATA LINES: S   –   choice of speed
                            N   –   speed of presentation
                            PH$ –   the phrase

PROGRAMMING LOGIC: The speed of presentation is controlled by N in lines 220, 240, 260, 280, and 300. The higher N is, the slower the speed of presentation. Forming a box in which to present the phrase assists students to focus their attention on the appropriate section of the screen.

HOW TO CHANGE THE DATA: 1. Change the phrases (lines 520-560).
                          2. Change the speeds (lines 220, 240, 260, 280, 300).
                          3. Make the phrases longer. (*Note:* Phrases must be thirty characters or less or box must be made bigger.)

4. Increase the difficulty of the phrases.

5. Change the number of the phrases (line 380).

```
10 CLEAR 500
20 CLS
30 PRINT a274, "PRACTICING FASTER READING"
40 PRINT TAB(18) "by Gloria Kuchinskas Ed.D."
50 FOR I=1 TO 1000 :NEXT I
51 CLS
52 PRINT TAB(10) "In this program, you can practice reading "
53 PRINT TAB(20) "10 sight words."
54 PRINT :PRINT TAB(10) "You can decide how fast to read."
55 PRINT TAB(15) "You have 5 choices of speed."
56 FOR I=1 TO 3000 :NEXT I
60 CLS
65 S=0
70 PRINT a 143, "How fast do you want to read "
80 PRINT TAB(25) "1. Very fast"
90 PRINT TAB(25) "2. Fast"
100 PRINT TAB(25) "3. Medium speed"
110 PRINT TAB(25) "4. Slow"
120 PRINT TAB(25) "5. Very slow"
130 PRINT
140 PRINT TAB(20) "Make a choice (1-5) ";
150 INPUT S
160 IF S>5 OR S<1 THEN 150
170 PRINT a 910, "Press any key when you are ready."
180 AK$=INKEY$
190 IF AK$="" THEN 180  ELSE 200
200 CLS
210 ON S GOTO 220  ,240  ,260  ,280  ,300
220 N=100
230 GOTO 320
240 N=150
250 GOTO 320
260 N=200
270 GOTO 320
280 N=300
290 GOTO 320
300 N=500
310 GOTO 320
320 PRINT a335, CHR$(191)+STRING$(33,131)+CHR$(191);
330 FOR W=399 TO 527 STEP 64
340 PRINT a W, CHR$(191)+STRING$(33,32)+CHR$(191);
350 NEXT W
360 PRINT a 527, CHR$(191)+STRING$(33,176)+CHR$(191);
370 FOR I=1 TO 500 :NEXT I
380 FOR Q=1 TO 10
390 READ PH$
400 PRINT a 408, PH$;
410 FOR I=1 TO N :NEXT I
420 PRINT a 408, CHR$(212);
430 NEXT Q
440 PRINT a 847, "Do you want to try again (Y/N) ";
450 INPUT Y$
```

```
460 Y$=LEFT$(Y$,1)
470 IF Y$="y" OR Y$="Y" THEN 480    ELSE 500
480 RESTORE
490 GOTO 60
500 IF Y$="N" OR Y$="n" THEN 510   ELSE 450
510 CLS :PRINT @346, "GOOD-BY !" :END
520 DATA "in the house","on the boat"
530 DATA "under the roof","at home"
540 DATA "next to me","behind the wall"
550 DATA "by my side","over my head"
560 DATA "inside the box","in front of the room"
```

13. PLURALS

SUGGESTED FILE NAME: PLURAL

SUGGESTED GRADE RANGE: 2–8

DESCRIPTION OF THE PROGRAM: This program provides guided practice informing regular plurals using -s and -es endings.

NEW PROGRAMMING STATEMENTS:

```
280 FOR Q = 380 TO 350 + LEN(W$) STEP -1
290 PRINT @Q, "s"
300 FOR I = 1 TO 20 :NEXT I
310 PRINT @Q, CHR$(193)
320 NEXT Q
```

Lines 280-320 move "s" backwards, (from right to left [-1]) to join the word (W$) to be made plural. Line 300 slows up the action. Line 310 makes "s" disappear. Line 320 makes "s" reappear in the next location.

EXPLANATION OF DATA LINES:

W$	–	the word
P	–	either 1 or 2 depending on the correct answer
X	–	the student's answer

PROGRAMMING LOGIC: Lines 360-410 perform the same function for the "es" ending as lines 280-330 perform for the "s" ending. Line 230 tells the program which ending to add.

HOW TO CHANGE THE DATA:
1. Change the words in lines 470-480.
2. Increase the difficulty of the words.
3. Change the number of words in lines 70, 240.
4. Use words from the content areas.

```
10  CLS
20  CLEAR 1000
30  PRINT a280, "PLURALS"
40  PRINT TAB(15) "by Gloria Kuchinskas Ed.D."
50  FOR I=1 TO 1000 :NEXT I
51  CLS
52  PRINT a74, "Read this carefully:"
53  PRINT TAB(15) "one house      two houses"
54  PRINT TAB(15) "house is singular - only one house"
55  PRINT TAB(15) "houses is plural  - more than one house"
56  PRINT :PRINT TAB(10) "Read this carefully:"
57  PRINT TAB(15) "boys     houses"
58  PRINT TAB(10) "Both are plural but boys ends in s"
59  PRINT TAB(10) "                        houses ends in es"
60  PRINT :PRINT TAB(10) "In this program, you will practice "
61  PRINT TAB(10) "forming plurals with 10 nouns."
62  GOSUB 440
63  CLS
70  FOR W=1 TO 10
80  READ W$,P
90  PRINT a350,W$
100 PRINT TAB(20) "Choose the plural ending:"
110 PRINT TAB(25) "1. add -s"
120 PRINT TAB(25) "2. add -es"
130 PRINT a665, "Pick 1 or 2 ";
140 INPUT X
150 IF X<>1 AND X<>2 THEN 130
160 IF X=P THEN 220  ELSE 170
170 PRINT TAB(25) "Try again."
180 FOR I=1 TO 500 :NEXT I
190 PRINT a704, CHR$(31)
200 PRINT CHR$(217);
210 GOTO 140
220 PRINT a384, CHR$(31)
230 ON X GOTO 280  ,360
240 IF W=10 THEN 270
250 CLS
260 NEXT W
270 CLS :PRINT a346, "GOOd=BY !" :END
280 FOR Q=380 TO 350+LEN(W$) STEP -1
290 PRINT aQ, "s"
300 FOR I=1 TO 20 :NEXT I
310 PRINT aQ, CHR$(193)
320 NEXT Q
330 PRINT 2346, "two ";W$;"s";
340 GOSUB 440
350 GOTO 240
360 FOR Q=380 TO 350+LEN(W$) STEP -1
370 PRINT aQ, "es"
380 FOR I=1 TO 20 :NEXT I
390 PRINT aQ, CHR$(194)
400 NEXT Q
410 PRINT a346, "two ";W$;"es";
420 GOSUB 440
430 GOTO 240
440 PRINT a917, "Press any key to go on."
450 A$=INKEY$
```

```
460 IF A$="" THEN 450  ELSE RETURN
470 DATA house,1,car,1,box,2,bus,2,clock,1
480 DATA dress,2,egg,1,flower,1,class,2,head,1
```

14. SIGNAL WORDS

SUGGESTED FILE NAME: SIGNAL

SUGGESTED GRADE RANGE: 2–8

DESCRIPTION OF THE PROGRAM: This program provides guided practice in identifying signal words (connectives, adjectives, prepositions, adverbs) that signal information about time, place, order, comparison, contrast, negative information, amount, and so forth. This is an important inferential comprehension skill.

NEW PROGRAMMING STATEMENTS:

170 IF RIGHT$(X$,1) . . . . . .

Look at one letter in string X$, the first one on the right.

170 . . . LEFT$(X$,INSTR(X$," ")-1)

Subtract one character if it is a space in the string (INSTR) X$, starting on the left of X$.

180 . . . X$ = MID$(X$,2)

The string X$ becomes the same string but with the first character eliminated; that is, start with the second (2) character from the left.

EXPLANATION OF DATA LINES:

S$	–	the sentence
A$	–	the signal word
B$	–	the information signaled
X$	–	the student's answer
N	–	the error counter

PROGRAMMING LOGIC: Line 170 examines the right side of the student's response to see if an extra space was typed in and then deletes it. Line 180 looks at the left side of the student's response and deletes the space if it is there.

HOW TO CHANGE THE DATA: 1. Change the sentences, signal words, and signals in lines 360-450.

2. Change the number of sentences in lines 70, 260.

3. Make the program easier by using sentences that all signal the same type of information, such as time.

4. Use sentences from content areas to make the sentences harder.

```
10 CLS
20 CLEAR 2000
30 PRINT @280, "SIGNAL WORDS"
40 PRINT TAB(18) "by Gloria Kuchinskas Ed.D."
50 FOR I=1 TO 1000 :NEXT I
51 CLS
52 PRINT @10, "Read this sentence:"
53 PRINT TAB(15) "The man went in the house."
54 PRINT :PRINT TAB(10) "The word   in   tells where the man w
ent."
56 PRINT TAB(10) "It signals place."
57 PRINT :PRINT TAB(10) "In this sentence:"
58 PRINT TAB(15) "He eats because he is hungry."
59 PRINT TAB(10) "The word  because  signals why."
60 PRINT :PRINT TAB(10) "In this program, you will try to find
 "
61 PRINT TAB(10) "10 signal words in 10 sentences."
62 GOSUB 330
63 CLS
70 FOR W=1 TO 10
80 N=0
90 READ S$,A$,B$
100 PRINT TAB(23) "SIGNAL WORDS"
110 PRINT TAB(18) STRING$(22,"*")
120 PRINT @265, S$
130 PRINT @385, "Type one word from the sentence that signals
";B$;"."
140 POKE 16409,0
150 PRINT CHR$(217);
160 LINEINPUT X$
170 IF RIGHT$(X$,1)=" " THEN X$=LEFT$(X$,INSTR(X$," ")-1)
180 IF LEFT$(X$,1)=" " THEN X$=MID$(X$,2)
190 IF X$=A$ THEN 260   ELSE 200
200 N=N+1
210 IF N=2 THEN 220   ELSE 240
220 PRINT TAB(15) "The ";B$;" signal is:   ";A$
230 GOTO 260
240 PRINT TAB(15) "Try again. Type carefully."
250 GOTO 150
260 IF W=10 THEN 300   ELSE 270
270 GOSUB 330
280 CLS
290 NEXT W
300 CLS :PRINT @346, "GOOD-BY !" : POKE 16409,1 : END
```

```
330 PRINT :PRINT TAB(20) "Press any key to go on."
340 A$=INKEY$
350 IF A$="" THEN 340  ELSE RETURN
360 DATA "Let's go to the movies tommorrow.",tomorrow,time
370 DATA "Put the book underneath the table.",underneath,place
380 DATA "I like movies but you like TV.",but,contrast
390 DATA "He looks like his mother.",like,comparison
400 DATA "We never eat raw meat.",never,a negative
410 DATA "The book is very funny.",very,how much
420 DATA "Write your name last.",last, order
430 DATA "Give him a piece too.",too,addition
440 DATA "Do it immediately.",immediately,when
450 DATA "Sit opposite John.",opposite,place
```

15. VISUAL MEMORY

SUGGESTED FILE NAME: VISMEM

SUGGESTED GRADE RANGE: 1–8

DESCRIPTION OF THE PROGRAM: This program assists students in developing short-term visual memory for words. It is not a spelling task because students are not required to retrieve the word from long-term memory without a clue. However it is a subskill necessary for spelling. It is an important skill for primary students to develop and will assist older students in the intermediate steps of learning their spelling words.

EXPLANATION OF DATA LINES: W$ –   the word

Y$ –   the student's response

PROGRAMMING LOGIC: Line 520 draws a line for the top of a box.

Lines 530-550 draw the left side of the box.

Lines 560-580 draw the right side of the box.

Line 590 draws the bottom of the box.

Using a box helps to focus the student's attention.

HOW TO CHANGE THE DATA: 1. Change the words in lines 610-620.

2. Change the number of words in line 70.

```
10 CLS
20 CLEAR 1000
30 PRINT @281, "VISUAL MEMORY"
40 PRINT TAB(19) "by Gloria Kuchinskas Ed.D."
50 FOR I=1 TO 1000 :NEXT I
60 CLS
70 PRINT @138, "In this program, you will be asked to look"
```

```
80 PRINT TAB(10) "at 10 words, remember them, and type them"
90 PRINT TAB(25) "from memory."
100 FOR I=1 TO 1000 :NEXT I
110 PRINT :PRINT TAB(18) "How fast do you want to go ?"
120 PRINT TAB(25) "1. Very fast"
130 PRINT TAB(25) "2. Fast"
140 PRINT TAB(25) "3. Slow"
150 PRINT TAB(25) "4. Very slow"
160 PRINT CHR$(220); :INPUT KK
170 ON KK GOTO 180  ,190  ,200  ,210
180 SP=100 :GOTO 220
190 SP=500 :GOTO 220
200 SP=1000 :GOTO 220
210 SP=1500 :GOTO 220
220 GOSUB 490
230 CLS
240 FOR W=1 TO 10
250 READ W$
260 PRINT @24, "Watch carefully."
270 PRINT @76, "You will be asked to remember the word."
280 GOSUB 520
290 FOR I=1 TO 500 :NEXT I
300 PRINT @475, W$;
310 FOR I=1 TO SP :NEXT I
320 PRINT @475, CHR$(204);
330 PRINT @658,"Type the word from memory."
340 POKE 16409,0
350 PRINT CHR$(219);
360 LINEINPUT Y$
370 IF LEFT$(Y$,1)=" " THEN Y$=MID$(Y$,2)
380 IF RIGHT$(Y$,1)=" " THEN Y$=LEFT$(Y$,INSTR(Y$," ")-1)
390 IF Y$=W$ THEN 450  ELSE 400
400 PRINT TAB(25) "Try again."
410 FOR I=1 TO 500 :NEXT I
420 PRINT @640, CHR$(31)
430 GOTO 300
450 GOSUB 490
460 CLS
470 NEXT W
480 CLS :PRINT @346, "GOOD-BY !!" : POKE 16409,1 : END
490 PRINT :PRINT TAB(20) "Press any key to go on."
500 A$=INKEY$
510 IF A$="" THEN 500  ELSE RETURN
520 PRINT @344, STRING$(16,176);
530 FOR Q=408 TO 537 STEP 64
540 PRINT @Q, CHR$(191);
550 NEXT Q
560 FOR Q=423 TO 552 STEP 64
570 PRINT @Q, CHR$(191);
580 NEXT Q
590 PRINT @600, STRING$(16,131);
600 RETURN
610 DATA boy,house,car,doll,toy
620 DATA dog,cat,bread,boat,girl
```

16. MULTIPLE MEANINGS

SUGGESTED FILE NAME: MULTIPLE

SUGGESTED GRADE RANGE: 3–8

DESCRIPTION OF THE PROGRAM: This program provides guided practice in using entries for words with multiple meanings. A sentence provides the context for which the student selects the correct meaning. Because approximately 75 percent of the words in a basic vocabulary have multiple meanings, the ability to use the sentence context is an important inferential skill. (See *The Ginn Word Book for Teachers: A Basic Lexicon*, D. Johnson, A.J. Moe & J.F. Baumann, Ginn and Company, 1983.)

EXPLANATION OF DATA LINES: ST$ – the sentence

XX – a number from 1-5 depending on the dictionary meaning that matches the sentence context

X – the student's response

N – an error counter

HOW TO CHANGE THE DATA:
1. Change the sentences and responses in lines 400-490.
2. Change the multiple meaning word in the DICTIONARY in lines 80-120.
3. Change the number of sentences in line 140.

```
10 CLS
20 CLEAR 2000
30 PRINT @275, "MULTIPLE MEANINGS"
40 PRINT TAB(15) "by Gloria Kuchinskas Ed.D."
50 FOR I=1 TO 1000 :NEXT I
51 CLS
52 PRINT @74, "Read these sentences:"
53 PRINT TAB(15) "1. I can jump rope well."
54 PRINT TAB(15) "2. Put the marbles in the can."
55 PRINT :PRINT TAB(10) "The word 'can'  has two meanings:"
56 PRINT TAB(15) "In sentence 1: able to"
57 PRINT TAB(15) "In sentence 2: a container"
58 PRINT :PRINT TAB(10) "Many words have more than one meaning
."
59 PRINT TAB(10) "In this program, you will try to find the "
60 PRINT TAB(10) "the meaning of 'run'  in 10 sentences."
61 GOSUB 370
62 CLS
70 PRINT "DICTIONARY MEANING:"
80 PRINT "run  v.  1. to move fast on the ground"
90 PRINT "          2. to follow a course of action"
```

```
100 PRINT "         3. to drive"
110 PRINT "         4. to stab"
120 PRINT "run  n.  5. a complete circuit of bases"
130 PRINT STRING$(63,"*")
140 FOR W=1 TO 10
150 READ ST$,XX
160 PRINT @522, ST$
170 PRINT
180 PRINT "Which meaning is correct in this sentence (1-5) ";
190 INPUT X
200 IF X=XX THEN 290  ELSE 210
210 N=N+1
220 IF N=3 THEN 230  ELSE 270
230 PRINT @576, CHR$(31)
240 PRINT TAB(10) "The correct meaning is number:   ";XX
250 GOSUB 370
260 GOTO 310
270 PRINT @572, CHR$(31)
271 PRINT TAB(5) "Read the sentence. Think about it. Try again
."
280 GOTO 190
290 PRINT TAB(20) "Good for you !"
300 GOSUB 370
310 POKE 16916,7
320 PRINT @448, CHR$(31)
330 N=0
340 NEXT W
350 POKE 16916,0
360 CLS :PRINT @346, "GOOD-BY !" :END
370 PRINT :PRINT TAB(20) "Press any key to go on."
380 A$=INKEY$
390 IF A$="" THEN 380  ELSE RETURN
400 DATA "Does he know how to run a train ?",3
410 DATA "Who runs faster, Mary or Jean ?",1
420 DATA "Let's run through your lines in the play again.",2
430 DATA "The pirate ran him through with his sword.",4
440 DATA "Run the wire along the ground.",2
450 DATA "Patty made a home run.",5
460 DATA "The race was run on grass.",1
470 DATA "The clock ran down.",2
480 DATA "Run the seam up on your sewing machine.",2
490 DATA "John ran into the chair.",1
```

17. SENTENCE COMBINING

SUGGESTED FILE NAME: COMBINE

SUGGESTED GRADE RANGE: 2–8

DESCRIPTION OF THE PROGRAM: This program provides practice in combining three short sentences into a compound or complex sentence. This skill assists students in both reading and writing more complex sentence structures.

NEW PROGRAMMING STATEMENTS:

> 290 IF ASC(X$)>=65...

If the decimal number (ASC) of the first letter in the string X$ is equal to or greater than the number 65

> 290...AND ASC(X$)<=90 THEN...

And the decimal number for the first letter in the string X$ is less than or equal to 90, then...

> 320 IF RIGHT$(X$,1)<>"." THEN...

If the rightmost character in string X$ is not a period, then

EXPLANATION OF DATA LINES:

S1$	–	the first short sentence
S2$	–	the second short sentence
S3$	–	the third short sentence
A1$	–	the first possible answer
A2$	–	the second possible answer
A3$	–	the third possible answer
X$	–	the student's answer
N	–	an error counter

PROGRAMMING LOGIC: The decimal numbers for capital letters are 65-90. Line 290 looks at the first word in the student's response to see if the student started the sentence with a capital. Line 320 looks at the end of the student's response to see if the student ended the sentence with a period. These two lines reinforce proper sentence formation.

HOW TO CHANGE THE DATA:
1. Change the sentences and responses in lines 500-790.
2. Change the number of trials in line 170.
3. Make the sentences longer and more difficult. (*Note:* The sentences will wraparound on the screen if there are more than sixty-four characters in each.)

```
10 CLS
20 CLEAR 2000
30 PRINT @276, "SENTENCE COMBINING"
40 PRINT TAB(16) "by Gloria Kuchinskas Ed.D."
50 FOR I=1 TO 1000 :NEXT I
60 CLS
70 PRINT @74, "Read these short sentences:"
```

```
80 PRINT TAB(15) "The man is tall."
90 PRINT TAB(15) "The man is working hard."
100 PRINT :PRINT TAB(10) "We can make a better sentence by put
ting"
110 PRINT TAB(10) "these two sentences together:"
120 PRINT TAB(15) "The tall man is working hard."
130 PRINT :PRINT TAB(10) "In this program, you will put 5 sets
 of short"
140 PRINT TAB(10) "sentences together to make better, longer s
entences."
150 GOSUB 470
160 CLS
170 FOR W=1 TO 5
180 N=0
190 READ S1$,S2$,S3$,A1$,A2$,A3$
200 PRINT TAB(15) S1$
210 PRINT TAB(15) S2$
220 PRINT TAB(15) S3$
230 PRINT
240 PRINT TAB(10) "Put these three sentences together."
250 PRINT TAB(10) "Keep the thoughts in the same order."
260 PRINT TAB(10) "Type them as one sentence."
270 POKE 16409,0
280 LINEINPUT X$
290 IF ASC(X$)>=65 AND ASC(X$)<=90 THEN 320  ELSE 300
300 PRINT TAB(5)"Start your sentence with a capital."
310 GOTO 280
320 IF RIGHT$(X$,1)<>"." THEN 330  ELSE 350
330 PRINT TAB(5) "End your sentence with a period."
340 GOTO 280
350 IF X$=A1$ OR X$=A2$ OR X$=A3$ THEN 420  ELSE 360
360 N=N+1
370 IF N=2 THEN 400  ELSE 380
380 PRINT TAB(20) "Try again."
390 GOTO 280
400 PRINT @256, CHR$(31)
410 PRINT A1$
420 PRINT TAB(20) "Good for you !"
430 GOSUB 470
440 CLS
450 NEXT W
460 CLS :PRINT @346, "GOOD-BY !" : POKE 16409,1 : END
470 PRINT :PRINT TAB(15) "Press any key when you are ready."
480 A$=INKEY$
490 IF A$="" THEN 480  ELSE RETURN
500 DATA "The man is big."
510 DATA "The man is in his car."
520 DATA "The man is driving west."
530 DATA "The big man is in his car driving west."
540 DATA "The big man is driving west in his car."
550 DATA "The big man is in his car and is driving west."
560 DATA "The pencil is mine."
570 DATA "Tne pencil is red."
580 DATA "The pencil is sharp."
590 DATA "My pencil is red and sharp."
600 DATA "My pencil is sharp and red."
```

```
610 DATA "I have a sharp, red pencil."
620 DATA "Look at the men."
630 DATA "They are in front of the house."
640 DATA "They are watching the policeman."
650 DATA "Look at the men in front of the house watching the p
oliceman."
660 DATA "Look at the men watching the policeman in front of t
he house."
670 DATA ""
680 DATA "The railroads are American."
690 DATA "They carry goods."
700 DATA "They go between big cities."
710 DATA "American railroads carry goods between big cities."
720 DATA "The railroads are American and carry goods between b
ig cities."
730 DATA "The railroads are American and they carry goods betw
een big cities."
740 DATA "The stove is white."
750 DATA "The stove has two ovens."
760 DATA "The stove is on sale."
770 DATA "The white stove with two ovens is on sale."
780 DATA "The white stove has two ovens and is on sale."
790 DATA ""
```

18. ANTONYMS

SUGGESTED FILE NAME: ANTONYM

SUGGESTED GRADE RANGE: 2–8

DESCRIPTION OF THE PROGRAM: This program provides practice in identifying antonyms in the context of a sentence. This is another important word relationship skill and helps develop vocabulary.

EXPLANATION OF DATA LINES:
ST$ – the sentence
A1$ – the first in the pair of antonyms
A2$ – the second in the pair of antonyms
X$ – the student's response
N – an error counter

PROGRAMMING LOGIC: Lines 380-590 draw a line under one of the pairs of antonyms in each sentence.

Line 110 tells the program which section of lines 380-600 will draw a line in the correct place for each sentence.

Lines 600-650 draw a box to focus on the antonyms.

Line 660 puts the antonyms in the box.

HOW TO CHANGE THE DATA: If any changes are made in the sentences in this program, new sets of underlines need to be drawn. Use the Video Display Worksheet in the Appendix to chart the sentences to do this.

1. Change the sentences and antonym pairs in lines 680-720.

2. Change the number of items in lines 70 and 280.

```
10 CLS
20 CLEAR 1000
30 PRINT @280, "ANTONYMS"
40 PRINT TAB(16) "by Gloria Kuchinskas Ed.D."
50 FOR I=1 TO 1000 :NEXT I
51 CLS
52 PRINT @266, "Read these sentences:"
53 PRINT TAB(15) "The sky is up."
54 PRINT TAB(15) "The ground is down."
55 PRINT :PRINT TAB(10) "Up and down are opposites."
56 PRINT TAB(15) "They are ANTONYMS."
57 PRINT :PRINT TAB(10) "In this program, you will practice"
58 PRINT TAB(15) "finding 5 sets of antonyms."
59 GOSUB 350
60 CLS
70 FOR W=1 TO 5
80 N=0
90 READ ST$,A1$,A2$
100 PRINT @261, ST$;
110 ON W GOSUB 400  ,440  ,480  ,520  ,560
120 PRINT @522, "Look at the underlined word."
130 PRINT TAB(10) "Type the word that means the opposite."
140 POKE 16409,0
150 PRINT CHR$(217);
160 LINEINPUT X$
170 IF X$=A1$ THEN 270 ELSE 180
180 PRINT @640, CHR$(31)
190 N=N+1
191 IF N=3 THEN 240 ELSE 200
200 PRINT TAB(15) "Try again. Type carefully."
210 FOR I=1 TO 500 :NEXT I
220 GOTO 150
240 N=0 :PRINT TAB(10)   "The antonym is ";A1$;"."
250 GOSUB 350
260 GOTO 120
270 GOSUB 600
290 GOSUB 350
300 POKE 16916,0
310 CLS
320 NEXT W
330 CLS :PRINT @346, "GOOD-BY !" :END
350 PRINT @911, "Press any key to go on."
360 A$=INKEY$
370 IF A$="" THEN 360  ELSE 380
380 PRINT @468, CHR$(31)
390 RETURN
400 FOR Q=329 TO 331
```

```
410 PRINT ƏQ, CHR$(131);
420 NEXT Q
430 RETURN
440 FOR Q=345 TO 348
450 PRINT ƏQ, CHR$(131);
460 NEXT Q
470 RETURN
480 FOR Q=341 TO 344
490 PRINT ƏQ, CHR$(131);
500 NEXT Q
510 RETURN
520 FOR Q=353 TO 354
530 PRINT ƏQ, CHR$(131);
540 NEXT Q
550 RETURN
560 FOR Q=330 TO 333
570 PRINT ƏQ, CHR$(131);
580 NEXT Q
590 RETURN
600 PRINT Ə512, CHR$(31)
610 PRINT Ə522, CHR$(191)+STRING$(33,131)+CHR$(191);
620 FOR Q=586 TO 660 STEP 64
630 PRINT ƏQ, CHR$(191)+STRING$(33,32)+CHR$(191);
640 NEXT Q
650 PRINT Ə650, CHR$(191)+STRING$(33,176)+CHR$(191);
660 PRINT Ə590, A1$;" and ";A2$;" are antonyms";
670 RETURN
680 DATA "The big boy stood next to the little girl.","little"
,"big"
690 DATA "The tap has hot and cold water.","hot","cold"
700 DATA "She runs up and down the stairs.","up","down"
710 DATA "Shut the screen when you go in and out.","out","in"
720 DATA "Look over the top and then under it.","under","over"
```

19. SEQUENCE

SUGGESTED FILE NAME: SEQUENCE

SUGGESTED GRADE RANGE: 3–8

DESCRIPTION OF THE PROGRAM: In this program, the student decides the sequences in which two sentences should appear based on logical order.

EXPLANATION OF DATA LINES:
S1$ – one of the two sentences
S2$ – the other sentence
AN – the number of the sentence that should come first
WR – the error counter

HOW TO CHANGE THE DATA: 1. Change the sentences.

2. Add an additional sentence to each set (change line 140; add line 165).

3. Make the sentences easier or harder to read.

```
10 CLEAR
20 CLEAR 1000
30 CLS
40 PRINT @284, "SEQUENCE"
50 PRINT TAB(17) "by Gloria A. Kuchinskas Ed.D."
60 FOR I=1 TO 1000 :NEXT I
70 CLS
80 PRINT TAB(16) "In this program, you will put 10"
90 PRINT TAB(16) "pairs of sentences in the proper"
100 PRINT TAB(29) "order."
110 GOSUB 350
120 FOR W=1 TO 10
130 CLS
140 READ S1$,S2$,AN
150 PRINT @64, "1. ";S1$
160 PRINT @128, "2. ";S2$
170 PRINT @256, "Which sentence should come first ";
180 INPUT X
190 IF X=AN THEN 300   ELSE 200
200 WR=WR+1 :IF WR=2 THEN 210   ELSE 260
210 WR=0 :PRINT @320, CHR$(31)
220 PRINT "The correct answer is sentence number: ";AN
230 GOSUB 350
240 PRINT @256, CHR$(31)
250 GOTO 170
260 PRINT TAB(20) "Try again."
270 FOR I=1 TO 500 :NEXT I
280 PRINT @320, CHR$(31)
290 GOTO 170
300 PRINT :PRINT TAB(20) "Good for you !"
310 FOR I=1 TO 500 :NEXT I
320 PRINT @256, CHR$(31)
330 NEXT W
340 CLS :PRINT @346, "GOOD-BY !" :END
350 PRINT :PRINT TAB(20) "Press any key to go on."
360 A$=INKEY$ :IF A$="" THEN 360   ELSE RETURN
370 DATA "Mother put the food in the refrigerator."
380 DATA "Mother brought the food in from the car.",2
390 DATA "Then paint birds in your sky."
400 DATA "Paint the sky blue.",2
410 DATA "Brush your teeth well."
420 DATA "Go to bed promptly.",1
430 DATA "Drive five blocks west."
440 DATA "When you come to main street, turn west.",2
450 DATA "The group checked their baggage at the counter."
460 DATA "They boarded the plane to Hawaii.",1
470 DATA "He put on black and white shoes."
480 DATA "He put on brown socks.",2
490 DATA "Finally, it was the new year !"
500 DATA "In October, he started counting the months.",2
```

```
510 DATA "The girls counted, '6, 7, 8, 9, 10.'"
520 DATA "The boys counted, '1, 2, 3, 4, 5.'",2
530 DATA "M N O P Q R S T"
540 DATA "V W X Y Z",1
550 DATA "Slowly the plane climbed up in the sky."
560 DATA "When it was high enough, it started to dive.",1
```

20. CONTRACTIONS

SUGGESTED FILE NAME: CONTRACT

SUGGESTED GRADE RANGE: 3–6

DESCRIPTION OF THE PROGRAM: This program provides guided practice in forming contractions with "not." The program illustrates the replacement of the "o" in not with the apostrophe and the joining of the verb and "n't" into one word by physical movement visible on the screen. This reinforces the word building aspects of contractions for students.

NEW PROGRAMMING STATEMENTS

$$110 \ V = 404 + LEN(V\$) + 1$$

This method of expressing a location allows for the variation in the length (LEN) of the verb (V$) and adds a space (+1).

EXPLANATION OF DATA LINES:
- S1$ – the first part of the sentence
- V$ – the verb to be contracted
- S2$ – the second part of the sentence
- CT$ – the contracted form of the verb
- V – a variable location on the screen
- C$ – the student's response

PROGRAMMING LOGIC: Lines 140-170 cause the o in not to move up the screen.

Lines 230-270 cause the ' to move down the screen to replace the o.

Lines 310-350 cause the contraction, n't, to move to the left to join the verb.

HOW TO CHANGE THE DATA:
1. Change the contraction to will, did, is, and so forth. This requires changes in many lines between 140 and 360 and changes in lines 610-650.
2. Change the number of items in lines 70 and 460.

```
10  CLS
20  CLEAR 500
30  PRINT @275, "CONTRACTIONS"
40  PRINT TAB(13) "By Gloria Kuchinskas Ed.D."
50  FOR I=1 TO 1000 :NEXT I
51  CLS
52  PRINT @266, "In this program, you will practice"
53  PRINT TAB(13) "forming contractions with not."
54  PRINT TAB(12) "You will have 5 examples to do."
55  FOR I=1 TO 2000 :NEXT I
60  CLS
70  FOR Q=1 TO 5
80  READ S1$,V$,S2$,CT$
90  PRINT @ 10, S1$+V$;" not ";S2$
100 PRINT @ 403, V$;
110 V=404+LEN(V$)+1
120 PRINT @ V, "not";
130 FOR I=1 TO 500 :NEXT I
140 FOR W=(V+1) TO V-(4*64) STEP -64
150 PRINT @ W, "o";
160 FOR I=1 TO 100
170 NEXT I
180 PRINT @ W, CHR$(193);
190 NEXT W
200 FOR I=1 TO 500 :NEXT I
210 PRINT @403, V$;
220 PRINT @ V, "n t";
230 FOR W=(V+1)-(4*64) TO V+1 STEP 64
240 PRINT @ W, "'";
250 FOR I=1 TO 100 :NEXT I
260 PRINT @ W, CHR$(193);
270 NEXT W
280 PRINT @ 403, V$;
290 PRINT @ V, "n't";
300 FOR I=1 TO 500 :NEXT I
310 FOR W=V TO V-1 STEP -1
320 PRINT @ W, "n't";
330 FOR I=1 TO 20 :NEXT I
340 PRINT @ W, CHR$(195);
350 NEXT W
360 PRINT @ 403, CT$;
370 FOR I=1 TO 500 :NEXT I
380 PRINT @458, S1$+CT$;" ";S2$
390 POKE 16409,0
400 PRINT TAB(10)  "Type the contraction carefully."
410 PRINT CHR$(212);
420 LINEINPUT C$
430 IF C$=CT$ THEN 440  ELSE 500
440 PRINT TAB(20) "Good work !"
450 GOSUB 570
460 IF Q=5 THEN 490
470 CLS
480 NEXT Q
490 PRINT TAB(20) "Good - by." : POKE 16409,1 : END
500 PRINT TAB(25) "Try again."
510 N=N+1
520 IF N=3 THEN 530  ELSE 410
```

```
530 PRINT @512,CHR$(31)
535 N=0
540 PRINT TAB(10) "The contraction is ";CT$;"."
550 GOSUB 570
560 GOTO 460
570 PRINT TAB(13) "Press any key to go on."
580 A$=INKEY$
590 IF A$="" THEN 580  ELSE 600
600 RETURN
610 DATA "The man ","could","work by himself.","couldn't"
620 DATA "People ","should","overeat.","shouldn't"
630 DATA "The children ","were","in the house.","weren't"
640 DATA "Mary ","did","meet her parents there.","didn't"
650 DATA "I ","have","enough crayons.","haven't"
```

21. SHOWING POSSESSION

SUGGESTED FILE NAME: POSSESS

SUGGESTED GRADE RANGE: 3–8

DESCRIPTION OF THE PROGRAM: This program provides guided practice in forming possessives with 's, and '. The visible formation of the possessive on the screen reinforces the word-building aspects of this program and aids in vocabulary development.

EXPLANATION OF DATA LINES: W$ – the word

RR – 1 or 2 depending on the correct way of forming the possessive

R – the student's response

PROGRAMMING LOGIC: Line 260 tells the program which ending ('s or ') is correct and therefore where the program should branch.

Lines 330-450 are for responses made with 's.

Lines 330-370 move "book" over to make room for the 's.

Lines 390-430 move the 's down into place.

Lines 460-580 are for responses with '.

Lines 460-500 move "book" over to make room for the '.

Lines 520-560 move the apostrophe down into place.

HOW TO CHANGE THE DATA: 1. Change the items in lines 630-640.

2. Change the number of items in lines 80 and 270.

```
10 CLS
20 CLEAR 1000
30 PRINT @275, "SHOWING POSSESSION"
40 PRINT TAB(16) "by Gloria Kuchinskas Ed.D."
41 FOR I=1 TO 1000 :NEXT I
42 CLS
43 PRINT TAB(10) "Read these sentences:"
51 PRINT TAB(15) "1. The red one is Mary's pencil."
53 PRINT TAB(15) "2. Those are the girls' pencils."
54 PRINT TAB(15) "3. The pencils are sharp."
55 PRINT :PRINT TAB(10) "In sentence 1, the pencil belongs to
Mary."
56 PRINT TAB(15) "The 's shows this possession."
57 PRINT TAB(10) "In sentence 2, the pencils belong to the gir
ls."
58 PRINT TAB(15) "Girls end in s, so the ' shows possession."
59 PRINT TAB(10) "In sentence 3, we don't know who owns the pe
ncils."
60 PRINT TAB(15) "The s is a plural ending."
61 PRINT :PRINT TAB(10) "In this program, you will decide the
proper ending"
62 PRINT TAB(15) "in 10 sentences."
63 GOSUB 600
64 CLS
70 W=0
80 FOR W=1 TO 10
90 READ W$,RR
100 PRINT @206, "It is ";
110 PRINT @212, W$;
120 PRINT @212+LEN(W$)+1, "book."
130 PRINT @329, "We show that the book belongs to ";W$
140 PRINT TAB(20) "1. by adding 's"
150 PRINT TAB(20) "2. by adding '"
160 PRINT TAB(20) "3. not possession"
170 PRINT @655, "Pick an answer (1-3) ";
180 INPUT R
190 IF R<>1 AND R<>2 AND R<>3 THEN 170
200 IF R=3 AND RR=3 THEN 300   ELSE 210
210 IF R=RR THEN 260   ELSE 220
220 PRINT TAB(25) "Try again.":FOR I=1 TO 800:NEXT I
230 PRINT @704, CHR$(31)
240 PRINT CHR$(217);
250 GOTO 170
260 ON R GOSUB 330   ,460
300 GOSUB 590
310 CLS
320 NEXT W
322 CLS :PRINT @346, "GOOD-BY !" :END
330 FOR Q=212+LEN(W$)+1 TO 212+LEN(W$)+3
340 PRINT @Q, "book."
350 FOR I=1 TO 100 :NEXT I
360 PRINT @Q, CHR$(197)
370 NEXT Q
380 PRINT @212+LEN(W$)+3, "book.";
390 FOR Q=20+LEN(W$)+1 TO 138+LEN(W$)+1 STEP 64
400 PRINT @Q, "'s"
410 FOR I=1 TO 100 :NEXT I
```

```
420 PRINT @Q, CHR$(194)
430 NEXT Q
440 PRINT @206, "It is ";W$;"'s book.";
450 RETURN
460 FOR Q=212+LEN(W$)+1 TO 212+LEN(W$)+2
470 PRINT @Q, "book."
480 FOR I=1 TO 100 :NEXT I
490 PRINT @Q, CHR$(193)
500 NEXT Q
510 PRINT @212+LEN(W$)+2, "book.";
520 FOR Q=20+LEN(W$)+1 TO 138+LEN(W$)+1 STEP 64
530 PRINT @Q, "'"
540 FOR I=1 TO 100 :NEXT I
550 PRINT @Q, CHR$(193)
560 NEXT Q
570 PRINT @206, "It is ";W$;"' book.";
580 RETURN
590 PRINT @320, CHR$(31)
600 PRINT @911, "Press any key to go on."
610 A$=INKEY$
620 IF A$="" THEN 610  ELSE RETURN
630 DATA John,1,the girls,2,a new,3,everyone,1,the boy,1
640 DATA the birds,2,the class,1,one,3,everybody,1,the ladies,2
```

22. PLAYING CONCENTRATION

SUGGESTED FILE NAME: CONCEN

SUGGESTED GRADE RANGE: 2–8

DESCRIPTION OF THE PROGRAM: This program builds short-term visual memory and attention span in students. It is a subskill of learning to spell and is especially valuable for students who are impulsive rather than reflective. A score is used to increase the desire to concentrate.

NEW PROGRAMMING STATEMENTS:

200 PRINT @389 + 11 + 11 + 11 + 11, W5$

This PRINT @ location ensures that the beginning of each word will be evenly spaced on the screen (11 spaces apart) without calculation. This location could have been expressed as 433.

EXPLANATION OF DATA LINES:

W1$, W2$, W3$, W4$, W5$ – The five words that appear on the screen

AN$ – the word the student is asked to remember

A – a number from 1-5 depending on the location of AN$

S – a counter for the score

PROGRAMMING LOGIC: Lines 210-250 draw lines under the five words.

Lines 260-300 number each word.

Lines 160-200 print a word over each line.

Lines 320-360 make the words disappear.

HOW TO CHANGE THE DATA: 1. Change the words in lines 610-700.

2. Change the number of trials in lines 90, 520.

3. Use words that are very much alike (same beginning or ending, for example) to make the game harder.

```
10 CLS
20 CLEAR 2000
30 PRINT @275, "PLAYING CONCENTRATION"
40 PRINT TAB(17) "by Gloria Kuchinskas Ed.D."
50 FOR I=1 TO 1000 :NEXT I
51 CLS
52 PRINT @74, "This game helps you build your visual memory sk
ills."
53 PRINT TAB(10) "You will be presented with 5 words at a time
."
54 PRINT TAB(10) "You will need to concentrate to remember whe
re"
55 PRINT TAB(20) "they all are."
56 PRINT :PRINT TAB(10) "You will have 10 sets of words to try
."
60 GOSUB 560
70 S=0
80 CLS
90 FOR W=1 TO 10
100 READ W1$,W2$,W3$,W4$,W5$,AN$,A
110 PRINT TAB(20) "CONCENTRATE !"
120 PRINT TAB(7) "You will need to remember where all the word
s are."
130 PRINT STRING$(63,"*");
140 PRINT @232, "Score:";S
150 GOSUB 560
160 PRINT @389, W1$;
170 PRINT @389+11, W2$;
180 PRINT @389+11+11, W3$;
190 PRINT @389+11+11+11, W4$;
200 PRINT @389+11+11+11+11, W5$;
210 PRINT @453, STRING$(8,131);
220 PRINT @453+11, STRING$(8,131);
230 PRINT @453+11+11, STRING$(8,131);
240 PRINT @453++11+11+11, STRING$(8,131);
250 PRINT @453+11+11+11+11, STRING$(8,131);
260 PRINT @520, "1";
270 PRINT @520+11, "2";
280 PRINT @520+11+11, "3";
290 PRINT @520+11+11+11, "4";
300 PRINT @520+11+11+11+11, "5";
310 FOR I=1 TO 1000 :NEXT I
```

```
320 PRINT @389, CHR$(200);
330 PRINT @389+11, CHR$(200);
340 PRINT @389+11+11, CHR$(200);
350 PRINT @389+11+11+11, CHR$(200);
360 PRINT @389+11+11+11+11, CHR$(200);
370 PRINT
380 PRINT @724, "Where was ";AN$;" (1-5) ";
390 INPUT X
400 IF X=A THEN 480  ELSE 410
410 S=S-500
420 IF S<0 THEN S=0
430 PRINT @238, CHR$(194);S
440 PRINT @793, "Try Again."
450 FOR I=1 TO 500 :NEXT I
460 PRINT @704, CHR$(31)
470 GOTO 160
480 PRINT TAB(15) "Good for you - ";AN$;" was in space ";A
490 S=S+500
500 PRINT @238, CHR$(194);S
510 GOSUB 560
530 CLS
540 NEXT W
545 CLS
550 IF S>4500 THEN PRINT "You are very good at concentrating !
" :ELSE 551
551 IF S<2000 THEN PRINT "You need to practice concentrating."
 :ELSE 552
552 CLS :PRINT @346, "GOOD-BY !" :END
560 PRINT @852, "Press any key to go on."
570 A$=INKEY$
580 IF A$="" THEN 570  ELSE 590
590 PRINT @852, CHR$(31)
600 RETURN
610 DATA green,yellow,blue,black,red,blue,3
620 DATA bird,bear,pig,cow,goose,bird,1
630 DATA truck,car,airplane,boat,sled,sled,5
640 DATA bread,milk,meat,apple,soup,milk,2
650 DATA shoe,glove,dress,coat,skirt,coat,4
660 DATA over,under,above,on,in,over,1
670 DATA pretty,silly,funny,happy,sleepy,sleepy,5
680 DATA they,she,we,he,you,he,4
690 DATA arm,leg,head,foot,eye,head,3
700 DATA bed,clock,chair,table,desk,clock,2
```

23. MAKING COMPARISONS

SUGGESTED FILE NAME: COMPARE

SUGGESTED GRADE RANGE: 2–8

DESCRIPTION OF THE PROGRAM: This program requires students to identify two words that are compared in a sentence. Both similes and metaphors are used. The program provides the attribute in which they are comparable. This skill aids inferential comprehension by helping students notice and interpret similes and metaphors in reading.

EXPLANATION OF DATA LINES: ST$ — the sentence

S1$ — the first word compared

S2$ — the second word compared

X$ — first student response

Y$ — second student response

PROGRAMMING LOGIC: Lines 160, 190, 270, 300 examine only the first four letters in the student's response and count the response correct if these four letters match the first four letters in either of the answers. This allows students to add to answers without penalty as long as the critical part of the answer (the first four letters) is identical.

Lines 150, 260 allow the student to type either correct response first.

Lines 340-380 draw a box.

Line 390 puts the two words compared and the attribute for comparison in the box.

Lines 340-390 must have semicolons at the end.

HOW TO CHANGE THE DATA:
1. Change the sentence and response in lines 530-570.

2. Change the number of items in lines 70, 470.

3. Increase the difficulty of the vocabulary.

4. Make all items similes to make the activity easier.

5. Make all items metaphors to make the activity of medium difficulty.

```
10 CLEAR 1000
20 CLS
30 PRINT @275, "MAKING COMPARISONS"
40 PRINT TAB(16) "by Gloria Kuchinskas Ed.D."
50 FOR I=1 TO 1000 :NEXT I
51 CLS
52 PRINT @266, "In the sentence:"
53 PRINT TAB(15) "Mary danced like a fairy."
54 PRINT TAB(15) STRING$(4,131);TAB(34) STRING$(5,131)
55 PRINT :PRINT TAB(8) "Mary and a fairy are compared."
56 PRINT TAB(15) "They dance the same way."
57 PRINT :PRINT TAB(8) "In this program, you will have 5 sets of"
58 PRINT TAB(17) "comparisons to find."
59 FOR I=1 TO 4000 :NEXT I
60 CLS
70 FOR Q=1 TO 5
80 READ ST$,S1$,S2$,CP$
```

```
90 PRINT ā335, ST$
100 PRINT
110 PRINT ā 458, "Type one word for one thing that is compared
."
120 POKE 16409,0
130 PRINT CHR$(217);
140 LINEINPUT X$
150 IF X$=S1$ OR X$=S2$ THEN 220   ELSE 160
160 IF LEFT$(X$,4)=LEFT$(S1$,4) THEN 170   ELSE 190
170 X$=S1$
180 GOTO 150
190 IF LEFT$(X$,4)=LEFT$(S2$,4) THEN 200   ELSE 430
200 X$=S2$
210 GOTO 150
220 PRINT ā 448, CHR$(31)
230 PRINT ā 458, "Type one word for the other thing that is co
mpared."
240 PRINT CHR$(217);
250 LINEINPUT Y$
255 IF X$=S1$ THEN Z$=S2$
256 IF X$=S2$ THEN Z$=S1$
260 IF LEFT$(Z$,4)=LEFT$(Y$,4) THEN 330 ELSE 270
270 IF WR=2 THEN 280 ELSE 290
280 WR=0 :PRINT ā537, Z$
285 FOR I=1 TO 2000 :NEXT I
287 GOTO 330
290 WR=WR+1
295 PRINT "Try again."
300 FOR I=1 TO 500 :NEXT I
310 GOTO 220
330 PRINT ā 448, CHR$(31)
340 PRINT ā 517, CHR$(191)+STRING$(54,131)+CHR$(191);
350 FOR W=581 TO 645 STEP 64
360 PRINT ā W, CHR$(191)+STRING$(54,32)+CHR$(191);
370 NEXT W
380 PRINT ā 645, CHR$(191)+STRING$(54,176)+CHR$(191);
390 PRINT ā 591, S1$;" and ";S2$;" are both ";CP$;
400 PRINT ā 847, "Press any key when you are ready."
410 AK$=INKEY$
420 IF AK$="" THEN 410   ELSE 470
430 PRINT TAB(20) "Try again."
440 GOTO 130
450 PRINT TAB(20) "Try again."
460 GOTO 240
470 IF Q=5 THEN 500   ELSE 480
480 CLS
490 NEXT Q
500 PRINT ā 832, CHR$(31)
510 CLS :PRINT ā346, "GOOD-BY !" : POKE 16409,1 : END
520 END
530 DATA "A snake is like a shiny twig.","snake","twig","shiny
"
540 DATA "Her eyes were blue lakes.","eyes","lakes","blue"
550 DATA "The snowy icing was white.","icing","snow","white"
560 DATA "The sun felt like fire on her skin.","sun","fire","h
ot"
570 DATA "The old man was as wise as an owl.","man","owl","wis
e"
```

24. WRITING POEMS

SUGGESTED FILE NAME: POEM

SUGGESTED GRADE RANGE: 4–8

DESCRIPTION OF THE PROGRAM: In this program, the computer produces a poem by selecting words at random from four dictionaries. Students are asked to critically analyze the poem produced, edit it, and copy their own version for later use in group activities. This program requires students to use critical reading skills, encourages poetry writing by providing a poetry starter, and improves editing skills.

NEW PROGRAMMING STATEMENTS:

    330 IF G = C THEN...

If the random number G is the same as the random number C, go back and select a new random number.

EXPLANATION OF DATA LINES:

A	–	number of adjectives
N	–	number of nouns
V	–	number of verbs
P	–	number of prepositions
A$	–	the adjectives
N$	–	the nouns
V$	–	the verbs
P$	–	the prepositions
C, G	–	random numbers for adjectives
D	–	a random number for nouns
E	–	a random number for verbs
F	–	a random number for prepositions

PROGRAMMING LOGIC: Lines 140-250 read the words in the four dictionaries.

Lines 260-290 assign a random number to each form of the word.

In effect, this tells the program which one of each kind of word to use.

Lines 330, 350, 380, 400 make sure the same word is not selected twice in the same poem by the computer.

Line 300 sets up the first line of the poem.

Line 310 sets up the second line.

Line 360 sets up the third line.

Line 410 sets up the fourth line.

HOW TO CHANGE THE DATA:
1. Change the words in the dictionaries in lines 620-650. (The mood, locale or visual images can all be changed when the words are carefully chosen by students.)
2. Change the number of words in each dictionary in line 610.
3. Change the meter by changing the line formations in lines 330, 350, 380, and 400.

```
10 CLS
20 CLEAR 2000
30 PRINT @277, "WRITING POEMS"
40 PRINT TAB(16) "by Gloria Kuchinskas Ed.D."
50 FOR I=1 TO 1000 :NEXT I
60 CLS
70 PRINT @340, "I can write a poem."
80 GOSUB 580
90 CLS :RESTORE
100 PRINT TAB(22) "THE DESERT"
110 PRINT TAB(20) "by the COMPUTER"
120 PRINT
130 READ A,N,V,P
140 FOR I=1 TO A
150 READ A$(I)
160 NEXT I
170 FOR I=1 TO N
180 READ N$(I)
190 NEXT I
200 FOR I=1 TO V
210 READ V$(I)
220 NEXT I
230 FOR I=1 TO P
240 READ P$(I)
250 NEXT I
260 C=RND(A)
270 D=RND(N)
280 E=RND(V)
290 F=RND(P)
300 PRINT TAB(18) "The ";A$(C);" ";N$(D);" ";V$(E)
310 PRINT TAB(18) P$(F);" the ";
320 G=RND(A)
330 IF G=C THEN 320  ELSE 340
340 H=RND(N)
350 IF H=D THEN 340  ELSE 360
360 PRINT A$(G);" ";N$(H);"."
370 I=RND(A)
380 IF I=C OR I=G THEN 370  ELSE 390
390 J=RND(N)
400 IF J=D OR J=H THEN 390  ELSE 410
410 PRINT TAB(18) "See the ";A$(I);" ";N$(J);"."
```

```
420 PRINT
430 PRINT TAB(5) "Do you want to change my poem to make it bet
ter (Y/N) ";
440 INPUT Z$
450 Z$=LEFT$(Z$,1)
460 IF Z$="Y" OR Z$="y" THEN 480   ELSE 470
470 IF Z$="N" OR Z$="n" THEN 500   ELSE 440
480 PRINT TAB(15) "Rewrite my poem on your paper."
490 GOSUB 580
500 PRINT TAB(15) "Do you want another poem (Y/N) ";
510 INPUT Y$
520 Y$=LEFT$(Y$,1)
530 IF Y$="Y" OR Y$="y" THEN 90    ELSE 560
560 IF Y$="N" OR Y$="n" THEN 570   ELSE 510
570 CLS :PRINT @346, "GOOD —BY !" :END
580 PRINT TAB(20) "Press any key to go on."
590 A$=INKEY$
600 IF A$="" THEN 590   ELSE RETURN
610 DATA 5,5,5,5
620 DATA dry,yellow,powdery,acrid,sandy
630 DATA rock,plateau,sand,view,plain
640 DATA drifts,spreads,lies,blows,heats
650 DATA on,in,over,under,near
```

25. VERB TENSES

SUGGESTED FILE NAME: TENSES

SUGGESTED GRADE RANGE: 2–8

DESCRIPTION OF THE PROGRAM: In this program, students identify the correct verb tense for a variety of verbs to use within a variety of sentence contexts. This is both a literal comprehension and a grammatical skill.

EXPLANATION OF DATA LINES: ST$ — the sentence beginning

A1$ — present tense of verb

A2$ — past tense of verb

A3$ — future tense of verb

A — a number from 1 to 3 depending on the correct answer

X — the student's response

PROGRAMMING LOGIC: Lines 730-770 remove A2$ from the screen.

Lines 790-830 remove A3$ from the screen.

Lines 850-890 remove A1$ from the screen.

Lines 290-430 move A1$ to join the sentence.

Lines 480-540 move A2$ to join the sentence.

Lines 590-700 move A3$ to join the sentence.

Line 190 tells the program the correct branch.

HOW TO CHANGE THE DATA: 1. Change the items in lines 960-1050.

2. Change the number of items in lines 70, 230.

3. Increase the difficulty of the sentences; the sentence stem must be twenty characters or fewer or the movement on the screen will be disturbed.

```
10 CLS
20 CLEAR 500
30 PRINT a277, "VERB TENSES"
40 PRINT TAB(15) "by Gloria Kuchinskas Ed.D."
50 FOR I=1 TO 1000 :NEXT I
51 CLS
52 PRINT TAB(10) "Read these sentences:"
53 PRINT TAB(15) "1. Tom played ball yesterday."
54 PRINT TAB(15) "2. Tom will play ball tomorrow."
55 PRINT TAB(15) "3. Tom is playing ball now."
56 PRINT :PRINT TAB(10) "The verb, play, means the same in all
 3 sentences."
57 PRINT TAB(10) "The form of the verb we use depends on the s
entence."
58 PRINT :PRINT TAB(10) "In this program, you will find the co
rrect form"
59 PRINT TAB(15) "of the verb in 10 sentences."
60 PRINT :PRINT :PRINT
61 GOSUB 920
62 CLS
70 FOR W=1 TO 10
80 READ ST$,A1$,A2$,A3$,A
90 PRINT a84, "VERB TENSES"
100 PRINT TAB(15) STRING$(21,"*")
110 PRINT a287, A1$;"          1";
120 PRINT a389, ST$;
130 PRINT a415, A2$;"          2";
140 PRINT a543, A3$;"   3";
150 PRINT
160 PRINT a645, "Which tense is correct (1-3) ";
170 INPUT X
180 IF X=A THEN 190  ELSE 210
190 PRINT a645, CHR$(31)
192 ON X GOTO 270,460,570
200 GOTO 240
210 PRINT TAB(20) "Try again."
212 FOR I=1 TO 500 :NEXT I
214 PRINT a645, CHR$(31)
220 GOTO 160
240 CLS
250 NEXT W
260 CLS :PRINT a346, "GOOD-BY !" :END
270 GOSUB 730
```

```
280 GOSUB 790
290 PRINT @287, A1$
300 PRINT @287+LEN(A1$)+7, CHR$(195)
310 FOR Q=287 TO 350 STEP 64
320 PRINT @Q, A1$
330 FOR I=1 TO 50 :NEXT I
340 PRINT @Q, CHR$(205)
350 NEXT Q
360 PRINT @389, ST$;
370 PRINT @415, A1$;
380 FOR Q=415 TO 389+LEN(ST$) STEP -1
390 PRINT @Q, A1$
400 FOR I=1 TO 50 :NEXT I
410 PRINT @Q, CHR$(205)
420 NEXT Q
430 PRINT @389+LEN(ST$), A1$
440 GOSUB 910
450 GOTO 240
460 GOSUB 790
470 GOSUB 850
480 PRINT @415+LEN(A2$)+7, CHR$(195)
490 FOR Q=415 TO 389+LEN(ST$) STEP -1
500 PRINT @Q, A2$
510 FOR I=1 TO 50 :NEXT I
520 PRINT @Q, CHR$(205)
530 NEXT Q
540 PRINT @389+LEN(ST$), A2$;
550 GOSUB 910
560 GOTO 240
570 GOSUB 730
580 GOSUB 850
590 PRINT @543+LEN(A3$)+8, CHR$(194)
600 FOR Q=543 TO 479 STEP -64
610 PRINT @Q, A3$
620 FOR I=1 TO 50 :NEXT I
630 PRINT @Q, CHR$(205)
640 NEXT Q
650 FOR Q=415 TO 389+LEN(ST$)+1
660 PRINT @Q, A3$
670 FOR I=1 TO 50 :NEXT I
680 PRINT @Q, CHR$(206)
690 NEXT Q
700 PRINT @389, ST$+A3$;
710 GOSUB 910
720 GOTO 240
730 FOR Q=415 TO 433
740 PRINT @Q, A2$
750 FOR I=1 TO 20 :NEXT I
760 PRINT @Q, CHR$(204)
770 NEXT Q
780 RETURN
790 FOR Q=543 TO 560
800 PRINT @Q, A3$
810 FOR I=1 TO 20 :NEXT I
820 PRINT @Q, CHR$(204)
830 NEXT Q
```

```
840 RETURN
850 FOR Q=287 TO 307
860 PRINT @Q, A1$
870 FOR I=1 TO 20 :NEXT I
880 PRINT @Q, CHR$(204)
890 NEXT Q
900 RETURN
910 PRINT @576, CHR$(31)
920 PRINT @783, "Press any key to go on."
930 A$=INKEY$
940 IF A$="" THEN 930  ELSE 950
950 RETURN
960 DATA "Yesterday he ","run.","ran.","will run.",2
970 DATA "Tomorrow he ","fly.","flew.","will fly.",3
980 DATA "He can ","add.","added.","will add.",1
990 DATA "Did he ","care?","cared?","will care?",1
1000 DATA "Last winter plants ","die.","died.","will die.",2
1010 DATA "What have the insects ","eat?","eaten?","will eat?"
,2
1020 DATA "Next June the test ","is given.","was given.","will
 be given.",3
1030 DATA "Mother said you can ","help.","helped.","will help.
",1
1040 DATA "The flowers are to ","pick.","picked.","will pick."
,1
1050 DATA "At noon the meat was ","turn.","turned.","will turn
.",2
```

chapter 8

25 PROGRAMS FOR MATHEMATICS AND SCIENCE ON THE TRS-80™

A program is more than a set of instructions to the computer; it is also a reflection of the inner workings of a person's mind. As such, programming logic often defies understanding. Therefore, don't be discouraged when you fail to fully comprehend the significance of all the statements in the programs in this chapter. You will find yourself in good company; we, the authors, cannot always interpret the products of one another's thinking. However, we have attempted to explain ourselves as much as possible without burdensome detail. We hope that we have given you enough clues so that you can understand some of the more obscure parts of the programs, and we hope that you will be able to design some programs of your own.

In this chapter you will find twenty-five programs for the TRS-80™ Model III or Model IV microcomputer. These programs are meant to serve two purposes.

1. They provide a practical means of learning beginning programming in the BASIC language. This book is not meant to provide a complete course in programming, but to introduce you to the BASIC language in an interesting and useful way.

2. The programs can serve as the beginning of your software library in that they provide short, concise exercises for specific skills in mathematics and science.

We recommend that the programs be typed in the order in which they are presented. They have been arranged in order of difficulty of programming techniques, not necessarily in order of concept difficulty. However, if you have a special need for a program that appears later on and are adventurous, please feel free to attempt the program in any order you wish.

To assist you in understanding the purpose of the programs before typing them into your computer, each program is preceded by the following information.

SUGGESTED FILE NAME: This is a suggested name to use when saving the program. The TRS-80™ computer allows file names of only eight characters or fewer with no punctuation marks. Usually, the title is too long to be used.

Caution: Each program must have a unique name when it is saved on a disk. If you try to save a program using the file name of a program already saved, the original program will be erased from the disk.

SUGGESTED GRADE RANGE: The grade levels at which a particular skill is taught and practiced.

DESCRIPTION OF THE PROGRAM: This paragraph describes the purpose of the program and some of its features.

NEW PROGRAMMING STATEMENTS: This section describes the functions of new programming statements that have not been used in a previous program.

EXPLANATION OF DATA LINES: The structure of the information in the data lines is explained in this section.

PROGRAMMING LOGIC: Here the authors attempt to explain their thinking. Program lines which might not be readily understood or that perform a special function are explained here.

HOW TO CHANGE THE DATA: It is possible to customize some of the programs to address the special needs of your students by changing data entries or certain lines of the program. The techniques needed to accomplish these changes are explained here.

A VERY IMPORTANT REMINDER

A computer line begins with the line number and ends with the last word or number before the next numbered line. *Do not press* <**ENTER**> *until you have typed the entire line.* When the cursor approaches the right side of the screen, just keep typing. Screen wraparound takes care of automatically moving the cursor down the screen.

For example, in the first program, "Guess the Mystery Number," line 60 will not fit on one line of the screen. Keep typing, and let screen wraparound take care of the problem. Press <**ENTER**> at the end of the word "INCLUSIVE." If you make a mistake and press <**ENTER**> too soon, retype the line.

MODEL IV USER: You must use a MODEL III TRSDOS disk (Cat. #26-0312), available from Radio Shack.

1. GUESS THE MYSTERY NUMBER

SUGGESTED FILE NAME: GUESS

SUGGESTED GRADE RANGE: 2–5

DESCRIPTION OF THE PROGRAM: This program provides practice in formulating a systematic method for solving a problem. The computer randomly chooses a number between 1 and 100. The student must guess it in the least number of tries. We hope that the student will discover that halving differences is the most efficient way to "guess."

PROGRAMMING STATEMENTS: RANDOM is a statement that turns on the random number generator. CLS clears the screen. The colon (:) separates one statement from the next. Theoretically, each BASIC statement should be on a separate line. However, several statements can be placed on the same line when separated by colons.

PRINT@ is a statement that forces messages to be printed at various locations on the screen. The screen is divided into 1023 locations. Look at the Video Display Worksheet in the Appendix. Each of sixteen rows on the screen has sixty-four locations. The first row starts with 0 and runs through 63; the second row begins with 64 and goes through 127; and so on. PRINT@270 causes the title in this program to be printed on the fifth row fourteen spaces from the left.

The FOR/NEXT loop makes the computer count to 1000 before continuing the program.

M = RND(100) chooses a number between 1 and 100 and assigns it to the variable M.

The variable, I, counts the number of guesses. I = 0 sets the counter at zero. I = I + 1 increases the counter by 1 each time a guess is made.

G is the guess; M is the mystery number. If G = M then the computer prints the message that the player has hit the number in I guesses.

If G < M (if G is less than M), the computer prints TOO LOW and each player is sent back to line 60 to make another guess.

Line 100 is executed if neither of lines 80 or 90 is true. In this case, the guess is TOO HIGH and the player is returned to line 60 for another guess.

In lines 110 through 140, the player can choose to play the game again.

HOW TO CHANGE THE DATA: You may want to adjust the program to use smaller numbers or larger ones. If so, change lines 40 and 60. For example, if you want the mystery number to be between 1 and 1000, change the lines to read

```
40 M = RND(1000)
60 CLS:PRINT"I'M THINKING OF A MYSTERY NUMBER BETWEEN 1 AND 1000
INCLUSIVE."
```

Be aware of the need to distinguish between the numeral zero and the letter o. The program listing does not have slashes through the zeros. Nevertheless, if "0" is in the context of a number, use the number, zero.

```
10 RANDOM : CLS
20 PRINT@275,"GUESS THE MYSTERY NUMBER"
30 FOR TI=1 TO 1000 : NEXT TI
40 M = RND(100)
50 CLS
60 PRINT "I'M THINKING OF A MYSTERY NUMBER BETWEEN 1 AND 100
   INCLUSIVE."
70 I=0
80 INPUT "GUESS";G
90 I = I + 1
100 IF G = M THEN PRINT "YOU HIT THE NUMBER IN ";I;" GUESSES
" : GOTO 130
110 IF G < M THEN PRINT "TOO LOW" : GOTO 80
120 PRINT "TOO HIGH" : GOTO 80
130 PRINT "DO YOU WANT TO PLAY THIS GAME AGAIN? (Y OR N)"
140 INPUT Z$
150 IF Z$ = "Y" THEN 40
160 IF Z$ = "N" THEN 190
170 PRINT "PLEASE TYPE Y OR N"
180 GOTO 140
190 PRINT "THAT'S ALL FOR NOW. BYE-BYE."
200 END
```

2. SOME—MORE OR LESS

SUGGESTED FILE NAME: SOMEMORE

SUGGESTED GRADE RANGE: 3–4

DESCRIPTION OF THE PROGRAM: The program gives students practice in adding to or subtracting from a given number when given the word "more" or "less." The student chooses a number from one to nine, which is the amount to be added or subtracted. This number is used in a statement that asks the student to type the number that is "more" or "less" than another.

NEW PROGRAMMING STATEMENTS: A$=INKEY$ allows the computer to accept a single character from the keyboard without requiring that <**ENTER**> be pressed. The statement

    IF A$="" THEN 70

will be executed repeatedly until a key is pressed.

    N=VAL(A$) assigns to N the numerical value of A$. Remember, a number assigned to A$ is stored as a word. In order to use it as a number, it has to be stored as a number. This is accomplished by N = VAL(A$).

```
10 RANDOM : CLS
20 PRINT@276,"SOME --- MORE OR LESS" : FOR TI=1 TO 1000 : NE
XT TI
30 CLS
40 PRINT "PROBLEMS OF THE FORM: <NUMBER> MORE/LESS THAN A GI
VEN NUMBER."
50 PRINT : PRINT"ENTER THE <NUMBER>, FROM 1 TO 9, TO BE USED
 IN THIS PROGRAM."
60 A$=INKEY$
70 A$=INKEY$ : IF A$="" THEN 70
80 IF VAL(A$)=0 THEN 70
90 N=VAL(A$)
100 O=RND(2) : IF O=2 THEN O$="LESS" ELSE O$="MORE"
110 V = RND(N * 10 + 9) + (N - 1)
120 IF O=2 THEN CA=V-N ELSE CA=V+N
130 CLS : PRINT
140 PRINT CHR$(23);TAB(3);"FIND THE NUMBER WHICH IS"
150 PRINT : PRINT TAB(7);A$;" ";O$;" THAN";V
160 FOR T=1 TO 200 : NEXT T
170 PRINT : PRINT : PRINT
180 PRINTTAB(2);"PLEASE TYPE YOUR ANSWER AND" : PRINTTAB(4);
" PRESS THE <ENTER> KEY."
190 INPUT A
200 IF A=CA PRINT : PRINT "GOOD ! !" : GOTO 220
210 PRINT : PRINT : PRINT "SORRY. THE NUMBER IS ";CA;"."
220 PRINT : PRINT "TYPE <G> TO GO ON--<S> TO STOP."
230 INPUT C$
240 IF C$="G" THEN 100
250 IF C$<>"S" PRINT "PLEASE TYPE <G> OR <S>." : GOTO 230
260 CLS : PRINT : PRINT : PRINT "SO LONG FOR NOW."
270 END
```

3. GREATER THAN–LESS THAN SYMBOLS

SUGGESTED FILE NAME: GRTRTHAN

SUGGESTED GRADE RANGE: 3–5

DESCRIPTION OF THE PROGRAM: This program gives the student practice using the greater than (>) and less than (<) symbols. The student chooses the largest number that he or she wishes to use in these exercises. The computer then displays two randomly selected numbers that are less than that larger number and asks the student to choose the symbol less than (<) or greater than (>) that correctly compares the two numbers.

NEW PROGRAMMING STATEMENTS: CLEAR 500 reserves space in the computer's memory for 500 characters (letters or numbers) of strings (words). Normally, the computer sets aside 50 spaces for words. Sometimes, when the computer might be asked to accept many typed-in words, you may want to reserve more than 50 characters of string space so you won't get the error "OUT OF STRING SPACE."

STRING$(4,95) tells the computer to print the special character for Code 95 four times. Refer to the Appendix in your computer manual for TRS-80 Model III or Model IV Character Codes. The character called CHR$(95) is a bar.

SC=INT(NC/T*100 + .5) computes the student's score. The INT (integer) function directs the computer to keep the integer part of a decimal number and drop the decimal part.

PROGRAMMING LOGIC: Notice in the score computation—INT(NC/T*100 + .5)—that .5 is added to the score before the decimal part is dropped. In effect, adding .5 rounds the number to the nearest ones place. For example, in rounding 88.7 to the nearest ones place, the computer calculates 88.7 + .5, then drops the decimal. Therefore, INT(88.7 + .5) = INT(89.2) = 89.

```
10 CLEAR 500 : RANDOM
20 CLS : PRINT@271,"GREATER THAN - LESS THAN SYMBOLS" : FOR TI
=1 TO 1000 : NEXT TI
30 CLS : PRINT "WHAT IS THE LARGEST NUMBER YOU WISH TO USE?"
40 PRINT : INPUT N : IF N<2 THEN 10
50 N1=RND(N) : N2=RND(N)
60 IF N1=N2 THEN 50
70 IF N1>N2 THEN CA$=">" ELSE CA$="<"
80 CLS : PRINT CHR$(23);TAB(8);N1;" ";STRING$(4,95);" ";N2
90 PRINT : PRINT
100 PRINT"TYPE THE CORRECT SYMBOL,"
110 PRINT : PRINT TAB(5);"> (GREATER THAN), OR"
120 PRINT TAB(5);"< (LESS THAN)" : PRINT
130 PRINT "TO FILL IN THE BLANK, AND PRESS"
140 PRINT "THE <ENTER> KEY."
150 INPUT AN$
160 T=T+1
170 IF AN$=CA$ THEN PRINT "CORRECT." : NC=NC+1 : GOTO 190
180 PRINT "SORRY, NOT CORRECT."
190 SC = INT(NC/T*100+.5)
200 PRINT "YOUR SCORE IS ";SC;"%."
210 PRINT : PRINT "PRESS <SPACE BAR> TO CONTINUE."
220 PRINT "PRESS <Q> TO QUIT.";
230 E$=INKEY$ : IF E$="" THEN 230
240 IF E$=" " THEN 50
250 IF E$<>"Q" THEN 210 ELSE 260
260 CLS : PRINT@405,"HAVE A HAPPY DAY ! !" : END
```

4. MORE THAN–FEWER THAN

SUGGESTED FILE NAME: MOREFEW

SUGGESTED GRADE RANGE: 3–5

DESCRIPTION OF THE PROGRAM: The student has the opportunity to practice the mathematical meaning of "more than" and "fewer than" in a counting context. The computer randomly chooses two letters and prints different amounts of the letters on the screen. The student then types the letter of which there are "more" or "fewer."

NEW PROGRAMMING TECHNIQUES: Sometimes it is convenient to enter values into the computer as lists (called arrays) that use the same variable. In this program there are four arrays: Q$, L, N, and L$. Each of these arrays has only two values in it. Each value is denoted by its numbered place in the list. For example, MORE is the first value in Q$ and is denoted Q$(1). The second value in array L is a random number between 1 and 26 added to 64.

RND(26)+64 is used to pick a letter of the alphabet randomly. Each character that can be typed into the computer from the keyboard is given a decimal code. This code is found in the Appendix of your computer manual in the table headed TRS-80™ Character Codes. The decimal codes for the letters of the alphabet begin with 65 and end with 90.

In lines 100 and 110, the letters stored in array L$ are obtained by taking the Character Code of the values in array L. For example, if $L(1) = 82$, then $L\$(1) = CHR\$(82) = R$.

PROGRAMMING LOGIC: In line 70 the computer is told to choose how many of each of the two letters to print on the screen. Line 90 tells the computer that if the two values chosen are the same, to go back to line 70 and choose again. The routine in lines 120-170 is to print the correct number of each of the two letters on the screen in random order. This loop of instructions will be executed over and over until all of the required letters appear on the screen.

```
10 RANDOM
20 CLS : PRINT@275,"MORE THAN - FEWER THAN" : FOR Z=1 TO 1000
: NEXT Z
30 CLS : Q$(1)="MORE " : Q$(2)="FEWER"
40 L(1)=RND(26)+64
50 L(2)=RND(26)+64
60 IF L(1)=L(2) THEN 40
70 N1=RND(8) : N2=RND(8)
80 N(1)=N1 : N(2)=N2
90 IF N(1)=N(2) THEN 70
100 L$(1)=CHR$(L(1))
110 L$(2)=CHR$(L(2))
120 LC=RND(2)
130 N(LC)=N(LC)-1
140 IF N(1)<0 AND N(2)<0 THEN 180
150 IF N(LC)<0 THEN 120
160 PRINT CHR$(23);L$(LC);" ";
170 GOTO 120
180 Q=RND(2)
190 PRINT : PRINT : PRINT
200 PRINT "TYPE THE LETTER OF WHICH THERE  ARE ";Q$(Q);" ABOVE
 AND PRESS THE"
210 PRINT "<ENTER> KEY."
220 INPUT AN$
```

```
225 IF AN$<>L$(1) AND AN$<>L$(2) PRINT "TYPE ";L$(1);" OR ";L$
(2);".":GOTO 220
230 T=T+1
240 IF Q=1 AND N1>N2 THEN CA$=L$(1) ELSE IF Q=1 AND N2>N1 THEN
    CA$=L$(2)
250 IF Q=2 AND N1<N2 THEN CA$=L$(1) ELSE IF Q=2 AND N2<N1 THEN
    CA$=L$(2)
260 IF AN$=CA$ THEN PRINT "CORRECT." : NR=NR+1 : GOTO 280
270 PRINT "SORRY, NOT CORRECT."
280 SC=INT(NR/T*100+.5)
290 PRINT "YOUR SCORE IS ";SC;"%."
300 PRINT : PRINT "PRESS <SPACE BAR> TO CONTINUE."
310 PRINT "PRESS <Q> TO QUIT."
320 X$=INKEY$ : IF X$="" THEN 320
330 IF X$=" " THEN CLS : GOTO 40
340 IF X$<>"Q" THEN 320
350 PRINT "THAT'S ALL FOR NOW. BYE-BYE."
360 END
```

5. CHOOSE THE LARGEST NUMBER

SUGGESTED FILE NAME: LARGEST

SUGGESTED GRADE RANGE: 3–8

DESCRIPTION OF THE PROGRAM: The object of this program is to choose the largest number from three numbers shown on the screen.

EXPLANATION OF DATA LINES: The two data lines contain a total of twenty numbers. The numbers are read into the computer; then, three of them are chosen randomly to appear on the screen.

HOW TO CHANGE THE DATA: The numbers in the data lines may be too difficult for your students. You can change the numbers simply by retyping the data lines. *You must be careful to use exactly ten numbers per data line and to separate each number from the next by a comma.*

```
10 DIM A(20) : R=0 : T=0
20 CLS : PRINT@275,"CHOOSE THE LARGEST NUMBER" : FOR TI=1 TO 1
000 : NEXT TI
30 FOR I=1 TO 20 : READ A(I) : NEXT I
40 CLS : INPUT "WHAT IS YOUR NAME";N$ : PRINT : PRINT "HAPPY T
O MEET YOU, "N$"."
45 PRINT:PRINT "I HAVE TWENTY EXERCISES FOR YOU TO DO." : FOR
TI=1 TO 1500 : NEXT TI
50 N=N+1 : RANDOM
60 B=RND(20) : C=RND(20) : D=RND(20)
70 IF B=C OR C=D OR B=D THEN 60
80 CLS : PRINT"#";N; : PRINT "   WHICH NUMBER IS LARGEST?"
90 PRINT : PRINT A(B) , A(C) , A(D)
100 PRINT : PRINT "TYPE YOUR CHOICE."
110 INPUT X : T=T+1
```

```
120 IF X<>A(B) AND X<>A(C) AND X<>A(D) PRINT : PRINT "PLEASE T
YPE ONE OF THE NUMBERS YOU SEE ON THE SCREEN." : FOR TI=1 TO 1
000 : NEXT TI : T=T-1 : GOTO 80
130 IF X>=A(B) AND X>=A(C) AND X>=A(D) THEN 140  ELSE PRINT "T
RY AGAIN, ";N$ : GOTO 110
140 R=R+1 : PRINT "YOU ARE CORRECT, ";N$ : PRINT : PRINT "YOUR
 SCORE IS ";INT((R/T)*100);"%."
145 IF N>=20 THEN 200
150 PRINT : PRINT "DO YOU WANT ANOTHER PROBLEM (Y OR N)"
160 INPUT Z$
170 IF Z$="Y" THEN 50
180 IF Z$="N" THEN 200
190 PRINT "PLEASE TYPE Y OR N, ";N$ : GOTO 160
200 FOR TI=1 TO 1000 : NEXT TI : CLS : PRINT "YOU HAVE FINISHE
D 20 PROBLEMS." : PRINT : PRINT "GOOD-BYE FOR NOW, ";N$;"."
210 PRINT : END
220 DATA -3,.5,13,0,-7,.44,.444,1.2,1.02,11
230 DATA -1.1,-1.11,.05,.112,.11,6,-4,-1,9,-8,7.2
```

6. UNDERSTANDING MULTIPLICATION
(ROWS AND COLUMNS)

SUGGESTED FILE NAME: UNDMULT

SUGGESTED GRADE RANGE: 3–5

DESCRIPTION OF THE PROGRAM: This program shows the connection between a rectangular display with rows and columns, and multiplication. The computer prints rows of squares on the screen. The student must count the rows of squares, count the columns, then count the squares. The student then multiplies the number of rows by the number of columns. The student should realize that multiplication of rows by columns is the efficient way to count items in a rectangular array.

NEW PROGRAMMING STATEMENTS: PRINT@660,CHR$(31) makes the computer clear the screen from location 660 to 1023 (the end of the screen). Likewise, PRINT@660,CHR$(30) would clear the line from location 660 to the end of the line.

PROGRAMMING LOGIC: The number of rows (NR) and the number of columns (NC) are chosen at random. Lines 70 through 130 draw the rows and columns on the screen. STEP 3 makes the rows print three spaces apart. STEP 4 makes the columns print four spaces apart. This is done so that the squares show up individually on the screen and the student can count them.

```
10 CLS : PRINT@272,"UNDERSTANDING MULTIPLICATION"
20 PRINT@340,"(ROWS AND COLUMNS)"
30 FOR I=1 TO 1000 : NEXT I : CLS
40 N=0 : T=0
50 NR=0 : NC=0 : CLS
```

```
60 R=RND(30) : C=RND(45)
70 FOR I=1 TO R STEP 3
80 NR=NR+1
90 FOR J=1 TO C STEP 4
100 NC=NC+1
110 SET (J+40,I)
120 NEXT J
130 NEXT I
140 PRINT@645,"HOW MANY ROWS"; : T=T+1 : INPUT A
150 IF A=NR THEN 160  ELSE PRINT@675,"COUNT THE ROWS AGAIN" :
GOSUB 310  : PRINT@660,CHR$(31) : GOTO 140
160 N=N+1
170 PRINT@709,"HOW MANY COLUMNS"; : T=T+1 : INPUT B
180 IF B=NC/NR THEN 190  ELSE PRINT@739,"COUNT THE COLUMNS AGA
IN" : GOSUB 310  : PRINT@727,CHR$(31) : GOTO 170
190 N=N+1
200 PRINT@772, A;" X ";B;" = "; : T=T+1 : INPUT C
210 IF C=NR*(NC/NR) THEN 220  ELSE PRINT@803,"NOT CORRECT -- T
RY AGAIN" : GOSUB 310  : PRINT@787,CHR$(31) : GOTO 200
220 N=N+1
230 PRINT@837,"HOW MANY SQUARES"; : T=T+1 : INPUT D
240 IF D=NR*(NC/NR) THEN 250  ELSE PRINT@867,"NOT CORRECT -- T
RY AGAIN" : GOSUB 310  : PRINT@855,CHR$(31) : GOTO 230
250 N=N+1
260 PRINT@901,"THAT'S RIGHT ! !"
270 PRINT@965,"YOUR SCORE IS ";INT((N/T)*100)"%."; : GOSUB 310

275 Z$=""
280 PRINT@965,"HOW ABOUT ANOTHER PROBLEM? (Y OR N)"; : INPUT Z
$ : IF Z$="Y" THEN 50
290 IF Z$="N" THEN CLS : PRINTTAB(19);"HAVE A SUPER DAY!!!!" :
 END
300 PRINT@965,"PLEASE TYPE Y OR N."; : GOSUB 310  : GOTO 280
310 FOR J=1 TO 500 : NEXT J : RETURN
```

7. UNDERSTANDING DIVISION

SUGGESTED FILE NAME: UNDDIV

SUGGESTED GRADE RANGE: 4–8

DESCRIPTION OF THE PROGRAM: This program shows the relationship between division and multiplication. A two-digit number is randomly chosen as the divisor. The products of the divisor and the digits, one through nine, are shown across the top of the screen. A division problem with the two-digit divisor is shown at the center of the screen. The student uses the products at the top of the screen to find the quotient.

NEW PROGRAMMING STATEMENTS: PRINT@832,CHR$(30) clears the line from location 832 to the end of the line. CHR$(31) clears the screen from a given location to the end of the screen.

LINEINPUT Q$ accepts input but does not show the question mark as INPUT does. The only kind of data that will be accepted with LINEINPUT is string data.

PROGRAMMING LOGIC: Lines 130 and 140 draw the box in the division problem. Line 270 uses LINEINPUT when asking for the quotient, and the cursor appears at the location in the problem for the quotient. Notice that line 280 draws part of the box again. The reason for this is that when something is printed on the screen, the computer erases the next line. With LINEINPUT, you cannot prevent this from happening. However, with plain print statements, you can prevent the computer from erasing the next line by ending the statement with a semicolon (;). This is shown in line 350: PRINT@352," ";. This statement erases an incorrect answer. The semicolon (;) prevents the computer from erasing the division box.

```
10 RANDOM : S=0
20 CLS : PRINT@276,"UNDERSTANDING DIVISION" : GOSUB 520
30 X=RND(89)+10
40 CLS : FOR I=1 TO 57 STEP 7 : PRINT@I,X : NEXT I
50 J=0
60 FOR I=65 TO 121 STEP 7 : J=J+1 : PRINT@I,"X";J : NEXT I
70 FOR I=128 TO 184 STEP 7 : PRINT@I,"====" : NEXT I
80 J=0
90 FOR I=192 TO 248 STEP 7 : J=J+1 : PRINT@I,J*X : NEXT I
100 Y=RND(9)
110 Z=RND(Y)-1
120 PRINT@472,X; : PRINT@477,(Y*X)+Z
130 FOR I=1 TO 5 : SET(56,23-I) : NEXT I
140 FOR I=57 TO 68 : SET(I,18) : NEXT I
150 PRINT@832,"TYPE THE PRODUCT NEAREST ";(Y*X)+Z;" WITHOUT
GOING OVER ";(Y*X)+Z;".";CHR$(31);
160 PRINT@896,""; : INPUT P
170 IF P<>Y*X AND S=1 THEN 180  ELSE 190
180 PRINT@896,"THE PRODUCT IS "; Y*X : GOSUB 520  : S=0 : GO
TO 150
190 IF P=Y*X THEN 220
200 PRINT@832,"NOT CORRECT -- CHECK THE ANSWERS AT THE TOP O
F THE SCREEN."
210 GOSUB 520  : S=1 : GOTO 150
220 PRINT@896,"THAT'S CORRECT ! !" : S=0
230 PRINT@541,Y*X;" = ";Y;" X ";X
240 PRINT@605,"===="
250 GOSUB 530
260 PRINT@832,CHR$(30);"TYPE THE QUOTIENT."
270 PRINT@352,""; : LINEINPUT Q$
280 SET(56,20) : SET(56,19) : FOR I=56 TO 68 : SET(I,18) : N
EXT I
290 IF VAL(Q$)<>Y AND S=1 THEN 300  ELSE 330
300 PRINT@832,CHR$(30);"THE QUOTIENT IS ";Y;"." : GOSUB 530

310 PRINT@352,"      "; : S=0 : GOTO 260
```

```
330 IF VAL(Q$)=Y THEN 370
340 PRINT@832,CHR$(30);"NOT CORRECT -- LOOK AGAIN." : GOSUB
530
350 PRINT@352,"        "; : S=1 : GOTO 260
370 PRINT@832,CHR$(30);"THAT'S RIGHT!!" : S=0
380 GOSUB 530
390 PRINT@832,CHR$(30);"WHAT IS THE REMAINDER?"
400 PRINT@672,CHR$(30); : LINEINPUT R$
410 IF VAL(R$)=Z THEN 430
420 PRINT@832,"NOT CORRECT -- SUBTRACT AGAIN." : GOSUB 530
: GOTO 390
430 PRINT@832,CHR$(30);"THAT'S CORRECT!!      ";
440 PRINT (Y*X)+Z;"= (";Y;" X ";X;") + ";Z : GOSUB 520
450 PRINT@896,"DO YOU WANT ANOTHER PROBLEM? (Y OR N)";
460 INPUT W$
470 IF W$="Y" THEN 30
480 IF W$="N" THEN 500
490 PRINT@896,CHR$(30);"PLEASE TYPE Y OR N." : GOSUB 530   :
GOTO 450
500 CLS : PRINTTAB(15);"I HOPE THIS IS A GREAT DAY FOR YOU!!
"
510 END
520 FOR I=1 TO 1000 : NEXT I : RETURN
530 FOR I=1 TO 600 : NEXT I : RETURN
```

8. FUN WITH DECIMALS

SUGGESTED FILE NAME: DECFUN

SUGGESTED GRADE RANGE: 5–8

DESCRIPTION OF THE PROGRAM: This program provides practice in decimal arithmetic using three-digit numbers with one decimal place.

PROGRAMMING LOGIC: In line 140, ASC is used in a different way from the previous program. Here the input for A$ is a letter. In line 140, 64 is subtracted from the ASC for A$. Then line 150 checks to see if the code is from 1 through 5. In your manual, you will find that the decimal codes for A, B, C, D, and E begin with 65 and end with 69. Subtracting 64 from the appropriate code leaves a number from 1 to 5.

If choice E is selected from the menu, the computer is directed to line 540. In line 540 a random value from 1 to 4 is selected. This value determines which operation is to be used in the next exercise. Depending on the value (1 to 4) selected, the computer is directed to go to line 500, 510, 520, or 530. For example, if the value chosen and stored in the variable O is 2, the operation indicated is subtraction and the computer is told to go to the subtraction routine beginning in line 510. This routine is rather complicated; don't feel bad if you can't follow it completely the first few times through.

```
10 RANDOM
20 CLS : PRINT@277,"FUN WITH DECIMALS"
30 FOR TI=1 TO 1000 : NEXT TI
40 CLS : PRINT : PRINTCHR$(23);TAB(7);"** PROGRAM MENU **"
50 PRINT : PRINT TAB(2);"A) ADDITION OF DECIMALS"
60 PRINT TAB(2);"B) SUBTRACTION OF DECIMALS"
70 PRINT TAB(2);"C) MULTIPLICATION OF DECIMALS"
80 PRINT TAB(2);"D) DIVISION OF DECIMALS"
90 PRINT TAB(2);"E) ALL OF THE ABOVE"
100 PRINT : PRINT : PRINT
110 PRINT "PRESS THE LETTER OF YOUR CHOICE"
120 A$=INKEY$
130 A$=INKEY$ : IF A$="" THEN 130
140 A=ASC(A$)-64
150 IF A<1 OR A>5 THEN 130
160 ON A GOSUB 500 ,510 ,520 ,530 ,540
170 N1=RND(999)*.1 : N2=RND(999)*.1
180 IF O=2 AND N1<N2 THEN 170
190 IF O=4 AND N1<N2 THEN 170
200 ON O GOSUB 550 ,560 ,570 ,580
210 CLS : PRINT CHR$(23);O$ : PRINT
220 PRINT TAB(6); N1; OP$; N2; "= ?"
230 PRINT : PRINT : PRINT TAB(4);"PLEASE TYPE YOUR ANSWER"
240 PRINT : PRINT TAB(4);"AND PRESS THE <ENTER> KEY."
250 PRINT : PRINT TAB(10);" "; : INPUT AV : PRINT
260 IF ABS(AV-AN)<.00005 THEN CA=1 : NC=NC+1 ELSE CA=0
270 T=T+1
280 SC=INT(NC/T*100+.5)
290 IF CA=1 PRINT TAB(11);"CORRECT!"
300 IF CA=0 PRINT TAB(5);"SORRY, ANSWER IS";AN
310 PRINT TAB(5);"YOUR SCORE IS";SC;"%."
320 PRINT : PRINT TAB(2);"PRESS <SPACE BAR> TO CONTINUE.";
330 PRINT TAB(2); "PRESS <Q> TO QUIT.";
340 D$=INKEY$ : IF D$="" THEN 340
350 IF D$=" " THEN 160
360 IF D$<>"Q" THEN 340
370 END
500 O=1 : O$="ADD" : OP$="+" : RETURN
510 O=2 : O$="SUBTRACT" : OP$="-" : RETURN
520 O=3 : O$="MULTIPLY" : OP$="x" : RETURN
530 O=4 : O$="DIVIDE" : OP$="/" : RETURN
540 O=RND(4) : ON O GOSUB 500 ,510 ,520 ,530 : RETURN
550 AN=N1+N2 : RETURN
560 AN=N1-N2 : RETURN
570 AN=N1*N2 : RETURN
580 AN=N1 : N1=N1*N2 : RETURN
```

9. PERIMETER AND AREA OF RECTANGLES

SUGGESTED FILE NAME: PERAREA

SUGGESTED GRADE RANGE: 6–8

DESCRIPTION OF THE PROGRAM: A rectangle is printed on the screen, and the student is asked to calculate the perimeter of the rectangle, then to calculate its area.

HOW TO CHANGE THE DATA: This program should not be changed.

```
10 RANDOM
20 CLS : PRINT@271,"PERIMETER AND AREA OF RECTANGLES"
30 FOR TI=1 TO 1000 : NEXT TI
40 L=RND(124)+3 : W=RND(37)+3
50 W = W / 2.5
60 A = 63 - L/2
70 B = 10 - W/2
80 CLS
90 FOR X = A TO A+L
100    SET(X,B) : SET(X,B+W)
110 NEXT X
120 FOR Y = B TO B+W
130    SET(A,Y) : SET(A+L,Y)
140 NEXT Y
150 PRINT@468,L;" BY ";W*2.5;" RECTANGLE";
160 GOSUB 360  : INPUT "PLEASE ENTER THE PERIMETER OF THIS R
ECTANGLE";P
170 IF P>(L+W*2.5)*2+.1 THEN GOSUB 360  : PRINT "YOUR ANSWER
 IS TOO LARGE.";  : GOSUB 340  : GOSUB 350  : GOTO 160
180 IF P<(L+W*2.5)*2-.1 THEN GOSUB 360  : PRINT "YOUR ANSWER
 IS TOO SMALL.";  : GOSUB 340  : GOSUB 350  : GOTO 160
190 GOSUB 360  : PRINT "VERY GOOD!!!  THAT IS CORRECT.";  : G
OSUB 300
200 GOSUB 360  : INPUT "PLEASE ENTER THE AREA OF THIS RECTAN
GLE";AR
210 IF AR>L*W*2.5+.1 THEN GOSUB 360  : PRINT "YOUR ANSWER IS
 TOO LARGE." : GOSUB 340  : GOSUB 350  : GOTO 200
220 IF AR<L*W*2.5-.1 THEN GOSUB 360  : PRINT "YOUR ANSWER IS
 TOO SMALL." : GOSUB 340  : GOSUB 350  : GOTO 200
230 GOSUB 360  : PRINT "EXCELLENT!!  YOU FOUND BOTH THE PERI
METER AND AREA CORRECTLY." : GOSUB 340
240 GOSUB 360  : PRINT "DO YOU WANT TO TRY ANOTHER RECTANGLE
? (Y=YES, N=NO)" : A$=INKEY$
250 A$=INKEY$ : IF A$="" THEN 250
260 IF A$="Y" THEN 40
270 IF A$<>"N" THEN 250
280 CLS : PRINT TAB(22);"HAVE A HAPPY DAY!!"
290 END
300 PRINT@976,"PRESS <SPACE BAR> TO CONTINUE . . .";
310 A$=INKEY$
320 A$=INKEY$ : IF A$="" THEN 320
330 IF A$=" " THEN RETURN ELSE 320
340 FOR T=1 TO 600 : NEXT T : RETURN
350 PRINT@832,"PLEASE TRY AGAIN . . .";  : GOSUB 300  : RETUR
N
360 PRINT@704,CHR$(31);  : RETURN
```

10. COMPUTER ROUNDING AID

SUGGESTED FILE NAME: ROUNDING

SUGGESTED GRADE RANGE: 5–8

DESCRIPTION OF THE PROGRAM: This program is a tool for the student to use when rounding numbers. The student types in a decimal number between 1 and 10,000, and the computer rounds the number to the place value selected by the student.

NEW PROGRAMMING STATEMENTS: In line 10, the statement DEFDBL N,R appears. The purpose of this statement is to tell the computer that the variables N and R are to have greater precision than normal. *Precision* is a mathematical term that refers to the number of digits in the numeral. The reason this statement is used in this program is that greater precision is required in order to perform the calculations used in this program.

Line 270 contains an arithmetic calculation using the symbol for exponent ([). In the arithmetic statement:

$$N*10\ [(RP-4)+.5$$

first, 10 is raised to the $(RP-4)$ power. That number is then multiplied by N. Finally, .5 is added to the product.

PROGRAMMING LOGIC: The calculations in line 270 perform the rounding of the number given to the place desired. First, the number entered is multiplied by a power of ten to move the decimal point to the desired position. Then, .5 is added to the result. When the INT function is applied to this value, the result is a whole number with the correct digits for the answer. Finally, the whole number result is divided by a power of ten to reposition the decimal point in the proper place.

HOW TO CHANGE THE DATA: This program should not be changed.

```
10 CLEAR 1000 : RANDOM : DEFDBL N,R
20 FOR X=1 TO 7 : READ RP$(X) : NEXT X
30 DATA THOUSAND,HUNDRED,TEN,UNIT,TENTH,HUNDREDTH,THOUSANDTH
40 CLS : PRINT TAB(15);">>>> COMPUTER ROUNDING AID <<<<"
50 FOR T=1 TO 1000 : NEXT T
60 CLS : PRINT TAB(20);"**** INSTRUCTIONS ****" : PRINT
70 PRINT TAB(5);"I WILL GLADLY ROUND ANY WHOLE OR DECIMAL NUMB
ER FOR YOU" : PRINT
80 PRINT "WHICH IS BETWEEN 0 AND 10000.  BE SURE WHEN YOU TYPE
 THE" : PRINT
90 PRINT "NUMERAL THAT YOU DO NOT INCLUDE A COMMA.  FOR EXAMPL
E, PLEASE" : PRINT
100 PRINT "TYPE ONE THOUSAND AS 1000 AND NOT AS 1,000.  BE SUR
```

```
E TO INCLUDE" : PRINT
110 PRINT "THE DECIMAL POINT IF THERE SHOULD BE ONE IN THE NUM
ERAL." : PRINT : GOSUB 320
120 CLS : PRINT "WHAT IS THE NUMBER YOU WOULD LIKE ME TO ROUND
"; : INPUT N
130 IF N<=0 THEN PRINT@896,CHR$(31);"THE NUMBER MUST BE GREATE
R THAN 0"; : GOSUB 320   : GOTO 120
140 IF N>10000 THEN PRINT@896,CHR$(31);"THE NUMBER MUST BE LES
S THAN 10000"; : GOSUB 320   : GOTO 120
150 IF N=INT(N) THEN P=0 : GOTO 190
160 FORX=0TO3
170 IF N*10[X-INT(N*10[X) >= .05 THEN P=X+1
180 NEXT X
190 CLS : PRINT TAB(5);"I CAN ROUND < ";N;" > TO THE NEAREST:"
200 FORX=1TO3+P
210 PRINT@64*(X+2)+20,X;")    ";RP$(X);
220 NEXT X
230 PRINT@972,CHR$(31);"PLEASE PRESS THE NUMBER OF YOUR CHOICE
. . ."; : A$=INKEY$
240 A$=INKEY$ : IF A$="" THEN 240
250 IF ASC(A$)<49 OR ASC(A$)>51+P THEN 240
260 RP=VAL(A$)
270 RV=INT(N*10[(RP-4)+.5)/10[(RP-4) : CH=RV
280 CLS : PRINT@210,"THE VALUE OF < ";N;" >"
290 PRINT@328,"ROUNDED TO THE NEAREST ";RP$(RP);" IS < ";CH;"
>."
300 GOSUB 320   : GOTO 120
310 END
320 PRINT@966,CHR$(31);"PRESS THE <SPACE BAR> TO CONTINUE OR <
Q> TO QUIT . . ."; : A$=INKEY$
330 A$=INKEY$ : IF A$=" " THEN RETURN
340 IF A$<>"Q" THEN 330
350 CLS : PRINT@463,"TRY TO BE A WELL ROUNDED PERSON."
```

11. THE LCM CHALLENGE

SUGGESTED FILE NAME: LEASTCOM

SUGGESTED GRADE RANGE: 5–8

DESCRIPTION OF THE PROGRAM: The LCM Challenge gives students practice in determining the least common multiple of two numbers. The program is written in a game format in which the student tries to achieve the best score given twenty-five exercises. The range of the values varies with the success the student has as the game is played. If the student gets the first five problems right, then the problems that follow may contain larger numbers and will be worth more points. If the student makes errors as the game is played, the range of the numbers and the point values of the questions will be reduced.

PROGRAMMING LOGIC: There are four levels of difficulty and point values used in this program. Level one, the least difficult, is found in lines 40-120; level two in lines 130-220; level three in lines 230-320; and level four in lines 330-400.

The first line in each of these routines sets the point value of the questions and stores that value in variable PV. The variable N is used to keep track of the total number of questions asked. The variables C1, C2, C3, and C4 are used to store the number of questions asked at each of levels 1-4.

The IF/THEN statements found in each of these routines determine whether the program should stay at the same level, move to the next higher level, or return to the previous level, based on the student's success rate. The last line in each of these program segments will send the computer to line 410 after twenty-five questions have been asked.

HOW TO CHANGE THE DATA: This program should not be changed.

```
10 CLEAR 1000 : RANDOM
20 CLS : PRINT@339,"<<< THE LCM CHALLENGE >>>" : FOR T=1 TO
1000 : NEXT T
30 C=0 : SC=0
40 PV=100 : N=0 : C1=0
50 C=C+1 : C1=C1+1
60 IF C=26 THEN 410
70 FV=RND(8) : SV=RND(8) : IF FV=SV THEN 70
80 GOSUB 540  : GOSUB 450
90 IF AN=LC THEN GOSUB 470  ELSE GOSUB 490
100 IF C1=5 AND N=5 THEN 130
110 IF C1=10 AND N>7 THEN 130
120 IF C<25 THEN 50   ELSE 410
130 PV=300 : N=0 : C2=0
140 C=C+1 : C2=C2+1
150 IF C=26 THEN 410
160 FV=RND(15) : SV=RND(15) : IF FV=SV THEN 160
170 GOSUB 540  : GOSUB 450
180 IF AN=LC THEN GOSUB 470  ELSE GOSUB 490
190 IF C2=5 AND N=5 THEN 230
200 IF C2=10 AND N>7 THEN 230
210 IF C2=10 AND N<4 THEN 40
220 IF C<25 THEN 140  ELSE 410
230 PV=700 : N=0 : C3=0
240 C=C+1 : C3=C3+1
250 IF C=26 THEN 410
260 FV=RND(25) : SV=RND(25) : IF FV=SV OR FV/SV=INT(FV/SV) O
R SV/FV=INT(SV/FV) THEN 260
270 GOSUB 540  : GOSUB 450
280 IF AN=LC THEN GOSUB 470  ELSE GOSUB 490
290 IF C3=5 AND N=5 THEN 330
300 IF C3=10 AND N>7 THEN 330
310 IF C3=10 AND N<4 THEN 130
320 IF C<25 THEN 240  ELSE 410
330 PV=1200 : N=0 : C4=0
340 C=C+1 : C4=C4+1
350 IF C=26 THEN 410
360 FV=RND(50) : SV=RND(50) : IF FV=SV OR FV/SV=INT(FV/SV) O
R SV/FV=INT(SV/FV) THEN 360
370 GOSUB 540  : GOSUB 450
380 IF AN=LC THEN GOSUB 470  ELSE GOSUB 490
390 IF C4=5 AND N<4 THEN 230
```

```
400 IF C<25 THEN 340
410 CLS : PRINT TAB(10);"THE << LCM CHALLENGE >> IS OVER.   Y
OUR SCORE IS"
420 PRINT : PRINT TAB(25);SC;"POINTS."
430 PRINT : PRINT TAB(15);"A PERFECT SCORE IS 17500 POINTS."
440 END
450 PRINT@320,CHR$(31);"ENTER THE LEAST COMMON MULTIPLE OF";
FV;"AND";SV;
460 INPUT AN : RETURN
470 SC=SC+PV : N=N+1
480 GOSUB 510  : RETURN
490 SC=SC-PV*.5 : IF SC<0 THEN SC=0
500 GOSUB 510  : RETURN
510 PRINT@42,CHR$(30);"SCORE =";SC;
520 PRINT@106,CHR$(30);"TURNS LEFT =";25-C;
530 RETURN
540 V1=FV : V2=SV
550 IF V1<V2 THEN TV=V1 ELSE TV=V2
560 LC=FV*SV
570 FOR X=TV TO 2 STEP -1
580    IF V1/X=INT(V1/X) AND V2/X=INT(V2/X) THEN V1=V1/X : V2
=V2/X : LC=LC/X
590 NEXTX
600 RETURN
```

12. BASIC NUMBER FACTS

SUGGESTED FILE NAME: NUMFACTS

SUGGESTED GRADE RANGE: 3–5

DESCRIPTION OF THE PROGRAM: This program provides practice with addition and multiplication facts. The student chooses either addition or multiplication. Numbers are presented randomly in a table with four numbers across the top and four down the side. The student fills in the body of the table.

PROGRAMMING LOGIC: The data lines are used to print the addends (or factors) horizontally and vertically on the screen. See lines 420 and 430.

There are two loops, lines 200-250 and lines 260-310, which illustrate how to choose numbers randomly so that no number is chosen twice. Each number that is chosen is checked against all numbers previously chosen to make sure it has not already been selected. If it has already been selected, the program cycles back to choose another number.

This routine is used several times, notably in the two programs "Twenty Science Questions" and "Abbreviations for Elements."

EXPLANATION OF DATA LINES: The data lines are used to print the factors (or addends) at the four horizontal or vertical locations in the table.

HOW TO CHANGE THE DATA: The data should not be changed.

```
10 RANDOM : DIM HP(16),VP(16) : PS$="< ? >"
20 CLS : PRINT@278,"BASIC NUMBER FACTS"
30 PRINT@521,"PRACTICE WITH ADDITION AND MULTIPLICATON FACTS"
: FOR TI=1 TO 2000 : NEXT TI
40 FOR X=1 TO 16 : READ VP(X) : NEXT X
50 FOR X=1 TO 16 : READ HP(X) : NEXT X
60 CLS : PRINT@140,CHR$(23);"*** PROGRAM MENU ***" : PRINT
70 PRINT TAB(6);"A) ADDITION FACTS" : PRINT
80 PRINT TAB(6);"B) MULTIPLICATION FACTS" : PRINT : PRINT
90 PRINT "TYPE THE LETTER OF YOUR CHOICE:" : A$=INKEY$
100 A$=INKEY$ : IF A$="" THEN 100
110 IF A$="A" THEN 130
120 IF A$="B" THEN 150    ELSE 100
130 O$="+" : OF=1 : P=0 : T=0 : GOSUB 190  : GOSUB 380   : GOSU
B 450
140 GOSUB 550  : GOTO 60
150 O$="x" : OF=2 : P=0 : T=0 : GOSUB 190  : GOSUB 380   : GOSU
B 450
160 GOSUB 550  : GOTO 60
170 DATA 3,1,2,4,1,2,3,2,1,4,4,2,4,3,3,1
180 DATA 2,3,1,4,2,4,1,3,1,3,1,2,2,4,3,4
190 H(1)=RND(9) : V(H)=RND(9)
200 FOR X=2 TO 4
210   H(X)=RND(9)
220   FOR Y=1 TO X-1
230     IF H(X)=H(Y) THEN 210
240   NEXTY
250 NEXTX
260 FOR X=2 TO 4
270   V(X)=RND(9)
280   FOR Y=1 TO X-1
290     IF V(X)=V(Y) THEN 270
300   NEXTY
310 NEXTX
320 FOR X=1 TO 4
330   FOR Y=1 TO 4
340     IF OF=1 THEN N(X,Y)=H(Y)+V(X) ELSE N(X,Y)=H(Y)*V(X)
350   NEXTY
360 NEXTX
370 RETURN
380 CLS
390 FOR X=20 TO 100 : SET(X,6) : NEXT X
400 FOR Y=1 TO 30 : SET(30,Y) : NEXT Y
410 PRINT@76,O$;
420 FOR X=1 TO 4 : PRINT@76+8*X,H(X); : NEXT X
430 FOR Y=1 TO 4 : PRINT@75+128*Y,V(Y); : NEXT Y
440 RETURN
450 P=P+1 : IF P=17 THEN RETURN
460 R=VP(P) : C=HP(P)
470 PRINT@75+R*128+C*8,PS$;
480 PRINT@832,CHR$(31);"ENTER THE NUMBER THAT BELONGS IN THE S
PACE SHOWN:";
490 INPUT AN$ : IF (ASC(AN$)>57 OR ASC(AN$)<47) THEN 480 ELSE
AN=VAL(AN$) : T=T+1
500 IF AN=N(R,C) THEN PRINT@832,CHR$(31);"VERY GOOD!!!!"; : GO
SUB 520  : GOSUB 600  : GOTO 450
510 PRINT@832,CHR$(31);"THINK CAREFULLY, THEN TRY AGAIN."; : G
```

```
OSUB 600  : GOTO 480
520 PRINT@75+R*128+C*8,"        ";
530 PRINT@76+R*128+C*8,AN;
540 RETURN
550 CLS : PRINTCHR$(23);TAB(2);"YOU TOOK";T;"TRIES TO ANSWER"
: PRINT
560 PRINT TAB(2);"THE SIXTEEN (16) PROBLEMS." : PRINT : PRINT
: PRINT : PRINT
570 PRINT TAB(2);"YOUR SCORE IS";INT(16/T*100+.5);"." : PRINT
: PRINT : PRINT
580 PRINT TAB(2);"PRESS THE <SPACE BAR> TO CONTINUE . . ."; :
A$=INKEY$"
590 A$=INKEY$ : IF A$=" " THEN RETURN ELSE 590
600 PRINT@960,CHR$(31);TAB(15);"PRESS THE <SPACE BAR> TO CONTI
NUE . . ."; : A$=INKEY$
610 A$=INKEY$ : IF A$=" " THEN RETURN ELSE 610
```

13. REDUCING FRACTIONS

SUGGESTED FILE NAME: REDFRAC

SUGGESTED GRADE RANGE: 5–8

DESCRIPTION OF THE PROGRAM: This program contains twenty-nine exercises in reducing fractions. The student is given a fraction and asked to type it in its reduced form.

EXPLANATION OF DATA LINES: Each exercise consists of three data items. The first two items are the numerator and denominator, respectively, of the fraction to be reduced. The third data entry is the answer. For example, in line 40, 3,6,1/2 defines the problem, three-sixths; 1/2 is the reduced form of the fraction.

HOW TO CHANGE THE DATA: You may substitute any fractions and their reduced form for those appearing in the data lines; make sure you enter them in the correct order: numerator, denominator, answer.

Remember to keep the same number of data entries in each line and to separate them with commas.

You may decide that twenty-nine problems are too many for your students. You can change the number of problems presented in each run of the program by changing line 210. For example, you may want each program run to contain only twenty problems. In that case, change line 210 to read:

```
210 FOR X = 1 TO 20
```

```
10 DIM N$(29), D$(29), LT$(29)
20 CLS : PRINT@277,"REDUCING FRACTIONS"
30 PRINT@524,"THERE ARE 29 EXERCISES IN THIS PROGRAM." : FOR T
I=1 TO 2000 : NEXT TI
```

```
40 DATA 3,6,1/2,8,10,4/5,12,14,6/7,6,9,2/3,12,15,4/5
50 DATA 21,30,7/10,15,20,3/4,25,35,5/7,45,50,9/10
60 DATA 8,12,2/3,20,24,5/6,40,44,10/11,18,24,3/4
70 DATA 30,36,5/6,12,15,4/5,24,30,4/5,80,90,8/9
80 DATA 49,70,7/10,28,30,14/15,20,45,4/9,12,28,3/7
90 DATA 6,48,1/8,24,60,2/5,7,42,1/6,24,64,3/8
100 DATA 50,90,5/9,42,66,7/11,28,98,2/7,105,120,7/8
110 FOR X = 1 TO 29
120    READ N$(X),D$(X),LT$(X)
130 NEXT X
140 CLS : PRINT : PRINT : PRINT TAB(5);"IN THIS PROGRAM YOU WI
LL BE ASKED TO REDUCE EACH"
150 PRINT : PRINT TAB(5);"FRACTION GIVEN TO LOWEST TERMS.  FOR
 EXAMPLE:"
160 PRINT : PRINT TAB(30);"6"
170 PRINT TAB(5);"EXPRESS THE FRACTION   ----    IN LOWEST TERM
S."
180 PRINT TAB(29);"10"
190 PRINT : PRINT : PRINT "YOU SHOULD TYPE THE ANSWER AS  3/5
 AND PRESS THE <ENTER> KEY."
200 PRINT : PRINT : PRINT TAB(10);"PRESS THE <ENTER> KEY TO CO
NTINUE."; : INPUT D$
210 FOR X=1 TO 29
220    CLS : PRINT "# ";X : PRINT : PRINT TAB(28)N$(X) : PRINT
 TAB(5);"EXPRESS THE FRACTION   -----   IN LOWEST TERMS."
230    PRINT TAB(28);D$(X)
240    PRINT : PRINT : PRINT "TYPE YOUR ANSWER IN THE FORM  N/D
  AND PRESS THE <ENTER> KEY."
245 AN$=""
250 PRINT@600,"";:INPUT AN$
255 IF AN$="" THEN 250
260    IF AN$=LT$(X) THEN CA=1 : NC=NC+1 ELSE CA=0
270    T=T+1
280    IF CA=1 THEN PRINT "THAT IS CORRECT!!!"
290    IF CA=0 THEN PRINT "SORRY, THAT IS NOT CORRECT."
300    IF CA=0 THEN PRINT : PRINT "THE CORRECT ANSWER IS ";LT$(
X);"."
310    PRINT : PRINT "PRESS THE <ENTER> KEY TO CONTINUE."; : IN
PUT D$
320 NEXTX
330 CLS : PRINT "THIS IS THE END OF THE PROGRAM . . ."
340 END
```

14. ADDITION OF INTEGERS

SUGGESTED FILE NAME: ADDINT

SUGGESTED GRADE RANGE: 5–8

DESCRIPTION OF THE PROGRAM: This program provides practice in the six forms of adding integers.

1. Both integers are positive or zero. For example, 13 + 28.

2. The first integer is positive and the second is negative. The absolute value of the first is greater than the absolute value of the second. For example, 28 + (−13).

3. The first integer is positive and the second is negative. The absolute value of the second is greater than the absolute value of the first. For example, 13 + (−28).

4. The first integer is negative and the second is positive (or zero). The absolute value of the first is greater than the absolute value of the second. For example, (−28) + 13.

5. The first integer is negative and the second is positive. The absolute value of the second is greater than the absolute value of the first. For example, (−13) + 28.

6. Both integers are negative.

EXPLANATION OF DATA LINES: The data lines contain the integers, −15 through 14. Two of the integers are selected randomly for each problem.

HOW TO CHANGE THE DATA: You may wish to use larger (or smaller) integers, or change the data to decimal numbers. Simply substitute data items one for one. Do not change the quantity of data items.

If you change the data to decimal values, be sure to change the title of this program to something more appropriate such as: "Addition of Decimal Numbers."

```
10 RANDOM : DIM A(30) : N=0 : X=0
20 CLS : PRINT@276,"ADDITION OF INTEGERS"
25 FOR TI=1 TO 1000 : NEXT TI
30 FOR I=1 TO 30 : READ A(I): NEXT I
40 CLS : N=N+1
50 J=RND(30) : K=RND(30)
60 IF A(J)>=0 AND A(K)>=0 THEN 110
70 IF A(J)>=0 AND A(K)<0 THEN IF (-1)*A(K)<A(J) THEN 130   ELSE
   150
80 IF A(J)<0 AND A(K)>=0 THEN IF (-1)*A(J)>A(K) THEN 170   ELSE
   190
90 IF A(J)<0 AND A(K)<0 PRINT "("A(J)") + ("A(K)") = -("(-1)*A
(J)" + "(-1)*A(K)") = "; : INPUT T : GOSUB 210 : ON FL GOTO 40
,280
100 CLS : GOTO 90
110 PRINT A(J)" + "A(K)" = "; : INPUT T : GOSUB 210 : ON FL GO
TO 40,280
120 CLS : GOTO 110
130 PRINT A(J)" + ("A(K)") = "A(J)" - "(-1)*A(K)" = "; : INPUT
 T : GOSUB 210 : ON FL GOTO 40,280
140 CLS : GOTO 130
150 PRINT A(J)" + ("A(K)") = "A(J)" - "(-1)*A(K)" = -("(-1)*A(
K)" - "A(J)") = "; : INPUT T : GOSUB 210 : ON FL GOTO 40,280
160 CLS : GOTO 150
```

```
170 PRINT A(J)" + "A(K)" = "A(K)" + ("A(J)") = "A(K)" - "(-1)*
A(J)" = -("(-1)*A(J)" - "A(K)") = "; : INPUT T : GOSUB 210 : O
N FL GOTO 40,280
180 CLS : GOTO 170
190 PRINT A(J)" + "A(K)" = "A(K)" + ("A(J)") = "A(K)" - "(-1)*
A(J)" = "; : INPUT T : GOSUB 210 : ON FL GOTO 40,280
200 CLS : GOTO 190
210 PRINT : IF T=A(J)+A(K) THEN 220 ELSE PRINT "NOT CORRECT.
THE ANSWER IS  ";A(J)+A(K);"." : N=N+1 : FOR I=1 TO 800 : NEXT
 I : FL=0 : RETURN
220 PRINT : PRINT "THAT'S RIGHT ! !" : X=X+1
230 PRINT : PRINT "YOU HAVE GIVEN ";N;" ANSWERS AND ";INT(X/N*
100);"% OF THEM ARE CORRECT."
240 PRINT : PRINT "DO YOU WANT ANOTHER PROBLEM? (Y OR N)" : IN
PUT W$
250 IF W$="Y" THEN FL=1 : RETURN
260 IF W$="N" THEN FL=2 : RETURN
270 PRINT "TYPE Y FOR 'YES' OR N FOR 'NO'." : INPUT W$ : GOTO
250
280 CLS : PRINT "IT'S BEEN A PLEASURE ADDING INTEGERS WITH YOU
."
290 PRINT "GOOD-BYE."
300 END
310 DATA -15,-14,-13,-12,-11,-10,-9,-8,-7,-6,-5,-4,-3,-2,-1
320 DATA 0,1,2,3,4,5,6,7,8,9,10,11,12,13,14
```

15. SUBTRACTION OF INTEGERS

SUGGESTED FILE NAME: SUBTINT

SUGGESTED GRADE RANGE: 6–8

DESCRIPTION OF THE PROGRAM: In this program, subtraction of integers is defined in terms of addition of integers. The student is given one addend, B, and the sum, C, and asked to fill in the missing addend, A. The problem is then restated as the sum, C, minus the addend, B, equals the difference, A. For example:

WHAT INTEGER ADDED TO -13 EQUALS 15?   Answer: 28

THEN $15 - (-13) = ?$ Answer: 28

EXPLANATION OF DATA LINES: The data lines contain the integers -15 through 14. You may wish to use integers with larger absolute values or decimal numbers. You can retype the data lines using any numbers. Just substitute your numbers, one for one, for the ones now in the program. Separate the data items with commas and make sure there are exactly thirty of them when you are finished.

If you change the data to decimal values, change the title of the program to reflect the new kind of problem.

```
10 RANDOM : DIM A(30) : W=0 : N=0
20 CLS : PRINT@275,"SUBTRACTION OF INTEGERS" : FOR TI=1 TO 100
0 : NEXT TI
30 FOR I=1 TO 30 : READ A(I) : NEXT I
40 J=RND(30) : K=RND(30)
50 Y=A(K)-A(J)
60 CLS : PRINT "WHAT INTEGER ADDED TO "A(J)" EQUALS "A(K)"?"
70 PRINT : INPUT X : N=N+1 : IF Y<>X PRINT "SORRY. THE ANSWER
IS:  ";Y;"." : FOR TI=1 TO 1000 : NEXT TI : GOTO 60
80 W=W+1
90 PRINT : PRINT "THEN "A(K)" - ("A(J)") = "; : INPUT T : N=N+
1
100 IF Y<>T PRINT "SORRY. THE ANSWER IS:  ";Y;"." : FOR TI=1 T
O 1000 : NEXT TI : GOTO 90
110 W=W+1 : PRINT : PRINT "THAT'S RIGHT ! !"
120 PRINT : PRINT "YOUR SCORE IS NOW ";INT((W/N)*100);"%"
130 PRINT : PRINT "DO YOU WANT ANOTHER PROBLEM? (TYPE Y OR N)"
140 INPUT M$
150 IF M$="Y" THEN 40
160 IF M$="N" THEN 180
170 PRINT "PLEASE TYPE Y OR N." : INPUT M$ : GOTO 150
180 CLS : PRINT : PRINT : PRINT TAB(22);"GOOD-BYE FOR NOW."
190 END
200 DATA -15,-14,-13,-12,-11,-10,-9,-8,-7,-6,-5,-4,-3,-2,-1
210 DATA 0,1,2,3,4,5,6,7,8,9,10,11,12,13,14
```

16. MULTIPLICATION OF INTEGERS

SUGGESTED FILE NAME: MULTINT

SUGGESTED GRADE RANGE: 6–8

DESCRIPTION OF THE PROGRAM: This program provides practice in multiplying integers. There are four forms of integer multiplication addressed by the program.

    1. Both integers are positive or zero.

      $(9)(13) = ?$ Answer: 117

    2. The first integer is positive or zero and the second is negative or zero.

      $(10)(-4) = -(10)(4) = ?$ Answer: -40

    3. The first integer is negative or zero and the second is positive or zero.

      $(-5)(12) = -(5)(12) = ?$ Answer: -60

    4. Both integers are negative or zero.

      $(-11)(-2) = (11)(2) = ?$ Answer: 22

EXPLANATION OF DATA LINES: The data lines contain the integers -15 through 14. Two of these numbers are chosen randomly for each problem.

HOW TO CHANGE THE DATA: If you want to use integers with a larger absolute value or decimal numbers, you may do so by retyping the data lines and substituting your values for the ones in the program. Make sure that you separate data items with commas and that there are exactly thirty data items in the program.

If you change the values in the program to decimal numbers, be sure to change the title to something such as: "Multiplication of Decimal Numbers."

```
10 RANDOM : DIM A(30) : R=0 : S=0
20 CLS : PRINT@275,"MULTIPLICATION OF INTEGERS"
25 PRINT@396,"YOU MAY DO AS MANY EXERCISES AS YOU LIKE." : FOR
   TI=1 TO 1000 : NEXT TI
30 FOR I=1 TO 30 : READ A(I) : NEXT I
40 CLS
50 X=RND(30) : Y=RND(30)
60 IF A(X)>=0 AND A(Y)>=0 THEN 100
70 IF A(X)>=0 AND A(Y)<=0 THEN 110
80 IF A(X)<=0 AND A(Y)>=0 THEN 120
90 IF A(X)<=0 AND A(Y)<=0 THEN 130
100 PRINT "(";A(X);")(";A(Y);") = "; : INPUT T : GOTO 140
110 PRINT "(";A(X);")(";A(Y);") = -(";A(X);")(";(-1)*A(Y);") =
    "; : INPUT T : GOTO 140
120 PRINT "(";A(X);")(";A(Y);") = -(";(-1)*A(X);")(";A(Y);") =
    "; : INPUT T : GOTO 140
130 PRINT "(";A(X);")(";A(Y);") = (";(-1)*A(X);")(";(-1)*A(Y);
    ") = "; : INPUT T : GOTO 140
140 S=S+1 : IF T=A(X)*A(Y) THEN 150  ELSE PRINT "NOT CORRECT.
    TRY AGAIN." : INPUT T : GOTO 140
150 R=R+1 : PRINT "THAT'S RIGHT ! !"
160 PRINT "YOUR SCORE IS ";INT((R/S)*100);"%"
170 PRINT : PRINT "DO YOU WANT ANOTHER PROBLEM? (Y OR N)"
180 INPUT Z$
190 IF Z$="Y" THEN 40
200 IF Z$="N" THEN 220
210 PRINT "PLEASE TYPE Y OR N" : GOTO 180
220 CLS : PRINT TAB(20);"PRACTICE MAKES PERFECT!"
230 END
240 DATA -15,-14,-13,-12,-11,-10,-9,-8,-7,-6,-5,-4,-3,-2,-1
250 DATA 0,1,2,3,4,5,6,7,8,9,10,11,12,13,14
```

17. DIVISION OF INTEGERS

SUGGESTED FILE NAME: DIVINT

SUGGESTED GRADE RANGE: 6–8

DESCRIPTION OF THE PROGRAM: This program gives students practice in division of integers.

PROGRAMMING LOGIC: The integers in this program are chosen randomly and no data lines are used. Line 40 shows two variables, X and Y, the values for which are assigned by the statement: RND(41) − 21.

RND(41) − 21 chooses a number from 1 to 41, then subtracts 21 from the number. In effect, this assigns values from − 20 to 20. For example, if RND(41) = 10, then RND(41) − 21 = − 11.

HOW TO CHANGE THE DATA: You may wish to modify the program to include division of integers by decimals or decimals by integers. You can accomplish this by changing one or both of the statements in line 40, which are mentioned above. For example, if you wish to divide a number in tenths by an integer, change line 40 to read:

```
40 CLS : X=RND(41)−21 : Y=(RND(41)−21)/10 : IF X=0 THEN 40
```

This will change the value for Y to a decimal number in tenths.

Also, change the title to something appropriate such as: "Division of Decimal Numbers."

```
10 RANDOM : DIM A(40) : R=0 : T=0
20 CLS : PRINT@277,"DIVISION OF INTEGERS"
30 FOR TI=1 TO 1000 : NEXT TI
40 CLS : X=RND(41)−21 : Y=RND(41)−21 : IF X=0 THEN 40
50 P=X*Y
60 PRINT P;" DIVIDED BY ";X;" = "; : T=T+1 : INPUT Q : PRINT
70 IF Q=Y THEN 110
80 PRINT "NOT CORRECT -- THE ANSWER IS:   ";Y;"."
90 FOR I=1 TO 600 : NEXT I
100 CLS : GOTO 60
110 R=R+1 : PRINT "THAT'S RIGHT ! !   ";INT((R/T)*100);"% OF YO
UR ANSWERS ARE CORRECT."
120 PRINT
130 PRINT "DO YOU WANT ANOTHER PROBLEM? (Y OR N)"; : INPUT Z$
140 IF Z$="Y" THEN 40
150 IF Z$="N" THEN 170
160 PRINT "PLEASE TYPE Y OR N" : GOTO 130
170 CLS : PRINT@405,"YOUR FINAL SCORE IS ";INT((R/T)*100);"%."
 : PRINT : PRINT "BYE-BYE."
180 END
```

18. THE CONCEPT OF PERCENT

SUGGESTED FILE NAME: PERCENT

SUGGESTED GRADE RANGE: 6–8

DESCRIPTION OF THE PROGRAM: The concept of percent is explained in terms of a set of items, each having a value that is a fractional part of one hundred. For example, in a set of twenty items, each item has a value of five, which is interpreted as 5% of the set.

EXPLANATION OF DATA LINES: In this program, three problems are based on the same set of items. Each data line contains entries for three problems. The set of items contains squares that are printed across the top of the screen.

Line 40 reads all the data items in one line. The data entries are as follows.

1. The number of squares to appear at the top of the screen.
2. The length of the set statement in lines 60 and 70. In line 430, L = 49. FOR I=1 TO L STEP 12, in line 80, makes a square appear on the screen at 1, 13, 25, 37, and 49, starting at 1 and adding 12 until you reach 49. Thus, L = 49 determines that five squares appear in the set.
3. The first question the student must answer.
4. The value of one square in the set.
5. The quantity of squares in the question. This number prints as the numerator of a fraction later on in the program.
6. The second question to the student.
7. The value of a second quantity of squares in the set.
8. The quantity of squares in the second question. This number prints as the numerator of a fraction later on.
9. The third question to the student.
10. The value of the squares in the third question.
11. The quantity of squares in the third question. This number prints as the numerator of a fraction later on in the program.

PROGRAMMING LOGIC: As you run the program, you will see that it is broken into two parts. In the first part, the value of each square appears under the square added together with a sum of 100. At the tenth problem, this doesn't happen anymore. Thus, there are some places in the program where there are several lines that appear to do the same thing, but do not; notably, 80 and 90; also, lines 290-310.

In lines 270 and 280, the program checks to see if the value of a square is less than ten or is a decimal number. If it is less than ten, then a zero is inserted between the value of the square and the decimal point. If it is a decimal number, then it is multiplied by ten. This is done so that the percent has the decimal point in the right location.

HOW TO CHANGE THE DATA: The data in this program should not be changed.

```
10 T=0
20 CLS : PRINT@275,"THE CONCEPT OF PERCENT"
30 PRINT@523,"YOU WILL DO 18 EXERCISES IN THIS PROGRAM." : F
```

```
OR TI=1 TO 2000 : NEXT TI
40 READ S,L,Q$(1),V(1),N(1),Q$(2),V(2),N(2),Q$(3),V(3),N(3)
50 CLS
60 PRINT "PERCENT IS A WAY TO COMPARE NUMBERS BASED ON 100."
70 IF T>=9 THEN 90
80 FOR I=1 TO L STEP 12 : SET(I+2,4) : NEXT I : GOTO 100
90 FOR I=1 TO L STEP 5 : SET(I+2,4) : NEXT I
100 PRINT@269,"HOW MANY SQUARES IN THE SET"; : INPUT A
110 IF A=S THEN 140
120 PRINT@269,"PLEASE COUNT THE SQUARES AGAIN."
130 GOSUB 490  : GOTO 100
140 PRINT@397,"100 DIVIDED BY ";S;" = "; : INPUT B
150 IF B=100/S THEN 180
160 PRINT@397,CHR$(30);"PLEASE DIVIDE AGAIN."
170 GOSUB 490  : GOTO 140
180 IF T>=9 THEN 220
190 E=125 : PRINT@(E+2),V(1)
200 FOR I=1 TO (S-1) : E=E+6 : PRINT@E," + ";V(1); : NEXT I
210 PRINT@(E+6)," = 100"
220 K=1
230 PRINT@525,Q$(K); : INPUT D
240 IF D=V(K) THEN 260
250 PRINT@525,CHR$(30);"LOOK AGAIN." : GOSUB 490  : GOTO 230
260 PRINT@652,N(K); : PRINT@661,V(K)
270 IF V(K)<10 THEN 310
280 IF V(K)/V(K) <> INT(V(K))/V(K) THEN 300
290 PRINT@716,"---   =   ----   =  .";V(K); : GOTO 320
300 PRINT@716,"---   =   ---   =  .";V(K)*10; : GOTO 320
310 PRINT@716,"---   =   ---   =  .0";V(K);
320 PRINT@743,"=  ";V(K);"%"
330 PRINT@780,S; : PRINT@790,"100"
340 T=T+1 : PRINT@909,"PRESS <SPACE BAR> TO CONTINUE."
350 X$=INKEY$ : IF X$="" THEN 350
360 IF X$= " " THEN 370 ELSE 350
370 IF T=18 THEN 410
380 PRINT@448,CHR$(31)
390 FOR I=1 TO 80 : NEXT I
400 K=K+1 : IF K=4 THEN 40    ELSE 230
410 CLS : PRINT@455,"YOU HAVE FINISHED ALL THE PROBLEMS IN T
HIS EXERCISE."
420 PRINT@602,"GOOD WORK ! !" : END
430 DATA 5,49,WHAT IS ONE SQUARE WORTH,20,1,WHAT ARE TWO SQU
ARES WORTH,40,2,WHAT ARE FOUR SQUARES WORTH,80,4
440 DATA 10,109,WHAT IS ONE SQUARE WORTH,10,1,WHAT ARE THREE
 SQUARES WORTH,30,3,WHAT ARE SEVEN SQUARES WORTH,70,7
450 DATA 4,37,WHAT IS ONE SQUARE WORTH,25,1,WHAT ARE 2 SQUAR
ES WORTH,50,2,WHAT ARE 3 SQUARES WORTH,75,3
460 DATA 20,96,WHAT IS ONE SQUARE WORTH,5,1,WHAT ARE NINE SQ
UARES WORTH,45,9,WHAT ARE FOURTEEN SQUARES WORTH,70,14
470 DATA 25,121,WHAT IS ONE SQUARE WORTH,4,1,WHAT ARE 15 SQU
ARES WORTH,60,15,WHAT ARE 20 SQUARES WORTH,80,20
480 DATA 8,36,WHAT IS ONE SQUARE WORTH,12.5,1,WHAT ARE THREE
 SQUARES WORTH,37.5,3,WHAT ARE SIX SQUARES WORTH,75,6
490 FOR I=1 TO 600 : NEXT I : RETURN
```

19. COMPUTER CHALLENGE

SUGGESTED FILE NAME: GESSGAME

SUGGESTED GRADE RANGE: 4–8

DESCRIPTION OF THE PROGRAM: In this challenge game, the student chooses a number for the computer to guess and the computer chooses a number for the student to guess. The challenge is that the student must guess the computer's number in fewer guesses than it takes the computer to guess the student's number.

```
10 RANDOM : CLS : DIM G(11),S(11),R$(11)
20 DATA 5000,4000,3000,2000,1500,1200,1000,750,500,250,0
30 FOR X=1 TO 11 : READ S(X) : NEXT X
40 FOR X=1 TO 20
50 PRINT@16,CHR$(31);"****  COMPUTER CHALLENGE  ****"
60 NEXT X : GOSUB 790  : PRINT
70 PRINTTAB(5);"YOU AND I ARE ABOUT TO TAKE PART IN A MENTAL
   CHALLENGE."
80 GOSUB 790  : PRINT
90 PRINT"YOU AND I WILL TAKE TURNS.  EACH OF US WILL CHOOSE
A NUMBER AND"
100 GOSUB 790  : PRINT
110 PRINT"THE OTHER WILL HAVE ONLY TEN CHANCES TO GUESS THAT
   NUMBER.  THE"
120 GOSUB 790  : PRINT
130 PRINT"NUMBER MAY BE ANY INTEGER FROM 1 TO 200.  THE SCOR
E WILL BE"
140 GOSUB 790  : PRINT
150 PRINT"BASED ON THE NUMBER OF GUESSES IT TAKES TO GET THE
   NUMBER.  THE"
160 GOSUB 790  : PRINT
170 PRINT"ONE OF US WITH THE HIGHEST SCORE AFTER FIVE TURNS
EACH IS THE"
180 GOSUB 790  : PRINT
190 PRINT"GREAT WIZARD OF THE MENTAL NUMBER GUESSING WORLD."
:GOSUB790  :GOSUB790
200 GOSUB 790  : GOSUB 790
210 PRINT@960,"<PRESS THE SPACE BAR WHEN YOUR BRAIN IS READY
   TO CHALLENGE ME.>";:A$=INKEY$
220 A$=INKEY$ : IF A$="" OR A$<>" " THEN 220
230 Y=0 : M=0 : YS=0 : MS=0
240 CLS : PRINT TAB(5);"DO YOU WANT TO CHOOSE THE FIRST NUMB
ER? (Y=YES, N=NO)"; : A$=INKEY$
250 A$=INKEY$ : IF A$="" THEN 250
260 IF A$="N" THEN 470
270 IF A$<>"Y" THEN 250
280 C=0 : CLS : PRINT "PLEASE ENTER YOUR NUMBER FROM 1 TO 20
0.  I PROMISE NOT TO PEEK."
290 INPUT N
300 CLS : IF N<1 OR N>200 OR INT(N)<>N THEN PRINT "YOUR NUMB
```

```
ER MUST BE AN INTEGER FROM 1 TO 200." : GOSUB 790  : GOTO 28
0
310 C=C+1 : IF C>10 THEN 420
320 IF C=1 THEN G(1)=RND(200) : GOTO 380
330 IF HF=1 AND C=2 THEN G(C)=INT((G(1)-1)/2) : GOTO 380
340 IF HF=0 AND C=2 THEN G(C)=G(1)+INT((200-G(1))/2) : GOTO
380
350 IF HF=1 AND C<10 THEN G(C) = G(C-1)-INT((ABS(G(C-1)-G(C-
2)))/2+.5) : IF G(C)<1 THEN G(C)=1 : GOTO 380   ELSE 380
360 IF HF=0 AND C<10 THEN G(C) = G(C-1)+INT((ABS(G(C-1)-G(C-
2)))/2+.5) : IF G(C)>200 THEN G(C)=200 : GOTO 380   ELSE 380
370 IF HF=1 THEN G(C)=1 ELSE G(C)=200
380 PRINT "MY GUESS #";C;"IS";G(C),
390 IF G(C)>N THEN PRINT "TOO HIGH" : HF=1 : GOTO 310
400 IF G(C)<N THEN PRINT "TOO LOW" : HF=0 : GOTO 310
410 PRINT "JUST RIGHT!!!!!!!!"
420 MS=MS+S(C)
430 PRINT : PRINT "I JUST EARNED";S(C);"POINTS."
440 PRINT "MY TOTAL SCORE IS NOW";MS;"POINTS."
450 M=M+1 : GOSUB 800
460 IF DF=1 THEN GOSUB 810  : GOTO 680  ELSE GOSUB 810
470 C=0 : CLS : N=RND(200)
480 PRINT "I HAVE CHOSEN MY SECRET NUMBER.  GOOD LUCK!!!" :
GOSUB 810
490 C=C+1 : IF C=11 THEN 590
500 CLS : INPUT "PLEASE ENTER YOUR GUESS";G(C)
510 IF G(C)>N THEN R$(C)="TOO HIGH" : GOTO 540
520 IF G(C)<N THEN R$(C)="TOO LOW" : GOTO 540
530 R$(C)="JUST RIGHT!!!!!!!!"
540 CLS
550 FOR X=1 TO C
560    PRINT "YOUR GUESS #";X;"WAS";G(X),R$(X)
570 NEXT X
580 IF G(C)<>N THEN GOSUB 810  : GOTO 490
590 IF C=11 THEN N=10 ELSE N=C
600 CLS
610 FOR X=1 TO N
620    PRINT "YOUR GUESS #";X;"WAS";G(X),R$(X)
630 NEXT X : YS=YS+S(C)
640 PRINT : PRINT "YOU JUST EARNED";S(C);"POINTS."
650 PRINT "YOUR TOTAL SCORE IS NOW";YS;"POINTS."
660 Y=Y+1 : GOSUB 800
670 IF DF=1 THEN GOSUB 810  : GOTO 680  ELSE GOSUB 810  : GO
TO 280
680 CLS : PRINT "YOUR TOTAL SCORE IS";YS;"POINTS." : PRINT
690 PRINT "MY TOTAL SCORE IS";MS;"POINTS." : PRINT : PRINT
700 IF MS>YS THEN PRINT "I AM THE VICTOR, THE WINNER, THE CO
NQUEROR!!!!!!!!!!!!!!!!" : GOTO 730
710 IF YS>MS THEN PRINT "SOMEHOW YOU MANAGED TO BEAT ME.  I'
LL GET YOU NEXT TIME!" : GOTO 730
720 PRINT "IT'S A TIE.  I THOUGHT SURE I HAD YOU THIS TIME."
730 GOSUB 810  : CLS : PRINT "WOULD YOU LIKE TO PLAY AGAIN?
 (Y=YES, N=NO)" : A$=INKEY$
740 A$=INKEY$ : IF A$="" THEN 740
750 IF A$="Y" THEN 230
760 IF A$<>"N" THEN 740
770 CLS : PRINT TAB(15);"YOU'RE VERY SMART FOR A HUMAN!!"
780 END
```

```
790 FOR T=1 TO 800 : NEXT T : RETURN
800 IF Y=5 AND M=5 THEN DF=1 : RETURN ELSE DF=0 : RETURN
810 PRINT@896,CHR$(31);"PRESS THE SPACE BAR TO CONTINUE ....
........" : A$=INKEY$
820 A$=INKEY$ : IF A$="" OR A$<>" " THEN 820  ELSE RETURN
```

20. READING A SCALE

SUGGESTED FILE NAME: SCALE

SUGGESTED GRADE RANGE: 6–8

DESCRIPTION OF THE PROGRAM: This activity is designed to give students practice in determining coordinates that correspond to points on a vertical scale. There are a total of thirty problems. A vertical scale is shown on which there are six coordinates; two of the coordinates are missing. The student must type the missing coordinates.

EXPLANATION OF DATA LINES: Each data line contains sufficient information for two problems on the same scale. Answers are printed on the screen at specific locations: 668, 540, 412, 284, 156, and 28. See the TRS-80™ Video Display Worksheet in the Appendix.

The first four data entries are the correct answers for two of the problems and their locations on the scale. For example, in line 440, the correct answers are 1 and 5. Their locations on the scale are 540 and 28.

P is the problem number.

The remaining six items are the coordinates on the scale. At two locations, the coordinates will be missing. The missing coordinates are denoted by "999." For example, in line 440, the second and sixth coordinates will be missing.

HOW TO CHANGE THE DATA: The data in this program includes decimal as well as integer data. You may want to change it so that all numbers are whole numbers, or you may want to use negative integers. The data in this program can be changed by replacing items one for one. Be very careful that screen locations match missing data items.

```
10 CLS : PRINT@279,"READING A SCALE"
20 FOR TI=1 TO 1000 : NEXT TI
30 CLS : PRINT "This computer program consists of thirty exerc
ises on"
40 PRINT "reading a scale." : PRINT
50 PRINT "Press the <SPACE BAR>  when you are ready to start."
60 X$=INKEY$ : IF X$="" THEN 60
70 IF X$=" " THEN 80    ELSE 60
80 CLS
90 FOR I=31 TO 0 STEP -1 : SET(50,I) : NEXT I
100 FOR I=0 TO 5 : SET(51,6*I) : SET(52,6*I) : NEXT I
110 P=1
120 PRINT@0,"#";P;
130 C=668 : N=1
140 READ L(1), A(1), L(2), A(2)
```

```
150 FOR I=1 TO 6 : READ V(I) : NEXT I
160 FOR J=1 TO 6
170 IF V(J)=999 THEN 190
180 PRINT@C,V(J);
190 C=C-128
200 NEXT J
210 FOR K=1 TO 5
220 PRINT@L(N)+5,"      "; : FOR I=1 TO 40 : NEXT I
230 PRINT@L(N)+5,"<---"; : FOR I=1 TO 40 : NEXT I
240 NEXT K
250 PRINT@768,CHR$(31);"What value corresponds to this point";
253 INPUT V$ : IF LEN(V$)=1 THEN 255 ELSE IF (LEFT$(V$,1)="-"
OR LEFT$(V$,1)=".") THEN V=VAL(V$) : GOTO 260
255 IF ASC(V$)>57 OR ASC(V$)<48 THEN 250 ELSE V = VAL(V$)
260 IF V=A(N) THEN 290
270 IF W=1 PRINT@768,CHR$(31);"The coordinate is ";A(N);"." :
FOR I=1 TO 600 : NEXT I : W=0 : GOTO 250
280 PRINT@768,CHR$(31);"Try again." : FOR I=1 TO 600 : NEXT I
: W=1 : GOTO 250
290 PRINT@768,CHR$(31);"That's right!!" : W=0 : P=P+1
300 PRINT@L(N)+5,"      "; : PRINT@L(N),A(N);
310 IF P=31 THEN 410
320 PRINT@896,"Press the <SPACE BAR> to continue . . ."
330 X$=INKEY$ : IF X$="" THEN 330
340 IF X$=" " THEN 350  ELSE 330
350 PRINT@768,CHR$(31) : PRINT@896,CHR$(31)
360 N=N+1
370 IF N=2 PRINT@0,"#";P; : GOTO 210
380 C=668
390 FOR I=1 TO 6 : PRINT@C,"      "; : C=C-128 : NEXT I
400 GOTO 120
410 FOR TI=1 TO 2000 : NEXT TI : CLS
420 PRINT@400,"That's all for now.  Bye-bye."
430 END
440 DATA 540,1,28,5,0,999,2,3,4,999
450 DATA 412,20,156,40,0,10,999,30,999,50
460 DATA 540,100,284,300,0,999,200,999,400,500
470 DATA 412,10,28,25,0,5,999,15,20,999
480 DATA 540,2,156,8,0,999,4,6,999,10
490 DATA 668,0,412,100,999,50,999,150,200,250
500 DATA 284,75,28,125,0,25,50,999,100,999
510 DATA 540,20,156,80,0,999,40,60,999,100
520 DATA 412,24,156,28,20,22,999,26,999,30
530 DATA 412,.2,284,.3,0,.1,999,999,.4,.5
540 DATA 540,.2,284,.6,0,999,.4,999,.8,1.0
550 DATA 540,.42,28,.50,.40,999,.44,.46,.48,999
560 DATA 668,2.1,284,2.4,999,2.2,2.3,999,2.5,2.6
570 DATA 412,1,28,2.5,0,.5,999,1.5,2,999
580 DATA 540,250,156,1000,0,999,500,750,999,1250
```

21. FEET PER SECOND AND MILES PER HOUR

SUGGESTED FILE NAME: FPS

SUGGESTED GRADE RANGE: 7–8

DESCRIPTION OF THE PROGRAM: This program is a simulation of a car traveling 1000 feet in periods of time measured in seconds. The student is asked to calculate its rate of speed in feet per second by dividing 1000 by the number of seconds. The student is then instructed to convert the rate in feet per second to miles per hour by using the fact that 88 feet per second is approximately 60 miles per hour. A calculator helps in this one.

NEW PROGRAMMING STATEMENTS: One of the features of Radio Shack BASIC, which is great fun, is character string graphics. In the Appendix of your owner's manual is a table called Graphics Characters (Codes 128-191). Each code represents a different configuration of quantities of lighted squares within a rectangle of six squares. There are sixty-four possible configurations. Single graphics characters can be added together to make pictures. In this program it is a picture of a car that moves across the screen. The picture of the car is accomplished by lines 220 and 230; the animation, by lines 240 through 310.

To make the picture of the car, each character code is used in a character string expression; then the expressions are added together. The sum is given the name A$.

To accomplish the animation, the car is moved across the screen by printing it, erasing it, then printing it again and erasing it again. This process simulates movement. In line 290, there is the statement: STRING$(D,128)=A$. This statement puts together the number "D" of character code 128, then adds on the picture of the car. Character code 128 is a blank space. Each time the loop is executed, D increases in value. This means that there are more blank spaces behind the car each time the loop is executed until the car is printed at its final destination.

```
10 CLEAR 1000 : RANDOM
20 CLS : PRINT@270,"FEET PER SECOND & MILES PER HOUR"
30 FOR TI=1 TO 1000 : NEXT TI
40 CLS : PRINT "In these exercises, a car is timed as it tra
vels 1000 feet."
50 PRINT : PRINT "You will be asked to state the speed of th
e car in feet per"
60 PRINT "second."
70 PRINT : PRINT "Using the fact that 60 miles per hour is a
pproximately"
80 PRINT "88 feet per second, you will be asked to convert t
he car's"
90 PRINT "speed in feet per second to miles per hour."
100 PRINT : PRINT "A calculator will be a big help to you."
110 PRINT : PRINT : PRINT : PRINT : GOSUB 600
120 PRINT "Press the <SPACE BAR> when you are ready to begin
 . . ."
130 X$=INKEY$ : IF X$="" THEN 130
140 IF X$=" " THEN 150  ELSE 130
150 CLS
160 FOR R=0 TO 120 : SET(R,13) : NEXT R
170 FOR R=1 TO 10 : SET(R*12,14) : NEXT R
180 PRINT@320,0;
```

```
190 FOR R=1 TO 5 : PRINT@318+R*12,200*R : NEXT R
200 PRINT@46,"SECONDS:";
210 K=RND(3) : T=0
220 A$=CHR$(171)+CHR$(131)+CHR$(151)+CHR$(26)+STRING$(K+3,24
)
230 A$=A$+STRING$(K,128)+CHR$(138)+CHR$(159)+CHR$(143)+CHR$(
159)
240 FOR I=0 TO 55 STEP K
250 X=RND(5)
260 IF X=2 OR X=3 THEN 280
270 T=T+1 : PRINT@55,T;
280 D=I+K
290 PRINT@128,STRING$(D,128)+A$;
300 FOR J=1 TO 15 : NEXT J
310 NEXT I
320 PRINT@448,CHR$(31);"How many feet per second to the near
est tenth";
330 INPUT FPS
340 IF ABS(FPS-(1000/T))<.05 THEN 400
350 IF W<>1 THEN 380
360 PRINT@448,CHR$(31);"Divide 1000 by";T;"."
370 GOSUB 600  : W=0 : GOTO 320
380 PRINT@448,CHR$(31); "Try again."
390 GOSUB 600  : PRINT@640,CHR$(31) : W=W+1 : GOTO 320
400 PRINT@576,"Way to go!!" : GOSUB 600   :W=0
410 PRINT@576,FPS;" feet per second is how many miles per ho
ur?"
420 PRINT@640,"Solve this proportion:";
430 PRINT@670,"60 MPH"; : PRINT@683,"?     MPH"
440 PRINT@734,"------  =  ---------";
450 PRINT@798,"88 FPS"; : PRINT@810,FPS;"FPS";
460 PRINT@832,CHR$(31); : PRINT "MPH  =  "; : INPUT S
470 IF ABS(S-(FPS*60/88))<.05 THEN 500
480 PRINT@896, "Multiply ";FPS;" by 60 and divide by 88."
490 GOSUB 600  : GOTO 460
500 PRINT@682,CHR$(30);S;"MPH"; : PRINT@832,CHR$(31);
510 PRINT@896,"That's correct!!";
520 PRINT@916,FPS;" FPS is ";S;" MPH." : GOSUB 600
530 PRINT@960,"Press <SPACE BAR> to continue or 'Q' to quit.
";
540 X$=INKEY$ : IF X$="" THEN 540
550 IF X$=" " THEN 570
560 IF X$="Q" THEN 580   ELSE 540
570 GOTO 150
580 CLS : PRINTTAB(15);"Remember, the speed limit is 55 MPH.
"
590 END
600 FOR I=1 TO 600 : NEXT I : RETURN
```

22. ABBREVIATIONS FOR ELEMENTS

SUGGESTED FILE NAME: ELEMENTS

SUGGESTED GRADE RANGE: 7–8

DESCRIPTION OF THE PROGRAM: A self-challenging game format is used in this program to help students learn the abbreviations for chemical elements. Each time the game is played, twenty elements are chosen randomly from a list of fifty. The maximum number of points a student can earn in one game is 10,000 (500 per element name). The faster and more accurately the student types abbreviations for the elements, the higher the score.

EXPLANATION OF DATA LINES: Each group of four data entries defines one problem. The first entry in the group is the element name; the second is the first letter in the abbreviation. The third data entry is the second letter in the abbreviation; if there is no second letter, 999 is used to fill that spot and clue the computer that there is no second letter. The fourth data entry is the second letter, if any, in lower case.

The program must be run in upper case. The student does not use upper/lower case and the <**ENTER**> key. In this program, INKEY$ is used. Therefore, the second letter in the abbreviation is given twice in the data. The first time, it is checked against the student's response; the second time, it is in lower case to be printed on the screen.

PROGRAMMING LOGIC: The FOR/NEXT loop in lines 100 through 150 chooses twenty different random numbers from one through fifty. These numbers are used to choose which elements will appear in the exercises in a game. In line 110, a number is chosen. Lines 120 through 140 check to see that the number has not already been chosen. If it has been, the program returns to line 110 to choose a different number.

There is an extra INKEY$ statement in line 270. This use of INKEY$ absorbs extra key strikes. For example, if an abbreviation is only one letter and the student types two letters, INKEY$ in line 270 absorbs the key stroke and prevents it from being interpreted as part of the answer for the next element name. To see how this functions, you may want to delete line 270 and try the program with extra key strikes. At Ready, type the line number (270) and press <**ENTER**> to delete the line.

The scoring technique is shown in line 280. The computer continually executes this line until a key is pressed. The maximum number of points that a student can get for each element abbreviation is 500. Each time line 280 is executed, a counter, C, is increased by one (1), then subtracted from 500. The score, S, is calculated by 500 − C. The score decreases as the student hesitates to type his or her answer.

Line 330 insures that the score for any single element abbreviation will not be less than zero. In line 340, the score, S, is added to the total score, SS, and SS is printed on the screen each time the student gives an answer. Of course, if the student gets a MISS!!, then the score remains the same as before.

```
10 POKE 16409,1
20 CLS : PRINT@274,"ABBREVIATIONS FOR ELEMENTS" : PRINT
30 PRINT "To successfully play this game, your computer shou
```

```
ld be in"
40 PRINT "UPPER CASE."
50 PRINT : PRINT "The faster and more accurate you are, the
higher your score."
60 DIM A$(50) , B$(50) , C$(50), D$(50) , A(50)
70 FOR J=1 TO 50 : READ A$(J) , B$(J) , C$(J) , D$(J) : NEXT
 J
80 A(1)=RND(50) : A(2)=RND(50)
90 IF A(1)=A(2) THEN 80
100 FOR Y=2 TO 20
110 A(Y)=RND(50)
120    FOR X=Y-1 TO 1 STEP -1
130     IF A(Y)=A(X) THEN 110
140     NEXT X
150 NEXT Y
160 PRINT@846,"Press the <SPACE BAR> to continue . . ."
170 Z$=INKEY$ : IF Z$<>" " THEN 170
180 CLS : PRINT@205,"Type the abbreviation for this element:
";
190 FOR K=42 TO 82 : SET(K,14) : SET(K,26) : NEXT K
200 FOR K=14 TO 26 : SET(42,K) : SET(82,K) : NEXT K
210 PRINT@788,"PERFECT SCORE:   10,000";
220 PRINT@852,"   YOUR SCORE:  ";SS
230 FOR T=1 TO 20
240 PRINT@0,"#";T
250 C=0 : Z=A(T)
260 PRINT@411,A$(Z);
270 X$=INKEY$
280 X$=INKEY$ : C=C+1 : S=500-C : IF X$="" THEN 280
290 IF X$=B$(Z) THEN 300  ELSE PRINT@665,"M I S S   !   !" :
 GOTO 370
300 IF C$(Z)="999" THEN 330
310 Y$=INKEY$ : IF Y$="" THEN 310
320 IF Y$=C$(Z) THEN 330  ELSE PRINT@665,"M I S S   !   !" :
 GOTO 370
330 IF S<0 THEN S=0
340 SS=SS+S
350 PRINT@665,"H I T   !   !"
360 PRINT@868,SS
370 IF C$(Z)="999" PRINT@475,B$(Z); : GOTO 390
380 PRINT@475, B$(Z) ; D$(Z);
390 FOR I=1 TO 600 : NEXT I
400 PRINT@640,CHR$(30) : PRINT@411,STRING$(11,128);
410 PRINT@475,STRING$(3,128);
420 NEXT T
425 PRINT@904,"To play another game, type RUN and press <ENT
ER>."; : FOR I=1 TO 500 : NEXT I : END
430 DATA Hydrogen,H,999,999,Magnesium,M,G,g,Aluminum,A,L,l
440 DATA Lithium,L,I,i,Silicon,S,I,i,Phosphorus,P,999,999
450 DATA Berylium,B,E,e,Sulfur,S,999,999,Chlorine,C,L,l
460 DATA Helium,H,E,e,Argon,A,R,r,Potassium,K,999,999
470 DATA Carbon,C,999,999,Calcium,C,A,a,Titanium,T,I,i
480 DATA Nitrogen,N,999,999,Chromium,C,R,r,Manganese,M,N,n
490 DATA Oxygen,O,999,999,Iron,F,E,e,Cobalt,C,O,o
500 DATA Fluorine,F,999,999,Nickel,N,I,i,Copper,C,U,u
510 DATA Neon,N,E,e,Uranium,U,999,999,Zinc,Z,N,n
520 DATA Sodium,N,A,a,Arsenic,A,S,s,Selenium,S,E,e
```

```
530 DATA Bromine,B,R,r,Krypton,K,R,r,Strontium,S,R,r
540 DATA Zirconium,Z,R,r,Molybdenum,M,O,o,Rhodium,R,H,h
550 DATA Silver,A,G,g,Cadmium,C,D,d,Tin,S,N,n
560 DATA Antimony,S,B,b,Iodine,I,999,999,Barium,B,A,a
570 DATA Tungsten,W,999,999,Platinum,P,T,t,Gold,A,U,u
580 DATA Mercury,H,G,g,Lead,P,B,b,Bismuth,B,I,i
590 DATA Radium,R,A,a,Plutonium,P,U,u
```

23. SOLVING PROPORTIONS

SUGGESTED FILE NAME: SIMILAR

SUGGESTED GRADE RANGE: 6–8

DESCRIPTION OF THE PROGRAM: Two similar rectangles are drawn on the screen to scale (more or less). The lengths of the sides of one rectangle can be multiplied by some number to obtain the lengths of the sides of the other rectangle. Three of the dimensions are given. The student must type the missing dimension.

EXPLANATION OF DATA LINES: Each data line contains the information for one problem. There are eleven entries in each data line. Each entry performs the function described below.

1. P is the problem number.
2. B1 is the number used in the SET statement (line 180) that draws the bases of the first rectangle.
3. X1$ is the length of the base of the first rectangle.
4. H1 is the number used in the SET statement (line 190) that draws the heights of the first rectangle.
5. Y1$ is the length of the height of the first rectangle.
6. B2 is the number used in the SET statement (line 210) that draws the bases of the second rectangle.
7. X2$ is the length of the base of the second rectangle.
8. H2 is the number used in the SET statement (line 220) that draws the heights of the second rectangle.
9. Y2$ is the length of the height of the second rectangle.
10. A is the correct answer.
11. W is the screen location at which the correct answer is to be printed.

```
10 CLS : PRINT@277,"SOLVING PROPORTIONS"
20 FOR TI=1 TO 1000 : NEXT TI
30 CLS : PRINT "The rectangles which you will see on the scr
een"
40 PRINT "are in proportion." : PRINT
```

```
50 PRINT "That is, the lengths of the sides of one rectangle
"
60 PRINT "can be multiplied by some number to obtain the len
gths"
70 PRINT "of the corresponding sides of the other rectangle.
"
80 PRINT : PRINT "Of the four dimension of the rectangles, t
hree"
90 PRINT "of them are given.  You must find the missing leng
th."
100 PRINT : PRINT "There are twenty exercises."
110 PRINT@896,"Press the <SPACE BAR> to continue . . ."
120 X$=INKEY$ : IF X$="" THEN 120
130 IF X$ <>" " THEN 120
140 CLS : Z=0
150 READ P, B1, X1$, H1, Y1$, B2, X2$, H2, Y2$, A, W
160 PRINT "#";P;
170 PRINT "  The sides of these two rectangles are in propor
tion."
180 FOR I=0 TO B1 : SET(10+I,9) : SET(10+I,9+H1) : NEXT I
190 FOR J=0 TO H1 : SET(10,9+J) : SET(10+B1,9+J) : NEXT J
200 PRINT@136,X1$; : PRINT@258,Y1$;
210 FOR K=0 TO B2 : SET(65+K,9) : SET(65+K,9+H2) : NEXT K
220 FOR L=0 TO H2 : SET(65,9+L) : SET(65+B2,9+L) : NEXT L
230 PRINT@164,X2$; : PRINT@285,Y2$;
240 PRINT@768, "What is the length of the missing side"; : I
NPUT S
250 IF S=A THEN 300
260 IF Z=0 PRINT@768,CHR$(31);"Not correct -- Try again."; :
 GOSUB 480  : Z=1 : GOTO 240
270 IF Z=2 PRINT@768,CHR$(31);"The answer is ";A;"." : GOSUB
 480  : Z=0 : GOTO 240
280 IF Z=1 GOSUB 380
290 GOTO 240
300 PRINT@896, "That's right!!"; : PRINT@W,A;
310 GOSUB 480  : Z=0
320 IF P=20 THEN 360
330 PRINT@896,CHR$(31);"Press the <SPACE BAR> to continue .
. ."; : X$=INKEY$
340 X$=INKEY$ : IF X$="" THEN 340
350 IF X$= " " THEN 140  ELSE 340
360 PRINT@896,"You have answered all twenty problems.  That'
s all for now."
370 GOSUB 480  : END
380 REM    ********** SUBROUTINE TO SHOW PROPORTION *********
*
390 Z=2 : PRINT@768,CHR$(31);"Solve this proportion:";
400 PRINT@807,X1$; : PRINT@817,X2$;
410 PRINT@870,"---   =   ---";
420 PRINT@935,Y1$; : PRINT@945,Y2$;
430 PRINT@896,"Press the <SPACE BAR> to continue . . .";
440 X$=INKEY$ : IF X$="" THEN 440
450 IF X$=" " THEN 460  ELSE 440
460 PRINT@768,CHR$(31)
470 RETURN
480 FOR TI=1 TO 800 : NEXT TI : RETURN
490 DATA 1,20,4,5,2,40,?,10,4,8,164
```

```
500 DATA 2,12,?,10,12,24,36,20,48,9,136
510 DATA 3,10,5,10,10,30,15,30,?,30,285
520 DATA 4,18,7,5,?,55,35,15,20,4,258
530 DATA 5,40,50,35,?,8,5,9,8,80,258
540 DATA 6,20,20,7,15,60,60,20,?,45,285
550 DATA 7,19,?,15,12,48,24,30,36,8,136
560 DATA 8,30,20,8,10,45,?,10,15,30,164
570 DATA 9,24,11,3,1,62,44,10,?,4,285
580 DATA 10,24,12,15,?,19,8,12,10,15,258
590 DATA 11,40,36,20,36,10,?,5,9,9,164
600 DATA 12,20,14,10,14,56,35,28,?,35,285
610 DATA 13,10,18,25,?,30,27,35,90,60,258
620 DATA 14,35,?,7,12,50,40,9,16,30,136
630 DATA 15,35,?,10,8,25,15,5,6,20,136
640 DATA 16,30,21,11,?,40,28,15,24,18,258
650 DATA 17,18,35,20,49,30,?,30,63,45,164
660 DATA 18,40,120,13,80,30,90,10,?,60,285
670 DATA 19,35,3.2,6,1,20,?,3,.5,1.6,164
680 DATA 20,35,.9,4,.2,60,?,8,.6,2.7,164
```

24. ESTIMATING MEASUREMENTS

SUGGESTED FILE NAME: ESTIMATE

SUGGESTED GRADE RANGE: 5–8

DESCRIPTION OF THE PROGRAM: Thirty exercises are presented in estimating measurements in one and two dimensions. Ten of the exercises compare two horizontal lines. The length of the first line is given. The student uses this measurement to estimate the length of the second line. Ten of the exercises compare two "boxes." The weight of the first "box" is given. The student uses this measurement to estimate the weight of the second "box." The final ten exercises compare two vertical lines. As before, the student must estimate the height of the second line when given the height of the first.

EXPLANATION OF DATA LINES: Each data line defines one exercise. The six data items for the first ten problems can be found in lines 710 through 800. Their explanations are as follows:

1. The problem number: P
2. The unit of measure: A$
3. The number which is used to draw the first line: A
4. The length of the first line: B
5. The number which is used to draw the second line: C
6. The length of the second line (the correct answer): D

The eight data items for the second set of ten problems can be found in lines 810 through 900. Their explanations are as follows:

1. The problem number: P

2. The unit of measure: A$

3. Height of first box: A

4. Length of first box: B

5. Height of second box: C

6. Length of second box: D

7. Weight of first box: E

8. Weight of second box (correct answer): F

The six data items for the third set of ten problems can be found in lines 910 through 1000. Their explanations are as follows:

1. The problem number: P

2. The unit of measure: A$

3. Number used to draw first line: A

4. Height of first line: B

5. Number used to draw second line: C

6. Height of second line (correct answer): D

```
10 CLS : PRINT@276,"ESTIMATING MEASUREMENTS"
20 FOR I=1 TO 1000 : NEXT I
30 CLS : PRINT "PLEASE TYPE YOUR NAME AND PRESS <ENTER>."
40 PRINT : INPUT N$ : PRINT : PRINT
50 PRINT "HAPPY TO MEET YOU, ";N$;"." : GOSUB 660
60 CLS : R=0 : T=0
70 PRINT "YOU WILL BE GIVEN A PICTURE OF AN OBJECT AND ASKED
 TO"
80 PRINT "ESTIMATE ITS LENGTH, WEIGHT, OR HEIGHT WHEN COMPAR
ED
90 PRINT "WITH ANOTHER OBJECT. THERE ARE 30 PROBLEMS."
100 PRINT : PRINT "HERE IS AN EXAMPLE, ";N$;":"
110 FOR I=1 TO 50 : SET (I,19) : NEXT I
120 PRINT@448,"12 INCHES"
130 FOR I=1 TO 75 : SET(I,28) : NEXT I
140 PRINT@640,"HOW MANY INCHES LONG?"
150 PRINT@768,"YOUR ESTIMATE SHOULD BE ABOUT 18."
160 PRINT@896,"PRESS <SPACE BAR> WHEN YOU ARE READY TO BEGIN
."
170 X$=INKEY$ : IF X$="" THEN 170
180 IF X$=" " THEN 190  ELSE 170
190 CLS : READ P, A$, A, B, C, D
200 PRINT "#";P
210 FOR I=0 TO A-1 : SET(I,7) : NEXT I
220 PRINT@192,B; : PRINT A$
230 FOR J=0 TO C-1 : SET(J,16) : NEXT J
240 PRINT@384,CHR$(31); "HOW MANY ";A$;" LONG";
250 INPUT N : T=T+1
260 IF N>=D-2 AND N<=D+2 THEN 290
```

```
270 IF N>D+2 SP=512 : GOSUB 670  : GOSUB 660   : GOTO 240
280 SP=512 : GOSUB 680  : GOSUB 660   : GOTO 240
290 SP=576 : GOSUB 690  : SP=704 : GOSUB 700  : GOSUB 660
300 IF P=10 THEN 320
310 GOTO 190
320 CLS : READ P, A$, A, B, C, D, E, F
330 PRINT "#";P
340 FOR J=16 TO 17-A STEP -1
350 FOR I=40 TO 39+B
360 SET (I,J)
370 NEXT I
380 NEXT J
390 PRINT@403,E; : PRINT A$
400 FOR J=16 TO 17-C STEP -1
410 FOR I=70 TO 69+D
420 SET (I,J)
430 NEXT I
440 NEXT J
450 PRINT@419,CHR$(31); "HOW MANY ";A$;
460 INPUT N : T=T+1 : IF N>=F-2 AND N<=F+2 THEN 490
470 IF N>F+2 SP=512 : GOSUB 670  : GOSUB 660   : GOTO 450
480 SP=512 : GOSUB 680  : GOSUB 660   : GOTO 450
490 SP=576 : GOSUB 690  : SP=704 : GOSUB 700  : GOSUB 660
500 IF P=20 THEN 510   ELSE 320
510 CLS : READ P, A$, A, B, C, D
520 PRINT "#";P
530 FOR I=19 TO 20-A STEP -1 : SET(26,I) : NEXT I
540 PRINT @ 460, B; : PRINT A$
550 FOR J=19 TO 20-C STEP -1 : SET(62,J) : NEXT J
560 PRINT@479,CHR$(31); "HOW MANY ";A$;" TALL";
570 INPUT F : T=T+1 : IF F>=D-2 AND F<=D+2 THEN 600
580 IF F>D+2 THEN SP=576 : GOSUB 670  : GOSUB 660  : GOTO 56
0
590 SP=576 : GOSUB 680  : GOSUB 660   : GOTO 560
600 SP=704 : GOSUB 690  : SP=832 : GOSUB 700  : GOSUB 660
610 IF P=30 THEN 620   ELSE 510
620 PRINT@704,"YOU HAVE ESTIMATED ALL THE MEASUREMENTS I HAV
E."
630 PRINT "YOUR FINAL SCORE IS";INT(R/T*100+.5);"%."
640 PRINT "GOOD-BYE, "N$"."
650 END
660 FOR I=1 TO 800 : NEXT I : RETURN
670 PRINT@SP,"TOO HIGH -- ESTIMATE AGAIN." : RETURN
680 PRINT@SP,"TOO LOW -- ESTIMATE AGAIN." : RETURN
690 PRINT@SP,"THAT'S A GOOD ESTIMATE, ";N$;"!!" : R=R+1 : RE
TURN
700 PRINT@SP,"YOUR SCORE IS";INT(R/T*100+.5);"%." : RETURN
710 DATA 1,INCHES,10,5,20,10
720 DATA 2,FEET,15,4,45,12
730 DATA 3,YARDS,60,20,30,10
740 DATA 4,CENTIMETERS,60,20,90,30
750 DATA 5,METERS,60,60,40,40
760 DATA 6,KILOMETERS,30,18,40,24
770 DATA 7,FEET,60,15,20,5
780 DATA 8,INCHES,40,12,60,18
790 DATA 9,METERS,80,80,20,20
```

```
800 DATA 10,CENTIMETERS,10,10,60,60
810 DATA 11,POUNDS,2,4,2,8,10,20
820 DATA 12,OUNCES,2,4,8,4,10,40
830 DATA 13,KILOGRAMS,4,8,4,32,20,80
840 DATA 14,MILLIGRAMS,12,12,12,9,40,30
850 DATA 15,OUNCES,5,10,10,20,25,100
860 DATA 16,GRAMS,16,4,16,12,25,75
870 DATA 17,POUNDS,6,8,12,16,8,32
880 DATA 18,TONS,5,10,15,10,2,6
890 DATA 19,OUNCES,16,12,16,3,40,10
900 DATA 20,GRAMS,16,4,8,4,30,15
910 DATA 21,CENTIMETERS,5,5,15,15
920 DATA 22,FEET,16,12,12,9
930 DATA 23,METERS,3,5,18,30
940 DATA 24,INCHES,15,9,10,6
950 DATA 25,KILOMETERS,8,4,16,8
960 DATA 26,MILES,10,2,15,3
970 DATA 27,YARDS,18,6,12,4
980 DATA 28,MILLIMETERS,8,8,12,12
990 DATA 29,INCHES,16,60,12,45
1000 DATA 30,METERS,4,7,16,28
```

25. TWENTY SCIENCE QUESTIONS

SUGGESTED FILE NAME: SCIENCE

SUGGESTED GRADE RANGE: 6–8

DESCRIPTION OF THE PROGRAM: This activity presents science facts in a game format. Twenty exercises are chosen at random from a set of forty-nine questions. The questions are to be answered "T" for true or "F" for false. As the program runs, a random amount of money is chosen for each question. As the student answers the questions correctly, his "jackpot" increases. Also, extra information is provided for most questions.

EXPLANATION OF DATA LINES: Each data line contains three entries that determine one science question. There are forty-nine data lines.

HOW TO CHANGE THE DATA: You may change data by simply retyping data lines and substituting your questions for the ones that are currently in the program.

You may wish to type the data and other messages so that all printing appears on the screen in upper and lower case. Use <**SHIFT**> **0** to switch back and forth from upper to upper/lower case.

```
10 SUM=0 : C=1 : CLEAR 3000 : RANDOM
20 DIM R(20),Q$(150)
30 CLS : PRINT@274,"TWENTY SCIENCE QUESTIONS"
40 FOR J=1 TO 147 : READ Q$(J) : NEXT J
```

```
50 R(0)=RND(48) : R(1)=RND(48)
60 IF R(0)=R(1) THEN 50
70 FOR X=2 TO 19
80 R(X)=RND(48)
90 FOR Y=X-1 TO 0 STEP -1
100 IF R(X)=R(Y) THEN 80
110 NEXT Y
120 NEXT X
130 CLS
140 FOR H=38 TO 80 : SET(H,0) : SET(H,8) : NEXT H
150 FOR V=0 TO 8 : SET(38,V) : SET(80,V) : NEXT V
160 FOR T=1 TO 20
170 PRINT@274,CHR$(31)
180 FOR I=1 TO 10
190 PRINT@91,"       "; : M=RND(1000)
200 PRINT@90,"$";M; : FOR J=1 TO 30 : NEXT J
210 NEXT I
220 PRINT@274,"ANSWER <T>RUE OR <F>ALSE."
230 A=3*R(T)+1 : PRINT : PRINT Q$(A)
240 A$=INKEY$ : IF A$="" THEN 240
250 IF A$<>"F" AND A$<> "T" THEN 240
260 PRINT A$
270 IF A$<>Q$(A+1) THEN 300
280 PRINT "THAT'S RIGHT!!      " : PRINT Q$(A+2) : SUM=SUM+M
290 PRINT "YOU WIN $";M,,"TOTAL WINNINGS = $ ";SUM : GOTO 33
0
300 PRINT "YOUR ANSWER IS NOT CORRECT."
310 PRINTQ$(A+2) : SUM=SUM-M
320 PRINT "YOU LOSE $";M,,"TOTAL WINNINGS = $ ";SUM
330 PRINT@912,"PRESS SPACE BAR TO CONTINUE . . ."
340 B$=INKEY$ : IF B$="" THEN 340
350 IF B$ <> " "THEN 340
360 NEXT T
370 CLS : FOR I=1 TO 80 : S=RND(959) : PRINT@S,"*"; : NEXT I
380 PRINT@331,"YOU HAVE PLAYED TWENTY SCIENCE QUESTIONS.";
390 PRINT@468,"YOU HAVE WON $";SUM;
400 PRINT@583,"YOU HAVE PROVED YOURSELF TO BE A WORTHY OPPON
ENT.";
410 FOR I=1 TO 2000 : NEXT I
420 END
430 DATA "A MUZZLE SETTING OF 45 DEGREES WILL GIVE A CANNON
ITS MAXIMUM    RANGE.",T,""
440 DATA "MANHOLES AND MANHOLE COVERS ARE CIRCULAR BECAUSE I
T IS EASIER TODIG CIRCULAR HOLES THAN RECTANGULAR ONES.",F,"
THEY ARE MADE IN THE SHAPE OF A CIRCLE SO THAT THE COVERS WI
LL  NOT FALL THROUGH."
450 DATA "THE EARTH IS SAID TO BE AN OBLATE SPHEROID.",T,"IT
 IS AN OBLATE SPHEROID, A SPHERE WHICH IS FLATTENED AT THE
  POLES."
460 DATA "THE DIAMETER OF THE MOON IS 2160 MILES.",T,"IT IS
2160 MILES, THE DISTANCE FROM SAN FRANCISCO TO CLEVELAND."
470 DATA "THE AVERAGE DISTANCE OF THE MOON FROM THE EARTH IS
  238,856      MILES.",T,"AT ITS FARTHEST POINT, IT IS 251,96
8 MILES FROM THE EARTH; AT   ITS CLOSEST POINT, 225,742 MILE
S."
480 DATA "THE MOON GIVES OFF NO LIGHT OF ITS OWN.",T,"IT REF
```

LECTS LIGHT RECEIVED FROM THE SUN."
490 DATA "ON THE MOON, YOU WOULD WEIGH SIX TIMES YOUR WEIGHT
 ON EARTH.",F,"YOU WOULD WEIGH ONE-SIXTH AS MUCH AS YOU WEIG
HT ON EARTH."
500 DATA "THERE ARE STORMS ON THE MOON.",F,"THE MOON HAS NO
WEATHER BECAUSE IT HAS NO ATMOSPHERE."
510 DATA "AN ECLIPSE OF THE MOON OCCURS WHEN THE SUN IS DIRE
CTLY BETWEEN THE EARTH AND THE MOON.",F,"AN ECLIPSE OF THE
MOON OCCURS WHEN THE EARTH IS DIRECTLY BETWEENTHE MOON AND T
HE SUN."
520 DATA "(1543) COPERNICUS THEORIZED THAT THE PLANETS AND T
HE SUN REVOLVEAROUND THE EARTH.",F,"COPERNICUS THEORIZED THA
T THE EARTH AND PLANETS REVOLVE ABOUT   THE SUN."
530 DATA "(1774) JOSEPH PRIESTLY DISCOVERED OXYGEN.",T,""
540 DATA "(1858) CHARLES DARWIN ADVANCED HIS THEORY OF EVOLU
TION OF PLANTSAND ANIMALS.",T,""
550 DATA "(1876) LOUIS PASTEUR DISCOVERED THAT VIRUSES CAUSE
 DISEASE.",F,"PASTEUR FOUND THAT MICROORGANISMS CAUSE DISEAS
E."
560 DATA "(1950) WILLIAM ROENTGEN DISCOVERED X RAYS.",F,"ROE
NTGEN DISCOVERED X RAYS IN 1895."
570 DATA "(1900) PAUL EHRLICH ORIGINATED CHEMOTHERAPY, THE T
REATMENT OF DISEASE WITH CHEMICALS.",T,""
580 DATA "(1905) ALBERT EINSTEIN PRESENTED HIS SPECIAL THEOR
Y OF   RELATIVITY.",T,""
590 DATA "(1960) ALEXANDER FLEMING DISCOVERED PENICILLIN.",F
,"FLEMING DISCOVERED PENICILLIN IN 1926."
600 DATA "(1942) ENRICO FERMI ACHIEVED THE FIRST SUCCESSFUL
NUCLEAR CHAIN REACTION.",T,""
610 DATA "(1953) FRANKLIN ROOSEVELT PRODUCED THE FIRST EFFEC
TIVE VACCINE AGAINST POLIO.",F,"JONAS SALK INVENTED THE FIR
ST POLIO VACCINE."
620 DATA "(1957) FRANCE LAUNCHED THE FIRST ARTIFICIAL SATELL
ITE.",F,"THE FIRST ARTIFICIAL SATELLITE WAS LAUNCHED BY RUSS
IA."
630 DATA "(1980) ARTHUR KORNBERG GREW DNA, THE BASE CHEMICAL
 OF THE GENE, IN A TEST TUBE.",F,"KORNBERG GREW DNA IN 1957.
"
640 DATA "MICKEY ROONEY AND LORNA DOONE (1961) BECAME THE FI
RST HUMANS TO FLY IN SPACE.",F,"THE FIRST HUMANS TO FLY IN S
PACE WERE YURI GAGARIN AND ALAN   SHEPARD."
650 DATA "NEIL ARMSTRONG (1969) BECAME THE FIRST PERSON TO W
ALK ON THE   MOON.",T,"HE SAID: ONE SMALL STEP FOR MAN; ON
E GIANT LEAP FOR MANKIND."
660 DATA "LIGHT TRAVELS AT 186,000 MILES PER HOUR.",F,"LIGHT
 TRAVELS AT 186,000 MILES PER SECOND."
670 DATA "ENIAC, THE FIRST ALL-ELECTRONIC DIGITAL COMPUTER,
WAS BUILT IN 1975.",F,"THE ELECTRONIC NUMERICAL INTEGRATOR
AND AUTOMATIC COMPUTER WAS BUILT IN 1946."
680 DATA "SOUND TRAVELS 1,100 FEET PER SECOND IN AIR.",T,"IT
 TRAVELS 1,100 FPS IN AIR BUT NOT AT ALL IN A VACUUM."
690 DATA "THE STARS ARE SUNS, VERY HOT MASSES OF GAS.",T,""
700 DATA "OUR SUN IS ABOUT 93 BILLION MILES FROM THE EARTH."
,F,"IT IS ABOUT 93 MILLION MILES FROM EARTH."
710 DATA "A MACH NUMBER IS A MEASURE OF SPEED.",T,"MACH 1 IS
 THE SPEED OF SOUND; MACH 2 IS TWICE THE SPEED OF   SOUND

, ETC. MACH IS NAMED FOR ERNST MACH (1838-1916)."
720 DATA "THREE SIMPLE MACHINES ARE: LEVER, PULLEY, WHEEL AN
D AXLE.",T,"THE SIX SIMPLE MACHINES ARE: LEVER, PULLEY, WHEE
L AND AXLE,   INCLINED PLANE, WEDGE, AND SCREW."
730 DATA "(1862) RICHARD GATLING INVENTED THE GATLING GUN.",
T,""
740 DATA "IRA GERSHWIN (1763) INVENTED THE STEAM ENGINE.",F,
"JAMES WATT INVENTED THE STEAM ENGINE."
750 DATA "THOMAS A. EDISON (1847-1931) PATENTED ONLY A FEW I
NVENTIONS.",F,"EDISON PATENTED MORE THAN 1,100 INVENTIONS IN
 60 YEARS."
760 DATA "ALEXANDER GRAHAM BELL INVENTED THE TELEPHONE IN 18
74.",T,""
770 DATA "THE SIZE OF AN ATOM IS ABOUT ONE-FIFTH ITS NUCLEUS
.",F,"THE SIZE OF AN ATOM IS ABOUT 50,000 TIMES THAT OF ITS
NUCLEUS."
780 DATA "THE EARTH IS ABOUT 4 1/2 BILLION YEARS OLD.",T,""
790 DATA "THE EQUATORIAL DIAMETER OF THE EARTH IS 7,926 MILE
S.",T,""
800 DATA "THE EQUATORIAL CIRCUMFERENCE OF THE EARTH IS 24,90
1 MILES.",T,""
810 DATA "50% OF THE EARTH'S ATMOSPHERE IS LESS THAN 100 MIL
ES ABOVE THE EARTH'S SURFACE.",F,"99% OF THE EARTH'S ATMOSP
HERE IS LESS THAN 100 MILES ABOVE THE EARTH."
820 DATA "THE EARTH TRAVELS 595 MILLION MILES AROUND THE SUN
 IN 365 DAYS, 6 HOURS, 9 MINUTES, AND 9.54 SECONDS.",T,"THAT
'S TRUE. ALSO, ITS SPEED IS APPROXIMATELY 66,600 MILES AN
HOUR."
830 DATA "SCIENTISTS ESTIMATE THE TEMPERATURE AT THE CENTER
OF THE EARTH TO BE AS HIGH AS 9,000 DEGREES FAHRENHEIT.",T,
""
840 DATA "DINOSAURS LIVED ABOUT 10 MILLION YEARS AGO.",F,"TH
EY LIVED ABOUT 180 MILLION YEARS AGO."
850 DATA "THE FIRST REGULARLY SCHEDULED TELEVISION BROADCAST
S BEGAN IN   1928.",T,"THAT'S TRUE. ALSO, NBC BEGAN TV BROA
DCASTS IN 1930 AND CBS,   IN 1931."
860 DATA "THOMAS A. EDISON INVENTED THE PHONOGRAPH IN 1870 A
ND THE   ELECTRIC LIGHT BULB IN 1879.",T,"HE INVENTED B
OTH OF THOSE AND, ALSO, MOTION PICTURES IN 1889."
870 DATA "ONE NAUTICAL MILE IS 1.151 STATUTE MILES OR 6,076
FEET.",T,""
880 DATA "ACCELERATION DUE TO GRAVITY AT SEA LEVEL IS 32.17
FEET PER   SECOND PER SECOND.",T,""
890 DATA "ONE KNOT IS 1.152 MILES PER HOUR.",T,""
900 DATA "OUR SOLAR SYSTEM AND THE EARTH REVOLVE AROUND THE
CENTER OF THE MILKY WAY GALAXY AT A SPEED OF 43,000 MILES AN
 HOUR.",T,""
910 DATA "THE INTEGRATED CIRCUITRY ON A SILICON CHIP WAS INV
ENTED IN 1958.",T, "ITS INVENTION IN 1958 IS CREDITED TO JAC
K KELLY OF TEXAS   INSTRUMENTS."

APPENDIX

TAB OR HTAB ⟶

| 1 | 2 | 3 | 4 | 5 | 6 | 7 | 8 | 9 | 10 | 11 | 12 | 13 | 14 | 15 | 16 | 17 | 18 | 19 | 20 | 21 | 22 | 23 | 24 | 25 | 26 | 27 | 28 | 29 | 30 | 31 | 32 | 33 | 34 | 35 | 36 | 37 | 38 | 39 | 40 |

VTAB ⟶

| 1 |
| 2 |
| 3 |
| 4 |
| 5 |
| 6 |
| 7 |
| 8 |
| 9 |
| 10 |
| 11 |
| 12 |
| 13 |
| 14 |
| 15 |
| 16 |
| 17 |
| 18 |
| 19 |
| 20 |
| 21 |
| 22 |
| 23 |
| 24 |

APPLE II +, APPLE IIe, and APPLE IIc
VIDEO DISPLAY WORKSHEET

272

TRS-80™ MODEL III and MODEL IV
VIDEO DISPLAY WORKSHEET

BIBLIOGRAPHY

Albrecht, B., Inman, D. & Zamora, R., *TRS-80 Level II BASIC*. John Wiley & Sons, Inc., 1980.

Apple II. *BASIC Programming Reference Manual*. Apple Computer, Inc., Cupertino, CA, 1978.

Apple II. *Apple II Reference Manual*. Apple Computer, Inc., Cupertino, CA, 1979.

Apple II. *The Applesoft Tutorial*. Apple Computer, Inc., Cupertino, CA, 1979.

Apple II. *The DOS Manual*. Apple Computer, Inc., Cupertino, CA, 1980.

Apple II. *DOS User's Manual*. Apple Computer, Inc., Cupertino, CA, 1983.

Apple II. *DOS Programmer's Manual*. Apple Computer, Inc., Cupertino, CA, 1982.

Apple IIe. *Owner's Manual*. Apple Computer, Inc., Cupertino, CA, 1982, 1983.

Apple II. *ProDOS User's Manual*. Apple Computer, Inc., Cupertino, CA, 1983.

Inman, D., Zamora, R. & Albrecht, B., *TRS-80 Advanced Level II BASIC*. John Wiley & Sons, Inc., 1981.

Lien, D. A., *Learning TRS-80 BASIC for Models I, II/16 and III*. Compusoft Publishing, 1982.

Radio Shack. *TRS-80 Model III Disk System Owner's Manual*. Radio Shack, A Division of Tandy Corporation, Fort Worth, TX, 1980.

Radio Shack. *TRS-80 Model III Operation and BASIC Language Reference Manual*. Radio Shack, A Division of Tandy Corporation, Fort Worth, TX, 1980.

Radio Shack. *Getting Started with TRS-80 BASIC*. Radio Shack, A Division of Tandy Corporation, Fort Worth, TX, 1981.

Richman, E., *Spotlight on Computer Literacy*. Random House School Division, New York, 1982.

SKILLS INDEX OF PROGRAMS

READING/LANGUAGE ARTS PROGRAMS

Skill Area	Program Number Apple	Program Number Radio Shack	Program Name	Grades
Alphabet	2	2	Alphabetizing	2–8
	6		Alphabetical Order	1–3
	8	10	Guessing Letters	2–6
Inferential Comprehension	5	6	Using Context Clues	2–8
	14	14	Signal Words	2–8
		19	Sequence	4–8
	19	23	Making Comparisons	2–8
	20		Analogies	4–8
Sight Words	1	1	Flash Cards for Sight Words	1–8
Structural Analysis (Grammar)		7	Making Sentences	4–8
	7	8	Pronouns	3–8
	13	13	Plurals	2–8
	18	20	Contractions	3–6
	21	21	Showing Possession	3–8
	24	25	Verb Tenses	2–8
		4	Parts of Speech	3–8
	25		Sentence Transformation	3–8
Speed Reading	11	12	Practicing Faster Reading	3–8
Visual Memory	15	15	Visual Memory	1–8
	9		Matching the Characters	1–5
	22	22	Playing Concentration	2–8
Vocabulary	4	5	Synonyms	3–8
		9	Compound Words	2–8
	10	11	Suffixes	3–8
	16	16	Multiple Meanings	3–8
	17	18	Antonyms	2–8
	12		Spelling and Typing	3–8
Writing (Interactive Language)	3	3	Writing A Story	3–8
		17	Sentence Combining	2–8
	23	24	Writing Poems	4–8

MATHEMATICS/SCIENCE PROGRAMS

Skill Area	Program Number		Program Name	Grades
	Apple	**Radio Shack**		
Addition/	2	2	Some—More or Less	2–5
Subtraction	3	3	Greater Than–Less Than Symbols	3–4
	4	4	More Than–Fewer Than	3–5
	12	12	Basic Number Facts	3–5
Decimals	8	8	Fun With Decimals	5–8
	18	18	The Concept of Percent	6–8
Fractions	13	13	Reducing Fractions	5–8
Geometry	9	9	Perimeter and Area of Rectangles	6–8
Integers	14	14	Addition of Integers	5–8
	15	15	Subtraction of Integers	6–8
	16	16	Multiplication of Integers	6–8
	17	17	Division of Integers	6–8
Multiplication/	6	6	Understanding Multiplication	3–5
Division	7	7	Understanding Division	3–5
Numeration	1	1	Guess the Mystery Number	2–5
	5	5	Choose the Largest Number	3–8
	10	10	Computer Rounding Aid	5–8
	12	12	Greatest Common Factor	7–8
	11	11	The LCM Challenge	5–8
Problem Solving (Logic)	19	19	Computer Challenge	4–8
Science	20	20	Reading a Scale	6–8
	21	21	Feet Per Second and Mile Per Hour	7–8
	22	22	Abbreviations for Elements	7–8
	23	23	Solving Proportions	6–8
	24	24	Estimating Measurements	5–8
	25	25	Twenty Science Questions	6–8

INDEX

A

Abbreviations for elements, 128–131, 258–261
Addition of integers, 114–116, 245–247
Alphabetical order, 54–56
Alphabetizing, 47–48, 175–177
Analogies, 79–81
Antonyms, 73–75, 206–208
Arrow keys, left and right:
  on the Apple, 7, 29
  on the TRS-80™, 145, 158

B

Backup copy, how to make a:
  of the ProDOS™, User's Disk, 20–22
  of the SYSTEM MASTER, 14–15
  of the TRSDOS, 151–152
Basic number facts, 110–112, 242-244
BASIC statements, 8
Booting:
  the DOS 3.3 SYSTEM MASTER, 13
  the ProDOS™, User's Disk, 19–20
  the TRSDOS, 150
BREAK key, 146, 149, 161
Bug, definition of, 9

C

CAPS LOCK key, 5
Catalog of programs, 13–14, 25
Central processing unit (CPU):
  on the Apple, 2
  on the TRS-80™, 142
Changing data:
  on the Apple, 39–40
  on the TRS-80™, 167–168
Choose the largest number, 98–99, 232–233
CLEAR key, 145, 149
Clearing the screen:
  on the Apple, 6, 8
  on the TRS-80™, 145, 149
CLS command, 159
Commas, use of, 28, 157
Comparisons, making, 77–79, 216–218
Compound words, 188–190
Computer challenge, 122–124, 253–255
Computer rounding aid, 106–108, 239–240
Context clues, using, 52–54, 183–184
Contractions, 75–77, 210–212
CONTROL key, 3, 4, 5, 11
CONTROL RESET key, 19, 20
COPYA, 15
Copying programs, how to do:
  on the Apple, 20–22, 37–39
  on the TRS-80™, 166–167
CRT, definition of, 143
CTRL key, 5
CTRL S key, 39

Cursor:
  definition of, 3, 5, 143
  how to move, 7, 145
  what to do if there is no, 41, 169

D

DATA statement:
  on the Apple, 35–37
  on the TRS-80™, 164–165
Decimals, fun with, 103–105, 236-237
Deleting copy, 18, 25, 39
DIR command, 151
Directory of programs, how to obtain, 151
Disk drive:
  definition of, 3, 143
  problems with, 42, 169–170
Diskette(s):
  booting a, 13, 150
  care of, 12, 150
  description of, 3, 12, 143, 149
  formatting, 22–24
  initializing, 16–17, 149
  labeling, 12, 15, 150
  saving copy on, 15–17
Division, understanding, 101–103, 234–236
Division of integers, 118–119, 249–250
$, string symbol:
  on the Apple, 32
  on the TRS-80™, 160–161

E

ENTER key, 143, 144, 146, 149
Erasing copy:
  on the Apple, 30
  on the TRS-80™, 153–154, 159
Errors, correcting, 40–41, 148, 168:
  arrow keys used in, 7, 29, 158
  in the PRINT statement, 9
  by retyping, 29, 158
ESC key, 6, 11

F

Feet per second and miles per hour, 126–128, 256–258
File, definition of, 19
Flash cards for sight words, 44–47, 173–175
Floppy. See Diskette(s)
Formatting a disk, 22–24
FOR/NEXT statements:
  on the Apple, 30–31
  on the TRS-80™, 159–160
Fractions, reducing, 112–114, 244–245

G

GOTO statement:
  on the Apple, 31–33
  on the TRS-80™, 160–162

Greater than–less than symbols, 95–96, 229–230
Guessing letters, 58, 190–191
Guess the mystery number, 92–94, 227–228

H

Hardware, definition of, 3, 143
HELLO program, 16
HOME command, 8, 30

I

IF/THEN statement:
  on the Apple, 33–34
  on the TRS-80™, 162–163
INIT HELLO, 16
Initializing diskettes, 16–17, 149
INPUT statement:
  on the Apple, 31–33
  on the TRS-80™, 160–162

L

LCM challenge, the, 108–110, 240–242
LET statement:
  on the Apple, 34–35
  on the TRS-80™, 163–164
LIST command, 29–30, 158
L key, difference between 1 key and the, 6, 145
Loading programs:
  on the Apple, 17–18
  on the TRS-80™, 153

M

Matching the characters, 59
Mathematical functions, how to do:
  on the Apple, 10–11
  on the TRS-80™, 147–148
Measurements, estimating, 133–135, 263–266
Monitor, definition of, 2
More than–fewer than, 96–98, 230–232
Multiple meanings, 71–73, 202–203
Multiplication, understanding, 99–101, 233–234
Multiplication of integers, 117–118, 248–249

N

NEW command:
  on the Apple, 30
  on the TRS-80™, 159
NEXT statement:
  on the Apple, 30–31
  on the TRS-80™, 159–160
Numbers, printing of, 10, 147

O

O key, difference between 0 key and the, 6, 145

P

Parts of speech, 179–181
Pathname, definition of, 19
Percent, concept of, 119–121, 250–252
Perimeter and area of rectangles, 105–106, 237–238
Playing concentration, 83–85, 214–216
Plurals, 66–67, 196–198
Practicing faster reading, 61–63, 194–196
PRINT statements:
  definition of, 7

PRINT statements *(cont'd)*:
  error using the, 9
  examples of, 8, 146–147
Program line, 10
Prompt, definition of, 3, 143
Pronouns, 56–57, 187–188
Proportions, solving, 131–133, 261–263

R

Reading a scale, 124–126, 255–256
READ statement:
  on the Apple, 35–36
  on the TRS-80™, 164–165
REM statement:
  on the Apple, 32
  on the TRS-80™, 161–162
Repeat a character, how to, 5–6
REPT key, 5–6
RESET key, 3, 4, 5, 11, 19, 20, 143
RETURN key, function of, 5, 7,
RUN command, 14

S

Saving copy:
  on the Apple, 15–17, 24–25
  on the TRS-80™, 152–153
Screen wraparound, 6, 144–145
Scrolling, 39
Semicolons, use of, 28–29, 157–158
Sentence combining, 203–206
Sentence transformations, 89–90
Sentences, making, 184–186
Sequence, 208–210
SHIFT key:
  on the Apple, 5, 11
  on the TRS-80™, 144, 145
Showing possession, 81–83, 212–214
Signal words, 67–69, 198–200
Software, definition of, 3, 143
Some—more or less, 94–95, 228–229
Spelling and typing, 63–65
Stopping a program, how to do, 41, 169
Subtraction of integers, 116–117, 247–248
Suffixes, 60–61, 191–193
Synonyms, 50–51, 181–182
Syntax error message, 7, 42, 170

T

Turning on a computer, how to do:
  on the Apple, 3–4
  on the TRS-80™, 143
Twenty science questions, 135–139, 266–269

U

Upper case letters, changing to lower case, 145

V

Verb tenses, 87–89, 221–224
Visual memory, 69–71, 200–201
Volume, definition of, 19

W

Writing a story, 49–50, 177–178
Writing poems, 85–87, 219–221